1991

This book is first and foremost an extended examination and discussion of the enslavement of men and women by others of their society, and in particular of the means and causes of the gradual end of slavery in early medieval Europe between 500 and 1200. Drawing upon a very wide range of primary archival sources, Professor Bonnassie places new findings about subjection, servitude and lordship in relation to the prevailing understanding of social history which has developed since the work of Marc Bloch. The author explains how slavery long persisted in southern France and Spain, as part of a public order that also sheltered free peasants, giving way in the tenth and eleventh centuries to a new regime of harsh lordships that mark the beginnings of feudalism. He shows that feudalism in south-western Europe was no less significant than in northern European lands.

In his introduction to the book Professor T. N. Bisson writes 'The achievements of this book are enhanced by two virtues not always joined in historians: analytical clarity and imaginative sympathy . . . A work of humane and powerful scholarship well conveyed in this translation, this book will be widely read and pondered.'

Past and Present Publications

From Slavery to Feudalism in South-Western Europe

This book is published as part of the joint publishing agreement established in 1977 between the Fondation de la Maison des Sciences de l'Homme and the Press Syndicate of the University of Cambridge. Titles published under this arrangement may appear in any European language or, in the case of volumes of collected essays, in several languages.

New books will appear either as individual titles or in one of the series which the Maison des Sciences de l'Homme and the Cambridge University Press have jointly agreed to publish. All books published jointly by the Maison des Sciences de l'Homme and the Cambridge University Press will be distributed by the Press throughout the world.

Cet ouvrage est publié dans le cadre de l'accord de co-édition passé en 1977 entre la Fondation de la Maison des Sciences de l'Homme et le Press Syndicate of the University of Cambridge. Toutes les langues européennes sont admises pour les titres couverts par cet accord, et les ouvrages collectifs peuvent paraître en plusieurs langues.

Les ouvrages paraissent soit isolément, soit dans l'une des séries que la Maison des Sciences de l'Homme et Cambridge University Press ont convenu de publier ensemble. La distribution dans le monde entier des titres ainsi publiés conjointement par les deux établissements est assurée par Cambridge University Press.

This book is also published in association with and as part of Past and Present Publications, which comprise books similar in character to the articles in the journal *Past and Present*. Whether the volumes in the series are collections of essays – some previously published, others new studies – or monographs, they encompass a wide variety of scholarly and original works primarily concerned with social, economic and cultural changes and their causes and consequences. They will appeal to both specialists and non-specialists and will endeavour to communicate the results of historical and allied research in readable and lively form.

For a list of titles in Past and Present Publications, see end of book.

From Slavery to Feudalism in South-Western Europe

PIERRE BONNASSIE

translated by JEAN BIRRELL

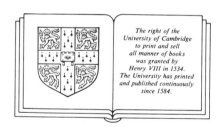

The right of the
University of Cambridge
to print and sell
all manner of books
was granted by
Henry VIII in 1534.
The University has printed
and published continuously
since 1584.

CAMBRIDGE UNIVERSITY PRESS
Cambridge
New York   Port Chester   Melbourne   Sydney

EDITIONS DE LA MAISON DES SCIENCES DE
L'HOMME
Paris

Published by the Press Syndicate of the University of Cambridge
The Pitt Building, Trumpington Street, Cambridge CB2 1RP
40 West 20th Street, New York, NY 10011, USA
10 Stamford Road, Oakleigh, Melbourne 3166, Australia
and Editions de la Maison des Sciences de l'Homme
54 Boulevard Raspail, 75270 Paris Cedex 06

First published 1991

Printed in Great Britain at the University Press, Cambridge

British Library cataloguing in publication data

Bonnassie, Pierre
   From slavery to feudalism in south-western Europe. –
   (Past and present publications).
   1. Spain, to 1479
   I. Title II. Series
   946'.01

Library of Congress cataloguing in publication data
   Bonnassie, Pierre.
      From slavery to feudalism in south-western Europe/Pierre Bonnassie:
   translated by Jean Birrell
   p.   cm. – (Past and present publications).
   ISBN 0-521-36324-1.
   1. Serfdom – Europe – History. 2. Slavery – Europe – History.
   3. Social history – Medieval. 500–1500. I. Title.
   HT757.B66 1990
   806.3'65'094 – dc20   89-23965

ISBN 0 521 36324 1 hardback
ISBN 2 7351 0406 0 hardback (France only)

WV

Contents

940.1
B716

139,660

Maps

Foreword

The studies gathered in this volume are changing our ideas about medieval social history. With the lone exception of Georges Duby, no one since Marc Bloch has done so much as Pierre Bonnassie to clarify big questions relating to the persistence and transformation of pre-millennial societies in France. When and how did ancient slavery end? When and how did agrarian labour assume the diverse forms of subjection commonly (and vaguely) labelled 'serfdom' by historians? How were such changes related to economic growth, to the restructuring of social power, and to the cultures and initiatives of peasants? These were questions about the history of people in the mass and they evoked equally capacious theoretical issues concerning the nature and stages of pre-industrial societies.

Such matters were not neglected by previous historians, least of all by Bloch, but their researches had not led to secure results. Everyone complained about the documents, too few (it was said) and too elitist to illuminate the scorned and voiceless many. It hardly helped to read the proliferating regional monographs, which seemed on the matter of serfdom to stress peculiarities at the expense of wider uniformities (and whose conclusions have to this day defied cogent summation). To build theories of feudalism on historical work was to build houses of cards. Non-Marxist historians themselves were in disagreement over the chronology of vassalage and feudal tenures. Nevertheless, a methodological milestone had been passed. It turned out that the only scholars for whom the questions given above held no terrors were those favoured few whose chosen regions were well documented for the tenth and early eleventh centuries. For Georges Duby working on the Mâconnais, for Pierre Toubert (Latium), for J.-P. Poly (Provence, though here less satisfactorily) the veil could be lifted on those obscure generations to reveal a profound rupture in social order and power. It became reasonable to suppose that the experience of these regions was not exceptional

Nowhere was this finding so spectacularly confirmed than for Catalonia. In his *thèse d'état* (1973; published 1975–6), Pierre Bonnassie exploited an incomparably rich documentation to show how an ancient public order persisted in the eastern Pyrenees down to the year 1000, how it was then threatened by heightened ambitions and economic growth, and how it collapsed in a paroxysm of competitive violence (1020–60) attended by the multiplication of castles, warriors, and fiefs. And Professor Bonnassie had only to fix on the social consequences of this evolution to see, for the first time anywhere, the starkly total – and brutal – transformation of a society of free peasant proprietors and slaves, its property protected by Visigothic law in public courts, into a new regime of peasant subjection to the oppressive lordships of castellans and knights bent on seizing whatever was left of public powers. 'From slavery to feudalism': it was a compelling demonstration for Catalonia.

Could the demonstration be replicated or generalised for neighbouring regions? Not easily, it seemed, whether for lack of evidence or lack of research. Yet to our good fortune Professor Bonnassie undertook such a study in two remarkable articles that form the coherent nucleus of this book. The first (in historical order) may well be the best study of medieval slavery (of any length) ever published; while the second is a pathbreaking essay on the chronology of militant feudalising in Spain (and Portugal) and southern France. These chapters (1 and 3 below), ranging backwards and forward in time, suggest that the crisis of the early eleventh century was indeed widespread, the sign of a seachange in medieval social structures. But there is caution here as well as forceful originality. Professor Bonnassie makes no claim that his conclusions apply generally north of the Massif Central, so that his work raises, amongst others, the question whether meridional structures of militant lordship conformed to some more profoundly cultural divide beween North and South after (or persisting after) the year 1000. In other studies, the author provides a fine survey of Visigothic Spain (chapter 2); compensates for the paucity of Occitanian evidence by wringing the singular testimony of the *Liber miraculorum Sancte Fidis* on the violent regime of castles (chapter 4); shows how the documentary forms of *convenientia* and *sacramentale* illustrate the categorical originality of the new Catalonian structures of alliance and commendation in the eleventh century (chapter 6); surveys the dynamics of feudalising in Catalonia down to 1150 (or beyond) with fine attention to the problems of class formation and enfranchisement (chapters 5, 7); and in highly resourceful essays on the status and economic (and political!) initiatives of peasants in Catalonia and early Capetian France, challenges us to think differently about the toilers so inexactly represented in the unsympathetic records of their masters (chapters 8–10). The valuable collaboration of Pierre Guichard in chapter 8 will not be overlooked. In chapter 10 a reflective review of the historical problem of servility not only underscores the reaffirmed need to think of post-millennial peasants as the successors of agrarian slaves, but fittingly evokes the abiding intelligence with which Marc Bloch broached the problematic of medieval slavery.

The feudalism Professor Bonnassie has recreated quite demolishes the old orthodoxy that depicted Mediterranean feudalisms as pale copies of northern ones. No regime of fiefs known to medieval Europe was so characteristic and original or so socially pervasive as that of Catalonia and much of Occitania by 1100. The evidence here adduced will be useful to historians of class formation, seigneurial exploitation, and peasant resistance; all the more so as this feudalism is no figment of sociological imagination. It was variable in incidence and chronology in ways yet to be explored; its discoverer has mapped out the heartlands for us while pointing helpfully to promising new directions of research.

The achievements of this book are enhanced by two virtues not always joined in historians: analytical clarity and imaginative sympathy. If Professor Bonnassie has improved our grasp of the larger history of slavery, servility, and economic change, it is because he has held insistently to his guiding questions no matter how thick the underbrush. And if his peasants seem more active, seem angrier, than those habitually portrayed (even caricatured) in our sources, it is because (one may feel) he has put himself in peasant shoes – and read between the lines. A work of humane and powerful scholarship well conveyed in this translation, this book will be widely read and pondered.

T. N. BISSON

Abbreviations

AC:	Arxiu Capitular
ACA:	Arxiu de la Corona d'Aragó, Barcelona
AHN:	Archivo Historico Nacional, Madrid
BN:	Bibliothèque Nationale, Paris
RB I, RB II etc:	Ramon Berenguer I, II etc
BR I:	Berenguer Ramon I

CPC: *Cartas de población y franquicia de Cataluña,* ed. J. M. Font Ruis, 2 vols. (in 3 parts) (Madrid, Barcelona, 1969–83)

ES: *España sagrada* . . ., ed. Henrique Florez et al., 58 vols. (Madrid, 1747–1918)

HGL: *Histoire générale de Languedoc* . . ., ed. Claude Devic, J.-J. Vaissete, 16 vols. (Toulouse, 1872–1904)

LFM: *Liber Feudorum Maior,* ed. F. Miquel Rosell, 2 vols. (Barcelona, 1945–7)

MGH: *Monumenta Germaniae Historica* (1823 to date)

AA: *Auctores Antiquissimi*

SS: *Scriptores*

PL: *Patrologiae cursus completus . . . Series latina,* ed. J.-P. Migne, 221 vols. (Paris, 1844–66).

Structures féodales: *Structures féodales et féodalisme dans l'Occident méditerranéen (Xe–XIIIe siècles). Bilan et perspectives de recherches* . . . (Rome, 1980)

Usatges: *Usatges de Barcelona,* ed. R. d'Abadal and F. Valls Taberner (Barcelona, 1913)

Annales: *Annales: Economies, Sociétés, Civilisations*

Settimane: *Settimane di studio del centro italiano di studi sull'alto medioevo* (Spoleto)

La Catalogne: Pierre Bonnassie, *La Catalogne du milieu du Xe à la fin du XLe siècle: croissance et mutations d'une société,* 2 vols. (Toulouse, 1976)

I. The survival and extinction of the slave system in the early medieval West (fourth to eleventh centuries)*

In memory of Marc Bloch

During the night of 16 June 1944, somewhere near Lyons, Marc Bloch died, shot by the Nazis. Among the many unpublished texts which he left was a study entitled 'How and Why Ancient Slavery Came to an End'. This article, later published in his journal, *Annales*,[1] was the outcome of many years of research into one of the problems which, throughout his life, most preoccupied him; in fact, for Marc Bloch, the disappearance of slavery constituted 'one of the most profound [transformations . . .] mankind has known'.[2] His article not only provided much information and formulated new hypotheses, but opened up many lines of research. To what

* This chapter comprises the revised text of three lectures given at the Centre d'Etudes Supérieures de Civilisation Médiévale, University of Poitiers, on 5, 6 and 7 July 1984, in commemoration of the fortieth anniversary of the death of Marc Bloch, and published in *Cahiers de Civilisation Médiévale*, 28 (Oct.–Dec., 1985), 307-43. Earlier versions were presented to the Society for the Study of Feudalism, the Autonomous University of Barcelona and the CESCM of the University of Poitiers, and, of course, my students at the University of Toulouse–Le Mirail; I would like to thank them all for their helpful comments and suggestions. Particular thanks are owed to my colleagues A. Mundó of the Autonomous University of Barcelona and P. Le Roux of the University of Toulouse–Le Mirail.

[1] *Annales* (1947), 30–43, 161–70. Reprinted in M. Bloch, *Mélanges historiques,* vol. 1 (Paris, 1963), pp. 261–85; also translated by William R. Beer in *Slavery and Serfdom in the Middle Ages* (Berkeley–Los Angeles, 1975), pp. 1–31.

[2] *Ibid.*, p. 1. Marc Bloch wrote other essays on servitude; amongst the most important are 'The Rise of Dependent Cultivation and Seignorial Institutions' in *The Cambridge Economic History of Europe*, vol. 1 (Cambridge, 1941), pp. 224–77, and 'Liberté et servitude personnelles au moyen âge, particulièrement en France: contribution à une étude des classes' in *Anuario de historia del derecho español* (1933), pp. 5–101. Both articles are reprinted in *Mélanges historiques*, vol. 1, pp. 210–58 and pp. 286–355; the latter also appears in *Slavery and Serfdom*, pp. 33–91. Nor should we forget *Rois et serfs* (Paris, 1921) and *La société féodale* (Paris, 1939/40), both of which devote many pages to this subject. The latter has been translated by L. A. Manyon as *Feudal Society* (London, 1961).

1

extent, in the forty years since his death, have these been explored and are we today in a position to answer the two questions he posed – why and how? Are we even able to determine *when* – this third question follows on from, but also determines, the other two – ancient slavery ended? My aim here is to review what we know (and do not know), and also to propose some new orientations and venture some answers; and this from a triple perspective – that of the factors in, and the forms and chronology of, the extinction of slavery in the rural societies of the early Middle Ages.

Forty years of research

Let us begin by looking at what Marc Bloch said. He asserted, firstly, something which was quite new at the time and is still far from being discredited, that 'at the time of the barbarian invasions and in the early days of their kingdoms, there were still many slaves in all parts of Europe ... more, it would appear, than during the early days of the Empire'.[3] Far from putting an end to slavery, the arrival of the Germans led, according to Bloch, to a revival of the slave trade, and this for two reasons: because the wars of the fifth century threw a large number of prisoners onto the market, and because the impoverishment caused by these wars drove many people to sell either themselves or their children. Thus, 'at the beginning of the Middle Ages, human merchandise had become abundant again at a reasonable price'.[4]

So there was an abundance of slaves around the year 500. They were, however, relatively rare three or four centuries later; in the Carolingian period, 'slavery was far from holding a place in European society comparable to that which it previously had held'.[5] Why had slavery so declined between the fifth and the ninth centuries? Marc Bloch put forward three possible reasons for its decline – religious, military and economic.[6]

As far as the Church was concerned, he was extremely cautious, emphasising the ambivalent character of its doctrinal positions. On the one hand, it proclaimed the equality of all men before God; on the other, it affirmed, quite unequivocally, the legitimacy of

---

[3] *Slavery and Serfdom*, p. 1.
[4] *Ibid.*, p. 3.   [5] *Ibid.*, p. 3.
[6] This is particularly clearly formulated in 'The Rise of Dependent Cultivation and Seignorial Institutions' (especially pp. 246ff.).

slavery, and this through the voices of its most celebrated teachers (St Augustine and Gregory the Great amongst others). In practice, however, the teaching of the Church tended to promote a decrease in the number of slaves, but in two ways only – by the encouragement given to manumission, which was included in the ranks of pious works, and, above all, by forbidding the reduction of Christians to slavery. This prohibition, which adversely affected the mechanics of capturing slaves by obliging raids for human cattle to be made often very far afield (in pagan countries), constituted 'the strongest action that Christianity had ever exercised'.[7]

As for the military situation, was it responsible for the failure of supply, and if so, to what extent? On this point, Marc Bloch referred, curiously, not to the early Middle Ages but to Roman Antiquity; it was the *pax Romana* of the two first centuries which might explain the relative decline in the number of slaves in the High Empire and the increase in their cost; conversely, the renewal of wars and internal troubles in the fourth and fifth centuries replenished the markets and reprovisioned the great estates with servile labour. For the early Middle Ages, Bloch was content to emphasise the persistence of the practice of capturing slaves, especially in the British Isles (during the wars between the Anglo-Saxons and the Celts) and Germany (during the wars of conquest of the first Carolingians and during the conflicts between Germans and Slavs).

But for Marc Bloch, neither religious nor military factors were sufficient to explain the reduction in the slave population. It could only really have been reduced through enfranchisement. Hence, of course, the importance of the Church's appeal for manumissions; but this could only be heard to the extent that the economic situation was favourable.

The question must, therefore, be argued in terms of profitability. The maintenance of immense herds of slaves was expensive, extremely so, and of all animal husbandry, that of human animals was the most difficult. The exploitation of the soil by systematic and intensive recourse to servile labour could thus only be contemplated in the context of an economy with a very open trade, procuring important outlets and assuring large profits. This type of exploitation had to be abandoned in the early Middle Ages

[7] *Slavery and Serfdom*, p. 25.

as a result of the recession which, for Marc Bloch, as for all historians of his time, characterised this period. Direct cultivation was succeeded by a system of tenure which allowed the master to free himself from the cares of feeding *servi* and *ancillae* and rearing their children. Slaves were settled on manses, and these *servi casati* were no longer completely slaves. Indeed, many were freed and turned into free, or more accurately, half-free, tenants. The early Middle Ages experienced, in fact, a great wave of manumission *cum obsequio* (with obedience and services retained), from which the large group of *colliberti* (slaves of the *familiae rusticae* freed collectively), benefited in particular.[8] Marc Bloch put great emphasis on this type of manumission for economic reasons. It is clear that for him, even if he avoided saying so explicitly, this type of enfranchisement went a long way towards answering the two questions which figured in the title of his essay. Why did ancient slavery end? Because many masters chose to free (at least partially) their slaves, reckoning it too costly to maintain a labour force which was not efficient in the new economic circumstances. How did it end? By giving way to a new class of dependants, the serfs, whose status was prefigured by that of those who were enfranchised *cum obsequio* (the *colliberti*, or future 'culverts'), and among whom was a mass of former free peasants fallen, for various reasons, under the subjection of a master.

In fact, Marc Bloch did not provide such a clear conclusion to his study. He opened up the enquiry, gathered information, and reflected deeply, producing a remarkable crop of new ideas, but he left the debate open, calling for further research.

FROM CHARLES VERLINDEN TO JEAN-PIERRE POLY

It must be said that this call for research was little heeded. Until recently, the problem of the end of slavery was for the most part ignored.[9] Little work has been done on the slavery of the early Middle Ages, with one exception, that of Charles Verlinden.

Verlinden has given us, in two stages, in 1955 (volume 1) and 1977 (volume 2), a veritable compendium on slavery in medieval

[8] 'Les "colliberti": étude sur la formation de la classe servile', *Revue historique* (1928), 1–48, 225–63, reprinted in *Mélanges historiques*, vol. 1, pp. 385–451, and in *Slavery and Serfdom*, pp. 93–149.

[9] Except by Marxist historians, of whom I shall speak below.

Europe.[10] The two thousand pages of this work, which are based on very considerable documentation, constitute a mine of information and an obligatory tool of reference for anyone working on this subject. That said, through the weakness of its problematic, the work is disappointing; written from an essentially juridical standpoint, it totally neglects the anthropological dimension of slavery. Its economic analysis is limited; we are spared nothing on the subject of variations in the market price of slaves, but the concept of a slave mode of production is totally lacking. The massive enterprise of Charles Verlinden represents, in fact, no advance as concerns the range of questions formulated by Marc Bloch. On the contrary, it tends to obscure the issue by treating without differentiating the two very different types of slavery known to medieval Europe, the rural slavery of the early Middle Ages (a dominant mode of production bequeathed by the ancient world) and the slave trade of the late Middle Ages (urban slavery, artisanal or domestic, a marginal phenomenon which really only affected the large Mediterranean ports). Further, on the specific issue of the end of ancient slavery, Verlinden's ideas were far from clear, much inferior to those of Marc Bloch. One gets the impression that, for him, the transition from slavery to serfdom was accomplished almost imperceptibly, even smoothly. But since he never defines either slavery or serfdom, his description of the transition fails to convince.[11]

So it is rather to the great syntheses of social history that we must turn to find answers to the questions posed by Marc Bloch. These answers are, it must be said, frequently allusive or confused, sometimes contradictory.

On the causes of the disappearance of slavery, there is general agreement in rejecting increasingly firmly the religious factor. According to Georges Duby, 'Christianity did not condemn slavery; it dealt it barely a glancing blow.'[12] Robert Fossier goes further: 'The Church played no role in the slow disintegration of

[10] Charles Verlinden, *L'esclavage dans l'Europe médiévale*, 2 vols. (Ghent, 1955/77).

[11] In this respect, chapter 2 of Book 2, 'De l'esclavage au servage', vol. 1, pp. 729–47, is certainly the weakest in the whole work.

[12] G. Duby, *Guerriers et paysans VIIe–XIIe siècle: premier essor de l'économie européenne* (Paris, 1973), p. 42, translated by Howard B. Clarke as *The Early Growth of the European Economy, Warriors and Peasants from the seventh to the twelfth centuries* (London, 1974), p. 32.

the servile system.'[13] And more recently, according to the same author, 'The progressive elimination of slavery was in no way the work of the Christian peoples. The Church preached resignation, promised equality in the hereafter, let people assume that God had singled out the wretched and, as it was of its time, felt no compunction about keeping large herds of animals with human faces.'[14]

The military situation (that is the cessation of razzia or raiding wars) is still cited to explain the dwindling recruitment of prisoners, but this factor appears less and less crucial. To explain the reduction in the number of slaves, it is rather the growing demand from the Muslim world (which meant that slaves captured in raids on the frontiers of the Carolingian world simply crossed the Empire to be sold in Islamic countries) which is emphasised.[15] Or else reference is made to the very low birth rate which must have prevailed amongst slaves, and which rendered problematic the reproduction of the herds of slaves working on the big estates.[16] It is economic explanations, in fact, which seem most plausible to contemporary historians and they continue to be formulated – in line with the writings of Marc Bloch – in terms of the costs of production. The basic idea is that gang slavery (or direct exploitation based on the maintenance of large slave *familiae*) was no longer profitable. The master of a large Carolingian estate had no interest in maintaining an abundant labour force that he could not employ all year round, but that he had nevertheless to feed throughout the dead seasons. His natural tendency was therefore to install his slaves on tenures, the well-known servile manses. For many authors, this process (visible as early as the Merovingian period, very common from then on)[17] constituted an essential stage in the withering away of ancient slavery. All this is in line with Marc Bloch.

Much newer are the ideas which are appearing with regard to

---

[13] R. Fossier, *Histoire sociale de l'Occident médiéval* (Paris, 1970), p. 65.

[14] R. Fossier, *Enfance de l'Europe*, vol 1, *L'homme et son espace* (Paris, 1982), p. 571.   [15] Duby, *Early Growth*, p. 40.

[16] *Ibid.*, pp. 183–4. Similarly, on the basis of a rigorous analysis of the demographic information in the polyptique of Saint-Victor of Marseilles, J.-P. Poly, 'Régime domanial et rapports de production "féodalistes" dans le Midi de la France (VIIIe–Xe siècles)' in *Structures féodales et féodalisme dans l'Occident méditerranéen*, Colloque de Rome, 1978 (Rome, 1980), pp. 57–84, especially pp. 67ff.

[17] See A. Verhulst, 'La genèse du système domanial classique', *Settimane*, 13 (1965), 135–60.

the modalities and the chronology of the extinction of the slave regime. On both these points, the revisions are due to Georges Duby. For him, it was not in the Merovingian, nor even in the Carolingian, period that ancient slavery ended, but later, in the eleventh century. 'Like Roman Gaul, like early Germany, France in the year 1000 was a slave society', he wrote in 1958.[18] He has since continued to reaffirm this position, supporting it with ever more rigorous proof. For him, in essence, the phenomenon of the disappearance of the old slavery has to be related to the emergence of a new structure, the *seigneurie banale*, which extended its grasp to all of the peasantry, without distinctions of juridical status. Under the iron heel of the lords possessed of the *ban*, the descendants of the old slaves of the early Middle Ages, were joined in a new form of dependence by a mass of free peasants who had fallen, in their turn, under the subjection of a master. In the tumult of the feudal revolution, the last *servi* were assimilated into the mass of the peasantry.[19]

These ideas of Georges Duby have continued and, indeed, still continue to gain ground. Nevertheless, though they have won complete acceptance amongst some historians,[20] they continue to provoke a certain unease amongst others. This is revealed by the difficulty that many of them experience in giving a name to the unfree of the Carolingian and post-Carolingian period: were they still slaves or already serfs? In his last work, Robert Boutruche, whilst aligning himself with Georges Duby, faltered when it came to the crunch, and was at a loss how to translate *servus* in the famous text of Adalbero of Laon.[21] Robert Fossier, for his part, has slaves and serfs in rather bizarre coexistence in the ninth and tenth centuries.[22] Jean-Pierre Poly and Eric Bournazel, finally,

---

[18] G. Duby and R. Mandrou, *Histoire de la civilisation française*, vol. 1 (Paris, 1958), p. 15.

[19] See, most recently, *Les trois ordres ou l'imaginaire du féodalisme* (Paris, 1978), pp. 183ff., translated by Arthur Goldhammer as *The Three Orders, Feudal Society Imagined* (Chicago, 1980). See also, among the same author's numerous writings on this subject, the article on 'Servage' in the *Encyclopaedia universalis*.

[20] For example, Renée Doehaerd, *Le haut moyen âge occidental: économies et sociétés* (Paris, 1971), p. 188; 'Everything seems to show that slavery remained alive in the West throughout the whole of the early Middle Ages: it only gradually disappeared in the following centuries, in a new demographic and economic environment.'

[21] R. Boutruche, *Seigneurie et féodalité*, vol. 1 (Paris, 1959), pp. 126–35, 371.

[22] Fossier, *Histoire sociale*, pp. 62–7. For the later period, his classification is clearer (*Enfance de l'Europe*, vol. 1, pp. 571–82).

whilst bravely posing the question ('Can one talk of slaves in the Carolingian period?'), dodge answering it, and use the word *servus* without translation.[23] This almost universal indecision on the part of medievalists with regard to a crucial problem for the period they are studying is, indeed, a curious phenomenon.

THE MARXISTS

Is enlightenment perhaps to be found elsewhere, that is, amongst those historians who invoke Marx? Their contribution deserves careful consideration because it is important and poses the question in very different terms from those examined so far. It is, in any case, natural for Marxists to take a particular interest in this question because it lies at the heart of the problematic developed by historical materialism. It concerns no less a matter than determining the causes and modalities of the passage from one mode of production (slavery) to another (feudalism). What is at issue is the whole problem of the models of transition (from feudalism to capitalism, from capitalism to socialism).[24] That said, it cannot be denied that it is rather artificial to oppose *en masse* Marxist and non-Marxist historians; while differences amongst the latter are considerable, they are even greater amongst the former, to the point where they have given rise to furious polemics. The Marxist historians can, in practice, be divided into two groups, those who are doggedly faithful to the letter of what Marx and Engels wrote on this subject (not, in fact, very much)[25] and those

[23] J.-P. Poly and E. Bournazel, *La mutation féodale, Xe–XIIe s.* (Paris, 1980), pp. 195–8, in particular p. 196, note 3. Poly had already, in his 'Régime domanial et rapports de production', entitled one section, 'When did ancient slavery end?' (p. 59). A good title, but the following pages, valuable though they are in other respects, tell us very little; yes, the Provençal *mancipium* of the ninth century was a *massip*, but what was a *massip*?

[24] The problem of the 'transition' or the '*voies de passage*' has given rise to many studies but mostly for later periods; see, in particular, *The Transition from Feudalism to Capitalism*, ed. R. H. Hilton (London, 1976); P. Vilar, 'La transition du féodalisme au capitalisme' in *Sur le féodalisme* (Paris, 1974), pp. 35–48; A. Soboul, 'Du féodalisme au capitalisme: la Révolution française et le problème des voies de passage', *La Pensée*, 196 (Nov.–Dec., 1977), 61–78. More generally, M. Godelier, 'D'un mode de production à un autre: théorie de la transition', *Recherches sociologiques*, 12 (1981), 161-93.

[25] The most important statements by Marx on this subject are found in *The German Ideology* and *A Contribution to the Critique of Political Economy*. His ideas were later developed and refined by Engels. These (and many other) texts have been collected by Maurice Godelier in *Sur les sociétés précapitalistes: textes*

who, without excessive reliance on these particular texts, apply to the problem the general schemas of the Marxist historical method.

The former attitude is found particularly among Soviet historians,[26] but also in certain German,[27] English,[28] and Spanish[29] writers. The basic idea, taken from Marx, is that the feudal mode of production is born of the synthesis of the pre- or proto-feudal elements which are found in previous modes of production, that is, the Roman slave mode of production and the Germanic mode of production, called 'primitive' or 'tribal'. The Germanic invasions engendered a process of interaction and fusion (of 'synthesis') which resulted in the birth of an economico-social formation which was radically new (feudalism), entailing at the same time the disappearance of the earlier social systems (and, in particular, slavery). On the basis of these premises, the literal Marxists have concentrated their attention on the study of the famous process of synthesis (their discussions focussing on the degree of 'balance' of this synthesis according to region)[30] and on the period during which it is considered to have happened, that is Late Antiquity, the period of the invasions and of the barbarian kingdoms. They tend, as a result, to minimise, even pass over in silence, the survival of slavery in early medieval Europe.[31]

choisis de Marx, Engels, Lénine (Paris, 1973) (with a long and valuable introduction).

[26] E. M. Staerman, 'La chute du régime esclavagiste' in Recherches internationales à la lumière du marxisme (Paris, 1957); Z. V. Oudaltsova and E. V. Goutnova, 'La genèse du féodalisme et ses voies en Europe', La Pensée, 196 (Nov.–Dec., 1977), 43–67. These articles, with other studies (generally of Marxist inspiration), appear in the collection edited by A. Prieto, Del esclavismo al feudalismo (Madrid, 1975, 4th edn 1980); not reading Russian, I have been able to consult only those works translated into a western language, which explains, obviously, the incomplete – and possibly unjust – nature of my references.

[27] E. Werner, 'De l'esclavage à la féodalité', Annales: ESC, 17 (1962), 930–9.

[28] P. Anderson, Passages from Antiquity to Feudalism (London, 1974).

[29] A. Barbero and M. Vigil, La formación del feudalismo en la Península ibérica (Barcelona, 1978).

[30] A 'balanced' synthesis in most of western Europe, because it integrates in equal parts the proto-feudal elements existing in the late Roman and the Germanic world; a synthesis with a predominance of 'Roman antique' elements in the Byzantine world; direct engendering ('almost without synthesis') by the Germanic-type societies in northern Europe (England, Germany, Scandinavia).

[31] For E. M. Staerman, the crisis of the slave system began in the second half of the second century; the third century saw 'the defeat of the old slave-owning groups', and, in the fourth century, 'the slave estate suffered a total collapse'. The fourth and fifth centuries, therefore, were the period of the transition to feudalism: after which, no more slavery (A. Prieto, Del esclavismo al

Other Marxist historians, especially in France, have adopted a different perspective. Choosing to disregard to some extent the famous pages of Marx on the 'synthesis' (pages which merely reflect the state of historiography at the time when Marx wrote), they have sought, and seek, to explain both the end of slavery and the appearance of feudalism by means of proper Marxist concepts, that is the development of the forces of production and the phenomenon of the class struggle.

The explanation of the extinction of the slave system by the development of the forces of production is essentially the work of Charles Parain. In a series of articles published between 1961 and 1977, he aimed to show that it was the improvement in the techniques of production (especially agricultural techniques) which rendered recourse to slavery less and less necessary, and eventually led to the disappearance of the slave mode of production.[32] The importance of technical innovations had not, in fact, escaped Marc Bloch (see, among others, his work on the water mill),[33] but he saw them as a consequence rather than as a cause of the reduction in the number of slaves. Parain altered the problematic: for him, it was the many improvements visible at the level of the rural economy (improvements to tools, in particular to scythes and sickles, diffusion of the flail, introduction of the wheeled plough and, above all, the conquest of water power) which, by saving on human labour, doomed slavery to disappear. But, faithful at this point to the chronology proposed by Marx, he dated these

feudalismo, pp. 103, 106–7). See also S. I. Kovialov, 'El vuelco social del siglo III al V en el Imperio romano de Occidente' in Prieto, *Del esclavismo*, pp. 109–29: the 'social revolution' of the third to fifth centuries finished off the slave system. Nor is the survival of slavery mentioned in the work of Anderson or Barbero and Vigil.

[32] 'De l'Antiquité esclavagiste au féodalisme' in *Quel avenir attend l'homme?*, *Rencontres internationales de Royaumont, May 1961* (Paris, 1961), pp. 36ff.; 'Le développement des forces productives en Gaule du Nord et les débuts de la féodalité' in *Sur le féodalisme, Recherches internationales à la lumière de marxisme*, 37 (1963), 37ff.; 'Le développement des forces productives dans l'ouest du Bas-Empire', *La Pensée*, 196 (Dec. 1977), 28–42. Most of Parain's articles have been republished in *Outils, ethnies et développement historique* (Paris, 1979).

[33] Especially, 'Avènement et conquête du moulin à eau', *Annales* (1935), 538–63, reprinted in *Mélanges historiques*, vol. 2, pp. 800–21. Also translated by J. E. Anderson in *Land and Work in Medieval Europe* (London, 1967), pp. 143–6. Discussed critically by Parain in 'Rapports de production et développement des forces productives: l'exemple du moulin à eau', *La Pensée*, 119 (Feb. 1965), reprinted in *Outils, ethnies et développement historique*, pp. 305–27.

improvements, in a highly questionable way, to the last centuries of the Roman Empire and not to the early Middle Ages; feudalism had, at all costs, to be born in the period of the invasions!

These views were opposed, and vehemently, by Pierre Dockès. In his *La libération médiévale*,[34] he made many criticisms of what he considered as a mechanistic view of history (as a 'mechanistic', even 'Stalinist' interpretation of historical materialism).[35] In making social changes follow automatically on technical changes, Parain forgot people; in this case, the slaves and their struggles for freedom.[36] But, in addition to the arguments of Parain, Dockès also took issue with the economic explanations for the extinction of slavery proposed by both Marc Bloch and Georges Duby.[37] The idea that the slave system had been abandoned because it was insufficiently productive appeared to him highly questionable; he showed this by reference to the studies of profitability made by American historians of slavery in the American South in the nineteenth century.[38] For Dockès, slavery could be and had been (in America as in the ancient world) a highly advantageous system of production. It thus could not be said to have failed because it no longer paid. Nor could it be said that it was abandoned because of the difficulties in recruiting servile labour. Even if these difficulties existed, it was always possible to rear young slaves; all slave societies have had recourse to this practice, and with success.[39]

Another explanation must, therefore, be sought. Dockès found it in the struggles of the slaves themselves. These appeared to him to be the prime (even the only) mover in the collapse of the slave regime. Which were these class struggles? For Dockès they were the revolts which took place from the third to the fifth centuries

[34] P. Dockès, *La libération médiévale* (Paris, 1979), translated by Arthur Goldhammer as *Medieval Slavery and Liberation* (London, 1982). It is worth noting, incidentally, that this is the only book entirely devoted to the subject of this article.
[35] Dockès, *La libération médiévale*, pp. 193–5.
[36] This reproach is not entirely justified; while he did not give class struggle a determining role, Parain did not ignore it; see 'Les caractères spécifiques des luttes de classes dans l'Antiquité classique', *La Pensée*, 108 (April 1963), 3–26.
[37] Dockès, *La libération médiévale*, pp. 145–79.
[38] See, in particular, R. Fogel and S. Engerman, *Time on the Cross* (New York, 1974).
[39] One only has to think of the importance of the *vernae* and *vernaculi* on the great Roman estates; and the American, Brazilian and African examples are well known.

within the Roman Empire, the uprisings of the Bacaudae, to which he had devoted another study,[40] and which he showed to have been, at least to a considerable extent, servile revolts. But it is at this point that his argument is weak or at least incomplete, because, according to him, the slave system foundered in the fifth century, as a consequence of the revolts of the Bacaudae. He tended, therefore, to minimise the survival of slavery into the early Middle Ages, and in this sense fell into the same error as those other Marxist historians he criticised. His failing, too, was a failing of chronology.

Overall, in spite of its often excessively polemical character, Dockès's book is stimulating both for the revisions he effects and for the new ideas he puts forward. Two of these seem to me particularly useful. The first is that when we speak of the end of slavery, it is a mistake to use the word 'end' in the singular; there were many 'ends' to slavery. A social regime of that type did not die from one blow, but as a result of very violent shocks, spread over time and interspersed with temporary revivals. Dockès identified two such crises, one in the third century, one in the fifth; there were others. The second idea worth retaining is that of the crucial importance of the role of the state to the functioning of the system. The slave mode of production implied norms of exploitation which were extremely cruel for those subjected to them. Isolated masters would have been unable to keep their slaves in subjection; it was absolutely essential for their authority to be buttressed by an efficient and coherent system of repression. Every crisis of state structures had as a corollary a crisis of the slave system. Every restoration of these same structures made possible a resurgence of slavery.

SUMMARY AND PERSPECTIVES

Our review of the research carried out since the death of Marc Bloch reveals totally contradictory conclusions.

Why did ancient slavery end? The traditional explanations (the action of the Church and the difficulties of recruitment), already called into question by Marc Bloch, have now been almost entirely

---

[40] P. Dockès, 'Révoltes bagaudes et ensauvagement, ou la guerre sociale en Gaule' in P. Dockès and J.-M. Servet, *Sauvages et ensauvagés* (Lyons, 1980).

abandoned, without ever having been shown to be false, and without having been replaced by more convincing arguments. The economic explanations which have, since Marc Bloch, succeeded them, have continued to gain ground, but contradict each other. Bloch described the transition from the large slave exploitation to the system of tenures as a consequence of the economic regression of the early Middle Ages. Contemporary historians (Georges Duby, Robert Fossier) retain the idea of slavery being abandoned because the costs of production were too high (which implies that the economy of the early Middle Ages was incapable of supporting such costs), even though they no longer describe this economy in terms of recession, but in terms of growth.[41] Charles Parain explains the end of slavery by growth alone, by the development of productive forces, but he clearly puts this too early, in the Late Empire. Finally, to cap them all, Dockès totally rejects these 'economist' arguments, which he describes, not without contempt, as 'mechanistic'. His own purely social explanation (the dynamic of the class struggle) is attractive, but seems too doctrinaire to carry conviction.

How did ancient slavery end? We have here the whole problem of the transition from slavery to serfdom. Marc Bloch argued that the two servitudes were different in kind, and observed a rupture, a discontinuity, between the slavery of the early Middle Ages and feudal serfdom (at most he found a foreshadowing of the status of serf in that of the Carolingian *colliberti*). But for him, the serfs of the twelfth century, whom he thought to be very much more numerous than the slaves of the early Middle Ages, must have had another origin. Against the views of Marc Bloch, the Belgian historians Charles Verlinden[42] and, above all, Leo Verriest[43] asserted, on the contrary, the primacy of continuity. The twelfth-century *servi* were the descendants of the Carolingian *servi*; Marc Bloch was wrong about their number; they in fact constituted only a tiny minority of the mass of the peasantry, and nothing preven-

---

[41] See the sub-title of Duby's *Guerriers et paysans*, i.e. *VIIe–XIIe siècle: premier essor de l'économie européenne* (and the title adopted for the English translation: *The Early Growth of the European Economy*).

[42] C. Verlinden, *L'esclavage dans l'Europe médiévale*, vol. 1, pp. 729ff.

[43] L. Verriest, *Institutions médiévales. Introduction au 'Corpus des records de coutumes et des lois de chefs-lieux de l'ancien comté de Hainault* (Mons, 1946). For the debate sparked off by the views of Verriest, see R. Boutruche, *Seigneurie et féodalité*, vol. 2, pp. 74–6.

ted their being seen as a relic of the slave system of early centuries. Georges Duby synthesised the two views; there were certainly descendants of the *servi* of the early Middle Ages among the serfs of the feudal period, but they had been joined in servitude by a mass of former free peasants submitted to the constraints of the *seigneurie banale*.[44]

Finally, when did ancient slavery end? At the end of Roman Antiquity and at the time of invasions, reply, with one voice, the Marxists, all remarkably faithful on this point to the letter of the writings of Marx.[45] In the eleventh century, according to Georges Duby. At some indeterminate date between the fifth and the eleventh centuries, say, lastly, with some embarrassment (if they say anything at all), most others.

Forty years after the death of Marc Bloch, the problem of the end of slavery in western Europe has thus reached a total impasse. How are we to proceed? How should we now orient our research? Three directions seem possible to me.

Firstly, there should be a return to the systematic examination of the sources; their alleged poverty is an argument rooted in laziness. They are numerous, indeed very numerous; the documentation of the early Middle Ages certainly provides more information about slavery than the whole of that for the Roman period. Also, it is extremely diverse: barbarian laws (which make it possible not only to establish a geography of slavery, since they concern the whole of western Europe, but which also provide precious chronological indications, since they were drawn up over the period from the sixth to the early ninth centuries), doctrinal texts of the Fathers of the Church (from St Paul to Burchard of Worms), conciliar acts, penitentials, formularies, literary and historiographical works, polyptiques, cartularies etc. The first task, therefore, should be to establish a corpus (or at the very least a catalogue) of written documents; then, to count, period by period, region by region, references to *mancipia*, *servi* and *ancillae*. The information gathered should be collated with that provided by archaeology; I am thinking, in particular, of excavations of sunken huts, which can tell us much about the relative import-

---

[44] This idea is developed in most of Duby's work. There is a useful summary of his views in his article 'Servage' in *Encyclopaedia universalis*.

[45] Though we should note that Dockès admits the existence of a phase of 'post-slavery' during the early Middle Ages (*La libération médiévale*, p. 298).

ance and the material conditions of existence of the servile labour on certain large estates.[46]

Secondly, more use should be made of regional research. Recent historical theses on the early Middle Ages discuss, in the nature of things, developments as regards slavery. They contain first-hand information, capable of renewing our problematic: theses on Aquitaine,[47] the Auvergne,[48] Latium,[49] Catalonia[50] the Charentais,[51] among others. Certain competent works of synthesis also make new contributions, especially for Italy.[52]

We need, lastly, to adopt a comparative approach. The slavery of the early Middle Ages cannot be understood in ignorance of the forms of slavery which preceded and followed it. Reading the works of specialists in Antiquity is clearly an imperative requirement.[53] But equally enlightening are the works of historians, and,

[46] There is a useful survey in Jean Chapelot, 'Le fond de cabane dans l'habitat rural ouest-européen: état des questions', *Archéologie médiévale*, 10 (1980), 5–57. This subject in itself merits extensive discussion. Whilst certain authors see the sunken hut as a typically servile dwelling structure (W. Winklemann, for example, for the site of Warendorf), others attribute to it other functions. It seems to me that, in general, the sunken hut has to be related either to slave lodgings or the artisanal labour required of them (hut-workshops for spinning and weaving for female slaves, sometimes grandly described as *gyneacea* in Carolingian texts).

[47] M. Rouche, *L'Aquitaine des Wisigoths aux Arabes: 418–719, naissance d'une région* (Paris, 1979).

[48] G. Fournier, *Le peuplement rural en Basse Auvergne durant le haut moyen âge* (Paris, 1962); also C. Lauranson-Rosaz, *L'Auvergne et ses marges (Velay, Gévaudan) du VIIIe au XIe siècle: la fin du monde antique* (Le-Puy-en-Velay, 1987).

[49] P. Toubert, *Les structures du Latium médiéval*, 2 vols. (Rome, 1973).

[50] Bonnassie, *La Catalogne*.

[51] A. Debord, *La société laïque dans les pays de la Charente, Xe–XIIe s.* (Paris, 1984).

[52] I have in mind, in particular, the Einaudi *Storia d'Italia* (Turin, 1974), which includes G. Tabacco, 'La storia politica e sociale: dal tramonto dell'Impero alle prime formazioni di Stati regionali', vol. 2, pp. 5–167 and K. Modzelewski, 'La transizione dall'antichità al feudalismo' *Annali*, 1 (1975).

[53] There is an immense bibliography; worthy of note, in particular, in addition to the *Actes des Colloques de Besançon* on slavery (1971, 1972 and 1973) are the works of Moses I. Finley, *The Ancient Economy* (London, 1973) and *Ancient Slavery and Modern Ideology* (London, 1980), also the recent article of Paul Veyne, 'Les esclaves-colons romains', *Revue historique*, 265 (1981), 3–25. The Soviet view is given in M. Raskolnikoff, *La recherche soviétique et l'histoire économique et sociale du monde hellénistique et romain*, AECR. (Strasbourg, 1957). To the bibliography on slavery has to be added that on the *colonus*, given that many authors have established a link between the decline of servitude (?) and the development of the *colonus* of the Late Empire. This whole question,

even more, ethnologists, who are interested in the phenomenon of slavery outside Europe: American slavery, obviously,[54] but also Brazilian[55] and African.[56] It is impossible, in fact, to pose the problem of the end of slavery without first giving a definition which is not only juridical and economic (as has always hitherto been the case), but also anthropological.

What is a slave?

I want to try to formulate a definition on the basis of the texts left by the barbarian monarchies, which will also incidentally serve to demonstrate to sceptics the survival of the phenomenon of slavery in the centuries following the great invasions.

There is no shortage of material! A simple count of the articles in the laws which, in the Germanic codes, refer directly to slavery, or at least contain clauses relating to slaves, is highly illuminating as regards the importance which the institution of slavery continued to hold in the societies of the sixth to the eighth centuries. In the laws of the Visigothic kingdom (I refer here to those promulgated from the reign of Leovigild to that of Egica, that is, between 567 and 700), the total is 229 out of 498 (46 per cent). Spain, it might be argued, an ancient land of servitude, provides too easy a proof. What about the northern Germans? The percentage is certainly less, but it is still considerable; in the law of the Bavarians (drawn up between 744 and 748), 64 articles out of 268 (24 per cent); in the Salic law (ms. *D*: recension of Pepin the Short, from 763/4), 13 articles out of 100. We should, perhaps, move on in time. The latest laws, codified on the orders of Charlemagne in

however, has recently been subject to radical revision, to the point where the very concept of the *colonus* has been questioned. Most recently: J.-M. Carrie, 'Le colonat du Bas-Empire: un mythe historiographique', *Opus. Riv. internaz. stor. econ. e soc. dell'Antiquità*, 1 (1982), 351–70, and his 'Un roman des origines: les généalogies du "colonat de Bas-Empire"', *ibid.*, 2 (1983), 205-51.

[54] In addition to the book by Fogel and Engerman already cited, worthy of note among recent studies are: A. Conrad and J. R. Meyer, *The Economics of Slavery* (Chicago, 1964); E. S. Morgan, *American Slavery, American Freedom* (New York, 1975); P. David and P. Temin, 'Slavery, the Progressive Institution', *Journal of Economic History* (Sept. 1974).

[55] See the classic work of G. Freyre, *Maîtres et esclaves* (Paris, 7th edn 1952), translated as *The Masters and the Slaves* (New York, 1946, 2nd edn 1956). See also: R. Mellafe, *Negro Slavery in Latin America* (Berkeley, 1975) and K. M. de Queiros Mattoso, *Etre esclave au Brésil (XVIe–XIXe s.)* (Paris, 1979).

[56] C. Meillassoux, ed. *L'esclavage en Afrique précoloniale* (Paris, 1975).

802/3, make this possible: 8 articles out of 59 in the law of the Thuringians (14 per cent) and 21 out of 91 in that of the Ripuarian Franks (23 per cent). Similar counts could – or rather should – be made from other barbarian codes, as well as in different types of source (formularies, conciliar acts); it seems likely they will provide similar results. And one finds a similar crop of mentions of slaves in the narrative texts – references are particularly numerous in Gregory of Tours, to cite only one example.

But are these creatures who continue to be called *mancipia*, *servi* and *ancillae* truly slaves? Was their lot not changed as compared with that of their predecessors in Antiquity? Here lies the nub of the problem. Let us start from the ultra-classical definition of Aristotle: that of the 'tool with a voice', making simply the correction – accepted, in any case, by both Aristotle and Plato – that this tool might also be regarded as an animal.[57] This is a useful correction given that, since the economy of the early Middle Ages was almost exclusively agricultural, the principal tools of labour were domestic animals employed in the fields.

From this perspective, there can be no doubt that the slaves of the sixth to eighth centuries were ranked with livestock. The clauses in the barbarian laws relating to the sale and theft of cattle apply equally, quite unequivocally, to the *mancipia*. Let us look, for example, at what the law of the Bavarians says about sales:

A sale once completed should not be altered, unless a defect is found which the vendor has concealed, in the slave or the horse or any other livestock sold . . .: for animals have defects which a vendor can sometimes conceal.[58]

This is confirmed by the rare tariffs of tolls which survive for such an early period: that of Arras, for example, deals with slaves under the rubric *De bestiis*.[59]

---

[57] The basic texts of Aristotle and Plato on slavery are found in *Politics*, Book 1 and *Laws*, Book 6, respectively. For the slave seen as cattle, there is a characteristic passage by Plato in the *Laws*, Book 1, *Oeuvres complètes de Platon*, pp. 776–7 (quoted by Dockès, *La libération médiévale*, p. 8).

[58] *MGH*, *Lex Baiwariorum*, XVI, 9: 'postquam factum negotium non sit mutatum, nisi forte vitium invenerit quod ille venditor celavit: hoc est in mancipio aut in cavallo aut in qualicumque peculio, id est cecum aut herniosum aut cadivum aut leprosum. In animalibus autem sunt vitia que aliquotiens celare potest venditor.'

[59] Published in *Cartulaire de l'abbaye de Saint Vaast d'Arras*, ed. E.-F. Van Drival (Arras, 1875), and quoted by Verlinden in *L'esclavage dans l'Europe médiévale*, vol. 1, p. 671. This tariff has come down to us in an eleventh-century version, but it is attributed to a *rex Theodericus*, which suggests a Merovingian origin.

Table 1. *The scale of values for animals and slaves according to Salic law*

	Pactus legis salicae	Lex salica (Pepin the Short)
pig (two-year old)	15 sous	15 sous
boar	17 sous	17 sous
ancilla	30 sous	35 sous
ox, cow, *servus*	35 sous	35 sous
horse	35 sous	45 sous
bull	45 sous	45 sous

In cases of theft, the laws generally make no distinction between slaves and cattle. Having stated that the theft of a horse was sanctioned by a reparation of three times the value of the stolen animal, the law of the Thuringians added: 'it is the same for slaves, oxen, cows, sheep and pigs'.[60] Only the price of composition differed; the law of the Burgundians was in this regard the most generous to slaves, estimating their value at twice that of a horse.[61] The Salic law, in its first edition, gave the same tariff (35 sous) for the *servus*, the *ancilla*, the *caballus* and the *iumentum*.[62] In its later versions, it established a scale of values for animals in general (see table 1).[63]

The Gallic laws (the fact that we are moving into the Celtic domain makes no difference in the way of thinking) went even further, if possible, in the process of assimilation; both slaves and cattle served indifferently as units of account in the payment of indemnities for murder and injury: .

[60] *MGH, Lex Thuringiorum*, arts. 32–3.
[61] *MGH, Lex Burgundiorum*, tit. IV (*De sollicitationibus et furtis*).
[62] *MGH, Pactus legis salicae*, X, 1.
[63] *MGH, Pactus legis salicae*, II, 8, 14; III, 4, 7, 8; X, 3, 4. *Lex salica*, II, 3, 4; XI, 1, 2. Two points should be made here. The first is that the price to be paid is the same, whether the animal (or slave) was stolen or killed (or resold by the thief or even, in the case of a slave, freed): the loss was, in effect, the same for the owner (X, 3: 'si quis servum alienum furaverit aut occiderit aut ingenuum dimiserit . . . solidos XXXV culpabilis iudicetur'). It should be noted, however, that certain categories of slaves (swineherds, hunters, smiths, millers, carpenters) were valued much more highly than ordinary slaves: the tariff of composition for them reached 70 sous in the *Pactus* (X, 6), 60 sous in the *Lex* (XI, 2): this is because the slaves were trained. But this does not imply that they were attributed with a more human condition; trained animals were also valued much more highly than ordinary animals (15 sous for a hunting dog as opposed to 3 sous for an untrained dog).

article 1. If someone voluntarily commits a homicide, let him give in reparation three female and three male slaves.

article 7. If someone injures a man to the extent of cutting off a hand or a foot, let him give in reparation one female or one male slave.

But, equally:

article 35. If someone strikes a man to the extent of breaking only one bone, let him give in reparation three cows.[64]

Such texts speak for themselves. If even more convincing testimony to the sub-humanity of the slave is required, two simple criteria can be employed: that of punishments and that of sexual relations between free and non-free (or rather, of their prohibition).

The history of punishments has never been written; this is unfortunate. Attempts to define liberty in the Middle Ages have been made in all sorts of ways without realising that, first and foremost, only the man who was not beaten felt himself to be free.[65] Slaves were beaten, and worse. Three types of punishment could be inflicted on them: blows, mutilation and death.

The number of blows that a slave might receive, as revealed by the barbarian laws, was appalling: dozens, hundreds of blows, as many as, and often many more than, for an ox or a dog. What with? Here, too, there is silence on the part of historians fascinated by the most esoteric institutional problems, but lacking any interest, it appears, in the manner in which their ancestors were beaten. Lashing with a whip was probably the normal practice; it was customary, at any rate, in Visigothic Spain.[66] Burgundian

---

[64] *Leges Wallicae*, ed. in F. H. W. Wasserschleben, *Die Bussordnungen der abendländischen Kirche* (Halle, 1851, reprinted Graz, 1958) pp. 124–36. Provisions of the same type are found in the *Canones Hiberenses, ibid.*, pp. 136–7.

[65] Or who at least could not receive corporal punishment except in consequence of a judicial decision. This remark applies equally to the slaves of the early Middle Ages and the villeins of a later period, the latter, too, being thrashed with impunity by the agents of their lord (as is amply demonstrated by the literature of the twelfth and thirteenth centuries). Does it not also apply to the domestic servants of the modern period? The thrashings inflicted on valets in comedies are the burlesque rendering of the sinister dependence in which servants of both sexes were often placed.

[66] In the Visigothic laws, the term *flagella* is used in 200 cases to indicate the sanction to be inflicted; the number of blows prescribed varied from 3 to 300. See, on this subject, Claude Nicolau, *Les systèmes de répression dans la législation wisigothique* (Mémoire de maîtrise, University of Toulouse–Le Mirail, 1977).

masters preferred a stick.[67] Salic law was more explicit; slaves were
tied to a ladder with their backs bare and struck with rods whose
thickness was normally that of a little finger.[68] And it should not be
thought that these corporal punishments existed only in the minds
of the jurists who compiled the Germanic codes; referring to the
great Spanish landlords, King Ervig commented: 'anxious to get
their fields worked, they thrashed their multitudes of slaves'.[69]

Mutilation was the practice everywhere, and is frequently
attested. A slave might have his hands cut off or his eyes put out
(amongst the Bavarians, for example),[70] but brutality of this sort
was generally avoided since it diminished, or even destroyed, the
victim's capacity for work. Facial mutilation was preferred (cutting
off the nose, the ears, the lips or scalping (*decalvatio*),[71] since,
whilst being spectacular, it did not take the worker from his work.
Castration was not uncommon, either in Spain or Frankish Gaul;
certainly it was not without risk (it was quite common for the
victim to die), but it presented the double advantage of severely
punishing the slave and softening his character. Both Salic and
Visigothic law obligingly tell us what was the equivalent for
women: 142 blows with rods north of the Pyrenees, cutting off the
nose to the south.[72]

Lastly, death. The master retained, of course, the power of life

---

[67] Burgundian law expressed the tariff of penalties to be inflicted on slaves in *ictus fustium*.

[68] *Pactus legis salicae*, ms. *S*, XLI, 9: 'Si vero in quolibet crimine servus compre-hendditur, dominus ipsius, si praesens est, ab eo qui repetit, admonere debet ut servum suum debeat suppliciis dare, ubi quis repetit et virgas paratas habere debet, quae ad magnitudinem minoris digiti minime sint et quoaequales, et scamno pristo ubi servo ipso tendere debeat.' In practice, Salic law measured the punishments in blows with rods (*colapos*) or whips (*flagella*).

[69] *Lex Visigothorum*, IX, 2, 9: 'laborandis agris studentes, servorum multitudines cedunt . . . '

[70] *Lex Baiwariorum*, II, 6, 11, 12 (mutilation of the hands) and I, 6 (ablation of the hands or the eyes). This last sanction was laid down in cases of burning churches: 'si servus est, tollatur manus eius et oculi eius, ut amplius non valeat facere' (for the same offence, a freeman was punished with a fine of 40 sous). Such disposi-tions speak volumes on the subject of the atmosphere of sweetness and light in which Christianity was imposed on Bavaria . . .

[71] The *decalvatio* (not to be confused with the *detonsio* – tonsure) was in fact the scalp; the hair was not cut off but pulled out. On this subject, see Nicolau, *Les systèmes de répression*, pp. 116–17, and for Merovingian Gaul, J. Hoyoux, 'Reges criniti: chevelures, tonsures et scalps chez les Mérovingiens', *Revue belge de philologie et d'histoire*, 26 (1948), p. 479.

[72] *Pactus legis salicae*, LXVII, 7; *Lex Visigothorum*, XII, 3, 4.

and death over his slaves. There was one exception to this rule: in Spain, around 650, a law of Chindaswinth abolished this right.[73] But, even in this case, ancient practices survived. The law was not observed, or, more accurately, it was got round, as we learn from a text of twenty years later (a law of Recceswinth on the same subject). Prohibited from killing recalcitrant slaves, masters, we are told, 'cut off a hand or the nose or the lips or the tongue or an ear or even a foot, or even put out an eye or severed some part of their body, or gave orders for them to be cut off, put out or severed'.[74]

How are these savage punishments to be explained? They did not spring simply from the sadism of masters, even though this was, in some instances, apparent.[75] They primarily served as examples, and by their terrifying character (the facial mutilations), were intended to discourage any spirit of insubordination amongst the slave population.[76]

It is not surprising that, ill-treated in this manner, slaves were prevented from frequenting free women. The question of sexual relations between free and slave constitutes, in fact, a privileged field of research, since the barbarian laws manifest a rare prolixity on this subject. The extreme precision and the abundance of the injunctions and prohibitions which they formulate, and the ruthless nature of the sanctions inflicted on offenders, constitute the best evidence of the barrier not only of class, but truly of race, even species, which free society wished to maintain between itself and the servile labour force.

In most cases,[77] unions between free and slave were considered

---

[73] *Lex Visigothorum*, VI, 5, 12: 'Ne domini extra iudicem servos suos occidant . . .; ut nullus dominorum dominarumque servorum suorum vel ancillarum seu qualiumcumque personarum extra publicum iudicium quandoquidem occisor existat.'

[74] *Lex Visigothorum*, VI, 5, 13, Recceswinth forbade such practices under pain of three years of penance (the form to be decided by the local bishop). His law on this subject was revoked by King Ervig before being restored by King Egica. Was it ever applied?

[75] See, in particular, Gregory of Tours, *Historia Francorum*, V, 3; the duke Rauching had torches put out between the naked thighs of his slaves; he had a young *servus* and an *ancilla* who had had the temerity to wish to marry buried alive, etc.

[76] It should be noted that facial mutilations constituted a frequent form of repression of an insubordinate peasantry throughout the Middle Ages. See, for example, the description in Wace of the repression of the revolt in Normandy in 997 (*Roman de Rou*, vv. 815–956).

[77] I will deal later with the question of sexual relations between a master and his own female slaves; see below, pp. 24–5 and note 88.

to be against nature. To be more precise – and on this point a comparison of the barbarian laws and penitentials is highly illuminating – they were treated as analogous to the offence of bestiality.[78] For the free woman who entered into carnal union with one of her slaves, reduction to slavery or, more often, death ensued. In Spain, the guilty couple were publicly whipped, then burned alive.[79] In Frankish Gaul, still in the eighth century, the free woman who gave way to this temptation became a slave of the fisc, unless her family preferred to kill her; her partner was condemned to the very harshest torture (*pessima cruciata*) and must die on the wheel.[80] As a general rule, the slave who laid a finger on a free woman could not hope to survive; it was lynch-law, characteristic of many other slave or post-slave societies. Also, and this shows clearly how slaves were less than human, a woman whose husband was reduced to servitude could remarry. Such remarriage was accepted both by civil and church law; in Spain, it was permitted at once,[81] in England, the clergy imposed a delay of one year, as in the case of a widow.[82]

Two consequences followed logically from the non-humanity of the slave: he could own nothing and he had no rights over his children.

The inability of slaves to own, certainly, poses problems, since some of them – in the early Middle Ages as in Antiquity – disposed of some property (moveable goods or money of which they enjoyed precarious possession).[83] But these things did not belong to the slave in law; he owned them no more than, for example, a dog owned its collar. In any case, he could alienate nothing of what he held. The Lombard king, Rothari, stated this formally in 643: 'A slave cannot sell anything. If someone buys something

---

[78] References to the sin of bestiality are very frequent in the penitentials; see, for example, Cumméan I, 28; III, 10, 28; Bede, III, 26, 28; Vigila, 90 . . . (Wasserschleben).

[79] *Lex Visigothorum*, III, 2, 2.

[80] *Novellae legis salicae*, III, 1.

[81] *Poenitentiale Vigilanum*, c. 72 (Wasserschleben, p. 532).

[82] *Poenitentiale Theodori*, II, 12, 8 (*ibid.*, p. 214).

[83] The existence of such property can be deduced from the possibility offered by the law to a slave of buying off certain sanctions inflicted on him. Salic law, for example, said that the slave should receive 120 blows with a whip or 'pay 3 sous for his back' (XIII, 1), that he should be castrated or pay 6 sous (XIII, 2; XXXV, 4).

from a slave, let him lose the price he has paid, and let what he bought revert to the slave's master.'[84]

That the slave had no power over his offspring resulted from the simple fact that unions between *servi* and *ancillae* were simply *de facto* unions. They were *contubernia*, a term used equally of the mating of animals. The offspring of slaves thus belonged to the master, like those produced by his domestic livestock. Children might therefore be separated from their parents, sold, or divided between different owners. In this last case, the law only intervened to resolve one specific difficulty: to fix the amount of the pecuniary compensation when there was an odd number of children to be shared out.[85]

It is time, with these remarks in mind, to come to the promised definition. This, for the slave of the sixth to eighth centuries, hardly differs from those which have been or could be proposed for his homologues in Antiquity or modern times:[86] the slave appears as a de-socialised being whose production and reproduction were entirely under the control of another. A being: certainly not, in the eyes of the free, a man or a woman. De-socialised: since placed on the margins of the human community; it is clear that free persons reduced to servitude lost their status, and no longer existed for the group, even the family, from which they came.[87] Whose production was alienated: inevitably, since they were tools of labour. But (and this differentiates slaves from other types of

---

[84] *Leges Langobardorum* (ed. Beyerle (1962)), *Edictum Rothari*, 233. The same provision existed amongst the Burgundians: *Lex Romana Burgondionum*, XIV.
[85] *Lex Visigothorum*, X, 1, 17.
[86] For this definition, I draw in particular on the introduction by Claude Meillassoux to *L'esclavage dans l'Afrique noire* (pp. 11–26). In these extremely suggestive pages, the author presents reflections inspired by the ethnographic research whose results are presented within the volume. See also Dockès, 'Définition de l'esclave' in *La Libération médiévale*, pp. 10–30.
[87] Meillassoux, *L'esclavage*, p. 21: 'By being snatched from his original social milieu, [the slave] was primarily "captive" . . . Removed from his original social milieu by violence, the captive was *de-socialised* by the brutal rupture of those relationships which characterise the social person: of family, of conjugality, of paternity etc. This de-socialisation is rendered in the new environment by a depersonalisation, further accentuated when the captive had been sold as merchandise, a process by which he was in addition reified. The de-socialisation and the depersonalisation are basic to the *condition* of the slave, a condition strictly negative and distinct in this from the *status* enjoyed by the free man.' This analysis resembles in some ways that of Dockès of the slave as 'dead to society', 'in suspended non-existence' and 'one of the living dead' (*La Libération médiévale*, pp. 11–16).

dependent worker) whose reproduction was also alienated – both
male and female slaves lacked the power either to choose their
partner or retain their children.[88]

This definition established, one observation, elementary but
crucial, must at once be made; the desire of the free to confine
slaves to a sub-human condition came up against an insurmount-
able obstacle. The obstacle was biological; objectively, slaves were
neither bovine nor porcine, but men and women. Hence the
impossibility experienced by *all* slave societies in maintaining the
definition of slavery in its full rigour. There resulted multiple contradictions which can be observed at leisure throughout the sixth
to eighth centuries, both in the formulation of legislation regarding
slaves and in the gap which separated this from reality.

Firstly, as far as punishments were concerned, it was for the
master alone to correct his slave, but the law came to prescribe
penalties for the *servus* accused of offences or crimes. This was to
recognise him, even if almost always to his detriment, as a juridical
person,[89] thus as an actual person.

Secondly, in the case of mixed unions, it is clear that the very
cruel sanctions repressing these applied almost exclusively to sexual relations between free women and male slaves.[90] On the other
hand, no barbarian law mentions the relations which a free man
might have with his *ancillae*; in such cases, the female slave ceased
to be a tool of labour and became a partner in pleasure.[91] It was
then the woman and not the beast in her which was appreciated,
and we know that certain masters went so far as to marry their

[88] Meillassoux, *L'esclavage dans l'Afrique noire*, p. 25: 'The control of the physical
reproduction of the slave is the condition of his exploitation as of his enslavement. This control is exercised with variations and more or fewer constraints
according to the society and the functions entrusted to the slave, but is always
present.'

[89] The problem of a possible 'juridical personality' of the slave has been the subject
of exhaustive study by legal historians. See, for example, for Visigothic Spain,
Verlinden, *L'esclavage dans l'Europe médiévale*, pp. 88ff.

[90] The free man was only punished if he copulated with a female slave who did not
belong to him; and, even in this case, only if the sexual act was accompanied by
physical maltreatment (damage to another's belongings) or happened in the
house of the master of the *ancilla* (violation of residence). See, for example, *Lex
Visigothorum*, III, 4, 15–16.

[91] Like the *bortmagad*, pleasure-slaves, which the law of the Frisians distinguished
from the *ancilla pecuariae*; union with the *bortmagad* of another man cost 12
sous, whilst anyone could use at will any *ancilla pecuaria* (a slave considered, in
any case, to be so repulsive that the law did not even envisage that she might
tempt a free man), *Lex Frisonica*, XIII, 1, *De stupro ancillarum*.

slaves (Clovis II marrying his Anglo-Saxon slave Bathilda, to quote a celebrated example).[92]

Further, whilst the servile *contubernium* was only a mating, some unions between *servi* and *ancillae* could present such an appearance of stability and durability that they were eventually assimilated into the *matrimonium* of the free.[93]

Lastly, contradictions show in the function of slave property; it might be in the interests of some masters, as was the case in Antiquity, to let their slaves carry out transactions, do business, and make money. In the last resort, the slave could buy his freedom with his hoard; the law of the Bavarians, for example, allowed this on the sole condition that the sum paid for the purchase had not been amassed without the master's knowledge.[94]

These contradictions, I repeat, are inherent to the nature of the slave system; they constitute, in a sense, the flaws in the system. All those factors which contributed to accentuating them can be regarded as causes of its decline.

The religious factor

Since Marc Bloch (and, indeed, following in his footsteps), all those historians who have dealt with the servitude of the early Middle Ages have tended to minimise the role played by the Church in its disappearance. They have correctly observed that, as an institution, the Church never opposed slavery, but, on the contrary, both approved it in principle and practised it.

Doctrinally, all the Church's thinking on this subject derived from St Paul, whose positions it is useful to recall in some detail. Three passages from the Apostle's Letters bear on slavery:

Every man should remain in the condition in which he was called. Were you a slave when you were called? Do not let that trouble you . . . For the man who as a slave received the call to be a Christian is the Lord's freedman, . . . Thus each one, my friends, is to remain before God in the condition in which he received his call. (First Letter to the Corinthians 7: 20-4)

---

[92] *Vita sanctae Bathildae* (*MGH, Scriptores Rerum Merovingicarum*, II, pp. 482ff.).
[93] In the edict of the Lombard King Rothari, the partners in a *contubernium* were sometimes incidentally described as *maritus* and *uxor* (*Edictum Rothari*, 98-9).
[94] *Lex Baiwariorum*, XVI, 7.

Slaves, obey your earthly masters with fear and trembling, single-mindedly, as serving Christ. Do not offer merely the outward show of service, to curry favour with men, but, as slaves of Christ, do whole-heartedly the will of God. Give the cheerful service of those who serve the Lord, not men . . . You masters, also, must do the same by them. Give up using threats; remember you both have the same Master in heaven, and he has no favourites. (Letter to the Ephesians 6: 5–9)

And, when Paul announces to Philemon that he is sending back to him one of his slaves, Onesimus, who had taken refuge with him, he prays Philemon to receive him gently, 'as a dear brother'. (Letter to Philemon, verse 16).

These texts of St Paul were constantly repeated in later centuries, but always interpreted in the sense least favourable to slaves, that is exclusively to legitimise slavery. See, for example, what has become of the words of the Letter to the Ephesians in a collection of sermons from the early Middle Ages:

Slaves, obey your masters single-mindedly, not offering merely the outward show of service, but in doing your work with love; because God has made them to be your masters, and you to serve them.[95]

This was by no means all. Listen to St Augustine himself, whose arguments similarly were endlessly repeated:

The first cause of slavery is the sin which has subjected man to man and this has not been done without the will of God who knows no injustice and knew how to apportion the penalties as the wages of the guilty.[96]

Two ideas are here developed and closely linked, that slavery is the penalty for the sins committed by men, and that it is just that this penalty strikes some men and not others because, since God is incapable of error, those it strikes are guilty.

This concept of the collective guilt of slaves was further developed by Isidore of Seville, who justified the right of masters to coerce by the need to improve slaves, and this for the general good:

Because of the sin of the first man, the penalty of servitude was inflicted by God on the human race: to those unsuited for liberty, he has mercifully accorded servitude. And although original sin has been removed for all

[95] Sermon wrongly attributed to St Augustine, in fact apocryphal (Ps. Aug., *Sermones*, CXVII, 12).
[96] *De civitate Dei*, XIX, 15.

the faithful through the grace of baptism, nevertheless the just God has apportioned different types of life among men, making some slaves and others masters, in such a way that the propensity of slaves to do wrong should be restrained by the power of the masters.[97]

The divine origin of slavery, the genetic perversity of slaves and the necessity of servitude as a means for the redemption of humanity through penitence – these were all ideas which became commonplace. In the Carolingian period, they are to be found in the writings of Alcuin, Jonas of Orléans, Regino of Prüm, Rabanus Maurus and many others.

In practice, the Church had, if it so wished, two means of contributing to the extinction of slavery: on the one hand, extending the right of sanctuary to fugitive slaves; on the other, encouraging manumissions by setting an example. What course did it adopt?

All the conciliar legislation of the fourth to ninth centuries was intended, by a variety of means, to exclude slaves from the right of sanctuary. St Paul had returned Philemon's slave, Onesimus, to his master; it was right, therefore, to return fugitive *mancipia* to theirs.[98] This rule was practised. The Life of St Pourçain, for example, tells us that he himself, having fallen into slavery and taken refuge in a monastery, was returned to his owner by its abbot.[99] At the most, certain councils (Orléans in 511, Clichy in 626) attempted to limit the results of such restitution for the slave by making the master swear not to take vengeance by killing or torturing him.[100] But woe betide the Christian who assisted the flight of a *servus*, or even just his disobedience; this was declared anathema. This was decided as early as the fourth century by the eastern council of Gangres, and this malediction was repeated century after century right down to Rabanus Maurus, who approved of it.[101]

---

[97] *Sententiae*, III, 47. For the familiar theme of the depravity inherent to the slave (*licentia male agendi servorum*) and its development in the literature of Visigothic Spain, see P. D. King, *Law and Society in the Visigothic Kingdom* (Cambridge, 1972), pp. 177–9.

[98] For the use of the Letter to Philemon as justification for such returns, M. Roberti, *La lettera di S. Paolo a Filemone e la condizione giuridica dello schiavo fuggitivo* (Milan, 1933).

[99] Gregory of Tours, *Vitae Patrum*, V, 1 (text quoted by G. Fournier, 'L'esclavage en Basse Auvergne aux époques mérovingienne et carolingienne', *Cahiers d'Histoire*, 6 (1961), 363.

[100] *MGH, Concilia Meroving.*, pp. 3, 198.

[101] Council of Gangres: Mansi, *Sacrorum Conciliorum*, II, col. 1100. The ideas of

However, the Church – here adopting the teaching of the Stoics – praised the practice of manumission, ranking it as a pious work. Saints' lives are frequently embellished with episodes of the redemption or manumission of slaves.[102] But, on closer reading, it can be seen that the principal end sought by the bishops was less to popularise manumission than to Christianise its methods, and integrate them into the liturgy. What was most strongly encouraged was the *manumissio in ecclesia*, already instituted at the time of Constantine, which now tended to be turned into a solemn ceremony with its own rite (celebration at the corner of the altar).[103] There seems to have been a move, in the seventh and eighth centuries, towards establishing a sacrament of enfranchisement, a new baptism sanctifying a new birth, that of the human animal into the ranks of men.

In any case, if the Church encouraged the laity to liberate their slaves, it remained, itself, openly slave-owning. Bishops and abbots were prohibited from emancipating the *mancipia* working on the demesnes in their charge. Councils repeatedly asserted this in the most explicit terms.[104] The reasons quoted were always the same: slaves, like the other possessions of the Church, belonged to God, and no one had the right to diminish the patrimony of the Lord. This was sometimes elaborated; it was by the labour of slaves that the Church could provide for the needs of the poor; to free slaves would be to harm the poor.[105] The argument is revealing – the beggars and the poor were at the very bottom of the social ladder, hence the solicitude lavished on them by the clergy. Where did this leave the slaves? Outside society.

In practice, the Church appears as the largest slave-owner.

Rabanus Maurus on slavery are particularly clearly shown in the *Comm. in Ecclesiasticum*, II, 8 and VII, 12 (*PL*, CIX, cols. 807–8, 1004–5).

[102] For example, for Aquitaine: Rouche, *L'Aquitaine des Wisigoths aux Arabes*, pp. 212–14 (lives of Saints Eloi, Cybard and Yrieix); also *Vita Tillonis, AA SS*, Janv. I, p. 377. For Provence, *Vita Caesarii, SSRM*, III, p. 493. For the Carolingian Auvergne, *Vita s. Geraldi*, III, 4 (*PL*, CXXXIII, col. 692).

[103] For the *manumissio in ecclesia*, Verlinden, *L'esclavage dans l'Europe médiévale*, vol. 1, p. 35. See also C. G. Mor, 'La manumissio in ecclesia', *Rivista storica diritta italiana* (1928), pp. 80–150. There is a good evocation of the rite in the formulary of Tours, form. 12, *MGH, Formulae Merovingici et Karolini*.

[104] For Septimania, Agde (506). For Spain: first council of Seville, council of Mérida, fourth and ninth councils of Toledo. For Gaul: Yenne, canon 8 (517), Clichy, c. 15 (626/627), Rheims, c. 13 (627/630).

[105] Conciliar canons of Agde, Clichy and Rheims cited above.

Virtually only parish churches, it seems, were without slaves. In Spain, for example, the sixteenth council of Toledo considered that a rural church could not support a full-time priest unless it had at least ten *mancipia* in its service (and if it had as few as ten, it was described as *pauperrima*).[106] In wills of abbots and bishops, slaves were counted in tens, even hundreds: 32 in the case of St Aredius (to which should be added 45 freed slaves), and 175 for St Cybard.[107] On monastic demesnes, the figures were even larger. When St Eligius endowed the monastery of Solignac, he enfranchised 'only' a hundred of the slaves he installed in its service.[108] In the Carolingian period, according to Elipandus of Toledo, the four abbeys ruled by Alcuin (Saint-Martin of Tours, Ferrières, Saint-Loup of Troyes and Saint-Josse) employed altogether over 20,000 *mancipia*.[109] And, finally, the papacy itself practised slavery. The correspondence of Gregory the Great contains orders to purchase slaves (which his emissaries must have procured in the markets of Gaul and Sardinia).[110] There is also the injunction addressed by the pope to the intendants of the patrimony of St Peter in Sicily to restore to their masters the *servi* who had sought refuge on the pontifical estates.[111]

One final question: were the slaves of the Church not treated more humanely than others? It must have varied from one case to another, but there is some suggestive evidence. First the council of Mérida, and then the eleventh council of Toledo, prohibited clerics from practising amputations (*truncationes membrorum*) on their slaves, proof that this practice was far from unknown.[112] The Church, then, from the highest to the lowest, far from fighting

---

[106] Toledo XVI, c. 5 (Mansi, *Sacrorum Conciliorum*, XII, 62).

[107] Rouche, *L'Aquitaine des Wisiogoths aux Arabes*, p. 212.

[108] *Ibid.*, p. 212.

[109] This figure is certainly exaggerated, since noted in a letter of a polemical nature. But Alcuin did not contest it; he was content to reply only that he had not himself made further purchases. For the *mancipia* of Alcuin, see Doehaerd, *Le haut moyen âge occidental*, pp. 187–8; Poly and Bournazel, *La mutation féodale*, p. 199.

[110] *MGH, Epistolae*, I, pp. 125 (purchases in Sardinia by the notary, Boniface) and 389 (purchases in Gaul by the priest, Candide, charged with acquiring some *pueros anglos qui sint ab annis decem et septem vel decem et octo*). For Gregory I and slavery, see Verlinden, *L'esclavage dans l'Europe médiévale*, vol. 2, pp. 92–6.

[111] *MGH, Epistolae*, I, p. 53.

[112] Mérida, c. 15; Toledo XI, c. 6. See also King, *Law and Society in the Visigothic Kingdom*, p. 151.

slavery, supported it; on the one hand, it justified it ideologically, on the other it based on it its material prosperity.

But is this all there is to be said? No, and Marc Bloch himself, though very critical of the Church's conduct, tempered his judgement: 'It was no small thing to have said to the "tool with a voice", as the old Roman agronomists called him: "you are a man" and "you are a Christian".'[113] The clergy of the sixth to eighth centuries were obliged to admit, despite an obvious reluctance, that slaves belonged to the Christian community. While they based the legitimacy of slavery on the words of St Paul, they could not forget the other aspect of the lessons of the Apostle, that is that God 'has no favourites'.[114] In fact, even if they appealed to the Old Testament, where they found models for reduction to slavery,[115] it was impossible for them to obliterate entirely the message of the gospels. Certainly, the Church behaved as if slaves were not complete Christians; Pope Leo I, in line with several councils, forbade them access to the priesthood.[116] A slave, with certain exceptions,[117] could not be a priest. But he was baptised, he could (indeed should) attend divine offices, he was admitted to the sacraments, he had a soul. He was, then, unambiguously a man. This categoric assertion was important at a time when the Church, in its efforts to destroy the pantheistic myths of Antiquity, was resolved to establish an absolute gulf between animality and humanity.[118] Slaves were on the right side of the dividing line.

Was this said to the *mancipia* in the churches? It is hardly likely. 'The churches', declared, for example, King Leovigild, 'should be the places where the need for obedience is taught and where examples of punishments are shown.'[119] In practice, the first Christian buildings erected in the countryside were private chapels built by great landowners on their slave-worked estates; the slave

---

[113] Bloch, *Slavery and Serfdom*, p. 14.

[114] Letter to the Ephesians, 6, v. 9, see above, p. 26.

[115] The examples most often quoted were Canaan and Joseph.

[116] *Can. apost.*, 81 (Mansi, *Sacrorum Conciliorum*, I, col. 46); Elvire, c. 80 (Mansi, II, col. 19). For Leo I, *PL*, 54, p. 611. There were similar provisions in civil legislation, from Valentinian III. On this subject, Verlinden, *L'esclavage dans l'Europe médiévale*, vol. 1, pp. 37–8.

[117] They were common in Spain. See, in particular, the will of Alfonso II, king of Asturias (died 842) which contains a long list of slave-priests and slave-deacons (*Diplomatica astur*, ed. A. C. Floriano (Oviedo, 1949), 1, no. 24, pp. 119–31).

[118] Hence the enormous attention paid by the penitentials to the sin of bestiality (see above, note 76).   [119] *Lex Visigothorum*, V, 4, 17.

labourers who were allowed to enter (on what conditions? or, to be more precise, in what grovelling posture?) were hardly likely to have heard there this liberating message. But they did enter and met there people who were free, if poor, and often workers in the same fields, subjected to the same harassment from the same masters. They knew each other; they learned to regard themselves as Christians, that is as men and women. It is hardly surprising, therefore, that mixed unions, however severely punished by the law, happened. There is evidence of them as early as the seventh century.[120] By the ninth century they had become common.[121] The Christianisation of the countryside – slow, haphazard, laborious[122] – must certainly have facilitated, without the knowledge of the hierarchy, the development of closer ties between the *servi* and the *pauperes*, encouraging a solidarity of the wretched.

But it had an even more decisive effect on the image slaves had of themselves. The very fact of entering a sacred building gave them proof of their humanity.[123] This conviction contradicted all the conditioning to which they were subjected, and which was designed to give them a repulsive, *vilissima*,[124] even bestial, iden-

---

[120] *Lex Visigothorum*, III, 2, 3 (law of Recceswinth). This law forbade mixed unions, but nevertheless implicitly recognised their existence. The couple concerned were brought before the judge three times: both were sentenced each time to receive 100 lashes. If they persisted three times in their will to live together – and survived the punishment – their union would be, though reluctantly, recognised (the free partner accepting reduction to slavery). Who can still claim that love was an invention of the twelfth century?

[121] Very numerous examples in all the polyptiques.

[122] If it was so slow (from the fourth to the ninth centuries: five hundred years!), it was perhaps because, for so long, the countryside knew no other places of worship than the private churches built by the great landowners. These edifices, situated on slave-estates, can have had little attraction for the local free peasantry. The Christianisation of the independent peasantry, in practice, was surely achieved by other means (I am thinking, in particular, of the apostleship of the hermits). It was only towards the end of a long evolution that the whole rural population was brought together in the same churches.

[123] In practice, even in Antiquity, slaves could be associated in certain forms of worship (Piganiol's idea of a religion specific to slaves is no longer accepted), but this was probably exceptional. On the importance attached by slaves to their integration into a community of worship, see the section devoted to this question by Gilberto Freyre for Brazil (*Masters and Slaves*, pp. 320ff.). Note this observation by a seventeenth-century traveller: 'The negroes who are not baptised think they are regarded as inferior beings . . . In reality, they are regarded less as men than as ferocious beasts until they enjoy the privilege of going to mass and receiving the sacraments.'

[124] In the Visigothic laws, the qualification *vilis, vilissimus* was regularly applied to the rural slave to distinguish him from the *idoneus*, or domestic slave.

tity.[125] Christian practice questioned the validity of the ideology promoted by the dominant class and mediated by the Church. It thus contributed to the destruction of one of its foundations – the 'ideal component', to employ the vocabulary of Maurice Godelier[126] – of the domination which the masters exercised over their wretched herds.

The consensus necessary to the maintenance of the slave system was thus undermined at two levels: the free poor ceased to see slaves as the cattle they were designated as by the rich and forbidden to frequent by the law; the slaves found in the sacraments which they received the justification for their aspiration to the human condition and, in consequence, to liberty.

Difficulties of supply

We come now to the demographic argument: that slavery ended thanks to a shortage of slaves. The diminution in the numbers of captures brought about a diminution in the stock of slaves. In other words, reductions to slavery ceased to be sufficiently numerous to compensate for the losses due to manumission or other factors. We must look, therefore, at the evolution of the phenomenon of enslavement.

War continued to be, as in Antiquity, the major supplier. Nevertheless, we need, in order to measure its effects, to distinguish between two periods, the age of the barbarian kingdoms and the Carolingian period.

From the fifth to the eighth centuries, war was permanent in western Europe and it remained fundamentally a manhunt. This is particularly clear in the case of England. The Anglo-Saxon conquest was accompanied by the large-scale enslavement of the Celtic population. All those Britons who had neither been massacred nor taken refuge in Brittany or the western provinces of Wales or Cornwall were reduced to slavery. But once the Celts were vanquished, peace did not follow, and the history of the

---

[125] See above, p. 17. In addition, 'Si servus aut ancilla aut equus aut bos aut quodlibet animal . . . ' (*Lex Frisonica*, *Additio*, tit. VII).

[126] M. Godelier, *L'idéel et le matériel* (Paris, 1984), p. 205; 'Every dominating power is composed of two inextricably mixed elements which give it its force: violence and consent. Our analysis inevitably leads to the conclusion that of the two components of power, the stronger force is not the violence of those who dominate, but the consent of those dominated in their domination.'

various Anglo-Saxon kingdoms is little more than the history of the interminable conflicts between them. These wars were also accompanied by more or less systematic enslavement and sale (often on the continent) of the captured labour force; the Anglian or Saxon slave was a common sight in the markets of Gaul.[127] As, indeed, were Celtic slaves, for the Celts were no kinder to each other than were their victors. Gaelic legends abound with stories of captures and there is an echo even in *Tristan and Isolde*; everyone knows that Tristan's first achievement was to kill Morholt of Ireland who came periodically to Cornwall to levy a tribute in young slaves of both sexes.

The wars which desolated Merovingian Gaul were also in effect razzias. One only needs to read the speech put by Gregory of Tours into the mouth of King Thierry I as he led his warriors into the Auvergne: 'Follow me and I will lead you into a country . . . where you will find cattle and slaves in abundance'.[128] The promise was kept; a large part of the population of Brioude and other places figured amongst the booty carried back to the Frankish lands.[129] War, in the Merovingian period, developed on many fronts, on the frontiers, of course (in Germany, on the confines of Brittany and Vasconia), but equally in the interior of the Frankish kingdom, in the course of the incessant conflicts between different kings (of Austrasia, Neustria, Burgundy etc.). And, above all, it was not only sovereigns who engaged in armed expeditions. The sixth to eighth centuries were a period of tribal wars which were waged from city to city, from province to province – Orléans

---

[127] For example: 'Erat tunc B. Eligius captivorum redemptor; habebat namque maximum in hujus modi opere studium. Sane ubicumque venundandum intellexisset mancipium, magna cum festinatione et misericordia accurens, mox dato pretio liberabat captivum; nonnumquam vero agmen integrum et usque ad centum animas, cum de navi egrederentur, pariter redimebat, sed praecipue ex genere Saxonum, qui abunde eo tempore veluti greges pecudum in diversa distrahebantur' (*Vita Tillonis, AA SS*, Janv. I, p. 377). For the trade in Anglian slaves, see the correspondence of Gregory the Great (see above, note 108). For the abundance of servile labour in England from the sixth to the eighth centuries, see M. Postan and C. Hill, *Histoire économique et sociale de la Grande Bretagne* (Paris, 1977), pp. 18–19 (first published as M. M. Postan, *The Medieval Economy and Society* (London, 1972). See in particular the laws of Ine, paras 23, 32, 33, 46, 74 (in D. Whitelock, *English Historical Documents*, 1 (1955), 364ff.).

[128] Gregory of Tours, *Historia Francorum*, III, 11.

[129] *Ibid.*, III, 12–13. For these events see Fournier, 'L'esclavage en Basse Auvergne', pp. 363–4. Bourges suffered a similar fate (*Historia Francorum*, VI, 31).

against Blois, Blois against Chartres, Chartres against Orléans etc.[130] In the time of Gregory of Tours, the region round Tours was pillaged ten times in seventeen years. This pillage was aimed at men as much as goods.

It may be thought, therefore, that from the fifth to the eighth centuries, the recruitment of slaves through war did not cease, but even – as Marc Bloch suggested – increased by comparison with ancient times. But this recruitment became localised, as a result of the small sphere of activity of these wars; slaves henceforward came, for the most part, from regions close to the region of their captivity. This was a crucial change, to which we will return.

With the accession to power of the Carolingians, these internal wars ceased (though there were still slave raids in Aquitaine under Pepin the Short).[131] One of Charlemagne's most obvious ambitions was to impose peace within the *regnum Francorum* and he was successful. Manhunts were confined to the frontiers of the Empire. They were at first productive, as long as the Franks were victorious. We know, for example, that many of the vanquished Saxons were transported into the interior provinces of the Empire to provide labour on the large estates.[132] But from the reign of Louis the Pious, wars, from being offensive, began to be defensive. In these circumstances, the number of captives certainly diminished. Should we see in this reduction in supply one of the causes (even the principal cause) of the decline of slavery? This would be to make too close a link between the fate of the slave mode of production and the military situation. It would amount to saying that slave regimes could only exist when states were always victorious. It would, above all, be to forget that war has only ever been one source of slaves. There are many other ways of procuring cheap servile labour. Early medieval Europe practised many of them.

Poverty was probably responsible for as much enslavement as war. It was almost general. The mass of *pauperes* lived in a state of endemic malnutrition and this state of penury was aggravated

---

[130] *Ibid.*, VII, 2.

[131] Fournier, 'L'esclavage en Basse Auvergne', p. 364 (reduction into slavery of the inhabitants of the castellany of Turenne during the campaign of Pepin against Waïfre).

[132] J.-P. Poly has discovered Saxon slaves even on the estates of Saint-Victor of Marseilles ('Régime domanial et rapports de production', p. 76, and note 50).

cyclically, every ten or fifteen years, engendering serious famines.[133] The only way to survive, for many of the poor, was to alienate their liberty. The modalities of these enslavements are plentifully described in chronicles and in collections of formularies.

One means of enslavement was debt; nothing had changed since Antiquity. Whoever borrowed and could not repay his debt was reduced into servitude for the benefit of his creditor. Hispanic law even spelled out that a debtor with several creditors became their joint property.[134] So in the eighth century you could become a slave for a few handfuls of grain or flour begged in hard times.[135]

Children were sold into slavery; this was authorised and practised everywhere. In all the early medieval penitentials, the rule is the same; it was not a sin for a father to sell sons or daughters as long as they were under fourteen; after that, their consent was necessary.[136] Some formularies (those of Angers and Tours, for example) tell us that bands of beggars, inscribed in the register of certain sanctuaries, specialised in the resale of such child labour.[137] This practice continued under Charlemagne. In 803, the capitulary additional to Salic Law stipulated that 'the fear of being sold as a slave could not excuse the murder of a father, a mother, an uncle, an aunt or other relative'.[138] This refinement is enough in itself to contradict the thesis of a 'softening' of servitude in the Carolingian period.

People sold themselves. When you were dying from hunger, how could you not agree to sell yourself in order to survive? 'Merchants', we are told by Gregory of Tours, 'reduced the poor to slavery in return for a morsel of food.'[139] The formularies vied with each other in providing models for such contracts of sale. They were authorised by the barbarian laws. They were sometimes

---

[133] In the reign of Charlemagne, for example, there were famines in 779–80, 792–3–4, 805–6 and 809, that is (not including local scarcities), eight years of general famine in forty-six years (texts collected by F. Curschmann, *Hungersnöte im Mittelalter* (Leipzig, 1900).   [134] *Lex Visigothorum*, V, 6, 5.

[135] As shown by some models of acts of enslavement preserved in the formularies (Formulaire d'Angers, 9; de Sens, 4).

[136] *Poenitentiale Theodori*, II, 13, 1; *Greg.* 183; *Dach.* 114; *Marlen.* 72; *Ps. Theod.* XIII, 28 (Wasserschleben).

[137] MGH, *Formulae Merovingici et Karolini, Form. Andecav.*, 49; *Form. turon.*, 11.

[138] MGH, *Capitularia regum Francorum.*, I, no. 39 (C. 5), p. 111.

[139] *Historia Francorum*, VII, 45.

even morally justified, as in the laws of the Visigoths: 'He who thinks of selling himself is unworthy to be free.'[140]

Judicial condemnations provided the last, but not the least important, of the mechanisms for enslavement. There were many crimes (or acts judged as such) for which the penalty was reduction to slavery. It appears, fairly regularly, as a substitute for the death penalty. It was more profitable to sell a guilty person than kill them.[141] But the crucial point is that every conviction, of whatever sort, could result in a poor person being enslaved. This was the effect of the system of 'wergild': every perpetrator of an injury who could not pay the pecuniary reparation due to his victim could be reduced into slavery to the benefit of the latter or his family. Unless a rich man paid the wergild instead; this often happened, on the evidence of the formularies, but only for the poor person to become the slave of his 'saviour' as a result of the debt he had contracted.[142] For all these reasons, it can be argued that the judicial machine, throughout the early Middle Ages, functioned as a system for the enslavement of the free poor. This was so to a very late date. In Catalonia, for example, the public tribunals were still pronouncing condemnations to slavery as late as 933, 987 and 988.[143] The same was true of León in 994.[144]

It appears, then, that early medieval society always disposed of a wide range of means for procuring slaves. The end of slavery cannot be explained in terms of the actual difficulties of recruitment. On the other hand, it must be emphasised that slaves were being recruited nearer and nearer to their place of servitude. In Antiquity, the *servus* was always almost a stranger, brought from afar (from the barbarian countries), entirely removed from his place of origin, ignorant even of the language of the land of his captivity. In the early Middle Ages, slave labour was frequently being procured from a neighbouring province (through the wars of

[140] *Lex Visigothorum*, V, 4, 11.
[141] Example of Gregory of Tours: *Historia Francorum*, VI, 36.
[142] Formulaire d'Angers, 2, 3.
[143] AC Vic, pergs. 152, 238; *Cartulario S. Cugat*, ed. Rius Serra (Barcelona, 1946), II, no. 218 (Bonnassie, *La Catalogne*, vol. 1, p. 299).
[144] Cl. Sánchez Albornoz, 'El "juicio del Libro" en León durante el siglo X' (annexe 2) in *Investigaciones y documentos sobre las instituciones hispanas* (Santiago de Chile, 1970), p. 290: 'fui mesta in adulterio cum Petro, que est meo compatre et marido alieno, et fuimus ad Librum, et iudicavit ut tradissent me servire sicut ancilla originale'.

razzia of the Merovingian period), even from the same locality (through the system of enslavement for debt, the sale of children and judicial condemnations). The slave who spoke the local language and who was familiar with local customs was a being who was *less and less de-socialised*. In a sense, he could be said to be now only arbitrarily de-socialised, by a sort of decree of the society of free men who rejected him. But such an exclusion could only operate if it was at least tacitly accepted, by the free as well as the slaves. Such a consensus, as we have seen, barely continued to exist.[145]

The role of productive forces: technical progress and economic growth

Contrary to what many historians have written, neither the Christianisation of the countryside nor the changes in the modes of recruitment were irrelevant to the process of the extinction of slavery. It simply needs to be emphasised that these two phenomena did not intervene directly, or mechanically, but through their consequences for the evolution of behaviour, by modifying the way in which slaves were regarded (as much by the free as by the slaves themselves). If it is the case, as we are told by Maurice Godelier, that every social reality is composed of an ideal part (images of man, of his links with nature and with other men) and a material part (the man himself and his tools),[146] it is clear that the first component of the reality at issue here (slavery) experienced profound transformations throughout the early Middle Ages. What happened to the second part?

Explanations for the end of slavery are today increasingly sought in the economic sphere. This was anticipated by Marc Bloch, for whom the essential factor was the settling of slaves on holdings; he saw in this the origins of their emancipation, and it appeared to him to be the inevitable consequence of the decline of the great estate in direct cultivation, a decline itself explicable by the economic recession of the early Middle Ages. This idea has been taken up by Georges Duby and most contemporary historians, even though they no longer believe in the recession.

[145] See above, p. 32.
[146] Godelier, *L'idéel et le matériel*, pp. 167–220 ('La part idéelle du réel', in particular p. 197).

Charles Parain, for his part, argued from within a perspective of growth. It was the increase in productive forces (and, in particular, technical progress) which, for him, brought about the extinction of the slave mode of production, but, persuaded that it disappeared in late Antiquity, he placed these great innovations, generators of freedom in the Late Empire.

We need, therefore, to pose once again the two questions which are at the heart of the debate, those of technical progress and of changes in the methods of cultivating the soil. We must take account of the most recent research, attempt to assess their relative importance and place the answers in as precise a chronological perspective as possible.

TECHNICAL PROGRESS

This is not the place to examine technical progress in all its aspects. I will deal only with its two most important manifestations, which are also those which have given rise to the most abundant historical literature – the domestication of water power and changes in methods of harnessing.

It is essential, even if commonplace, to emphasise the importance of the revolution constituted by the diffusion of the water mill.[147] Just how important this was becomes apparent when we call to mind what it replaced, that is the hand mill. This rotating drum, in almost universal use in the Roman world from the second century AD, was in practice almost exclusively worked by slaves (mostly female) and the work was long (hour after hour, day and night), tedious and exhausting. Its employment thus supposed the existence of a large labour force exclusively devoted to it. The diffusion of the water mill, therefore, for thousands and thousands of human beings, had a beneficial effect; it greatly lightened their labour. When did this happen? Its chronology is becoming clear,

---

[147] We should remember that the *invention* of the water mill took place in the first century BC. It was almost immediately hailed as a great victory for humanity; a Greek poem from the time of Augustus, often quoted, hymns 'the corn-grinding nymphs', whose industry will henceforward assure long hours of sleep for servants (*Antholog. Palat.*, IX, 418. See Bloch, *Mélanges historiques*, vol. 2, pp. 801, 838). But the *diffusion* of this new technique was much later; throughout almost the whole of the Roman period, the water mill was really only seen as a curiosity, without practical application.

thanks, in particular, to two recent studies.[148] According to these, we may agree with Parain that the water mill appeared in the countryside of Gaul in the Late Empire and that some large milling complexes, such as that of Barbégal, near Arles, were constructed at this period.[149] But its use was not common till later. The first phase of its diffusion came between the sixth and the eighth centuries. Its propagation was still far from rapid; references to mills begin to appear here and there in the texts, but this new instrument was still considered by its owners as something rare and extremely precious.[150] It was only during a second phase, from the ninth to the eleventh centuries, that the water mill achieved a dominant position.[151]

Progress in methods of harnessing consisted in the adoption of the frontal yoke for oxen and the invention of the shoulder collar for horses; the latter a decisive innovation because it made possible the use of this animal in agriculture. While, in the case of the ox, the chronology of progress remains unclear,[152] it seems now to

[148] But not yet published: H. Amouric, *Moulins et meunerie en basse Provence occidentale, du moyen âge à l'ère industrielle* (thèse 3e cycle, University of Provence, 1984), 4 vols. (forthcoming, Aix-en-Provence); P. Dockès, '"Grands" moulins hydrauliques, rapports sociaux et systèmes d'exploitation' (to appear in *Mélanges I. Wallerstein*). See also, R. Philippe, *L'énergie au moyen âge; l'exemple des pays d'entre Seine et Loire* (thèse d'Etat, mss., Paris, 1980).

[149] F. Benoit, *L'usine de meunerie hydraulique de Barbégal* (Paris, 1940).

[150] In Spain, a law of Recceswinth punished the theft of the *ferramenta* of a mill very severely: restoration of the stolen material, a heavy fine and 100 lashes (*Lex Visigothorum*, VII, 2, 12). Up to the ninth–tenth centuries, the use of hand mills was still much more important; in Frisia, some *ancillae* continued to operate them (*Lex Frisonica*, XIII, 1: *ancilla quae molere solet, ancilla in usum molae*); in Provence, they continued to be made and exported (in the ninth century?), as is shown by the excavation of a Saracen wreck off Agay (A. G. Visquis, 'Premier inventaire de l'épave dite des Jarres, à Agay', *Cahiers d'archéologie subaquatique*, 2 (1973), 157–8).

[151] In the ninth century, mills were still fairly rare on the demesnes described by the *Brevium Exempla* and the polyptiques. For their diffusion in Catalonia in the tenth–eleventh centuries, see Bonnassie, *La Catalogne*, vol. 1, pp. 459–64, and for Picardy in the eleventh–twelfth centuries, Fossier, *La terre et les hommes*, vol. 1, pp. 382–4. Domesday Book records 5624 water mills.

[152] From lack of documents. The horn yoke seems to spread from the eleventh century at the latest; it enabled better use to be made of the motor power of the animals than did the neck yoke in use in previous centuries. Nevertheless, teams with neck yokes are still occasionally pictured in the twelfth century, at Pérouse and Lucca, for example. See Perrine Mane, *Calendriers et techniques agricoles (France, Italie, XIIe–XIIIe s.)* (Paris, 1983); also G. Fourquin, in *Histoire de la France rurale* (Paris, 1975), vol. 1, p. 412.

be well established in the case of the horse. The use of the latter as a beast of the plough became general between the second half of the ninth and the second half of the eleventh century.[153]

It is striking that in both cases the innovations concerned the exploitation of energy; on the one hand, water power, and, on the other, an increased return accrued from animal labour (the return was quintupled in the case of the horse) took the place of human energy (represented by slave labour) in the most laborious and common of tasks. What is more, human labour itself was more efficiently used thanks to decisive improvements visible in the domain of tools – diffusion of the flail, appearance of the plough with mould-board and, above all, essentially from the tenth century, the increasing substitution of tools of iron for the paltry wooden tools which had been mainly used hitherto. We may conclude that technical progress – slow to manifest itself, but experiencing a marked acceleration at the end of the ninth and in the tenth centuries – made a significant contribution to lightening those tasks devolved to the servile labour force.

The mistake would be once again to make the disappearance of the slave system follow automatically from factors of a technical order. This is the error into which fell old authors such as Lefebvre des Noëttes, who made, as is well known, the end of slavery a direct consequence of the invention of the horse collar.[154] It is also the error which can be held against historians as far apart ideologically as Parain[155] and Lynn White.[156] Technical progress constitutes, in effect, only one of the aspects of the development of the productive forces. It can only be made to intervene convincingly as the explanation of social changes by being located in the wider context of economic changes. We need, therefore, to

---

[153] The first mention of horses used for ploughing is in the last third of the ninth century, in a text of Alfred the Great referring to Norway and written to accompany an Anglo-Saxon translation of Orosius. For the progress of the use of the horse and its chronology, Lynn White, *Medieval Technology and Social Change* (Oxford, 1962).

[154] Lefebvre des Noëttes, *La force motrice animale à travers les âges* (Paris, 1924). Marc Bloch was much interested in this work to which he devoted two reviews: 'Techniques et évolution sociale; à propos de l'histoire de l'attelage et de celle de l'esclavage', *Revue de synthèse historique*, 41 (1926), 256–9, and 'La force motrice animale et le rôle des inventions techniques', *ibid.*, 43 (1927), 83–91.

[155] See 'Rapports de production et développements des forces productives: l'exemple du moulin à eau' in *Outils, ethnies et développement historique*, pp. 305–27.

[156] *Medieval Technology and Social Change*.

examine how these, by changing the way in which the soil was cultivated (in other words, for the period in question, the essential basis of material life), involved a redeployment of labour, which itself generated a liberation of rural slaves.

ECONOMIC GROWTH

We need to look first at the chronology of economic growth. All recent studies of the early Middle Ages have questioned the concept of a global economic recession as characterising this period. If this recession can be seen in the sphere of trade (especially long-distance trade), it is entirely absent at the level of the basic activity, that is, the rural economy. Very much to the contrary, the early Middle Ages appear as the point of departure for a long-term expansion which had as its consequence (but consequence only) the large-scale assarting of the eleventh to thirteenth centuries.

This growth may have begun during the Late Empire. The Celtic peasantries of the west of the Roman world seem to have demonstrated considerable dynamism at this period.[157] The evidence for this very early period is, however, too slight to insist upon. In any case, after the period of troubles (essentially the sixth and the beginning of the seventh centuries, which were marked by all sorts of calamities including epidemics of bubonic plague which decimated a large part of the European population),[158] very clear signs of agrarian expansion appear throughout the west. In England, the arable clearings were being expanded from the seventh century; it was at this period that the heavy soils of the Midlands, in particular, began to be won for agriculture.[159] In Germany, pollen analysis dates the first advance of cereals at the expense of the forests to the period 550-750.[160] In Picardy, place-name studies demonstrate an intensive occupation of the soil before the

---

[157] C. Parain, 'Le développement des forces productives dans l'ouest du Bas-Empire', Outils, ethnies et développement historique, pp. 405–24.

[158] J.-N. Biraben and J. Le Goff, 'La peste dans le haut moyen âge', Annales, 24 (1969), 1484–508.

[159] Postan, The Medieval Economy and Society, p. 15. See also Duby, Early Growth, pp. 21–2.

[160] See, in particular, the pollen diagrams of Rotes Moor reproduced in R. Delort, Introduction aux sciences auxiliaires de l'histoire (Paris, 1968), p. 157, and in Duby, Early Growth, p. 9. Also, R. Noël, Les dépôts de pollens fossiles (Turnhout, 1972).

Carolingian period.[161] In the south-west of Gaul, the evidence of saints' lives and place-names combines to attest to numerous assarts in the sixth to eighth centuries, whilst local Roman law adapted to the phenomenon of assarting.[162] In Italy, the pioneer role of certain *curtes* is clearly visible from the eighth century, in both coastal plains (the Lower Po) and the Apennine foothills (the eastern Sabina).[163] In sum, the seventh and, above all, the eighth centuries clearly emerge, despite the shortage of documents, as the age of the 'early growth of the European economy'.

Did this growth continue uninterrupted? It is impossible to be sure. Certainly the ninth century was a period of expansion in Italy. In Gaul, especially in the north, things are less clear; the reappearance of famine at the time of Charlemagne and Louis the Pious is a disquieting indicator.[164] In any case, the polyptiques testify to a stagnant demographic situation. The first half (or first two-thirds) of the ninth century seem to mark a lull in the process of expansion.[165] It was, however, only temporary; a resumption was clear well before 900 and in the tenth century developed into what has been called the 'great expansion', which was to last in some regions until the middle – even the end – of the thirteenth century. In Catalonia, the apogee of assarting was between 870 and 950; this was the age of the *aprisiones*, the *rupturas* and the *arrancationes*.[166] It was the same in north-west Spain, with the colonisation of the plain of the Duero and many other uncultivated areas during the century from 850 to 950.[167] For Latium, Pierre Toubert did not hesitate to use the word revolution to characterise

[161] Fossier, *La terre et les hommes*, vol. 1, pp. 155–9.

[162] Rouche, *L'Aquitaine des Wisigoths aux Arabes*, pp. 229–39.

[163] P. Toubert, 'L'Italie rurale aux VIIIe–IXe siècles: essai de typologie domaniale', *Settimane*, 20 (1973), 105ff. (with reference to the works of V. Fumigalli on the plain of the Po). For the Sabina, Toubert, *Les structures du Latium*, vol. 1, pp. 461ff.

[164] See Curschmann, *Hungersnöte*, pp. 89–96. Also Doehaerd, *Le haut moyen âge occidental*, pp. 58–66.

[165] This lull is clearly shown for Picardy by Fossier, *La terre et les hommes*, vol. 1, pp. 203–7.

[166] Bonnassie, *La Catalogne*, vol. 1, pp. 99ff. See also R. d'Abadal, *Els primers comtes catalans* (Barcelona, 1958) (chapter 6: L'ocupació i repoblació de les comarques d'Osona i Bages', pp. 73–114), and the same author's *Catalunya carolingia*, 3, *Els comtats de Pallars i Ribagorça* (Barcelona, 1955), intr.

[167] C. Sánchez Albornoz, *Despoblación y repoblación del Valle del Duero* (Buenos Aires, 1966); S. de Moxó, *Repoblación y sociedad en la España cristiana medieval* (Madrid, 1979), in particular part 1, pp. 17–198.

the growth of the tenth century.[168] Many more examples could be quoted. Let it suffice to say that the years preceding 1000 saw a generalisation of the application of the new techniques developed during the early Middle Ages; tools improved in quality and quantity, the use of iron spread throughout the countryside, cultivated surfaces were enlarged, crops were less meagre. Slavery became extinct against a background of an almost continuous and increasingly more marked development of the forces of production.

Important though it is, however, to establish the chronology of expansion, it is equally so to define its context. On this point, one anachronism must be avoided at all costs. It is one of which most historians who have discussed this subject for at least a century have been guilty. It consists of applying to the medieval agrarian revolution the patterns of development of the modern industrial revolution. This has the effect of making it impossible to conceive of economic progress except within the context of highly concentrated enterprises. Applied to the Middle Ages, this assumption makes the great estate the obligatory context for expansion.[169]

But, looked at more carefully, it is apparent that the great estate was ill-adapted either to experimenting with new techniques or expanding the cultivated area. One reason was its rigid structures,

[168] Toubert, *Les structures du Latium*, vol. 1, p. 330.

[169] The primacy of the large estate has remained dogma until the last few years for the large majority of historians, non-Marxists as much as Marxists. The attitude of the latter is, in fact, surprising inasmuch as F. Engels attacked precisely this primacy, with great force and clarity (and basing himself on examples bearing on the Middle Ages), in the course of his polemic with Dühring (*Anti–Dühring* (French translation, 1968), pp. 208–15). If these fine pages have been forgotten, it is no doubt because they went too contrary to received ideas. Even today, a study such as that of Claire Billen and Christian Dupont, 'Problématique marxiste et histoire rurale (VIIIe–XIIIe s.) entre Loire et Rhin', (*Acta histor. Bruxellensia*, 4 (1981), 89–128), though highly estimable and well-documented, almost totally ignores the existence of an independent peasantry. Voices are now, however, beginning to be heard emphasising the importance of the 'peasant economy' of Late Antiquity (Mireille Corbier, 'Propriété et gestion de la terre: grand domaine et économie paysanne' in *Aspekte der historischen Forschung in Frankreich und Deutschland, Schwerpunkte und Methoden* (Göttingen, 1981), pp. 11–29 and of the early Middle Ages (Poly and Bournazel, *La mutation féodale*, pp. 362–3). The latter observe, for example: 'the debate about technical innovations seems in every way vitiated by the strange idea that the lord was the entrepreneur and the great estate the location. In contrast, there is a tendency to see the peasantry, no doubt unconsciously, as a class which is weak and anaemic, lacking resources and initiative.'

characterised by inflexible units of exploitation (the manses). Another was the general lack of interest on the part of the 'elites' (in practice, the great landowners) in anything to do with work on the land.[170] And, lastly, there was the inertia of a workforce subject to forced labour, who not only showed no initiative but frequently sabotaged the tasks imposed on them. The recriminations of Charles the Bald against the tenants on the royal and ecclesiastical *villae* are pertinent here; they refused to 'thresh in the barn' (with flails) or to 'spread marl', thus they opposed the application of new techniques, because they involved extra work.[171] For all these reasons – and many others – it is easy to explain why it was on the great estates that the most meagre yields were found, those famine-level yields which can be calculated on the basis of information in the polyptiques.[172]

In practice, it was on small holdings that progress was made, especially on peasant allods. One of the major discoveries of the research of recent years has been that of the great dynamism of the small peasant holding in the early Middle Ages. It was by the creation of thousands and thousands of allods that the frontiers of colonisation were pushed back in the eighth to tenth centuries; in

---

[170] The objection may be made that only the 'great' circulated, and were thus in a position to achieve the diffusion of innovations. Maybe, but did counts and abbots, when they met, discuss ploughshares?

[171] Edict of Pîtres, *Cap.* 29 (*MGH, Capitularia regum Francorum.*, II, 311–28); translated in Duby, *Economie rurale et vie des campagnes dans l'Occident médiéval* (Paris, 1962), vol. 1, p. 293, translated by Cynthia Postan as *Rural Economy and Country Life in the Medieval West* (London, 1968), p. 373.

[172] Such a calculation has been made by Duby for the royal demesne of Annapes; in the year when the inventory was drawn up (a year of poor harvest, in fact), the yields seem to have varied between 1 and 1.8 to 1 (*Rural Economy and Country Life*, pp. 25–6). Georges Duby has been the subject of quite unjustified attacks on this question of yields (in particular by R. Delatouche, 'Regards sur l'agriculture aux temps carolingien', *Journal des Savants* (1977), pp. 73ff.). In fact, the very reliable information furnished by the Italian polyptiques (especially that of San Tommaso of Reggio Emilia, which gives for the same year the quantities of grain sown and cropped) leads to conclusions similar to those of Duby: the yields varied between 1.7 to 1 and 3.3 to 1. The texts are in *Inventari altomedievali di terre, coloni e redditi*, ed. A. Castagnetti, M. Luzatti, G. Pasquali, A. Vasina (Rome, 1979) (for the inventory of Reggio, which can be dated to the tenth century, pp. 195–8). Calculation of yields and comments by V. Fumagalli, 'Rapporti fra grano, seminato e grano raccolto nel politico del monastero di San Tommaso di Reggio', *Rivista di storia d' agricultura*, 6 (1966), 350–62; and 'Storia agraria e luoghi communi', *Studi medievali*, 3rd ser., 9 (1968), pp. 359–78. See also M. Montanari, *L'alimentazione contadina nell' Alto Medioevo* (Naples, 1979).

León and Castile by the system of *pressura*,[173] in Catalonia by the *aprisio*.[174] This proliferation of allods is to be seen not only in the marginal zones, but also in the most ancient heartlands of the west, in the Picardy of Robert Fossier,[175] and the Auvergne of Christian Lauranson.[176] Everywhere, the first wave of agrarian expansion originated in the initiatives of the free peasantry – extremely poor, but free – who, in their struggle against hunger, cleared forests, drained marshes, terraced hillsides, ploughed virgin lands and improved their tools and cultural practices. The peasant allod was even the site of the most complex technical innovations; in both Latium and Catalonia, most water mills built in the ninth and tenth centuries were the work of associations of small landowners.[177] The same was true of the construction of the first irrigation networks.[178]

In the face of these successes on the part of the peasant allod, how could the great estates respond? They were decentralised, broken up and dispersed. They, too, established offshoots. They were surrounded by clusters of autonomous exploitations, first small domanial satellites, such as the *villaria*, *curticellae* and *mansionilia* found by Robert Fossier in Picardy,[179] and then, and principally, by the colonising tenures (*coloniae*, *casae colonicae*, *colonges*) established in profusion on the new lands.[180] These hold-

---

[173] Sánchez Albornoz, *Despoblación y repoblación*. See also his 'Repoblación del reino asturleonés', *Cuadernos de historia de España*, 53–4 (1971), pp. 236–375, 380ff., and his *El régimen de la tierra en el reino asturleonés hace mil años* (Buenos Aires, 1978), pp. 199–242; de Moxó, *Repoblación y sociedad*. From a more juridical point of view, I. de la Concha, 'La pressura', *Anuario de historia del derecho español* 14 (1942–3), 445ff.

[174] Abadal, *Els primers comtes catalans*, pp. 96–110; Bonnassie, *La Catalogne*, vol. vol. 1, pp. 99–118. The *aprisio* (like the *pressura*) was the ascription of a piece of land in full ownership to someone who had occupied it, brought it into use and cultivated it without interruption for thirty years.

[175] Fossier, *La terre et les hommes*, vol. 1, pp. 210–11 ('The preponderance of small holdings').

[176] Lauranson, *L'Auvergne*, pp. 429–32.

[177] Toubert, *Les structures du Latium*, vol. 1, pp. 460–1, note 3: 'In the middle decades of the ninth century, the rural mills known were external to the structure of the *curtis*, sometimes held in co-ownership by the small communities of allod owners'; Bonnassie, *La Catalogne*, vol. 1, pp. 459–64.

[178] Bonnassie, *La Catalogne*, vol. 1, pp. 464–9.

[179] Fossier, *La terre et les hommes*, vol. 1, pp. 161–2.

[180] For Latium, Toubert, *Les structures du Latium*, vol. 1, pp. 479–87 and *passim*. For Italy in general, Toubert, 'L'Italie rurale', pp. 118–28. For Provence, Poly, *La Provence*, pp. 103–6, etc.

ings were exempt, or almost, from labour services; their lords relinquished the archaic system which involved imposing forced labour. But they were burdened with rents proportionate to the crop; the lords taxed the fruits of labour. The reign of share-cropping tenures began in the early Middle Ages.

These processes of agrarian expansion were clearly in total contradiction to the slave system. They assumed a highly mobile labour force which had to be established far from the estate centres, where assarting was taking place. They implied that the initiative had in the main to be left to the actual cultivators, who were extremely difficult to control on holdings which retained only the most tenuous links with the *curtis* (or what remained of it). They required, in fact, a transformation of the servile labour force which could only be achieved through enfranchisement.

It is at this point that we find those enfranchisements for economic reasons whose importance Marc Bloch appreciated. But they are found in a very different context than the one he described – in a climate of growth, not recession. The phenomenon has been clearly demonstrated by Pierre Toubert for Latium and, more generally, for Italy; according to him, the first agrarian expansion was to a large extent the work of the 'small proletariat' of the enfranchised.[181] It was achieved in the context of contracts designed to install former slaves of the *familia* on tenures of a colonising type, contracts which 'made it possible to channel towards the frontiers of colonisation a surplus of enfranchised labour from the most anciently settled and densely populated regions'.[182] This says it all.

I would like to add only that the settlement of former slaves on new lands sometimes assumed even simpler forms, as is shown by the charter of liberties of Cardona, in Catalonia, conceded around 880 by Count Guifred. This granted complete freedom to fugitive slaves who, without the knowledge of their masters, had or would come to settle on the frontier lands he wished to populate.[183] This reference to the phenomenon of escapes brings us to the question of the extent to which the emancipation of the slaves was the consequence of their own endeavours.

[181] Toubert, 'L'Italie rurale', p. 121.
[182] *Idem, Les structures du Latium*, 1, p. 471.
[183] Font Rius, *CPC*, 1, document no. 9, pp. 14–18.

Freedom: a victory

The emphasis put by Pierre Dockès on class struggle[184] as a factor in the extinction of slavery is fully justified if one starts from one simple assertion: that the slave system is a particularly cruel and degrading system of oppression to which men and women can only be subjected, and in which they can only be maintained, by force. The pressure exercised by slaves to achieve freedom and accede to human dignity is constant, and can only be contained by an efficient system of repression, that is by a state system. One might, therefore, expect every period experiencing a weakening of state structures to be characterised by struggles on the part of slaves; these may take different forms according to circumstances, sometimes open revolt, sometimes – most often – disguised disobedience and latent subversion.

True servile revolts are almost only found in Late Antiquity. They were part of the famous 'wars of the Bacaudae' (which brought together in revolt, as well as slaves, numerous bands of poor free peasants).[185] They culminated in two principal phases, one in the third century (between 250 and 286), the other in the middle of the fifth century (between 435 and 454). Their violent character did not prevent their defeat; they were bloodily put down and the slave system, re-established in the hands of new Germanic masters, survived them unharmed.

From then on, open revolts were rare. They were not, however, completely unknown in the early Middle Ages. The slaves of the kingdom of Asturias rose around 770; their troops were beaten (probably in Galicia) by King Aurelius, who restored to the masters all their powers.[186] Other rebellious movements occurred in Gaul, at the time of the Norman invasions. The latter had, in practice, two contradictory consequences; the Vikings carried off large numbers of human cattle, but the disorganisation provoked

---

[184] Dockès, *La libération médiévale* (esp. pp. 249ff.).

[185] Dockès, 'Révoltes bagaudes et ensauvagement'. There is a similar approach in Finley, *The Ancient Economy*, pp. 117–18. See also E. A. Thompson, 'Peasant Revolts in Late Roman Gaul and Spain', *Past and Present* (1952), 11–23.

[186] According to the *Chronicon Albeldense* (ed. Gómez Moreno, 'Las primeras cronicas de la Reconquista', *Boletín de la Real Academia de Hist.* (1932), p. 612). On this revolt, also cited by other sources, Cl. Sánchez Albornoz, *Origenes de la nación española: estudios critecos sobre la historia del reino de Asturias*, vol. 2 (Oviedo, 1974), pp. 335–47.

by their attacks favoured the emancipation of the local slaves. At any rate, we learn that slaves killed their masters and reduced them to servitude during the great raid of 885 in the Parisian basin.[187]

In normal times, the assassination of a master tended to be presented as an individual act of insubordination. This was the case, in particular, in the Lombard laws of Kings Rothari and Liutprand, which, between 643 and 733, made several references to such murders.[188] *Servi*, driven mad by their humiliations, strangled their persecutors. *Ancillae* poisoned their masters or mistresses; some were even seen as *strigae*, a sort of vampire which devoured men, and it was by no means uncommon for them to be put to death for this, so much so, indeed, that King Rothari was obliged to intervene to put a stop to the practice.[189] Such behaviour is a clear indication of the fear which must have reigned in some slave-owning circles.

But the insubordination of slaves generally took more oblique forms, and also more concerted. One of these – and no doubt the most important – was ill-will shown in carrying out the tasks demanded. But how can we observe manifestations of this, and how, indeed, can the history of the power of inertia be written?

Another, more striking, form of insubordination was flight. The flight of slaves was a constant phenomenon, referred to in all the barbarian laws.[190] But some periods saw the process accelerate and hence, in consequence, left fuller documentation, which throws light on both its methods and implications. This was the case in the seventh and early eighth centuries in both Italy and Spain. The times were propitious for such ventures. The great plagues of the sixth and early seventh centuries had decimated the population;

---

[187] As in the poem of Abbo of Saint-Germain-des-Prés on the siege of Paris by the Normans (ed. H. Waquet (Paris, 1942), p. 30, verses 184–5):

Efficetur servus liber, liber quoque servus
Vernaque fit dominus, contra dominus quoque verna.

[188] *Leges Langobardorum*, ed. Beyerle (2nd edn, 1962); *Edictum Rothari*, 142 (643), *Liutprand*, 21 (721) and 138 (733).

[189] *Edictum Rothari*, 376.

[190] It was, in fact, responsible for many assarts of the early Middle Ages. Fugitive slaves hid in deserted places in the middle of great forests where their survival depended on opening up and cultivating new clearings. For the Carolingian period, the *Vita Geraldi* evokes such clandestine assarts somewhere in the Massif Central; in this case, they were operated by runaway *coloni*, not slaves, but the result was the same (*Vita Geraldi*, I, 24).

labour was in short supply and runaway slaves found it easy to find work as free labourers. The law recognised, but could not prevent, this:

> If a runaway slave says he is free, if he is not recognised and if he is hired for a wage in the house of a free man, the latter cannot be charged because he did not know it was a matter of a runaway slave.[191]

In Italy, the edict of King Rothari of 643 devoted a score of articles to suppressing escapes.[192] It punished collusion which was common, including amongst the free population; it organised pursuit; it provided rewards for captures. It also reveals that runaway slaves were forming bands (*concilia*) and engaging in a sort of mass brigandage in Lombard Italy; on occasion, these bands even attacked slave-run great estates and freed the *mancipia* working there.[193] A little later, the edict of Grimoald (662–71) recorded that certain slaves 'through pride or as a result of ill treatment' left their masters *per pugna* and went off to settle elsewhere.[194] The laws of Liutprand of 717 and 727 returned to the question; escapes had not ceased and were now happening on a large scale. Slaves from Lombardy crossed the Apennines to settle in Tuscany, even in the duchies of Spoleto and Benevento.[195]

The situation in Spain was similar, if not worse. Throughout the seventh century, laws repressing the flight of slaves, punishing accessories and instituting bounties for information received multiplied without tangible result.[196] In 702, King Egica recognised that 'there was now no city, no suburb, no *vicus*, no *villa* where runaway slaves were not concealed'. Appalled by the 'growing vice' (*increscens vitium*) of escapes, he decided to promulgate a truly extreme law which mobilised the whole free population of Spain in a sort of social police devoted to hunting down slaves. Every inhabitant of a place where a suspicious (that is, poorly clothed) person arrived must seize, interrogate and torture him to make him confess to being a slave and name his master. If they failed to do this, they were all, men and women, to be

---

[191] *Lex Visigothorum*, IX, 1, 12.   [192] *Edictum Rothari*, 256–80.

[193] *Edictum Rothari*, 279 (*De concilio rusticanorum*) and 280 (*De rusticanorum seditione*).

[194] *Grimvaldi Leges*, 1.

[195] *Edictum Liutprandi*, 44 and 88.

[196] The whole of book IX of the Visigothic Code is devoted to the repression of the flight of slaves.

punished with two hundred lashes. The local agents of the king and the village priests were charged with carrying out this sentence; if they failed to inflict it, they were themselves to receive three hundred lashes with the whip, on the orders of the royal justices and the bishops. If these last covered up for their subordinates, they, too were to be punished, though less severely: thirty days on barley and bread and water.[197] This was undeniably a panic measure, revealing the depth of the social crisis into which Spain was plunged nine years before the arrival of the Muslims.

There is less direct evidence of the flight of slaves from the Carolingian period, but the phenomenon continued. One very significant indication of it can be detected in the high number of manses described as *absi* in the polyptiques; many tenures were empty of occupants on the lands of Saint-Victor of Marseilles in 813/14.[198] The cartulary of Beaulieu-sur-Dordogne spelled out in the tenth century that manses had been abandoned by *servi in fuga lapsi*.[199] In the same way, it seems very likely that some populations of the high Alpine valleys, called *Marruni* in the *Life* of Gerald of Aurillac, were in fact groups of 'maroons', or runaway slaves.[200] And flight was certainly facilitated by the destabilisation – at least temporary – of society consequent on the new invasions of the ninth and tenth centuries.

By around 1000, it was no longer only a question of escapes, but of a general attack on the very concept of servitude by the slaves themselves – the last in rural Europe. The rejection of the slave condition was then so strong, and so openly expressed, that the emperor Otto III decided, during a synod held at Pavia in 998, to promulgate a capitulary designed to check the tendency – an act which was quite extraordinary in a century when legislative practice was almost non-existent, and an act whose solemnity proves the urgency of the situation. The text was issued, said the

---

[197] *Lex Visigothorum*, IX, 1, 12.

[198] Deserted tenures represented as much as 84 per cent of the total in the estates owned by the monastery in western Provence (15 out of 22 at Lambesc, 27 out of 28 at Bedada, 5 out of 7 at Domado, 10 out of 11 at Marciana etc.). See Poly, *La Provence*, p. 101.

[199] *Cartulaire de l'abbaye de Beaulieu en Limousin*, ed. M. Deloche (Paris, 1859), nos. 55, 186.

[200] *Vita Geraldi*, I, 17. The hypothesis of J.-P. Poly, who sees in them fugitive slaves, is very plausible (*La Provence*, p. 27 and note 109); 'Régime domanial et rapports de production', p. 80 and notes 54–5.

emperor, at the request of the great men of the Empire, ecclesiastical and lay, and of all the landowners (*possessores*), great, middling and small, who lamented their inability to retain the *obsequium* (respect, obedience and services) which they were owed by their slaves. These, escaping the vigilance of their masters, were proclaiming themselves to be free. 'They lie', said the capitulary. But, as it was impossible to provide proof of their servitude, it would henceforward be for the *servus* who claimed to be free to prove his liberty; to do this, he had to beat in judicial combat a champion designated by his master. An unequal combat, obviously, but even this procedure, though so favourable to the masters, did not apply to ecclesiastical estates; the slaves of the Church could not be freed on any pretext. 'Let it not be legal for any slave belonging to a church to quit his servitude; let no priest attached to a church be able henceforward to free a single slave from servitude; and we order that if such a slave has been enfranchised in any manner, this enfranchisement should be regarded as null and the slave should return under the law and into the servitude of the church to which he belongs.'[201]

They were fighting a rearguard action. The edict of Otto III constituted the last attempt to restore a slave regime. It was clearly doomed to failure.

Towards a chronology of the extinction of slavery

The history of the extinction of the slave regime is a long one, extending over the whole of the early Middle Ages. But it is not a linear history. Ancient slavery did not die of its own accord, smoothly and imperceptibly. It was destroyed by a series of increasingly serious upheavals, brought about by the conjuncture of all those factors discussed above.

The first shocks were certainly experienced in the Late Empire. Already at that period, questions began to be asked, if not about the legitimacy of servitude, at least about its modalities; appeals to treat slaves humanely, for long made by various moralists (the Stoics, Seneca, Pliny the Younger and also St Paul) began to

---

[201] M. Uhlirz, 'Die Regesten des Kaiserreiches unter Otto III' (Böhmer, *Regesta Imperii*) (Graz, 1957), p. 697. This capitulary is discussed by Tabacco in 'La storia politica e sociale: dal tramonto dell'Impero alle prime formazioni di Stati regionali', pp. 159–60.

disturb the good conscience of the slave-owning society. Already, technical progress which reduced the role of human labour in the most tedious activities was apparent. Already, perhaps, there were appearing locally the first signs of the growth of the rural economy. Above all, the slave state was considerably weakened by the crises which, in the third and fifth centuries, shook the Empire: civil wars, barbarian penetration etc. Hence the two first serious shocks to the system, one in the second half of the third century, the other in the mid fifth century, inflicted by the two major revolts of the Bacaudae. There had been, in the meantime, a first phase of recovery for the slave order, under Diocletian and his successors.[202]

But ancient slavery did not disappear with Antiquity; far from it. The slave regime was reconstituted more solidly than ever by the barbarian monarchies. The Germans (in this case, Goths) who, in 545, defeated the Bacaudae revolt of the Tarraconensis, were policing the social order.[203] Everywhere, the Germanic kings encouraged slavery by promulgating measures whose ferocity exceeded that of Roman law. This legislation was particularly voluminous in Spain and Italy, ancient lands of servitude. But it is striking that it also developed (in Salic law in its various versions, in the Anglo-Saxon laws, in the Bavarian laws etc.) in the countries of northern Europe. It appears both as witness to and instrument of the diffusion of slavery throughout northern Europe, where it had previously been relatively rare. At the same period, a vast enterprise to justify slavery within the framework of the Christian society was carried to a successful conclusion by the most prestigious doctors of the Church within the orbit of the barbarian monarchies (Gregory the Great, Isidore of Seville etc.). For all these reasons, the sixth and the beginning of the seventh centuries may be regarded as the period of the maximum diffusion of the institution of slavery in western Europe.

But new, and more serious, problems emerged. A new phase of crisis afflicted the system in the second half of the seventh century

---

[202] These two revolts and the Diocletian restoration are discussed in Dockès, 'Révoltes bagaudes et ensauvagement'.

[203] This revolt and its repression are described by Idatius, *Chron. an.* 454 (*MGH, AA, Chronica minora*, vol. II, p. 158). The struggle against the Bacaudae appears to have determined the conclusion of the *foedus* of 452/3 between Rome and the Visigoths. See Dockès, *La libération médiévale*, p. 235, and L. Musset, *Les invasions: les vagues germaniques* (Paris, 1965), p. 227.

and at the beginning of the eighth. At this period, the slaves, all baptised, and participating in Christian worship alongside the free, no longer accepted being treated like animals. They rebelled against some masters, or, more often, took flight. The demographic and economic situation was favourable to their emancipation; the plagues of the end of the sixth and the early seventh centuries had cut a swathe through the ranks of the active population. Labour was in short supply, just as the first signs of economic recovery became apparent. Hence those fugitive slaves hired as free workers, and hence the waves of desertion of slave estates; the attempts made, especially in Spain and Italy, to prevent this at all costs by multiplying repressive measures were in vain. At the turn of the seventh century, the system seemed on the brink of collapse.

But it is noticeable that this crisis affected principally the Mediterranean region, perhaps also, to a lesser extent, Gaul. No trace of it can be detected in northern Europe, where the slave regime, established more recently, resisted much better. This can be seen in the British Isles, in reading the Anglo-Saxon laws (those of Ine,[204] in particular) and the Gallic laws. In Germany, slaves were extremely numerous, as is shown by the surviving charters; the rich documentation of the abbey of Fulda, in particular, provides from the eighth century long lists of *mancipia* owned, given and exchanged by landowners of all types; it shows quite unambiguously that the practice of slavery was diffused through all ranks of society.[205]

The elements for a new (and last) revival of the system, therefore, existed. This was attempted, especially under Charlemagne,

---

[204] Laws of Ine on slavery: 23, 32, 33, 46, 74 (in Whitelock, *English Historical Documents*, vol. 1, pp. 364ff.).

[205] *Urkundenbuch des Klosters Fulda*, ed. E. Stengel (Marburg, 1958). See in particular, no. 22: 13 *mancipia* (754); no. 37: 10 *mancipia* (762); no. 40: 22 *mancipia* (763); no. 71: 18 *mancipia* (775); no. 85: 9 *mancipia* (778); no. 87: 30 *mancipia* (779); no. 90: 66 *mancipia*, 16 *lides* (779); no. 126: 58 *mancipia* (750/779); no. 195: 13 *mancipia* (792); no. 200: 18 *mancipia* (776/796); no. 202: 62 *mancipia* (776/796); no. 203: 28 *mancipia* (776/796); no. 237: 38 *mancipia* (796) and also no 491: 49 *mancipia* (780/802) etc. No other labour than these slaves, always called *mancipia*, was found on the lands bequeathed to the monastery. Slaves were also employed by the poor; a certain Ota, who possessed nothing other than the little house where she lived, nevertheless willed two *mancipia* (no. 49: 754/759). See O. Bruand, *Le domaine foncier de l'abbaye de Fulda au VIIIe siècle* (mémoire de maîtrise, University of Toulouse–Le Mirail, 1980).

in parallel with the reconstruction of the state. The restoration of the slave system was particularly marked in the drafting in 802/3 of the last Germanic Codes (the laws of the Thuringians, the Ripuarian Franks and the Frisians, the capitulary additional to Salic Law). It can also be seen in the resumption of efforts to legitimise slavery made by men such as Alcuin, Regino of Prüm and Rabanus Maurus. It is to be seen also, of course, in the enslavement of the Saxons. It even, in part, inspired the compilation of the polyptiques; we should not forget the title of the polyptique of Saint-Victor of Marseilles: *Descriptio mancipiorum ecclesie Massiliensis*.

But conditions were no longer so favourable. The institution of slavery was increasingly attacked. For the first time, voices were heard in the very heart of the Church demanding the complete abolition of slavery. Agobard of Lyons, paraphrasing St Paul, but going further, demanded the suppression of all juridical distinctions between free men and slaves.[206] Abbot Smaragde of Saint-Mihiel said: 'Prohibe, clementissime rex, ne in regno tuo captivas fiat!'[207] And, most of all, amongst the lower ranks of the population, slavery lost its significance; mixed marriages were common, servile manses were occupied indifferently by free or servile tenants. Manifestly, the institution of slavery, rejected by the slaves, no longer made sense to the free poor. In these circumstances, the regime restored by Charlemagne could only be, in the words of Jean-Pierre Poly, 'an ersatz slave regime'.[208]

Nevertheless, slavery was not yet dead. It is clear from a text such as the *Life* of St Gerald of Aurillac that the estates of this large landowner in the Auvergne were still, at the end of the ninth and the beginning of the tenth centuries, populated by 'innumerable slaves'. At his death, in 909 or 910, Gerald enfranchised one hundred, but he could, according to his hagiographer, have

---

[206] Agobard, *Liber adversus legem Gundobaldi* (*PL*, CIV, col. 115: 'All men are brothers, all invoke one same Father, God: the slave and the master, the poor man and the rich man, the ignorant and the learned, the weak and the strong, the humble worker and the sublime emperor. None of them disdains the other, none judges himself inferior to another, none has been raised above the other . . . There is no Gentile or Jew, circumcised or uncircumcised, Barbarian or Scythian, Aquitainian or Lombard, Burgundian or German, slave or free, but in all things and always there is only Christ.'

[207] In his *Via Regia*, dedicated to Charlemagne (text quoted by Verlinden, *L'esclavage dans l'Europe médiévale*, vol. 1, p. 705, note 220).

[208] Poly, *La mutation féodale*, p. 368.

liberated many more if the law had permitted.[209] Also, according to the same source, it appears that the behaviour of masters had hardly changed; his sanctity notwithstanding, Gerald threatened certain recalcitrant slaves with mutilation.[210] It is true that, in the Carolingian period, many of these slaves were settled on holdings. Does this mean, as is often claimed, that their condition was assimilated to that of the free tenants? The documents suggest caution on this point; on the estate of the abbey of Staffelsee, in Bavaria (to take a classic example), the servile manses owed 145 days of labour a year, whereas the free manses owed only between none and 36.[211]

The slave system, in fact, only succumbed to a final crisis which occurred at the end of the tenth and the beginning of the eleventh centuries. At this point, everything combined to promote the extinction of slavery, all the factors tending to its disappearance operated simultaneously. Adherence to Christian beliefs, for long formal or hesitant, became general amongst the rural population; this carried the seeds of the birth of the first 'popular religious movements', and promoted, above all, the spiritual unification of the peasantry in all its component elements. The technical progress which lightened human labour became more widely diffused. The expansion of the agrarian economy, increasingly apparent, necessitated an ever greater mobility on the part of the rural workers, which required enfranchisement. The state structures broke down in the wake of the new invasions, and with them the whole repressive apparatus which depended on them. There developed everywhere, in consequence, what Giovanni Tabacco has called for Italy 'a spontaneous movement of liberation'.[212]

This definitive process of the extinction of rural slavery can be traced, region by region. In Latium, slaves became much fewer from the middle of the tenth century; references to *servi* become exceptional in the second half of this century, and disappear at the beginning of the eleventh century (with a last isolated example in

[209] *Vita Geraldi*, III, 4.
[210] *Ibid.*, II, 11. The persistence of the practice of mutilation is also attested by Jonas of Orléans (quoted by Verlinden, *L'esclavage dans l'Europe médiévale*, vol. 1, p. 703).
[211] *MGH, Capitularia* I, pp. 251–2. Text translated and discussed by Duby, *Rural Economy and Country Life*, pp. 364–6.
[212] Tabacco, 'La storia politica e sociale: dal tramonto dell'Impero alle prime formazione di Stati regionali', pp. 158–61.

1031/32).[213] In Catalonia, the chronology is similar, but slightly delayed; there were seven mentions between 1000 and 1025, with a last one in 1035.[214] In the Auvergne, for which there are fewer documents, six groups of slaves are mentioned in the second half of the tenth century, one only after 1000 (in 1031/55).[215] In the Charente region, words with servile connotations (*mancipium*, *servus* and *ancilla*) are found in 15 per cent of the acts surviving from between 950 and 1000, but in only 1 per cent of those surviving from between 1000 and 1050.[216] More generally, a survey of all the acts emanating from the Frankish monarchy from the reign of Louis the Pious to that of Philip I makes it possible to quantify the decline in the institution of slavery; the use of the word *mancipium* (unequivocal indicator of the slave-owning mentality) becomes increasingly rare in the second half of the tenth century, and almost disappears after 1030 (see table 2).[217]

Everywhere, the slave system was in its death throes in the second half of the tenth century, to expire, at the latest, at the beginning of the eleventh. From this perspective, the capitulary of Otto III which, in 998, tried for the last time to restrain the 'appetite for liberty' of the last slaves can be seen as its death certificate in western Europe.

One last problem remains to be examined, that of the transition from slavery to serfdom, or, if preferred, from the slave to the feudal mode of production. This is an immense problem which can only be touched on here.

Basically, we can agree with Marc Bloch who, with great intuition, denied all continuity between these two systems of exploiting labour, and showed differences of origin and nature between the slavery of the ancient type and the serfdom of feudal times. It can even be shown that in one whole part of Europe (that is, the whole

[213] Toubert, *Les structures du Latium*, vol. 1, pp. 510–11, note 3.

[214] Bonnassie, *La Catalogne*, vol. 1, pp. 298–302 (table of the last references to Christian slaves, p. 301).

[215] Lauranson, *L'Auvergne*, pp. 422ff. (table of the last references to slaves, facing p. 426).

[216] Debord, *La société laïque dans les pays de Charente*, pp. 314–15 (in particular diagram on p. 315).

[217] Diagram based on the researches of Véronique Sablayrolles, *De l'esclavage au servage, de Louis le Pieux à Philippe Ier. d'après les actes royaux* (mémoire de maîtrise, University of Toulouse–Le Mirail, 1982).

Table 2. *Percentage of the number of references to* mancipia *in relation to the number of royal acts*

	Royal acts	Percentage of references to *mancipia*
814–77	Louis the Pious Charles the Bald	42.1
877–935	Louis II Charlemagne Charles the Fat Charles the Simple Raoul	41.5
935–87	Louis IV Lothar Louis V	20.7
987–1031	Hugh Capet Robert the Pious	17.3
1031–1108	Henry I Philip I	1.5

of southern Europe), there was a real chronological hiatus in the history of servitude; ancient slavery disappeared before the new version was born. To quote once again from Pierre Toubert: 'In preparation over a long period, the liquidation of slavery was achieved everywhere in Latium by, at the latest, 1000, and without any serfdom having emerged to take its place.'[218] In Catalonia, where the last references to *servi* or *mancipia* date from the beginning of the eleventh century, we have to wait until the years 1060/80 for the first signs of the new servitude to appear.[219] The chronology is very similar in the Auvergne.[220] It is the case, therefore, that throughout southern Europe, there existed a privileged moment (at the end of the tenth or the beginning of the eleventh centuries, give or take a few years according to region) when society was free (juridically) from any form of servitude, where the tendency was towards a total emancipation of the peasant class. This situation was intolerable for the ruling class, who reacted extremely violently by the imposition of the *seigneurie banale*, that is the imposition on this free peasantry (anciently or recently free)

[218] Toubert, *Les structures du Latium*, vol. 1, p. 510.
[219] Bonnassie, *La Catalogne*, vol. 1, pp. 298–302 and chapter 7 below, pp. 221–4 (table of the earliest donations of *homines proprii*, p. 223).
[220] Lauranson, *L'Auvergne*, pp. 439–42.

of radically new burdens which the documents call 'exactions, new usages, new customs, bad usages, bad customs'. These burdens, as they became heavier, paved the way for a new servitude, transforming the descendants of the free peasantry of the year 1000 into *manants*, villeins, or worse, into *hommes propres* and *hommes de corps*, in brief, into serfs.[221]

In northern Europe the change is less clear, in that here, rural slavery, later in being widely established, was slower to disappear completely. Hence, at the period of the imposition of the *ban*, and the establishment of a new servitude, there still existed in these regions groups of *servi* who were descended from the old rural slaves; Domesday Book, in 1086, recorded about 25,000 of these dependants of ancient origin who represented between 1 and 16 per cent of the rural population of the English counties.[222] These last *servi* were caught in the meshes of a new subjection and integrated (with titles such as, for example, in England, neifs (*nativi*)) into the mass of *manants*, villeins and 'serfs' of the feudal period. But, as Leo Verriest demonstrated (correcting Marc Bloch on this point), these *servi* were never other than a tiny minority in the countryside of the twelfth and thirteenth centuries in relation to the dependent peasantry of more recent origins.[223] Here and there, therefore, a continuity between slavery and serfdom can be detected,[224] but this phenomenon (which has done so much to obscure the problem and caused so much controversy amongst historians) was always small-scale and rare.

It should not be permitted to obscure the essential truth, that is of a discontinuity – the death of a very old social order (the slave system) and the forms of subjection associated with it, the birth of

---

[221] I am using the word 'serf' in the broad meaning it had in the spoken language, a much wider meaning than that of the word *servus*, which, in the Latin charters, seems to be reserved for the descendents of the old slaves of the early Middle Ages (see below).

[222] The percentages by county are given by Fossier, *Enfance de l'Europe*, vol. 1, p. 573, who took them from H. L. Loyn, *Anglo-Saxon England and the Norman Conquest* (3rd edn, London, 1972).

[223] Verriest, *Institutions médiévales*.

[224] Poitou provides a good example of an intermediate situation between the southern model (complete break) and the northern model (indications of a secondary phenomenon of continuity). In Poitou, the word *mancipium* disappeared between 960 and 976/77; the word *servus*, on the other hand continued in use right up to the middle of the eleventh century, whilst the first mention of the *homines proprii* appeared as early as 1032 (information kindly communicated by M. Georges Pon).

a new society (feudal society) and new types of dependence. The transition from one to the other constitutes what we may, with Georges Duby, call the Feudal Revolution.[225]

[225] I am not dealing here, obviously, with the urban slavery of the last centuries of the Middle Ages. This form of slavery, of restricted geographical extent, purely domestic and artisanal, seems to be a by-product of Mediterranean trade. From the eleventh century, slavery was no longer relevant to the basis of the economy, that is agriculture. With the advent of feudalism, it was marginalised. From the fifteenth to sixteenth centuries, it was exported: Europe finally rid itself of all vestiges of the slave regime, but introduced this system of exploitation into the countries it colonised.

2. Society and mentalities in Visigothic Spain*

On 1 January 414, a splendid wedding took place in Narbonne: Athaulf, King of the Visigoths, married Galla Placidia, daughter of Theodosius the Great and sister of Honorius, Emperor of the Roman West. The German king wore a toga, poets chanted nuptial songs and fifty young slaves dressed all in silk presented the bride with fifty plates laden with gold and silver. The marriage was symbolic and immensely famous at the time; it was seen as the achievement at long last of a union of Rome and Germany, of the Latin and barbarian worlds. Some, like the historian Idatius even regarded it as the fulfilment of the prophecy of Daniel foretelling the marriage between the king of the North and the daughter of the South. Alas, within two years, Athaulf was dead, stabbed by one of his warriors at Barcelona, and Galla Placidia, beaten and violated, was eventually sent back to her brother for a ransom of 6,000 barrels of corn. Thus, between Narbonne and Barcelona, began the 300-year-long history of Visigothic Spain, a history whose beginnings, in their high hopes and high drama, seem like an encapsulation of all that followed. It was a brutal history; a time of senseless violence, cruel tortures and plunder (Galla Placidia herself, along with the gold and silver displayed at her wedding, was part of the booty seized by the Visigoths when, four years earlier, they had captured and sacked Rome). But the wedding was also an ostentatious and a prophetic event; it revealed the desire for a rapprochement between two hostile peoples, or, rather, between two cultures. It expressed, in its own way, a longing to lay the basis for a new age. Despite many and bloody setbacks, its promise was fulfilled.

By the time of the ceremony in Narbonne, the Germanic incursions into Spain were already under way. The raiders were mounted horsemen brandishing swords and scramasaxes, who burned

---

* First published in *Histoire des Espagnols, dir.* B. Bennassar (Paris, A. Colin, 1985), vol. 1, pp. 15–51.

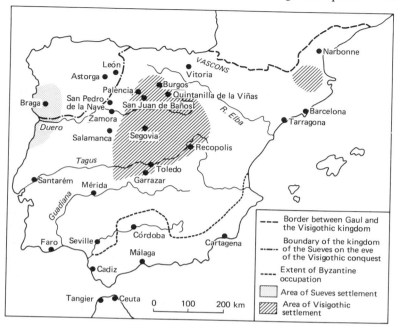

1. Visigothic Spain

town suburbs and massacred the files of fugitives so as to clear their way. But there were also heavy convoys of wagons carrying women and children, domestic animals and some small, indeed very small, provisions. The invaders were as poor as the people they were invading.

VANDALS, SUEVES AND VISIGOTHS

The Vandals came first, in 409. They have a bad reputation, probably not wholly deserved. They pillaged and destroyed – though quite what is not known – but hardly more than any other occupying force camping in a hostile country. And they did not stay long, only twenty years. One group, the Hasdings, established themselves in the North-West, the others, the Silings, in the South, but without making any mark on the country; Andalusia, at any rate, contrary to a widespread belief, does not owe them its name. In 429, they moved on to Africa. They subsequently only manifested themselves in occasional raids on the Balearic Islands, which they briefly incorporated into the maritime empire, or, to be more precise, the pirate kingdom, which they had established from Carthage in the western Mediterranean.

They were accompanied in 409 by the Sueves, an old, but much enfeebled, people, who settled in Galicia and in the north of what is now Portugal (around Braga). Their rule, chaotic and little known, was maintained, for better or worse, for almost two centuries, and perhaps contributed to the formation of the region's identity. Their occupation came to an end in 585 at the hands of the Visigoths.

It was the latter who, for good reasons, were most important. Like their cousins the Ostrogoths, established in Italy, the Visigoths were clearly distinct from the other Germanic peoples. They were distinguished, in the first place, by their language, which belonged to a group of East Germanic languages (a linguistic group which has today disappeared), which possessed an alphabet. Further, they came from a long way away, from the shores of the Black Sea. And they were remarkable, lastly, for their history; since settling in Dacia in 271, they had lived in constant contact with the Roman world, maintaining peaceful and mutually beneficial relations with it the length of the Danube, from the Pannonian basin to the delta. It was under attack from the Huns that they crossed the river Danube in 376 and penetrated the Empire, starting on an interminable flight. They sought a home first in the Balkans, then in Italy, before arriving in Narbonne in 414, where they hesitated whether to settle north or south of the Pyrenees. There were some in Barcelona, and others crossed the peninsula as far as Tarifa, but it was in Aquitaine that they settled for three quarters of a century, and where, round Toulouse and Bordeaux, they founded a kingdom which did not lack splendour, and which prefigured their future Iberian monarchy. Finally, in 507, beaten at Vouillé by the Franks under Clovis, they moved definitively into Spain.

The peninsula was lucky to fall to the Visigoths, who were far removed from Frankish and Saxon savagery. It is true that they had not yet lost their original characteristics. Their physical appearance and customs (long hair and the use of butter in cooking) could still shock the Hispano-Romans. Their family and social organisation (based on the *sippe*, or clan) was largely strange to the structures of the Mediterranean region. Their art, a direct product of the world of the steppes, and revealed by the remarkable finds (buckle-plates from sword-belts and fibulas) discovered in their tombs, was ornamental, employing geometric and animal designs with consummate skill; it was diametrically opposed to the monumental and anthropomorphic art cultivated in the Roman world. Their law, finally, based on the simple principle of compensation for the victim (wergild), retained in its inspiration many of its original Germanic features. But their leaders understood and spoke Latin, surrounded themselves with poets and orators, and occasionally read Virgil in the original. The Visigoths, far from destroying, conserved things Latin, and the Hispano-Roman writers, on this as on many other points, paid them homage. To mention only the greatest of them, Isidore of Seville was happy to write a *History of the Goths*, in which he unequivocally embraced their cause.

The assimilation of the Visigoths was made all the easier by two factors; they were relatively few – between 70,000 and 200,000 according to the estimates, as hypothetical as varied, advanced by different historians – and they were spread over what was, by contemporary standards, an immense kingdom which included Septimania, that is the region extending from the Pyrenees to the Rhône, as well as Spain. The only real concentrations of Germanic population were found, to judge by known burial sites, on the Meseta, and particularly on the plateau of Old Castile, between the Ebro and the Tagus, in a triangle formed by the towns of Palencia, Toledo and Calatayud. At the very most, on the basis of place-name evidence, a secondary zone of dispersal in Catalonia (the western Pyrenees and the province of Girona) can be added to this main nucleus. In any case, the new arrivals seem to have been easily accepted everywhere. Their settlement was organised through the Roman system of the *hospitalitas*; they received portions of estates called *sortes* (that is, two-thirds for the Gothic occupant, with one-third remaining to the old Hispano-Roman proprietor). But these arrangements applied only to a very small amount of the land, in particular of the pasture lands belonging to an aristocracy very well endowed in other respects, and only the leaders of the immigrants benefitted from them.

THE HISPANO-ROMANS

The Hispano-Romans were in the vast majority, but the word used for them, though convenient, is ambiguous. To what extent were they Spanish, to what extent Roman?

In the Roman period, Spain did not exist. The peninsula was divided into provinces (six by the time the Germans arrived: Baetica, Lusitania, Galicia, Tarraconensis, Carthaginiensis, the Balearic Isles) which were simply administrative circumscriptions of the Empire. A diocese of the Spains had existed since Diocletian, but, quite apart from the fact that it also included Mauretania Tingitana (Morocco), it was attached to the prefecture of the Gauls and the vicars who ruled it were only intermediaries; decisions were taken in Rome and carried out within the framework of the different provinces.

Though there was no true Iberian particularism within the Roman world, it cannot as a result be assumed that the peninsula was deeply Romanised. It certainly participated with distinction in the growth of Latin scholarship, providing some of its most illustrious representatives (Seneca, Lucian, Quintilian, Columella and Prudentius). But the diffusion of this culture was limited to very narrow circles and in any case hardly extended beyond the towns. These were the original centres of Roman civilization and they continued in this role under the Visigoths. The municipal magistrates survived, but were dominated by a tightly closed aristocracy which controlled the town councils (*curiae*) and filled the administrative posts: quaestors, aediles and *duoviri*. The *cursus honorum* was invariably the rule and it was necessary to have proceeded right through it to accede to the highest posts of *curator* or *defensor civitatis*. But, even in the towns, this system tended to become a mere façade, with real power passing to the counts (designated by the monarchy) or the bishops. The municipal officers were left with little more than the responsibility, less and less appreciated, of using their wealth to guarantee tax levies.

Further, the towns declined, as everywhere in the Empire, if to a lesser extent. This decadence began as early as the third century (the ruin of Empúries (Ampurias), for example) and was accentuated from the fifth century. Urban functions were increasingly confined to the provision of defence (ramparts were built everywhere in the Late Empire) and ecclesiastical administration (bishops lived in towns). It is worth noting, nevertheless, that this decline was not universal, and that there were some fortunate exceptions, the most notable being the successive capitals chosen by the Visigothic kings – Barcelona, Mérida and Toledo. Barcelona, in particular, which has retained vestiges of its sixth-century royal palace, experienced at this period its first phase of growth, at the expense of Tarragona, the old Roman metropolis.

But the crucial development remains the rise to pre-eminence of the countryside. In practice, the countryside, whose history is overshadowed throughout Antiquity by the brilliance, to some extent illusory, of urban civilisation, was only recovering the place it had always occupied: approximately 95 per cent of the inhabitants were rural. What was new was that its pre-eminence became apparent; the Hispano-Roman aristocracy, fleeing fiscal burdens, removed to their rural villas; the Goths themselves preferred the country to the town. But the Iberian countryside was only partly Romanised in the fifth century. While the plains of the east and south of the peninsula had received numerous Roman colonies and had their landscapes transformed by centuriation, the impact of Rome declined as one moved west or north. Everywhere things began to revert to their original state, most completely towards the Pyrenees and the Cantabrian Sea.

THE BASQUES

The Basques had never really been subjugated by the Romans; nor were they by the Visigoths. It was not for want of trying, but the numerous expeditions made to this end in the sixth and seventh centuries usually ended in disaster (just as did those organised from north of the Pyrenees by the Frankish kings). And giving the name Vitoria (*Victoria*) to the citadel founded in 581 by King Leovigild to contain them, was not enough in itself to achieve this.

The domain of the Basque language in the fifth to seventh centuries was much larger than today. In addition to the Basque country and modern Navarre, it seems to have extended some considerable distance into the central, even western, Pyrenees. The evidence for its boundaries is lacking. However, the place-name studies made by linguists such as J. Coromines and G. Rohlfs clearly show that the pre-Indo-European dialects related to

Basque continued to be spoken in most of the high Pyrenean valleys long after their supposed date of Romanisation. Place-names of Basque type represent 30 per cent of the total in upper Aragon, 35 per cent in upper Ribagorça and as much as 54 per cent in upper Pallars (90 out of 168 names of communes). They are found even further west, in the *conca* of Urgell, in Andorra (with, in particular, the names Urgell and Andorra) and as far east as Cerdanya (Cerdagne), where they are very numerous (Urtg, All, Alp, Creixenturri etc.). It is highly significant that the forms of these place-names often represent a late stage in the evolution of the Basque language. It is more remarkable still that in these same regions, the Latin roots entering into the composition of certain place-names have been distorted (substitution of *p* for *f*, for example), as if men had forced them to follow rules of evolution foreign to the Romance languages. One can deduce that the adoption of a Latin speech (or Romance-derived languages) was very slow to be imposed here. In Cerdanya, it goes no further back than the fifth century; sometimes, even, as for example in upper Pallars, the population continued to employ a Basque idiom, an astonishing mixture of Basque and Low Latin, right up to the tenth or eleventh centuries.

This linguistic originality is completed by a number of specific traits which made the mountainous Basque region, which preserved traditions dating back to pre-history, even the Neolithic period, a world totally distinct from the Spanish peninsula. These special features, which found their religious expression in a tenacious paganism, and which are visible in all areas of social organisation (large families, matriliny etc.), explain the implacable hostility which was forged between the Euskarian population and Hispano-Gothic society, rendering any attempt at integration vain. In fact, the Basques, who experienced from the fifth to the seventh century one of the most dynamic periods in their history, far from being on the defensive, were conquerors. To the north of their original home, they extended their domination over all the territory between the Garonne and the Pyrenees, and this subject region took their name: Gascony (Vasconia). To the south, though not achieving territorial aggrandisement, they nevertheless constituted a constant threat to the fragile frontiers of the Visigothic kingdom, reaching, for example, as far as Saragossa in 653.

THE JEWS

It would be impossible to complete this overview of the ethnic elements composing Visigothic Spain without reference to the Jews. Along with other Orientals (Syrians and Greeks), they were numerous in all the cities, where they were involved in every sort of commercial and artisanal activity. Information about them is, it must be admitted, very sparse; even archaeology (in spite of the discovery at Elche of a synagogue from this period) has told us little. In practice the Jews are largely only known indirectly, through Christian sources and, in particular, through the abundant legislation applying to them as a result of their religious practices.

It is possible to distinguish two phases in the attitude of the Visigothic monarchy towards the Jews; the first, before the conversion of the Visigoths to Catholicism, was broadly tolerant; the second, following the conversion of the Visigoths in 587, was one of increasingly cruel persecution.

In the sixth century, the Jews continued to live under the same regime as during the Roman Empire. No changes were made to the measures regarding them taken by the Emperor Theodosius, which were continued unmodified by the first Visigothic kings. They enjoyed a high degree of autonomy, along with some discriminatory measures. Their communities were responsible for their own administration and had their own courts which, sovereign in civil matters, had jurisdiction in all cases not meriting the death penalty. Their right to worship was recognised, rest on the Sabbath respected, and, though the construction of new synagogues was forbidden, those in existence enjoyed the protection of the law. On the other hand, religious proselytism was frowned on and mixed marriages forbidden in principle (although this prohibition seems in practice to have been little observed).

The growth of anti-Semitism in the seventh century was the consequence of a combination of several different factors. Economic reasons certainly played a part; at a time when the economy was contracting, the profits from the extensive trade of the Jews attracted envy and easily appeared scandalous in the eyes of a society sunk into ruralism. There were also cultural reasons; the Hebraic schools provided an education of high quality and the rabbis were often better educated than the Catholic priests, with whom they often competed successfully. Some Christians, certainly, were converted to Judaism. It was these 'Judaisers' who first bore the brunt of the law; from the reign of Chindaswinth (642-53), any baptised person who adopted the Hebraic religion was punished by death and the confiscation of his possessions, and the same applied to the Jew responsible for the conversion. Converts were attacked first, the Jews themselves soon after. They were prohibited from employing Christian domestic servants, they were excluded from all public responsibilities, their capacity to bear judicial witness was restricted, and limitations were imposed on their commercial activities, particularly its most lucrative element, the trade in slaves. The seventh century saw the development of an increasingly repressive anti-Jewish legislation, and the final crisis of the Visigothic regime took place in a climate of fierce anti-Semitism.

Free and slave

It is impossible, given the sources available, to make even a rough estimate of the population of Visigothic Spain. The figures which have sometimes been put forward (and which vary considerably from author to author) are based on no firm evidence. At the very most, it is possible to discern the main demographic trends. From the third century at least, the whole of western Europe experienced a period of demographic stagnation, even decline; mortality was high, chiefly as a result of chronic malnutrition, whilst the replacement of generations was threatened by Malthusian practices such as abortion and infanticide. In Spain, as throughout the Mediterranean basin, the situation was aggravated in the sixth century by deadly epidemics of bubonic plague. This plague, which decimated Constantinople in 542, was at its worst in the peninsula between 570 and 588, afflicting especially the maritime zones of the east and the north-east. The streets of towns and villages alike were so littered with corpses that it was difficult to find space to bury them. But though flaring up again from time to time, the plague disappeared fairly early in the seventh century, not to reappear in Spain for seven hundred years. The population recovered and, it seems, entered a new phase of growth. This was a shift of direction, tentative and barely perceptible in the short run, but whose impact continued to grow up to the end of the thirteenth century.

While the demography of Visigothic Spain remains essentially a matter for conjecture, its social organisation is rather better known. It was a slave society. From this point of view, the arrival of the Germans, who themselves practised slavery, changed nothing. As in Antiquity, a clear dividing line, juridically defined with absolute precision, separated the free and the non-free worlds. On one side were those whose status and existence was surrounded by, at the very least, elementary safeguards; on the other were creatures who were totally subject to the arbitrary authority of their masters. But this crucial division was not the only one. On all sides, new barriers were erected which made of this society one of the most rigidly hierarchic that has ever existed.

THE POWERFUL AND THE POOR

The social category of the free was far from homogeneous; the most blatant wealth existed side by side with the most abject poverty.

At the top was an aristocracy which was small but immensely rich. The magnates who composed it were dignified with laudatory titles: they were the Premiers (*priores, primates, proceres*), the Best (*optimates, honestiores*), the Illustrious (*viri illustres*) or the Generous (*generosae personae*). Some were Goths, the rest Hispano-Romans, the two in any case being soon united by marriage.

The Goths were dominated by a small number of families whose roots were lost in a mythical past and who often opposed each other in fierce inter-family wars; it was from this group that the kings were chosen. In the course of time, a certain number of other clans were attached to these tutelary families by matrimonial ties and military alliances; together they constituted the nobility of blood. It was from this tribal group, strongly imbued with the spirit of clientage, that were recruited the trusted officers who, in the name of the sovereign, controlled and administered the kingdom. First came the men closest to the king, the warriors of his personal guard (*gardingos, leudos*); they were both dear to and feared by the king, whom they protected, but killed when he transgressed. Next came the officers responsible for central administration: the palatine counts. Lastly, there were the dukes and counts despatched to the provinces to see that the wishes of the king were respected, and who were invested with the royal *bannum*, that is with the discretionary power to command, judge and punish; they formed a military nobility, constantly mobilised in the defence of the regime, but also the prime beneficiaries of royal munificence.

They were in close contact with the representatives of the Hispano-Roman aristocracy. The latter were still called senators, a reminder that their ancestors had belonged to the old Roman senatorial class. They possessed huge landed estates with a vast labour force. But their power was by no means only economic; they maintained on their estates veritable private armies, as much as two thousand strong. They were the first to rally to the invaders, enthusiastically collaborating so as to preserve their privileges. They baptised their children with Germanic names and gave their daughters to Gothic leaders. They offered their own services, which were accepted, and many senators retained or obtained important administrative responsibilities. Did this add up to a complete fusion of the two aristocracies? It is by no means certain. Unlike what happened in Gaul, for example, no Hispano-Romans achieved the very highest posts in the administration of the kingdom, and the end of the Visigothic period seems to be marked by a hiatus in the process of amalgamation, as if the great Gothic families had realised the dangers for them of too complete an integration into the native milieu.

Those free who were not noble comprised the majority of the population. They were called the Inferiors (*inferiores*), the Lesser Ones (*minores, humiliores*) or the Poor (*pauperes*). They were for the most part peasants (*rustici, rusticani*), small landowners descended from the *possessores* of the Late Roman Empire. They lived on isolated rural holdings or in little agglomerations (*vici*). They enjoyed some administrative and judicial autonomy, with their own deliberative assemblies (*conventus publicus vicinorum*) which regulated local affairs. Sometimes this communal organisation went further, especially in the less Romanised regions. Here, in the Cantabrian mountains and the high Pyrenean valleys, some villagers still collectively owned, by a custom which dated back to prehistory, at least some of their lands and flocks. Communal and private property co-existed in Visigothic Spain.

But these free communities were experiencing hard times. Exposed to the rapacity of an aristocracy which retained all the power, which it both used and abused, many of them had been driven to revolt. Spain, like Gaul, experienced real social wars in the fifth century, the wars of the Bacaudae (the name given to the insurgents). There can be no doubt that these, by disrupting military organisation, helped to facilitate the penetration of the Germans. On the other hand, the latter were able to appear as potential saviours in the eyes of a landed aristocracy gripped by panic. It was, in effect, the Goths who crushed the Bacaudae of Tarraconensis in 454.

The Visigothic regime, then, operated solely to the benefit of the powerful. The lot of the poor in these times of poverty and insecurity was hard. Hunger was widespread and it only needed bad weather for endemic shortage to turn into harsh famine. What could they do? Some waited outside church doors in the hope of a meagre pittance. Others joined the private armies being organised by the rich; the name given to these domestic fighting men – *bucellarii*, or dry biscuit-eaters – is suggestive of their status. The poorest of all, lastly, had no alternative but to alienate their liberty and sell themselves as slaves – themselves and their children – for the few bags of corn which would enable them to survive.

THE SLAVES

The persistence of a slave economy constitutes one of the chief features of Visigothic Spain. It is clearly visible in legislation; out of 498 texts of laws which have survived from this period, 229 refer, wholly or in part, to the question of slavery. Slaves existed in large numbers; it was not uncommon for a large landowner or ecclesiastical establishment to own several hundred, even several thousand, slaves. It is significant that the sixteenth Council of Toledo laid down that a rural church could not support a full-time priest without at least ten slaves (and where there were only ten, the church would be 'very poor').

Who were these slaves? The majority were slaves by birth. Servitude was hereditary; it only needed one servile parent for the children to be slaves. 'The rule is that the new-born assume the vilest condition of their parents', declared Isidore of Seville. The continuation of the slave population was thus assured by natural growth alone. But this was not the only source of slaves; for a variety of reasons, slaves by birth were joined by many other unfortunates. Poverty was the chief cause; the poor sold themselves, as we have seen, in times of famine. The law authorised such sales, even justified them doctrinally: 'He who thinks of selling himself is unworthy to be free.' The sale of children by their parents was, if not formally authorised, at least tolerated. The slave trade, also, continued to supply Spain with foreign slaves (from, for example, the British Isles and Sardinia). War, too, played a part, particularly those civil wars which were often in practice tribal conflicts whose main purpose was to capture from the opponent's territory the largest possible number of cattle, human or animal. But it seems to have been judicial sentencing which was responsible for the greatest number of reductions to slavery. The principle was quite simple: any condemned person who could not pay the indemnity due to his victim or his victim's family was handed over to them as a slave, even when the damage inflicted was minor, even imaginary. The judicial system functioned to a large extent as a machine to enslave poor free men.

Any person reduced in this way to the rank of slave lost his identity and found himself de-socialised. He had no further link with his former family. His wife (or husband) could, for example, remarry after one year. It was as if he was dead. He was, in fact, dead to the society of the free and even, in the view of the legislators, to society itself. One of the essential features of Visigothic legislation was to relegate the slave to a sub-human condition. The term used for him – *mancipium* – was neuter in gender, as if it applied to an object. The slave was, in effect, a thing. Or, more exactly, an animal; the barrier which separated him from the society of the free was conceived as separating not only two races, but two species. Nothing shows this more clearly than the fierce determination with which sexual relations between the free and slaves were prohibited, and assimilated with practices which were against nature, indeed bestial. They were punished with the utmost cruelty:

If a free woman mates with her slave or with a free man who has been her slave, or marries him, and this is proved, she must die. She and he should be whipped in front of the judge and burnt. If the guilty woman is a widow or a virgin, she will suffer the same penalty . . . If a free woman marries a slave belonging to someone else, or mates with him, the judge, as soon as he is informed, should separate them and inflict on them the punishment they deserve, that is one hundred lashes each. If they mate again, the judge should have them brought before him again and have them given a further one hundred lashes each. And if at the third time they do not wish to separate, the judge should have them given a further hundred lashes and return the woman to the power of her parents. And if her parents let her return once more to the slave, she should be handed over as a slave to the latter's master. The children born of this iniquitous mating will be slaves like their father and the woman's belongings should go to her nearest family . . . And we determine that this same law should apply to free men who mate with the female slaves of the king or another master.

The one exception to this rule, phallocratic in the strict sense of the term, was that masters were left to dispose as they wished of their own female slaves. In this, as in other spheres, no restriction was put on the arbitrary power of the slave-owner.

This arbitrary power was particularly visible in the punishments inflicted on slaves. They were beaten and whipped like recalcitrant beasts. But, for some masters, blows were not enough. They resorted to mutilation. There was a clear preference for methods which did not deprive the slave of his ability to work. These were of two types: facial mutilation and castration. Or there was death; slave-owners retained, as in Antiquity, the power of life and death over their human cattle. Around 650, a law of Chindaswinth attempted to abolish this power. But old practices died hard; the law was not respected, or, to be more precise, it was got round, as we learn from a text of twenty years later (a law of Recceswinth on the same subject); forbidden from killing recalcitrant slaves, masters, we are told, 'cut off a hand or the nose or the lips or an ear or even a foot, or even put out an eye, or severed some part of their body, or ordered that something should be cut off or put out or severed'. How are these savage punishments to be explained? They do not result simply from the sadism of masters, though this is, in some cases, apparent. They had, above all, the value of example, and, by their spectacular character (the facial mutilations), were intended to discourage all spirit of insubordination.

Should this very bleak picture of the servile condition in the Visigothic period be tempered at certain points? It is clear that not all slaves suffered the same lot. Those belonging to the king, for example, were relatively protected. Above all, it was customary to distinguish two categories within the servile population: the 'good' or 'qualified' (idonei) and the 'vile' (vili). The former served in the households of the mighty; the women were chambermaids or concubines, the men footmen or specialised craftsmen; some even bore arms (in bodyguards or private armies) or worked in the offices of the royal chancellery. But they were only a minority compared with the 'vile' or the 'ugly', that is those worn out with toil labouring on the big estates.

The effect of the Church on the fate of slavery is ambiguous. Bishops certainly encouraged enfranchisement, even, at one point, considering making it a sacrament. It is also the case that Christianity tended to detach slaves from the animality in which they were confined, to make of them – an immense step forward – human beings, Christians in the full sense. But, on the other hand, blatantly abusing certain words of St Paul, the clergy legitimated slavery, and made it an institution of divine origin. For Isidore of Seville, slavery had as its role the expiation of original sin, it derived from a providential programme for the salvation of humanity through penitence, and masters were justly invested with the power of coercion over their servile labourers for the greater good of all. Another idea given wide currency was that slavery was synonymous with baseness. Slaves were collectively guilty and thus responsible for their lot; if, in effect, they were not intrinsically perverse, it was impossible to understand why God kept them in such a condition. And finally, on the concrete level, the Church was reluctant to enfranchise its own slaves (how could the poor be fed without the labour of slaves?) and seems by no means always to have treated them gently. One example, amongst many others: first the Council of Mérida and then the ninth Council of Toledo prohibited clerics from mutilating their slaves, evidence that this practise was by no means unknown.

The alleviation of the servile condition came about, in practice, by other routes. It was to some extent a consequence of a deterioration in the lot of the poor free. Maltreated and humiliated in their turn, they eventually joined their lot with that of the slaves. The fact of working together, depending on the same master, receiving from him or his agents the same punishments and frequenting the same church (and it is in this sense, at the level of popular religious practice, that Christianity played a part) all contributed to breaking down the old barrier of blood between free and non-free. It should also be added that the emancipation of slaves, particularly at the end of the Visigothic period, assumed an even simpler form: for many, flight was the most direct route to freedom.

Table 3. *The price of life by age and sex (in sous)*

Age	Men	Women
0–1	0	0
1–2	60	30
2–4	70	35
4–7	80	40
7–10	90	45
10–11	100	50
11–12	110	55
12–13	120	60
13–14	130	65
14–15	140	70
15–20	150	250
20–40	300	250
40–50	300	200
50–60	200	200
60–65	200	100
over 65	100	100

MEN AND WOMEN

Men and women were no more equal in free society than amongst slaves. An objective indicator of the respective regard in which the two sexes were held is provided by the tariffs of composition in case of murder (see Table 3). They set a price on life, to be paid to the parents of the victim.

Table 3 is very revealing. We should note first the lack of importance accorded to babies; mortality in the first months of life was so high that no price was attached to creatures whose chances of survival were slim (all the more so, given that infanticide was widespread). It was at the age of one year that the human being began to acquire value. This value increased fairly slowly up to the age of ten, much faster afterwards, that is from the time when the work which could be required of the child became significant. It was between 15 and 40 years of age in the case of women, and between 20 and 50 in the case of men, that the price of life reached its highest level. It then declined with the approach of old age, the threshold of minimal value being at 60 for women and 65 for men. Old people, contrary to what is often thought today, were little valued in ancient societies.

The differences between the sexes are considerable. A woman

aged 70, for example, was worth less than a man for fifty years of his life; she was worth only half as much, both in her childhood (up to the age of 15) and when aged between 60 and 65. But it would be a mistake to place too much emphasis on these differences. The undervaluation of women was general at the period, and much less marked in Spain than in most other kingdoms of the West. It is rather the relative smallness of the margin separating masculine and feminine values which is striking. For most of her adult life (from 20 to 40), a women was costed at five-sixths of a man (250 as opposed to 300 sous). From 50 to 60 and after 65 she was on a level with him. And there was even a brief period in her life (between 15 and 20) when she was much more valuable (250 as against 150 sous). Crudely, these figures reveal the existence as early as the Visigothic period of a constant which is visible throughout the history of Spanish women: the high regard enjoyed by two categories, widows and virgins.

CHILDHOOD, MARRIAGE AND ADULTHOOD

'In the inheritance of the father the children come first'; Visigothic law gave absolute priority to the direct line of succession. Anyone who died leaving sons or daughters was bound to bequeath them four-fifths of his possessions. Another fundamental principle, directly derived from Roman law, and persisting unchanged until the feudal period, was equal division between children. Boys and girls were on a strictly equal footing. Children were often very young when they received their promised inheritance, either because of the early death of one of their parents (a frequent occurrence), or because the latter had forfeited their maternal or paternal authority. This might result from adultery by the father or the mother, the mother's remarriage before one year of widowhood had elapsed, or cohabitation by the widowed mother with a slave or a freedman.

Further, children were protected. The law attempted, admittedly without great success, to check the practice of infanticide by punishing it severely. Putting children out to be nursed could not turn into abandonment in disguise; natural parents who failed to make the annual allowance to the nursing parents were reduced to slavery to the latter's benefit. Greedy guardians or those who abused their position were liable to fines which were often heavy. Lastly, though the sale of children into slavery by their own parents was tolerated, they could not be sold by anyone outside the family. The sale and theft of free children was punished without mercy; anyone committing this crime had to pay 300 sous – much more than if he had 'only' killed the child – to its parents or was handed over to them for them to choose between putting him to death or selling him as a slave.

Emancipation, on the other hand, came very early. At 10 years old, a child who was ill could make a will. At 13, he could testify and take an oath. At 14, he came of age. In the case of slaves, children remained with their mother till the age of 12; at that age, they were sold or began to work for their master.

Marriage was a matter of the utmost importance. This was not the case with slaves, who had the right only to *contubernium* (a term used without distinction for the mating of humans and animals), made or unmade at the whim of the master, whether there were children or not. But it was very much so among the free. The preliminaries were crucial, in particular, the choice of spouse, a long and complicated procedure, undertaken by the family. In this sphere, the father's word was law; a daughter who married against the wishes of her father was disinherited. The young girl was permitted, nevertheless, a degree of initiative; if, said the law, she was attracted by a young man, he might seek an interview with the parents, and, if he was accepted, a dowry was fixed. If both mother and father were dead, the young woman had even greater room for manoeuvre; if she twice objected to a partner chosen by her brothers, she could choose her own husband. Lastly, there was always a means for young couples resolved to bypass family opposition – to simulate abduction. This was, in fact, a part of the primitive matrimonial ritual of the Germans, and still practised, even though the law endeavoured to prohibit it.

Also of Germanic inspiration were the customary marriage procedures. These began with the exchange of rings; it was the ceremony of the *arrae* which amounted to a reciprocal commitment and corresponded to a solemn engagement. There was not as yet, indeed not for a long time, anything Christian about the marriage itself. The blessing of a priest was optional and rarely sought. What made the marriage was its consummation and public recognition of this the morning after the wedding night. This was the hour of the *morgengabe*, the morning gift. This present from the husband to the young wife was originally nothing other than the price of her virginity. It became the marriage settlement in favour of the wife, the dowry. It was the man who endowed the woman; this remained the case for centuries (at least until the twelfth century). The amount of the dowry varied; tiny to begin with (a thousandth of the husband's possessions), it grew steadily throughout the Visigothic period. King Ervig codified it: ten male slaves, ten female slaves and twenty horses, or – and it was the ratio which was maintained for centuries – one-tenth of the husband's wealth. The aim was to assure 'the future dignity of the marriage', in other words, to guarantee the material security of the wife. In this it was successful. For centuries Spanish women not only enjoyed complete control over their own property (that is to say, their share of their inheritance, often received through an anticipatory transfer at the time of the marriage), but had a permanent right to oversee the property of their husband. In practice, in most cases, the dowry was not effectively handed over to the wife at the time of the wedding; what she received (often by written charter) was the virtual possession of a tenth of the wealth of her partner; he, in consequence, could not make any gift, sale or alienation of his own patrimony without the agreement of his wife.

We must not, though, paint too idyllic a picture of the position of women in the Visigothic period. The laws themselves suggest caution, and, directly or indirectly, reveal much misery and unhappiness. Adultery was common, and severely punished in principle, but it is significant that only women appear as guilty in the repressive legal provisions. Male unfaithfulness was tacitly accepted, unless by a poor man (in which case the law authorised seizure of his meagre patrimony or reduction to slavery). In high society, and particularly within the royal family, the result was virtual polygamy. It also led to repudiation, which was authorised up to the middle of the seventh century. Chindaswinth then forbade it, though retaining some exceptions (fornication by the woman, or the husband's wish to enter religion). In practice, it continued to be possible for a man to get rid of an old wife so as to take a younger one. Or he might prefer to frequent prostitutes. Prostitution was common everywhere, in the towns, as one would expect, but even in small country towns (*vici*), even in the smallest *villae*. It was encouraged by slavery; many a master found it financially profitable to exploit his young female slaves this way. Rape, lastly, to judge by the frequency of references to it in the legislation, seems to have been common amongst all social categories.

It was during adolescence or in old age, as we have seen, that the value attributed to women came closest to that of men, sometimes even exceeding it. The special esteem paid to widows and virgins was not only a product of civil society, but something strongly preached by the Church. It was at this period that Pope Gregory the Great laid down a hierarchy of value within mankind; at the base were married persons, sullied by sex, even if within legitimate marriage; at an intermediate level were those who were continent, who had experienced sexual activity but no longer practised it; at the top came virgins.

Widows were continent, at least in theory. For St Braulio, they were like Judith, invested with every virtue. They were protected by the law in the same way as young women, for example in cases of rape or violation. Above all, on the death of her husband, a widow acquired real economic independence. The dowry, till then in effect possessed only in theory, at that point became fully hers, added to her own possessions. Further, she had the use for life of a part of the inheritance of her dead husband, a part equal to that which went to each of their children. Lastly, it was the widow who, if the children were minors, managed the whole of the family patrimony. The law in effect made widows into heads of families, conferring on them all the authority previously held by the father. It was through widowhood and it alone that Spanish women of that period – as later – could bank on achieving full equality with men.

The high esteem for virginity sprang from a number of different factors. In lay society, and especially amongst the aristocracy, the young woman was a prize to be contended for. At this period more than any other, marriage was the surest way for an individual to rise in status, and for a family to increase its distinction. If it was through men that nobility was transmitted (which is not completely certain at this period – historians disagree), its degree was determined by women. The illustriousness of a family was in proportion to the marriages it made. It is striking, for example, to see many nobles attach themselves from choice to their maternal ancestry, proof that this brought them greater glory. In these circumstances, it was in the interest of families offering their daughters to push up the bids (in the strict sense of the term, since the dowry came from the husband). Hence complex strategies were deployed in the exchange of women – to use a term dear to ethnologists – which was central to social life. The price of virginity was monetarised, and high.

Some clerics denounced this trade in virgins. According to Leander of Seville: 'Men who take wives are accustomed to provide dowries, offer rewards and donate their patrimonial possessions, so that they seem to buy rather than choose their wives.' However, the Church, in its own manner and to a quite excessive degree, contributed to this exaltation, and so to raising the price of virginity. Leander himself, in his *De institutione virginium*, made himself its inspired poet. Eve, he said, by defiling herself, was responsible for original damnation: 'What she lost in Eden is repaired in you, O virgins . . . in you God recognises His work, He sees you just as He made you.' But the preservation of virginity was not only the means to preserve an immaculate integrity, it was also a method (there were others, such as fasting and confinement, but it was the best) of achieving detachment from the world. The salvation of the soul began with contempt for the flesh. How did marriage fit in? Leander had difficulty in understanding how God could permit anything so repugnant: 'Marriage is straightaway corruption, the weight of the fertilised womb, the pain of childbirth.' But, after much searching, he found a justification: without marriage no more virgins would be born.

Pagans and Christians

Christianity, authorised by Constantine (Edict of Milan, 313), became the state religion of the Roman Empire under Theodosius, who, in 391, formally prohibited the practice of any other form of worship. But religion is not imposed by decree. In Spain as elsewhere in the West, Christianity was slow to take root; the ancient gods obstinately refused to die. Paganism survived; or rather several paganisms – beliefs and practices derived from different cultures.

PAGANISMS

The religion of the Basques, its origins lost in the mists of time, was certainly unique and highly original. It was, as far as can be judged from the traces it left in folklore, pure pantheism. Dominated by the mighty figure of Jaungoika, the Master of Heaven, divinities populated the forests and mountains. For a long time, indeed for a very long time, the Basques remained fiercely attached to these gods; the rare attempts to evangelise them (St Amand) failed miserably. On the contrary, Euskarian paganism was on the offensive, and posed a constant threat to the frail Christianity of the adjacent regions. The Basques enjoyed a reputation as 'scourges of churches'. As late as the tenth century, the first pilgrim routes to St James of Compostela made the long detour through Somport to avoid the Basque country.

Hispano-Latin paganism was more diffuse, but it still strongly influenced mentalities in all social categories. It derived from two sources: an ancient base of native beliefs, on which were superimposed Graeco-Roman myths. It was a potent mixture; Christian baptism was ineffective in the face of such deeply rooted customs. The bishops bemoaned this. Polemius, bishop of Astorga, despairing of the conduct of his flock, wrote to his archbishop, Martin of Braga, for advice. The latter's reply has survived; it consisted of a veritable treatise – the *De correctione rusticorum* – on rural paganism and how to combat it. It also included a model sermon whose purport is highly revealing as regards the practices of the peasantry of León – or Portugal – in the mid sixth century:

How many of you, who have renounced the devil, his angels, his worship and his evil works, have gone back to worshipping the demon? Because burning candles to stones and trees and springs and at cross-roads, what else is this but devil-worship? Practising divination and taking the augurs, honouring the days dedicated to idols, what else is this than devil-worship? Celebrating the festivals of Vulcan and the Kalends, adorning tables, arranging laurels, studying footprints, pouring wine over a log in the hearth, putting bread in springs, what else is this than devil-worship? Women who, before their toil, invoke the name of Minerva, who marry on the day of Venus, who wait for that day to make a journey, what else are they doing but worshipping the devil? Casting spells on herbs to render them baleful, invoking the name of the demons for this purpose, what else is it than devil-worship? And there are very many other things which it would take too long to enumerate. And all this you do after having been baptised and having renounced the devil; in this way, returning to the evil works of the demons, you deny your faith and the pact you have received in baptism, and you pay heed to other signs, which are the signs of the devil, and which you see in the flight of birds and sneezing and many other things . . . Similarly, you abandon the practice of the holy incantation, which is the symbol of the Creed, and you forget the prayer of our Lord, which is the Our Father, to indulge in diabolical incantations and the songs of the demon.

The ancient gods were clearly still present, or at least those who had known how to adapt to the needs of an increasingly peasant society: Vulcan helped in the manufacture of tools, Venus made women fertile, and the wise Minerva now protected the humble toil of village women. Above all, nature remained an immense temple where primordial elements were adored – water, fire, stones, plants, not to speak of the earth itself. The sphere of the sacred was enormous, and Christian priests had great difficulty in confining it within the special buildings set aside for it – the churches. All the more so since Christianity, though it promised salvation, had little to offer as regards people's most pressing anxieties: fear of drought and storms, fear of sickness and famine, fear of night-time, of wolves and monsters. Certainly, the saints would soon take on many of the tasks now assumed by genies, would cause rain to fall and crops to grow, protect cattle and little children. But this had not yet happened, and the new religion was very far from being a rural one.

Meanwhile, people held to their ancient practices. Sorcerers and sorceresses, enchanters, Magi, diviners and augurs still peopled the Iberian countryside, and wielded great influence, whether for good or for evil. Under pressure from the bishops, the Visigothic monarchy pursued them relentlessly, especially towards the end of the period. This attempt at repression is well illustrated by some of the laws of Ervig dating from the end of the seventh century:

Firstly, those who make potions of herbs and give them to people to drink ought to receive a punishment such that, if their victim dies, they should die themselves, horribly. If their victim does not die, they will be committed to his power, and he can do with them what he pleases.

Those who conjure up storms, and cause hail to fall on vines and harvests, and those who speak with devils, and those who alter the desires of men and women, and those who make circles in the night, and those who make sacrifices to the devils, let all such, if they are taken, receive two hundred lashes, and be scalped, and be horribly branded on their foreheads, and be shown in this condition in ten villages round the town, so that people are frightened by this punishment. And let those who have sought their advice receive two hundred lashes.

Let every free man or slave who, by enchantment or ligature, has harmed men or animals . . . or has rendered a man mute receive in his body the same harm he caused to others.

If a man gives a potion of herbs to a woman to make her abort and her child does, he will be put to death. As for the woman who has drunk the potion so as to abort, let her receive two hundred lashes if she is a slave, or be reduced to servitude if she is free.

THE CHURCH

In practice, the civil authorities seem only to have attacked pagan practices to the extent that they had harmful effects. Such reserve was not, naturally, present in the attitude of the Church, which attacked them at every opportunity and in whatever form they appeared. Their manifestations were various and often strange, to judge from the (unfortunately very incomplete) picture conveyed by a document from a slightly later period. This dates from the eighth century, but is based on earlier sources: a Manual of Penitence compiled by a clerk called Vigila, which lists all the possible sins, indicating in each case, the number of days of fasting on bread and water to be prescribed by the priest:

If a Christian consults diviners, enchanters, sorcerers, augurs or those who examine entrails or other such people: five years of penitence.
If anyone, to perform some magic or for any other reason, bathes by swimming on his back: eighteen days of penitence.
If anyone, to cure some infirmity, bathes under the jetty of a mill: fifteen days of penitence.
For those who, in dances, dress like women or disguise themselves in a monstrous fashion, as *majas* or as ogres or clothe themselves with animal skins: one year of penitence. (*Maia*: originally the divinity of the month of May; *orcos*: monsters who obeyed Orcus, that is, Pluto.)
If anyone is an emissary of storms: fifteen years of penitence.

This is, indeed, an oddly disparate collection of prohibitions, but one in which two of the great phobias of the medieval Church, and in particular of the Spanish Church, nevertheless emerge – those of bathing and dancing. Water, which invited nudity, spring water especially, domain of nymphs and naiads, and which healed and regenerated, was of all the elements the one which remained most closely connected with pagan rites; offerings continued to be made at springs (coins and crowns of flowers were thrown in, ritual loaves were left) and, well into the sixth century, people still observed the summer solstice which celebrated the marriage of fire and water (with so-called 'St John's Day' fires, but also with suspect midnight baths in lakes and streams). Bathing was long seen in Spain as a sign of doubtful piety, almost a licentious act.

Dancing was even less amenable to Christianisation. Unlike singing and music, for example, which were easily integrated into the liturgy, it was impossible to assimilate, it seemed to be an irreducible fact of paganism. Dancing was, and remained in the sixth and seventh centuries, the primordial manifestation of a sacred alliance between man and nature. Between, for example, men and animals: the animal skins worn by dancers on certain days in the year (on the calends of January, in particular, to greet the New Year) refer back to immemorial totemic myths. More dangerous still were the dances of spring, the May festivals, rites of sexual liberation which celebrated the fecundity of the earth and of women. The month of May would, of course, later be Christianised, retaining its feminine connotations (the month of Mary), but at the cost of a complete reversal of its meaning (a celebration of virginity), with, naturally, all dancing excluded.

The battle against pagan practices carried the Christian Church onto what was, for it, dangerous ground. It was tempting to respond to magic with magic. One curious example involved the struggle against divining, especially by means of the interpretation of sneezes. What did a sneeze represent to a diviner? It was a manifestation of the spirits which lodged in the human body. From the nature and intensity of the act, it was possible to understand the wishes of the spirit. What did Christian priests do to fight this practice? They encouraged the faithful to call on the name of the Lord when anyone they were speaking to sneezed: 'Jesus!' The meaning of this exorcism has been lost in modern Spain, but the practice has survived, testimony to remarkable pagan–Christian syncretism.

This profound saturation with paganism is visible even within the clergy, giving rise to a veritable 'ecclesiastical sorcery' which was denounced by the councils. Some priests, for example, suspended the divine offices, hid the liturgical objects and installed the hangings of mourning in their churches, in the hope of forcing God, by depriving Him of His worship, to punish their enemies. Others celebrated requiem masses on behalf of the living, so as to bring about their death. Such aberrations are to be explained by the ignorance of the lower clergy, who still received no doctrinal training and whose members were chosen, sometimes from amongst freed slaves, more for their docility towards the authorities than for their knowledge of the sacred texts. The bishops themselves were often distressingly credulous; a certain Bishop of Ibiza discussed in his sermons a letter sent from heaven by Christ to one of his faithful.

On the question of morality, the least said the better. On, for example, the subject of the penchant for drink exhibited by many clerics, it is enough to quote without comment the first lines of Vigila's penitential:

1. If a bishop or a priest indulges, inveterately, in the vice of drunkenness, let him resign or be deprived.
2. If a priest or a deacon or a monk drinks to the point where he is disgustingly drunk, twenty days of penitence.
3. If he vomits when he is drunk, a further fifteen days.
4. If he vomits up the Eucharist, sixty days.
5. If a dog eats the vomit, one hundred days.

We must beware, however, of generalising. It is true that contemporary sources, particularly those emanating from the councils, present the clergy of the Visigothic period in a very bad light; nevertheless, had they all been unworthy, the progress made by Christianity would be impossible to explain. Though limited, this was real. It was achieved from the towns and the monasteries.

Worship and religious practice

Christian worship in the fifth century was an almost exclusively urban phenomenon. The parish was merged with the diocese and all religious life was organised round the cathedral. The ecclesiastical personnel consisted almost exclusively of the bishop and his immediate assistants. It was from this urban base that, slowly and laboriously, the countryside was populated with places of worship: first in the *vici*, small country towns of some importance, then on the *villae*, that is the estates of the aristocracy. In the latter case, the action of the bishops was reinforced by that of the great landowners, who built chapels intended to receive their labourers, and whose priests they themselves nominated. These were pious works, but not entirely without ulterior motive: 'The churches', declared a text of King Leovigild, 'should be places where discipline is taught, where obedience is learned, and where examples of punishments are displayed.' Nevertheless, these private churches, which to begin with hardly differed from the other demesne buildings (ovens, mills, stables etc.), soon became the centres of new rural parishes, and as such, the centres of a community life which was not necessarily – far from it – respectful of authority. By bringing together all those who worked the land, free and non-free, they were places where a new peasant identity was formed.
But the monks, too, built churches. The origins of Iberian mon-

asticism may date back to the fourth century, but it is not until the sixth, even the seventh, century that it really began to flourish. It took two forms: eremitic and cenobitic. Large numbers of hermits, eager for solitude and mortification, constantly in search of the most inhospitable 'deserts', had no other ambition than to be dead to the world. Some of them are known to us: Valerius, passionate imitator of the Egyptian anchorites, whose exemplary life gave rise to many vocations, and made Bierzo, to which he retired, a new Thebes; and Nanctus, a wandering solitary, who, to be sure of neither seeing any women nor being seen by them, was preceded and followed by two disciples whose job it was to chase the female race out of his path. And there were those anonymous recluses (voluntarily anonymous) who spent their whole lives confined in minuscule enclosures in which they could hardly move.

Like eremitism, Spanish cenobitism was of oriental inspiration. Throughout the Visigothic period, it developed without any set plan, at the mercy of vocations. Monasteries were created here and there, developing their own customs, and at most forming loose groups. In the seventh century, the disorder was such that Isidore of Seville and Fructuosus of Braga both decided to produce monastic rules (the rule of St Benedict was not yet common in the peninsula), but each in a very different spirit. The rule of Fructuosus, inspired by the eremitic model, emphasised the necessity of living as far as possible 'in the solitude of the cell'. That of Isidore, in contrast, gave priority to community life. But whether they joined the one or the other obedience, monasteries were founded in large numbers. Some became famous, such as Biclar in Catalonia and Asan in the Aragonese Pyrenees, and became, in their turn, centres of evangelisation, with the monks both creating and serving in parish churches. To take one example, the slow and difficult Christianisation of the Catalan Pyrenees was probably due to the activities of the monasteries of Pallars and Ribagorza (Alaó, Senterada, Taverna), themselves born of the apostleship of St Victorianus and his disciples.

Arians and Catholics

THE ARIAN CHURCH

One of the principal difficulties encountered by the Catholic Church in establishing its authority in Spain lay in the competition it for long faced from a rival, the Arian Church. The Goths were Arians, that is they professed a deviant form of the Christian faith, which had been preached in the early fourth century by the priest, Arius of Alexandria. Arianism was, in fact, a simplified version of Christianity, stripped of many of its mysteries. In the Holy Trinity, only the Father was one, not created and eternal. The Son proceeded from the Father, and the Spirit, in its turn, proceeded from the Son. In other words, only the Father was truly God, the Son and the Spirit enjoying only a delegated divinity. Christ, in particular, appeared in this conception as a created being, the first such. Though condemned by the Council of Nicaea in 325, Arianism continued to gain ground, thanks largely to the preaching of a Gothic bishop, Ulfilas, who translated the gospel and liturgical texts into the Gothic language and persuaded his compatriots to accept his Arian interpretation. From the Goths, Arianism was then transmitted to most of the Germanic peoples, with the exception of the Franks and the Saxons.

The consequence was that two antagonistic Christian practices coexisted in Spain. There were Catholic bishops but also Arian bishops, and both held councils and nominated priests and deacons. There was an Arian liturgy as well as the Catholic liturgy, and the former diverged at many points: the Arian offices were celebrated at night, the liturgical language was Gothic, and even baptism was performed according to a different rite, by triple immersion. Catholic and Arian priests even differed in the way they wore their hair: the former cut the hair on their heads very short, but sported long beards; the latter let their head hair grow long and flowing, but shaved their faces closely.

The kings, of course, protected the Arian Church. Their attitude to the Catholic clergy fluctuated. Whilst it was, in general, fairly tolerant, there were occasional phases of disguised persecution, in particular for reasons of foreign policy. To the north, the Pyrenean frontier was threatened by the Franks, who were Catholics. To the east, a whole area of the Spanish Levant had been occupied since the reign of Justinian by the Byzantines, who were also anti-Arian. In these circumstances, the Spanish Catholics were easily suspected of colluding with the enemy. This was often brought home to them, by individual acts of harassment (when Queen Clothilde, a daughter of Clovis and a Catholic, attended mass, her husband, King Amalric, got the onlookers to throw 'dung and various other muck' in her face), or by legislation, sometimes quite rigorous (Alaric II and some of his successors took steps to limit the judicial privileges of the Catholic clergy).

Above all, both sides aimed to provoke defections from the opposing camp. Some Catholics were re-baptised according to the Arian rite, especially in the north-west of the peninsula. On the other hand, some well-known Goths embraced Catholicism: John of Biclar, for example, distinguished representative of the Gothic nobility; and Masona, made Catholic bishop of Mérida; and, most of all, Hermenegild, son of King Leovigild. It was his conversion which precipitated a crisis. Allied to the Byzantines, Hermenegild roused Andalusia to revolt in 579–80 and proclaimed himself king in opposition to his father. Defeated and captured, he was assassinated in obscure circumstances in 585, his death making him a martyr in Catholic eyes.

From this point, the story was soon concluded. Leovigild tried to come to terms with his Catholic subjects, and attempted to establish a unity of faith on the basis of an expurgated Arianism. There were concessions in the practice of conversion: a simple declaration of intent was all that was needed to be admitted to the Arian cult, instead of a new baptism as before. Above all, there were concessions with regard to dogma: the equality of the Father and the Son was admitted, with only the Holy Spirit relegated to inferior rank. These advances to Catholicism were not without effect; certain chroniclers were uneasy that there might be a new wave of adhesions to Arianism. But, most importantly, they had the effect of causing confusion in Arian consciousness; the differences between the two faiths were increasingly less understood. It was King Reccared who took the vital step; second son and successor to Leovigild, he rallied to Catholicism on the urging of Archbishop Leander of Seville. His conversion (586 or early 587) brought in its wake that of all the Gothic magnates and the whole Arian episcopate. The Third Council of Toledo (589) proclaimed unity of religion throughout the kingdom. From that day on, Spain was to know no other faith than Roman Catholicism.

THE CATHOLIC VISIGOTHIC KINGS

From 587 to 711 a new conception of the relation between Church and state, pregnant with consequence, was born. The two institutions grew ever closer, tending even to become identified, to the point where some historians have been able to talk of a theocratic regime.

The Church was strictly subordinate to the sovereign. The latter was held to derive his power from God. He was accountable only to Him for the salvation of his people, and, in consequence, responsible for the conduct of the clergy. He regarded himself – and was regarded by the clergy – as invested with a divine right to intervene in ecclesiastical affairs. When he acceded to the throne, the bishops acclaimed him with the name of apostle: 'He merits the name of apostle who fulfils the office.' From 672 (accession of Wamba), he was sacred, the first of the western monarchs to receive unction. In the logic of this latent Cesaro-Papism, relations with Rome became both distant and discordant. The Spanish Church isolated itself, defined a liturgy of its own (which survived the Mozarabic period) and affirmed its particularism. The archbishop of Toledo, directly subject to the king, tended to substitute his authority for that of the Pope, to become in the peninsula, in a sense, the homologue of the Patriarch of Constantinople in the Eastern Empire. To talk of schism would be to exaggerate, but the tendency was very definitely towards the constitution of a national church.

The most striking expression of the union of the political and the religious appeared in the holding of councils, both the provincial councils, which in principle met every year, on All Saints' Day, and, most of all, the general Councils of Toledo; from 589 (Third Council) to 702 (Eighteenth Council), they can be regarded as the most important institution of Visigothic Spain. Bringing together, in theory, all the bishops of the kingdom (punishments as severe as excommunication might be inflicted on absentees), but assembling alongside them the high lay dignitaries, they constituted veritable legislative organs, not only in ecclesiastical matters, but also in subjects affecting civil society. It was the king alone who convoked them, who presided at the opening ceremony, who fixed the order of the day (in the *Tomus regius*, a written programme distributed at the beginning of the sessions), and, finally, it was he who, in giving the force of law to the conciliar canons, implemented the decisions of the bishops.

The civil power thus acquired the habit of depending on the Church. The latter appeared as the guarantor of the loyalty of its subjects. It was the priests who, within each parish, were responsible for collecting the oaths of obedience which all free men ought to make to the king as their legitimate and natural leader. It was the bishops who, when necessary, pronounced excommunication against those who dared to rebel against the monarch or who, more mundanely, broke the laws, including the civil laws. It was the Councils of Toledo which endowed with their moral authority the power of the sovereign, a legitimation often welcome when accession to the throne was the consequence of usurpation, even assassination.

On the other hand, the king was invested with the mission to defend the faith, to secure it against all attack from whatever source, to prohibit, even, any debate on that subject. The civil power had a duty to destroy heresy and heretics, apostasy and apostates, to punish severely the sacrilegious, even simple blasphemers. As did King Ervig:

If anyone blasphemes the name of Christ, son of God, or refuses to receive his holy body or his holy blood, or rejects it after taking it, or utters some blasphemy or insult with regard to the Holy Trinity, let this blasphemer be shamefully scalped and receive one hundred lashes and be thrown into irons and, finally, condemned to perpetual exile. Let his possessions be handed over to the king who will give them to whoever he pleases.

Thus a theocratic conception of Spanish society was asserted in the Visigothic period, of a unified body joined in a single faith, subject to a single law and tolerating no deviance.

Spain united and Spain torn apart

'HOLY AND HAPPY SPAIN'

Of all the lands which lie between the West and India, you are the most beautiful, O holy and happy Spain, mother of nations, you who illumine not only the Ocean but the Orient. You are the honour and ornament of the world, the most illustrious region of the earth, where flourishes the creative glory of the Gothic people.

This love-song addressed to the land of Spain is the work of Isidore of Seville, and dates from the beginning of the seventh century. The sentiment he expressed was something new at this period; two centuries earlier, another writer, Orosius, though also born on Spanish soil, wrote, 'I am Roman and only Roman and I rejoice at the birth which gave me this Roman fatherland.' The appearance of the very concept of Spain was the work of the Goths: 'It can justifiably be said', wrote R. d'Abadal, 'that in creating their *regnum Gothorum*, the Visigoths created *Hispania*.'

This creation was in the first place the result of territorial unification. The disparate Roman provinces were succeeded by a single kingdom with its capital at Toledo. The whole of the peninsula was gradually subjected to one single authority; the Suevian kingdom of Galicia and Lusitania was conquered, then annexed in 585; the Byzantine domination of the coastal regions of the south-west – imposed in 550 by the troops of the Emperor Justinian, and extending at one point from Denia to the Algarve – was bit by bit reduced, then destroyed. From the reign of Suinthila (621-30), the Gothic kings could legitimately proclaim themselves kings of the whole peninsula, 'from sea to sea'.

The standardisation of the law completed the unification of the country. Nothing is more impressive, and nothing left a more lasting mark, than the work of the Visigothic monarchy in the field of law. At the beginning, there were diverse customs, varying from region to region and from ethnic group to ethnic group, disparate codes for the use of the Hispano-Romans (Breviary of Alaric) or the Goths (Code of Euric), and procedures of Roman, Germanic or native inspiration. By the end, there was one single code, applicable throughout the land and to all its peoples. The development of this code was the fruit of a legislative activity without parallel in the Europe of the time: 324 laws were promulgated by Leovigild (or collected by him from his predecessors), 99 by Chindaswinth, and 87 by Recceswinth, who also gathered them all together in a *Liber judicorum*, which seems to have been completed in 654. This book, a synthesised and ordered collection of all the existing legislation, was also added to by Kings Ervig and Egica. In its definitive form, it was destined to constitute, under various names (*Fuero juzgo* in Castile, *Llibre dels jutges* in Catalonia), the basis for all judicial practice in Christian Spain for many centuries to come. The origins of this law have been, indeed still are, much debated; it drew its inspiration, in point of fact, both from Roman legislation (the Theodosian Code) and from very ancient native customs, with some intermingling of Germanic elements. The main point to note is the veneration in which it was held, in the Spain of the Reconquest and long after.

Lastly, a new culture was born, in the Visigothic period, apparent as early as the sixth century. The ancient municipal schools and masters of rhetoric were succeeded by ecclesiastical schools and the teaching of bishops. The Second Council of Toledo called on the latter to receive pupils in every cathedral church and train them by the use of Latin authors, the Bible and the Fathers. A few writers' names already emerge, such as those of four brothers, all bishops: Justinian of Valencia (author of a *Sermon on St Vincent*), Justus of Urgell (who wrote a *Commentary on the Song of Songs*), Nebridius of Egara and Elpidius. In Lusitania, Martin of Braga, not content with combatting rural paganism, produced moralising works, adapting the precepts of Seneca to the new Christian context (*Formulas for an Honest Life, Treatise on Anger, Book of Morals* and *Treatise on Poverty*).

But it was Seville which, at the end of the sixth and in the seventh centuries, became the principal cultural centre. This was to a large extent under the impetus of Archbishop Leander, who organised teaching of a high quality. Leander had travelled widely; to Rome, where he met Pope Gregory the Great (it was at Leander's instigation, it seems, that Gregory wrote his famous *Moralia in Iob*), to Constantinople, to which he was sent by King Leovigild on a diplomatic mission, and where the Patriarch John the Faster dedicated one of his works to him. The school of Seville was therefore open to the external world; Greek was read there, and sometimes Hebrew. Its library was one of the richest in the West.

It was this favourable milieu which produced Isidore, younger brother of Leander, and, in his turn, archbishop of Seville. With Isidore, who was archbishop for forty years from 599, Hispano-Roman culture attained its apogee. 'Glory of Spain and Pillar of the Church', according to his disciple, Braulio of Saragossa, Isidore produced an encyclopaedic, *œuvre*, chief amongst which was his gigantic work (in twenty volumes) of *Etymologies*, a veritable summation of all the knowledge of his time. From cosmology to gardening, from jurisprudence to cooking, Isidore tried to encompass everything which was done, said, written or simply existed in the world. From God to minerals, by way of the angels, men, animals and vegetables, nothing escaped him. He was interested in history, to which he devoted two fundamental works: a *History of the Goths* and a *History of the Vandals and Sueves*; also in theology (his *Sententiae* and, in a more polemical spirit, his *Catholic Faith against the Jews*), and in biblical exegesis (*Commentary on the Book of Numbers, Forty Questions on the Old and New Testaments*), and, lastly, in canon law (*On the Ecclesiastical Offices*). This was an immense endeavour, which impresses even more when one remembers that Europe was then still in the middle of a cultural depression. It was a corpus which would be endlessly re-copied and expounded, and which would constitute for the whole West one of the fundamental sources of the new Christian learning.

Was Isidore's Spain, then, holy and happy? We must be aware of the limits of this culture, as of the limits of the unity allegedly achieved between all the Spanish. The later renown of Isidore's culture should not deceive us. In the seventh century, it still affec-ted only a very narrow learned elite – a few bishops and their entourage, at the most a few high dignitaries of the royal court. It was never intended to be revealed to the masses. The books were treasures which were jealously guarded; access to them was reserved for rare initiates. As for the unity of the kingdom, it was above all that of a ruling caste, turned in on itself out of fear. Its basis was fragile, even illusory. The Visigothic political structure rested on an iniquitous social system, on the savage dictatorship of a tiny minority of privileged persons. The insubordination of the subjugated classes, long contained but always latent, emerged into the light of day at the end of the period. It started with the revolt of those very slaves the legitimacy of whose condition Isidore had tried to prove by fierce argumentation.

THE CRISIS OF THE SLAVE SYSTEM

The maintenance of the slave system supposed, as a first condition, that the slave remained a de-humanised being. From the moment when the slave was integrated, in however small a way, into society, his chains began to sunder. The Greeks and Romans understood this, and recruited their slaves from distant lands and totally alien languages and customs, and kept their servile herds in conditions of strict segregation.

In Visigothic Spain, the barrier between free and non-free became increasingly fragile. This was the result, in the first place, of the methods of recruitment. Slaves from abroad became rare;

most people reduced to slavery were from the native population: captives seized on raids into neighbouring provinces or poor wretches reduced to selling themselves or condemned to slavery for having been unable to make pecuniary recompense for an injury. These new slaves were in no way cut off, except by juridical expedients, from the society which surrounded them. But a similar development was affecting the mass of slaves by birth. The latter, descendants of the servile populations of the Late Empire, were, generation by generation, completely assimilated into the milieu in which they lived – the same language, the same customs, the same labours. It became increasingly absurd to regard them only, according to the definition of Aristotle, as tools with human voices, or to see them only, as bidden by Gothic law, as animals. The masters themselves were well aware, from their frequenting of servile concubines, that, on this point, anatomy defied the law. And baptising slaves, lastly, served to make one fact blindingly obvious: creatures who received a sacrament were men and women like the rest.

In these circumstances, the consensus necessary for the maintenance of slaves in a sub-human condition gradually broke down. The slave system could only be maintained by force, even by terror. The law played its part, as we have seen, attempting, by stipulating cruel punishments, to prevent any coming together of free and slave, and making persistent efforts to forbid what was in its eyes the aberration of mixed marriages. The great landowners did not lag behind, and redoubled their harsh treatment to extract obedience. According to one official document, 'They thrashed the multitude of slaves who worked their fields.' Further, the practice of chaining, not in evidence since the heyday of the Roman Empire, reappeared in the seventh century:

Every free man who has liberated from his chains or other bonds a slave belonging to another will pay, for the folly of his act, ten sous to the slave's master; if he cannot pay, he will receive one hundred lashes; if it is a slave who commits such a deed, one hundred lashes.

This increase in repression achieved, as is often the case, the exact opposite of what was intended. It incited slaves to flee. And circumstances, in the seventh century, favoured escapes. The successive plagues which, since 570, had desolated the peninsula, had thinned out the ranks of a labour force which was already small.

The fugitive slave who succeeded in reaching a region sufficiently distant not to be recognised, could, once there, easily hire himself out as a free worker. The legislators were appalled, but could achieve little against market forces:

If a runaway slave says he is free, if he is not recognised and if he is hired for a wage in the house of a free man, the latter cannot be charged because he did not know it was a matter of a runaway slave; but if the slave is recognised and taken back by his master, it is the latter who should receive the promised wage.

In fact, fugitive slaves received help from various sources. In the first place, from their fellow-slaves; it is clear that active solidarity was manifested within the servile herds (the law punished with two hundred lashes any slave who gave a fugitive information about the best route to take). But they also received assistance from many free peasants; how otherwise can we explain the fact that a suspicious unknown person could be received into the midst of a community, settle down there and even marry?

It often happens that slaves flee from their masters, say they are free and marry free women. In such cases, we ordain by this law that the children born of such mating should be slaves like their father. And the master who finds his slave can reclaim both the father and the children and the slave's property. The same as regards female slaves who flee and marry free men.

The problem of fugitive slaves was at the forefront of the preoccupations of the slave-owning class throughout the seventh century; repressive laws accumulated without having any great effect. Rewards for informers, harsh punishments for those who aided and abetted – nothing could stop a movement which, to judge by the Lombard laws, was equally serious in Italy at the same period.

In 702, appalled by what he called the 'growing vice' of escapes, and remarking that 'there was now no city, no suburb, no small town, no village where runaway slaves were not concealed', King Egica decided to take decisive action. Recognising the ineffectiveness of the repressive measures taken so far, he decreed a sort of general mobilisation of Spanish society. He promulgated a truly extraordinary law which speaks volumes about the depth of the crisis; all the inhabitants of any place where a suspicious individual, that is a stranger who was poorly clothed, arrived, were enjoined to seize him, and interrogate and torture him until he confessed his servitude and the name of his master; if the inhabitants failed to do this, they were collectively regarded as accomplices and were all – men and women, whatever their status – to receive two hundred lashes. The local royal agents were responsible for inflicting this punishment on the villagers; if they were reluctant to do this, they were themselves to receive three hundred lashes of the whip, on the orders of the bishops and royal judges; and, finally, if the latter, 'out of interest or fear', covered up for their subordinates, they were themselves to be punished severely: thirty days on barley bread and water.

This was a panic measure. On the one hand, the crisis of the slave system was so deep, and escapes of slaves so numerous, that even those responsible for public order ceased to act against them, unless compelled by force; on the other, the ruling class, in a last effort to preserve its domination, tried to organise the whole population of free Spain into a sort of gigantic social police. This happened only nine years before the arrival of the Muslims from Africa; it is clear that Spanish society was already tottering.

HUNTING DOWN THE JEWS

The same panic and, in consequence, the same savagery, can be seen in the anti-Semitic legislation of the last Visigothic kings. Ever since the conversion of Reccared to Catholicism, the Jewish communities had been subjected to increasingly open persecution. Their 'execrable perfidy' and their 'detestable customs' were denounced ever more vehemently. The monarchy ordered ever more discriminatory measures against them. It also tried to sow discord amongst them: a law of Recceswinth incited Jews to stone alive any among them who violated the laws of the kingdom, and then share out his possessions. It was an attempt to range good Jews against bad Jews, a manoeuvre destined to fail pitiably.

Anti-Semitism had become, by the end of the seventh century, an obsession within the entourage of the Visigothic kings and the archbishops of Toledo. The attack on the Jews was systematically pursued through the councils, and repressive laws, ever more brutal, multiplied; there were at least forty between 681 and 694. What was the reason for this fierce determination to be rid of the Jews? It was, primarily, because their presence on Spanish soil and their obstinate loyalty to their faith appeared as the last obstacle to the unification of the kingdom, the identification of *regnum* and *ecclesia*, and the construction on earth of that City of God which, uniting all men in one single faith, ought to prefigure the Heavenly City. The illusion that, by persuasion or force, the Jews could be converted persisted for a long time, at least a century. Disappointment to some extent explains the anger against them: if they could not be converted, they must be eliminated. But this was a far from easy task, because the activities of the Jews were indispensable to the economy of the kingdom; they alone were skilled in long-distance trade, they alone competent to manage the large estates of the aristocracy and even the Church. There were many bishops who, with efficient administration in mind, chose Jews as the stewards of ecclesiastical fortunes. This scandalised others. Integrist circles in the capital, led by Archbishop Julian of Toledo (himself of Jewish origin!), persuaded the kings to commit themselves, in defiance of all reason, to a disastrous policy of the total eradication of Judaism. The kings were all the more inclined to listen because, in the climate of political and social crisis which characterised the regime's last days, they needed scapegoats to deflect the wrath of the people.

'Come on, I say, come on! Extirpate the Jewish plague which is these days intensifying in madness!' King Ervig's appeal to the Fathers of the Twelfth Council of Toledo in 681 marked the opening of the great Jew hunt. According to the terms of the decisions made at this assembly, promulgated as laws of the kingdom, all Spanish Jews were instructed to have themselves baptised within one year, under pain of whipping (one hundred lashes), scalping, perpetual exile and the confiscation of their goods to the benefit of the king. But, curiously, the council, admitting in advance the likelihood of failure, ordained a whole range of other measures. Circumcision was prohibited; in case of violation, both the circumciser and the circumcised were to be castrated (the penis was to be cut off at the roots, the law spelled out); if a woman had her child circumcised, castration was commuted to cutting off the nose. The celebration of the Passover or any other Hebraic festival was punished by flogging, scalping and the confiscation of possessions. The same punishment applied for observing the repose of the Sabbath, respecting ritual dietary customs, and reading or simply keeping books contradicting Christian doctrine. The movement of Jews was restricted; every Jew travelling had to announce his journey to the priests of the villages through which he passed. The same applied with residence; all Jews, male or female, had to present themselves every Saturday to the local bishop, or village priest, or, if there was no priest, to some good Christian.

On the other hand, moving on to the attack against those Christians who were on friendly terms with Jews, an attempt was made to prevent all possibility of good relations between the communities. Henceforward, any Christian who gave lodgings to a Jew, or shared a meal with or accepted a present from a Jew, was liable to one hundred lashes and confiscation of his possessions. A Jew could no longer own Christian slaves: by the mere fact of confessing, they were to be freed. Further, the great landowners and the bishops and the abbots who had entrusted the management of their patrimonies to Jewish stewards were threatened with confiscation of half of the goods farmed out. In the case of the possessions of the Church, the fine would apply to the personal fortune of the guilty bishop or abbot. Finally, fearing some want of vigour on the part of the lay administration, the king entrusted control of the implementation of the anti-Jewish laws to the bishops alone. As a further precaution, each bishop was to be supervised by another bishop. The law even envisaged the circumstance of a 'perfidious Jew' corrupting the episcopate; in such a case, the king himself assumed direct responsibility for the execution of these repressive measures. Such dispositions characterise, in the words of a contemporary historian, the ideology of a totalitarian state which lacked the means for a totalitarian policy.

The Jews resisted. King Egica – the very same king who distinguished himself in the pursuit of runaway slaves – stepped up the persecution. At his instigation, the sixteenth Council of Toledo (693) tried to destroy the Jewish communities, this time by the expedient of economic ruin. The doors were closed to the Jews, all trade with Christians was prohibited, and, in addition, the acquisitions of landed property which they had been able to make, at whatever period, were declared illegal; the possessions concerned – land, houses, vineyards, olive groves – were all confiscated by the king. Even this was not enough. In 694 Egica proposed to the seventeenth Council of Toledo the final solution, which was adopted: all Spanish Jews were to be reduced to servitude and handed over to such rich and pious Christians as would swear to prevent them from practising the Jewish religion. Jewish children up to the age of seven were to be taken from their parents to be brought up in Christian families.

What was the effect of such measures? We do not know, since no document concerning their application survives. It is true that the Christian population may have been impelled into destroying the synagogues, which, if we believe the acts of the sixteenth Council, were all in ruins in 693. It does not, however, seem that official anti-Semitism found much support amongst the population as a whole. Two facts tend to suggest this; on the one hand, the difficulties encountered by the crown in getting its own agents to put its decisions into practice, proof that they did not respond to popular aspirations; on the other, the rapid return to a climate of cordial relations between Jews and Christians after the collapse of the Visigothic monarchy. But, in spite of everything, the Jews were afraid, and one can understand why they welcomed the Muslims as liberators; the chroniclers are unanimous in telling us that it was they who were first to open the gates of the towns.

A SELF-DESTRUCTIVE FRENZY

The frenzied attacks made by the ruling class, in effect the high Gothic aristocracy in particular, on the most defenceless social categories can be seen as, to some extent, distractions from the crisis with which it was itself afflicted. Throughout the seventh century, the clans who shared power fought each other in constant, bitter battles, in which the supreme prize was the acquisition of the royal title. Of thirteen kings between 612 and 711, six acceded to the throne by usurpation, four were deposed and two assassinated. Political instability appeared to be a congenital disease of the Visigothic monarchy, the *morbus gothorum*, to use the term of a contemporary Frankish chronicler.

One cause of this instability was institutional in nature; it lay in the principle of the election of the king – an old custom of the Germanic nobility, which became law by the decision of the fourth Council of Toledo in 663. The king was chosen by the assembly of bishops and magnates. The only conditions for election were that the king must belong to the 'nobility of the Gothic race', have long hair (a sign of honour: it was therefore only necessary to cut off a pretender's hair to deprive him of the throne, or that of a king to depose him) and not owe his accession to 'the seditious tumult of the rural masses' (from fear of possible peasant uprisings). The field was thus open to every sort of fratricidal strife, conspiracy and revolt; no usurper failed to arrange some assembly of bishops and magnates to give legitimacy to his conquest of the throne.

Power was thus won by the sword. This conception of royal successions accorded with the nature of the Visigothic aristocracy, which had always preserved its character of a military nobility. Each clan possessed its armed retinue of *gardingos*, warriors fanatically faithful to their leaders. These armies clashed in an indefinite and chaotic succession of tribal conflicts. The lot of the losers was not happy: when Chindaswinth prevailed in 642, he had two hundred magnates and five hundred *gardingos* from the opposing party executed; Egica resorted to summary executions throughout his reign ('he pursued the Goths with a harsh death', said one chronicle). The dominant caste, then, far from saving its fire for those it governed, tore itself to pieces.

If internal strife was exacerbated towards the end of the period, it was because the stakes were higher. The accumulation of riches attached to the royal function continued to increase. This included the gold, silver and precious stones with which the king covered his favourites and his concubines, or used in magnificent votive crowns, some of which have survived; also cash, which he bestowed on his warriors, and with which he bought alliances; but, above all, landed property: the public estate (the 'royal fisc') which was entirely at the disposal of the king, grew steadily. Constituted originally from the remains of the old imperial Roman demesne, it was constantly increased by the confiscations operated by successive sovereigns – fines inflicted by the courts, ransoms of Jews, but also booty plundered from vanquished adversaries. Leovigild set the example; the Frankish chronicler, Gregory of Tours, said of him sarcastically that 'he left not even enough to piss against a wall' to the magnates he had despoiled. His successors only extended this system, and the regime entered the infernal cycle which characterised the last days of its history: confiscations, revolt of the despoiled, new confiscations to punish the rebels, new rebellions etc. The canons of the last Councils of Toledo are cluttered with dispositions regarding these dispossessions: legitimations by the bishops of confiscations practised by the king, cession to the Church of part of the goods concerned, threats of anathema against anyone seeking to recover confiscated possessions etc. The history of the ruling class – lay and ecclesiastical – was now no more than that of a clash of egos.

The collapse of the Visigothic monarchy was inherent in these contradictions. To assure decisive support in the division of plunder, they did not shrink from provoking foreign intervention. To vanquish rivals, Athanagild called on the Byzantines, Sisenand on the Franks, and Froia on the Basques. In 711, Achila and his brothers, sons of the dethroned Wittiza, called on the Muslims of the Maghreb to crush the usurper, King Roderic. Once he had been beaten and killed, they were quite ready to renounce the throne, on condition that their new Arab masters confirmed them in possession of the 3,000 agricultural holdings belonging to the royal demesne. They got what they wanted: in the words of R. d'Abadal, 'the endowment amply compensated for the loss of the royal title, it was worth more than the title itself'.

The Visigothic era thus ended as it had begun, in blood and terror. The three centuries between 414 and 711 had without doubt been one of the darkest periods in the history of the peninsula, at least for the majority of the population: the thrashed and mutilated slaves, the small peasants humiliated and dispossessed, the Jews hunted down and flogged. Plague had raged, as had hunger. For many people at that time, existence had been little more than a harsh struggle to survive. Women had been forced to kill their new-born babies, men to sell themselves or their children.

But the battle had been won. It may seem paradoxical to talk of victory at the moment when the Visigothic monarchy collapsed before the Muslims. But it was the kings who lost, betrayed, to a large extent, by an aristocracy blinded by its own privileges. The people of Spain, on the other hand, began to see light at the end of the tunnel. The crisis of the seventh century was a serious blow to the slave system which had relegated men to the level of beasts. Rural slavery did not, of course, collapse from one blow; there was a slave revolt in Asturias as late as 770, under King Aurelius, and the last references to Christian slaves in Galicia and Catalonia are from the beginning of the eleventh century. But fewer and fewer men and women suffered this fate, and its rigours steadily diminished. Also, once the great epidemics of the late sixth and early seventh centuries were over, the demographic situation began to improve. The eighth century already gives an impression of renewed vitality. The first signs of growth, of both population and resources, are visible; this became increasingly marked and developed into the great expansion which sustained the Reconquest.

A new culture was also in the process of being born. It was a juridical culture, composed of innumerable references to Visigothic law and a literary culture, with Isidore of Seville as its crowning glory; but it was also a fundamentally Latin and Christian culture. It was, in fact, long after the fall of Rome, in the Visigothic period, that Spain was truly and profoundly Romanised. And this Romanisation went hand in hand with Christianisation.

What was the role of the Visigoths in all this? It was at one and the same time both insignificant and crucial. It was insignificant if measured by the specifically Germanic contributions to Iberian civilisation: a few words (very few) which have passed from Gothic into Spanish, rather more personal names (Roderic/Rodrigo, for example, in Castile; Hermengald/Armengol in Catalonia etc.), some juridical practices (above all in the field of matrimonial and family law) and certain forms of art (but very localised in time and space). It was crucial, on the other hand, in that the Goths performed the function of catalyst; they were the instruments of the first unification of Spain. It would, of course, be anachronistic to suggest that the Spanish nation was born in the sixth and seventh centuries, but it was at this period that the concept of Spain was forged.

This is what would be remembered by posterity. The men of the Reconquest were not mistaken when, in their Cantabrian or Pyrenean redoubts, they vowed a 'fanatical attachment' (to use the words of Sánchez Albornoz) to the memory of the Visigothic Age. It was an age of much misery and hardship, but they made it their Golden Age.

Sources and bibliography

Principal sources used:

Leges Wisigothorum, ed. K. Zeumer, (*MGH, Leges*, 1) (Leipzig, 1902)

Formulae wisigothicae, ed. K. Zeumer (*MGH, Leges*, 5, *Formulae . . .*) (Hanover, 1886)

Martin of Braga, *De correctione rusticorum*, ed. R. Jove Clols (Barcelona, 1981)
Poenitentiale Vigilanum, in F. H. W. Wasserschleben, *Die Bussordnungen der abendländischen Kirche* (Halle, 1851, reprinted Graz, 1958)
J. Vives, *Concilios visigóticos y hispanoromanos* (Barcelona, 1963)

Brief bibliography:

R. d'Abadal, 'El regne hispànic dels Gots' in *Dels Visigots als Catalans* (Barcelona, 1969)
J. Coromines, 'La toponymie hispanique préromane et la survivance du basque jusqu'au bas Moyen Age (phénomènes de bilinguisme dans les Pyrénées centrales') in *VI Intern. Kongress für Namenforschung*, vol. 1 (Munich, 1960)
J. Fontaine, *Isidore de Séville et la culture classique dans l'Espagne wisigothique* (Paris, 1959)
P. D. King, *Law and Society in the Visigothic Kingdom* (Cambridge, 1972)
E. James, ed. *Visigothic Spain: new approaches* (Oxford, 1980)
A. Linaje Conde, *Los origenes del monacato benedictino en la península iberica*, 3 vols. (León, 1973)
E. Llobregat, *La Primitiva Cristiandat valenciana, segles IV al VIII* (Valencia, 1977)
S. MacKenna, *Paganism and pagan survivals in Spain to the fall of the Visigothic Kingdom* (Washington, 1930)
R. Menéndez Pidal, ed. *Historia de España*, vol. 3, *España visigoda* (Madrid, 1963)
J. Orlandis, *Historia de España. La España visigótica* (Madrid, 1977)
E. A. Thompson, *The Goths in Spain* (Oxford, 1969)
E. N. Van Kleffens, *Hispanic Law until the End of the Middle Ages* (Edinburgh, 1968)
Visigodos (Los), Historia y civilización (Actes de la Semanza Intern. de estudios visigóticos, 1985) (University of Murcia, 1986)
H. Wolframm, *History of the Goths* (Berkeley, Calif., 1988)

3. *From the Rhône to Galicia: origins and modalities of the feudal order**

I would like to begin by referring to the proceedings of the conference with a similar theme held in Toulouse in 1968,[1] and by attempting to assess what progress has since been made. Important additions to our knowledge of the social structures of the French Midi and northern Spain from the tenth to the twelfth centuries were made at the 1968 conference, but the discussion also revealed differences, often quite sharp, between historians from north and south of the Pyrenees.[2] These differences mainly concerned the degree of feudalisation of the regions concerned. Have they since diminished? It appears not; they seem rather to have increased. The dominant trends in the recent historiography of feudalism on either side of the Pyrenees appear diametrically opposed.

With regard to southern France, and especially Languedoc, the general tendency now is to emphasise the specificity – or, if one prefers, the atypical nature – of these regions central to the feudal world. This, at any rate, is the impression given by the thesis of Mme Magnou-Nortier, whose conclusion describes the county of Toulouse as 'a great medieval state . . . knowing, till the twelfth century and certainly up to the Capetian conquest . . . neither vassalage nor feudalism'.[3] This is also what is suggested, though with certain qualifications, by Thomas Bisson in an important paper published in 1977, in which he sought the foundations of the politico-social order in eleventh- and twelfth-century southern

---

* First published in *Structures féodales et féodalisme dans l'Occident Méditerranéan* (*X–XIIIe siècles*) Actes du colloque de Rome, 1978 (Rome, 1980), pp. 17–44.
[1] *Les structures sociales de l'Aquitaine, du Languedoc et de l'Espagne au premier âge féodal* (*Toulouse, 28–31 mars 1968*) (Paris, CNRS, 1969).
[2] See, in particular, the debate between the late Robert Boutruche and Hilda Grassotti, *ibid.*, pp. 105ff.
[3] E. Magnou-Nortier, *La société laïque et l'Eglise dans la province ecclésiastique de Narbonne* (*zone cis-pyrénéenne*) *de la fin du VIIIe à la fin du XIe siècle* (Toulouse, 1974), p. 651.

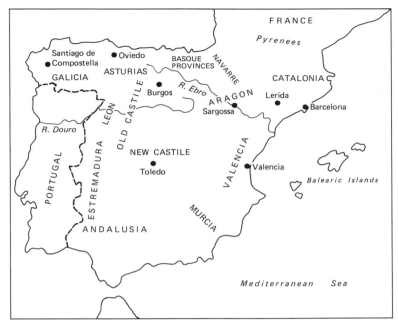

2. Early medieval Spain

France in the institutions of peace, rather than the feudal–vassalic structures.[4] The extreme statement of this position is to be found in a theoretical article by Elizabeth Brown which invites us simply to expunge words such as *féodalité* and feudalism from the vocabulary of medieval history.[5]

In Spain, ideas have evolved in the opposite direction. It is in relatively old works that one has to look for categorical assertions of Iberian specificity in the feudal period. They can be found, for example, in the work of Cl. Sánchez Albornoz, who, though he detected a degree of proto-feudalisation in Visigothic Spain,[6]

---

[4] T. N. Bisson, 'The organized peace in southern France and Catalonia, ca. 1140–ca. 1233', *American Historical Review*, 82 (April 1977), 290–331, esp. p. 291.

[5] E. A. R. Brown, 'The tyranny of a construct: feudalism and historians of medieval Europe', *American Historical Review*, 79 (October, 1974), 1063–88.

[6] Cl. Sánchez Albornoz, *En torno a los orígenes del feudalismo*, vol. 1, *Fideles y gardingos en la monarquía visigoda* (Mendoza, 1942); *idem, El 'stipendium' hispano-godo y los orígenes del beneficio prefeudal* (Buenos Aires, 1947); *idem*, 'El ejército visigodo: su protofeudalización, *Cuadernos de Historia de España*, 43–4 (1968).

insisted that this trend was stopped sharp by the Arab conquest and the imperatives of the Reconquest; in these conditions, he argued, the societies of north-west Spain were organised on a basis which was largely alien to feudalism.[7] Recent works, in contrast, beginning with the fine synthesis on the medieval history of the peninsula produced in 1973 by García de Cortazar,[8] continue to emphasise the strict parallelism existing between the evolution of Hispano-Christian and other European societies.[9] Such an approach inevitably leads to emphasising those feudal features which were found in the Iberian world. At its most extreme, in the most recent work on this question, by A. Barbero and M. Vigil, Spain appears as totally feudalised.[10]

In short, the numerous studies which have appeared in the last ten years tend to oppose a southern France that was little or not at all feudalised, to a strongly feudalised northern Spain. It is clear that such a contrast is both paradoxical and exaggerated. It can only be explained, it seems to me, by disagreements with regard to, on the one hand, the vocabulary employed and, on the other, the chronology of the process of feudalisation. It is a question of vocabulary because historians opposing each other in this way are in some cases discussing a very narrowly defined feudalism and in others the general problem of feudal society. It is a matter of chronology because they are often not speaking about the same period. But chronological questions are essential to a proper understanding of the genesis of the feudal system. None of the societies considered here remained unchanged from the tenth to the twelfth centuries; I would even argue – since we must examine the problem as closely as possible – that their structures differed

---

[7] Cl. Sánchez Albornoz, 'Conséquences de la Reconquête et du Repeuplement sur les institutions féodo-vassaliques de Léon et de Castille' in *Les structures sociales de l'Aquitaine, du Languedoc et de l'Espagne*, pp. 18–28. In particular, p. 19: 'The war against the Saracens could not provide conditions favourable to the strengthening or even the continuation of the feudalising process which had begun in the seventh century.' This idea is also developed in the same author's magisterial *España, un enigma histórico*, 2 vols. (1967).

[8] J. A. García de Cortazar, 'La época medieval' in *Historia de España Alfaguara*, 2 (1973).

[9] See, for example, *ibid.* p. 222: 'debe subrayarse de una vez por todas el parelelismo que, con las inevitables diferencias propias de un mundo de unidades escasamente articuladas, mantiene en todos sus aspectos el proceso histórico de la Península con el del resto de la Cristiandad latina'.

[10] A. Barbero and M. Vigil, *La formación del feudalismo en la Península ibérica* (Barcelona, 1978).

perceptibly depending on whether one considers the beginning or the end of the eleventh century. Accordingly, I will attempt to analyse, period by period, the often radical transformations experienced by the societies of the whole Hispano-Occitanian world between the years 1000 and about 1150. I will begin by looking at the best-known case, that of Catalonia – best known because illumined by a very abundant documentation, and perhaps also the most interesting because it was a region situated at the junction of the Hispanic and Occitanian spheres. I will then try to establish to what extent the lessons drawn from the Catalan example can, or cannot, be applied to either the Languedocian or the other Hispano-Christian societies.

I

Study of the fifteen thousand or so documents surviving from tenth- and eleventh-century Catalonia makes it possible to distinguish three quite distinct phases in the genesis of the feudal order.[11]

The first phase lasted till about 1020-30. The documents for this period, particularly rich for the years around 1000, show a society still fundamentally unaffected by feudal practices and vassalage. They make it possible to refute the old idea, already attacked by R. d'Abadal, according to which Catalan feudalism was only an imported feudalism, introduced by the Carolingian conquest.

The way power was organised reflected the permanence of very old traditions. Its basis remained the application of a written law, of essentially Roman inspiration, the *lex Visigothorum* still frequently cited in charters and, in many of its prescriptions, still literally observed. Similarly, the political ideal remained that formulated by Isidore of Seville, which made the prince the *rector*, that is the guarantor of legality. From this juridical base, the authority of the counts, and in particular of the counts of Barcelona, was further strengthened by the need for solidarity dictated by the Arab threat, which drew the population together

---

[11] These sources are discussed in my thesis, *La Catalogne*, to which I refer once and for all what follows. For the period before 950, see the magisterial works of Ramón d'Abadal, in particular *Catalunya carolingia*, 3 vols. (in 5 parts) (Barcelona, 1926–86) and *Els primers comtes catalans* (Barcelona, 1958). More recently, J. M. Salrach, *El procés de formació nacional de Catalunya (segles VIII–IX)*, 2 vols. (Barcelona, 1978).

round its traditional leaders. The agents of the counts – viscounts and vicars – remained, absolutely unambiguously, public officers (the texts call them *personae publicae*), even though they were recruited hereditarily from the same families. Their remuneration consisted of an endowment of public property and revenues; called the *fevum*, this was originally part of the fiscal demesne (*fevum sive fiscum*, say the documents) assigned to public officers as payment for their service. Certain aspects of the management of this *fevum* remained, however, subject to the control of the comital courts. The private fief did not exist.

The same phenomenon of continuity can be observed in the social structures. Catalan society in the ninth and tenth centuries was still a slave society. The old rural slavery bequeathed by Antiquity was not finally extinguished till the first third of the eleventh ✦ century. The free, here as elsewhere, were divided by the gulf separating the noble and the non-noble. The latter were for the most part independent peasants, usually possessing their own allods and often of free status. The nobles, for their part, possessed, by right of birth, the monopoly of command, but only exercised it under the superior authority of the count. They owed the count fidelity, not by virtue of homage or an oath of vassalage, but simply by reason of the obligation of every subject to obey his natural leader. Private clienteles existed, it is true, but they were little structured, included only a very limited number of dependants, and were seldom found except around very high dignitaries, principally the counts.

This socio-political equilibrium was broken during the crisis which marked the period 1020-60 and which constituted the second and central phase in the genesis of the Catalan feudal system. This is not the place to describe once again the origins of this crisis; let us, for the sake of simplicity, say that it appears as a consequence of growth (or, put another way, of the increase of productive forces): growth of agricultural production, associated with land clearance, which here, as, for example, in Latium,[12] began very early, by the beginning of the ninth century; and growth of trade, stimulated from 980/90 by the massive introduction of Muslim currency. The phenomenon of enrichment, clearly

---

[12] P. Toubert, *Les structures du Latium médiéval*, 2 vols. (Paris, 1973), vol. 1, pp. 339ff.

visible from the early years of the eleventh century, had the effect of provoking acquisitiveness and setting one aristocratic lineage against another. Hence the first manifestation of the crisis took the form of an outbreak of private wars within the nobility. But these wars were accompanied by social wars which opposed the aristocracy generally against the peasantry, over the appropriation of the fruits of growth. On the one hand, the aristocracy were imposing increasingly heavy levies on peasant production (the imposition of new usages, bad customs etc.), in short the obligations of the *seigneurie banale*; on the other hand, the peasants resisted, the most characteristic manifestation of this resistance being the movement of the Peace and Truce of God, whose popular origin is here clearly revealed. To be sure, these struggles ended in victory for the specialist fighters – the nobles – and in a general enserfment of the old free peasantry. Such was the arrival in Catalonia of what we are entitled to call feudalism (*féodalisme*). And the crisis was also felt on another level, that of political power, where it gave rise to a long and violent revolt of the nobles against comital authority, now chiefly seen by the aristocracy as an obstacle to the satisfaction of their new appetites.

The consequences of the crisis were immediate and spectacular. The shock experienced in the space of a generation was expressed in a veritable revolution which entirely remodelled the social structure. The wars had entailed the formation of a large number of armed clienteles, hence the recruitment of private warriors, called *milites*, or, more correctly, since they garrisoned the castles, *milites castri*. These *milites* were now linked to their chiefs by means of homages and oaths of vassalage: the first mention of homage in Catalonia is around 1020,[13] while the Catalan archives have preserved over a hundred examples of oaths of vassalage from the second third of the eleventh century alone.[14] These *milites* were also now remunerated for their armed service by the grant of authentic fiefs, called *caballarias* for simple knights and *castlanias* for the leaders of the castle garrisons (*castlans*). Finally, it is clear that the whole ancient public judicial system had been swept aside; relations between lineages were now based on the practice of private pacts, concluded at will: these were the *con-*

---

[13] *LFM*, 1, no. 157 (between 1018 and 1023).
[14] Ninety-one in the comital archives of Barcelona alone for between 1041 and 1076 (Bonnassie, *La Catalogne*, vol. 2, p. 706).

venientiae which, with homage and the oath of fealty, now constituted the basis of social relations.

The third phase, beginning around 1060, was characterised by a process of crystallisation. The new structures, spontaneously generated in the fever of violence, were consolidated and institutionalised. The agents of this normalisation were essentially the counts of Barcelona, whose wealth (in gold and men) enabled them to weather the storm relatively unharmed and overcome the noble insurrection. The counts established themselves at the head of the networks of loyalty which had been formed and acquired the means to retain their control. They did this in a number of ways; amongst the most original and systematically employed were 'solid' homage and the money-fief. 'Solid' homage (analogous to the Angevin and Norman liege homage and appearing at the same period) linked to the count personally a growing number of *milites* (usually of modest birth) and placed them entirely at his disposal. These *milites* were often remunerated with a money-fief, consisting of an annual cash rent, and thus capable of being immediately confiscated if the vassal was unfaithful. At a higher level of society, the great aristocratic lineages were induced to make their submission to the count by means of *convenientiae*, the principal clause of which consisted of the transformation of fortresses previously held as allods into fiefs held of the count. There was a multiplication of these 'taken back' fiefs (*fiefs de reprise*), which may be assimilated to 'free fiefs' inasmuch as the count often imposed no other duty on his new feudatories than the surrender of their castles on request. Nevertheless, the whole of the Catalan aristocracy was by this means integrated into a system of feudo-vassalic relations completely dominated by the count of Barcelona. The compensatory feature of these submissions was the acknowledgement in favour of this same aristocracy of rights and powers over the old free peasantry and the onerous impositions laid on them in the form of *questias, toltas* and various services. Thus, by 1100, Catalonia has the appearance of a fully feudal society.

II

Let us now adopt a wider perspective and consider the group of countries relatively close in language and habits of life which extended from the Rhône to Galicia, and ask to what extent, by what means and according to what chronology the process described for Catalonia can be applied to them. Up to about 1000, it is the similarities that prevail. The phenomenon of continuity, of the survival of very ancient structures, visible in Catalonia is to be found in all these countries. The most obvious sign was their common attachment to Romano-Visigothic juridical traditions; from the Rhône to Galicia, the *lex Visigothorum* still retained all its prestige and vigour in the tenth century.[15] There were some exceptions, it is true. North of the Pyrenees, the Toulousain, which had never, in practice, been part of the kingdom of Toledo, was exposed to strong Frankish influence; in 933, for example, Count Raymond III of Toulouse quoted Salic law in judicial proceedings.[16] Similarly, on the eastern fringe of Septimania, around Nîmes, it seems that oral procedures, associated with certain ritual practices of Frankish origin, were more important than strict respect for the written law.[17] South of the Pyrenees, the chief exception was the Basque-Navarrese region, for which there is, in fact, little evidence, but which appears to have remained faithful to an oral tradition, inherited from the remote Basque past, and pointing to a highly original form of law.[18] The influence of this Basque-Navarrese custom may also have affected the neighbouring county of Castile, where there was a substantial Basque population; here, under the impulse of Count Fernán Gonzalez, the Romano-Visigothic tradition and even any reference at all to written law were fiercely rejected in favour of arbitration procedures (*albedríos*).[19]

But with practically only these exceptions, the sway of Gothic law – now known as the *Liber Iudicum* – was universal. In Septi-

---

[15] In addition to the general histories of Spanish law, see E. N. Van Kleffens, Hispanic *Law until the End of the Middle Ages* (Edinburgh, 1968) and W. Kienast, 'La pervivencia del derecho godo en el Sur de Francia y Cataluña', *Boletín de la Real Academia de Buenas Letras de Barcelona* 35 (1973–4), 265–95. There are also numerous references in various regional studies.

[16] *Gallia Christiana . . .*, 16 vols. (Paris, 1715–1865), vol. 6, 423, no. 14; *HGL*, 5, 160, no. 57; Kienast, 'La pervivencia del derecho godo', pp. 266, 276 note 33.

[17] Case in 876 (with reference to a throw of *festuca*) analysed by Magnou-Nortier, *La société laïque et l'Eglise*, pp. 273–4.

[18] For Basque law, see the excellent study by J. Poumarède, *Les successions dans le Sud-Ouest de la France au Moyen Age* (Toulouse, 1972), especially pp. 296ff., 328–34.

[19] Van Kleffens, *Hispanic Law*, pp. 131–5. Fernán Gonzales had all the copies of the *Liber Iudicum* he could find in his county burned in the cathedral of Burgos.

mania, from Elne to Maguelonne, an unbroken succession of
references from the beginning of the ninth to the end of the tenth
centuries shows that its prescriptions were consistently applied in
both public trials and private acts, and especially in last wills.[20]
One can only agree with Walter Kienast when he says that Gothic
law represented a barrier cutting Septimania off from the Frankish
world.[21] The kingdom of Asturias and León, for its part, demonstrated, in the words of Claudio Sánchez Albornoz, an almost
fanatical attachment to memories of the kingdom of Toledo and
made determined efforts to restore its institutions.[22] Even the most
westerly lands – Galicia and Portugal – bore the same imprint, as is
shown by the research into Portuguese society from the tenth to
the twelfth centuries now being carried out by Robert Durand. In
sum, it seems clear that the respect accorded to a law whose
precepts were chiefly based on the two Roman concepts of public
sovereignty and private property was incompatible with the
development of feudal attitudes, which by their very nature
represented a negation of such concepts.

An examination of the way power was organised supports this
impression. Everywhere the lawful authorities retained their
power in the tenth century. In Languedoc, this was the case with
the counts of Carcassonne, of Melgueil and, above all, the counts
of Toulouse-Rouergue, whom Madame Magnou-Nortier could
describe as 'quasi-kings'.[23] As their wills reveal,[24] the resources at
their disposal were considerable, whether in the form of their
patrimonial possessions or the fiscal demesnes and revenues, full
possession of which they had often been able to acquire from the
Carolingian kings.[25] Their delegations of power were still within
the context of the law, and their representatives – viscounts and
vicars – were seen by them much more as public officers than as

---

[20] Magnou-Nortier, *La société laïque et l'Eglise*, pp. 263–73; Kienast, 'La
   pervivencia del derecho godo', pp. 267–9, 274, notes 21–3.
[21] *Ibid.*, p. 269.
[22] Cl. Sánchez Albornoz, *Origenes de la nación española: estudios críticos sobre el
   reino de Asturias*, 3 vols. (Orviedo, 1972–5), especially vol. 2, pp. 623–40.
[23] Magnou-Nortier, *La société laïque et l'Eglise*, p. 521. See also pp. 232–42.
[24] Wills of Raymond I of Rouergue in 961 (*HGL*, 5, no. 111) and of the Countess
   Garsinde in 972 (*ibid.*, no. 126).
[25] Precepts of Charles the Bald for Oliba II of Carcassonne in 870 and 877. See on
   this subject, A. R. Lewis, *The Development of Southern French and Catalan
   Society, 718–1050* (Austin, 1965), p. 162 and Bonnassie, *La Catalogne*, vol. 1, p.
   212 and note 32.

private servants. In two documents of 961 and 965, for example, making dispositions with regard to Nîmes, the count of Toulouse was careful to describe his viscount in that town by the expression *'ipsa potestas de Nemauso publica'*.[26] As for the monarchy of Oviedo, then of León, its power, assured and strengthened by the necessities of the resistance to Islam, extended to every aspect of the life of the country – army, justice, administration, ecclesiastical life.[27] The king of Asturias-León nominated, replaced and dismissed at will the *comites* or *potestates* (this word was still used to indicate the representatives of authority!) who governed the various territorial circumscriptions (*commissa, comitatos*) in his name.[28] In Galicia he continued to levy a tax of Roman origin,[29] and in León he promulgated decrees which, for example in 1017 and 1020, could appear as legislative texts.[30] In these circumstances, it is impossible to discern any trace of that characteristic phenomenon of feudal epochs, the collapse of power. On the contrary, the *iussio regis* – like the *iussio comitis* in Catalonia – dominated from on high the lives of men.[31]

On the institutional plane, in fact, the only arguments for a feudalisation of society are to be found in vocabulary, that is in the diffusion in the tenth century of the words *vassus* and *fevum*. But we should note both that this diffusion remained very incomplete and that the meaning of these words was a long way from what it was in classical feudal language. The word *vassus*, extremely rare in Septimanian documents (where it almost only applies to

[26] *Cartulaire de l'église cathédrale N. D. de Nîmes*, ed. E. Germer-Durand (Nîmes, 1874), nos. 60, 61. Lewis, *The Development of Southern French and Catalan Society*, p. 206.

[27] Sánchez Albornoz, 'Conséquences de la Reconquête et du Repeuplement', p. 19: 'In the mortal combat against the Muslims, the monarchy organised and directed the resistance, but in return this resistance confirmed and strengthened the monarchy.'

[28] Sánchez Albornoz, '"Imperantes" y "postestates" en el reino asturleonés' in *Cuadernos de Historia de España*, 45–6 (1967), 352–73; Hilda Grassotti, *Las instituciones feudo–vasalláticas en León y Castilla*, vol. 2 (Spoleto, 1969), pp. 929ff.

[29] Cl. Sánchez Albornoz, 'El "tributum quadragesimale": supervivencias fiscales romanas en Galicia' in *Mélanges Louis Halphen* (Paris, 1951), pp. 645–58.

[30] For 1017, Sánchez Albornoz, 'Un texto desconocido del Fuero de León', *Revista de Filología Española*, 10 (1922), 317–23. For 1020, see the critical edition of the Fuero de León by Vasquez de Parga, *Anuario de Historia del Derecho Español*, 15 (1944).

[31] Grassotti, *Las instituciones feudo-vasalláticas*, vol. 2, pp. 931ff.; also her 'La ira regia en León y Castilla' in *Cuadernos de Historia de España* (1965), pp. 5–135.

dependants of notables of Frankish origin) and almost unknown in Catalonia (one single reference in the tenth century), was only in at all common use in north-west Spain, where its meaning remained very fluid. The term was only ever used of persons of modest or inferior rank, and Hilda Grassotti sees it as little more, in the tenth century, than a late equivalent of the word *bucellarius*.[32] In reality, whether in Septimania, Catalonia, Aragon or the kingdom of Asturias and León, the services owed by the nobles to the superior representatives of authority were due not as a result of some contract of vassalage but by virtue of what historians writing in Castilian call the *relación de naturaleza*, that is the 'natural' loyalty that every free man owed to his 'natural' leader.[33] Whereas the word *fevum*, used only in Septimania and Catalonia, meant even in 1020, to quote almost word for word the definition given by Mme Magnou-Nortier, 'a tenure conceded in a piece of public land by the public authority to an agent of that authority'.[34]

The grants of land made by the kings of Aragon or the kings of Asturias and León were little different in type: *honores* in Aragon, *prestámos* or *atónitos* in León and Galicia.[35] These concessions were normally intended to remunerate a public service and they continued, as has been shown by Cl. Sánchez Albornoz, the payments (*stipendia*) accorded by the kings of Toledo *pro exercenda publica expeditione*.[36] It should be added that they were always temporary in the kingdom of Asturias and León and could be revoked at will by the monarchy.[37] To sum up: from the Rhône to Galicia, the politico-juridical tradition inherited from the Visigothic kingdom (and, through it, from the Late Roman Empire) remained very much alive and none of the characteristic features

[32] Grassotti, *Las instituciones feudo-vasalláticas*, vol. 1, pp. 44–5.

[33] On this subject, see Bonnassie, *La Catalogne*, vol. 1, pp. 142–3.

[34] E. Magnou-Nortier, 'Sur le sens du mot "fevum" en Septimanie et dans la Marche d'Espagne à la fin du Xe et au début du XIe siècle', *Annales du Midi*, 76 (1964), 141–52; Bonnassie, *La Catalogne*, vol. 1, pp. 209–14.

[35] J. M. Lacarra, ' "Honores" et "tenencias" en Aragon (XIe siècle)' in *Les structures sociales de l'Aquitaine, du Languedoc et de l'Espagne*, pp. 143ff.; Grassotti, *Las instituciones feudo-vasalláticas*, vol. 2, pp. 558–60.

[36] Sánchez Albornoz, *El 'stipendium' hispano-godo y los origenes del beneficio pre-feudal*.

[37] H. Grassotti, 'La durée des concessions bénéficiaires en León et Castille: les cessions "ad tempus"' in *Les structures sociales de l'Aquitaine, du Languedoc et de l'Espagne*, pp. 79–113.

of feudalism were yet visible, except sporadically, in the institutional order.

Does this mean that, on a more general level, the basis of feudalism did not already exist? Or, in other words, is it not already possible to discern the existence of relations of production of the type which in, for example, the twelfth and thirteenth centuries, linked peasants and lords within a seigneurie? It would appear not. On the contrary, the two dominant features which appear to characterise both Languedocian and Hispano-Christian society in the ninth and tenth centuries are the survival of ancient slavery and the existence of an active independent peasantry.

In both Septimania and Catalonia the persistence of the slave mode of production on many large estates seems to be proven. The number of slaves was certainly diminishing, especially in the tenth century, as a result of manumission and flight. But the squads of slaves belonging, for example, to the counts of Toulouse, the viscounts of Béziers and Carcassonne, the monasteries or the principal representatives of the high aristocracy were far from negligible.[38] South of the Pyrenees, Visigothic Spain's enormous population of *mancipia* was also a long way from extinction. Asturias, indeed, seems to have been the only region in Europe to have known a slave revolt in the early Middle Ages.[39] And slaves were still to be found in the tenth century not only in Asturias but in León, Galicia and even Castile, despite its reputation as a land of freedom.[40] The exploitation of the great estates was based at least in part on the toil of a servile labour force which worked the demesnes. It also depended on the rents from the lands remaining in the hands of the free peasantry.[41] But the latter, often local allod-holders, generally owed only a rent in kind for the lands they worked; their lot was little different from that of the Italian *livellarii*. There was no real complementarity

---

[38] See the texts quoted by Magnou-Nortier, *La société laïque et l'Eglise*, pp. 219–23.

[39] Sánchez Albornoz, *Origenes de la nación española*, vol. 2, pp. 335ff.

[40] Ch. Verlinden, *L'esclavage dans l'Europe médiévale*, vol. 1, *Péninsule ibérique, France* (Bruges, 1955), pp. 136–9. For example, Sánchez Albornoz, *Una ciudad de España cristiana hace mil años; estampas de la vide en León* (Madrid–Mexico, 5th edn, 1966), pp. 124–5 and note 71. For Castile, J. A. García de Cortazar, *El dominio del monasterio de San Millán de la Cogolla (siglos X–XIII)* (Salamanca, 1969), pp. 106–7 (the forty *casatos* quoted in this passage seem to be *servi casati*).

[41] Sánchez Albornoz, 'Contratos de arrendamiento en el reino asturleonés' in *Cuadernos de Historia de España*, 10 (1948), 142–79.

between demesne and rented holdings, that is, no 'manorial system' in the classic sense.

Moreover, there existed true peasant landownership. Lack of evidence makes it difficult to detect in Septimania (though one suspects it was there), but it is clearly visible south of the Pyrenees. There, as Barbero and Vigil have recently shown,[42] it sometimes took the form of collective ownership; this must have been the case in particular in some very archaic regions of Basque or Cantabrian settlement. But almost always, in Asturias, León and Catalonia alike, it was a question of individual ownership, and there can be no doubt that the existence of these small peasant proprietors constitutes the major fact of the agrarian history of this period.[43] Certainly, these peasant allods were under threat, the prey, frequently, through purchase or judicial confiscation, of the great landowners (both lay and ecclesiastical) who integrated them into their large estates.[44] But – and this crucial fact must be emphasised – they were constantly reconstituted through assarting (the conquest of the waste in Septimania and of the frontier 'no man's land' in Spain),[45] and by means of the Catalan *aprisiones*, the *excalios* of Aragon and the *pressuras* of Castile. It was this stubborn resistance of peasant landownership which, at least up to the beginning of the eleventh century, prevented the establishment of a true seigneurial regime, hence of feudalism. This resistance was also found at the level of social organisation, in the birth and proliferation, particularly in the frontier regions, of autonomous communities of free villagers: the famous *concejos*, so well described by Maria del Carmen Carlé,[46] which constituted both the bulwark of Christianity against Islam and the strongest prop of the monarchy of Asturias and León in the face of aristocratic ambition.[47]

---

[42] Barbero and Vigil, *La formación del feudalismo*, pp. 354–80 (but considerable caution is needed with regard to the sections devoted to the *Hispani*).

[43] Sánchez Albornoz, 'Pequeños propietarios libres en el reino asturleonés' in *Settimane*, 13 (1965). For Catalonia, Bonnassie, *La Catalogne*, vol. 1, pp. 219ff.

[44] Examples of concentration of landownership in Barbero and Vigil, *La formación del feudalismo*, pp. 362–80. For Catalonia, Bonnassie, *La Catalogne*, vol. 1, pp. 236–42.

[45] For Septimania, Magnou-Nortier, *La société laïque et l'Eglise*, pp. 200–2; for Spain, numerous studies, amongst the best of which is Sánchez Albornoz, *Despoblación y repoblación del valle del Duero* (Buenos Aires, 1968).

[46] M. del C. Carlé, *Del concejo medieval castellano-leonés* (Buenos Aires, 1968).

[47] Sánchez Albornoz, 'Conséquences de la Reconquête et du Repeuplement',

Up to the beginning of the eleventh century, then, from the Rhône to Galicia, a number of factors successfully prevented the establishment of a regime of fiefs. Some were the result of the inertia of societies strongly attached to the past (an attachment to juridical precepts bequeathed by ancestors, and the survival of the slave tradition), others were newer (the vitality of the allod-holding peasantry in the frontier zones). All combined to maintain the existing order, under the watchful supervision of the *potestas publica*, whether this took the form of counts, as in Septimania, Catalonia, Aragon and Castile, or of kings, as in Navarre and León.

In these circumstances, it is difficult to imagine that the transition to a new politico-social order, the feudal order, could be achieved without serious tensions. How and when were these tensions, visible in Catalonia in the second third of the eleventh century, manifested in Languedoc and in north-west Spain? Before attempting to answer this question, the point should be made that economic conditions everywhere favoured the eruption of the crisis; while politico-social structures remained almost unchanged, the economy underwent a profound transformation under the double impact of the expansion of the cultivated area and the growth of trade. Little is known about assarting in Languedoc, for lack of evidence, though it can be detected, nevertheless, in the tenth century;[48] in the Iberian peninsula, it happened on a large scale in the ninth and tenth centuries with, in particular, the colonisation of the Duero basin (70,000 square kilometres repopulated and brought into cultivation between 850 and 910),[49] as well as Rioja[50] and the foothills of the Pyrenees:[51] it is reasonable to assume a very large increase in agricultural production. But the expansion took many forms, the development of

---

pp. 26–7: 'It was because the kings disposed of the military and fiscal power of the *concejos* . . . that they had at their disposal forces of warriors of non-vassalic type'; and: 'This mass of large and small *concejos* . . . contributed to counteracting, and not only with their militias, the feudalisation of the country.'

[48] Magnou-Nortier, *La société laïque et l'Eglise*, pp. 200–2.

[49] Sánchez Albornoz, *Despoblación y repoblación*. The estimate of area is from García de Cortazar, 'La época medieval', p. 135.

[50] See in particular García de Cortazar, *El dominio del monasterio de San Millán de la Cogolla*, pp. 97ff.

[51] For Catalonia, Bonnassie, *La Catalogne*, vol. 1, pp. 106ff. For Ribagorza and Aragon, examples in Barbero and Vigil, *La formación del feudalismo*, pp. 362–74.

regional and local trade (in salt, in particular),[52] for example, or of long-distance trade.[53] And from the beginning of the eleventh century, Muslim gold began to penetrate north-west Spain and Catalonia in massive quantities, in the form of wage payments from 1009 at least, in the form of *parias* from 1060 at the latest.[54] Some of this gold crossed the Pyrenees and circulated in southern France.[55] One would expect this enrichment, here as in Catalonia, to lead to covetousness, and consequently conflicts, and produce upheavals in the socio-political system.

In Languedoc, this was first apparent in the functioning of the judicial institutions. From the beginning of the eleventh century, the courts were no longer orderly and justice became a veritable free-for-all. This decay is demonstrated by an affair which clearly aroused strong feelings, since it led to three successive law-suits, of which two separate accounts have survived: the affair of the *villi* and salt-pans of Pallas, in the diocese of Agde.[56] It was a dispute in which considerable interests were at stake (it concerned, in fact, a substantial part of the salt marshes of the Etang de Thau) and which opposed, at various stages, members of the comital families of Toulouse-Rouergue and Carcassonne and the monastery of Conques. What does this trial, held around 1013, reveal? Firstly, professional judges have disappeared; the dispute was submitted

---

[52] See the substantial study by Reyna Pastor de Togneri, 'La sal en Castilla y León: un problema de la alimentación y del trabajo y una política fiscal (siglos X al XIII)' in *Cuadernos de Historia de España*, 37, 38 (1963).

[53] Trade with Muslim Spain, in particular. For imported goods, Bonnassie, *La Catalogne*, vol. 1, pp. 417ff.; Sánchez Albornoz, *Una ciudad de España cristiana*, passim.

[54] The year 1009 was the year of the great expedition of the count of Castile, Sancho García, to Cordova (first example of a Christian army paid by a Muslim prince). It was towards 1060 that the payment of tributes (*parias*) by the Taifa kings to Ferdinand I of Castile began. On *parias*, H. Grassotti, 'Para la historia del botín y de las parias en León y Castilla' in *Cuadernos de Historia de España* (1964), and J. M. Lacarra, 'Aspectos económicos de la sumisión de los reinos de taifas' in *Homenaje a J. Vicens Vives*, 1 (1965). For Catalonia, Bonnassie, *La Catalogne*, vol. 2, pp. 665–72.

[55] P. Bonnassie, 'La monnaie et les échanges en Auvergne et Rouergue aux Xe et XIe siècles, d'après les sources hagiographiques', *Annales du Midi*, 90 (1978), pp. 275–88.

[56] Record of a lawsuit held at Béziers in 1013 in *HGL*, 5, no. 171, cols. 358–61. Reference to a court held at Conques and account of another trial convoked on the site of the dispute in *Liber miraculorum sancte Fidis, ed.* A. Bouillet, II, 12 (Paris, 1897). Magnou-Nortier's discussion (*La société laïque et l'Eglise*, pp. 277–8) is based only on the text in the *HGL*.

to arbitrators chosen by the parties and recruited from the local nobility. Secondly, the law was no longer invoked, but a solution sought in a negotiated compromise, that is in the material compensation of the unsuccessful party by the winners. Thirdly, the debates took place against a background of total confusion and were constantly interrupted by violent incidents; each party, in fact, appeared at the trial accompanied by a strong armed escort and faced a disorderly public. The negotiated settlement was itself challenged and some of the participants called for a judicial duel. Finally, the monks from Conques, in theory the victors, had to make a precipitate flight in the face of threats uttered against them, and even then only a miracle by St Foy enabled them to escape retaliation at the hands of the knights despatched in pursuit.

This degradation of the public judicial system very quickly developed into a series of private wars, conflicts tending to be settled at the point of a sword rather than before the courts. The importance of these private wars was emphasised as early as 1880 by Auguste Molinier, in a study of Languedocian feudalism remarkable for the period.[57] They are relatively well known to us through a double series of sources: on the one hand, the *convenientiae* – that is the negotiated treaties which ended them – preserved in southern archives,[58] on the other, narrative texts and particularly the accounts in a work of hagiography of the highest interest: the Book of Miracles of Sainte-Foy of Conques, compiled partly between 1013 and 1020, and partly towards the middle of the eleventh century.[59]

This *Liber miraculorum*, many episodes in which concern Languedoc,[60] provides a very full picture of all the various types of violence practised at that period,[61] and thus makes it possible to establish a veritable typology of exactions by nobles in the eleventh century. Let us look briefly at its dominant features.

---

[57] A. Molinier, *Etude sur l'administration féodale dans le Languedoc (900–1250)* in *HGL*, 7 (1899), 132–213. For the private wars, see pp. 142–4.

[58] Most of those which survive are published in *HGL*, 5.

[59] *Liber miraculorum sancte Fidis*. The first part is the work of a master of the cathedral school, Bernard of Angers, the second of an anonymous monk.

[60] Stories concerning Languedoc (still called 'Gothie': II, 4): I, 3, 12, 19; II, 2, 10; III, 18, 20, 21; IV, 22; App. III, 1.

[61] See in particular: I, 1, 23; II, 7; III, 4, 5, 10, 13, 14, 15, 17; IV, 4, 5, 8, 9, 10, 16, 17; App. I, 2, 4; App. II, 3; App. IV, 2, 4, 6.

Wars might result from inter-family hatred, each aggression leading to vengeance, each vengeance to a new vengeance; the mechanism of these vendettas is well known. More often, however, the causes were material; what motivated the armed expeditions was the quest for booty, whence their character as razzias in the form of attacks on villages, pilgrims and processions of relics, innumerable thefts of livestock, especially horses, and – perhaps most of all – taking hostages for ransom. The bases from which the raids were made were always the castles which the viscounts and vicars, former public officers, had converted into family allods: the wars raged, then, from castellany to castellany, or, less often, from province to province.[62] They might result in sieges (of fortresses), but more often took the form of ambushes or murderous raids into the countryside. The agents of this violence were always called *milites*, or, as in Catalonia, *milites castri*, because they consisted of the permanent garrisons of the fortresses; they operated in groups and their bands might number as many as several dozen, even – but here the texts surely exaggerate – several hundred, mounted men.

It is hardly necessary to describe in detail the nature of the violence, even the atrocities, perpetrated (arson, murders, mutilations etc.). It is more important to note that to noble violence there sometimes responded – as in Catalonia – a peasant counter-violence which might go so far as the assassination of particularly odious castellans.[63] There thus developed class conflicts which represent the bloody imprint on the social fabric of the advent of feudalism.

It remains to establish the chronology of this crisis in eleventh-century Languedoc, but it has to be admitted that on this point research has made little progress. Archibald R. Lewis tried to give an approximate chronology, based on the growth of the number of castles, a clear sign of a 'militarisation' of society. According to him, the number grew very rapidly between 975 and 1050: counting for this latter date thirty-one fortresses in western, and forty-three in eastern, Languedoc, he reasonably concluded that the castle had become, by the middle of the eleventh century, 'the

---

[62] We should note, however, the wars between the men of Rouergue and Quercy (IV, 17), and Albi and Quercy (App. I, 4).
[63] For a particularly significant story: IV, 3.

predominant factor in the social life of Southern France'.[64] Nevertheless, it appears that Lewis's figures are very incomplete; in an article which appeared in 1976,[65] Frederick Cheyette was able to list over forty fortresses and more than seventy fortified villages (which raises, in passing, the problem of *incastellamento* in Languedoc) for the region between Carcassonne and Béziers alone; and his figures based both on texts and aerial photography have been further increased since the publication of his work. It remains almost impossible at present to assign even a very approximate date to the construction of these fortresses.

Archaeology may at some stage come to our aid, but meanwhile we have to make do with what the written documents say in an attempt to trace the chronology of the violence. Like Auguste Molinier, I tend to see two key stages in the development of these private wars: the first round about 1035 (the period which saw serious troubles erupt in Razès and the Albigeois),[66] the second later in the century, from 1082 and the assassination of Ramon Berenguer II, during the struggles over the succession to the counties of Carcassonne and Razès.[67] These two key periods, however, have to be seen against the background of a very long phase of social instability, beginning, according to A. R. Lewis, as early as the last quarter of the tenth century, and prolonged, with the rivalry between the houses of Toulouse and Barcelona for southern supremacy,[68] into the twelfth century. In sum, then, Languedoc may have been feudalised in rather different conditions from those experienced by Catalonia: not in a short, sharp shock, but after a long and difficult gestation lasting many decades.

[64] A. R. Lewis, 'La féodalité dans le Toulousain et la France méridionale (850–1050)', *Annales du Midi*, 76 (1964), 247–59.
[65] F. Cheyette, 'The castles of the Trencavel: a preliminary aerial survey' in *Order and Innovation in the Middle Ages. Essays in Honor of Joseph R. Strayer*, ed. W. C. Jordan *et al.* (Princeton, 1976), pp. 255–72 (in particular the map on pp. 264–5).
[66] Molinier, *Etude sur l'administration féodale dans le Languedoc*, pp. 142–3. For the Razès, *HGL*, 5, col. 402, no. 199. For the Albigeois, *ibid.*, col. 411, no. 203.
[67] A later account in *ibid.*, cols. 31–4, no. 6. See also R. d'Abadal, 'A propos de la domination de la maison de Barcelone sur le Midi de la France', *Annales du Midi*, 76 (1964).
[68] Ch. Higouet, 'Un grand chapitre de l'histoire du XIIe siècle: la rivalité des maisons de Toulouse et de Barcelone pour la prépondérance méridionale' in *Mélanges Louis Halphen* (Paris, 1951), pp. 313–22. See also Abadal, 'A propos de la domination de la maison de Barcelone'.

In north-west Spain, the advent of a feudo-vassalic society followed a still different route. Here, there was no brutal rupture during the eleventh century. There were, of course, changes. They are visible above all at the level of basic social relations, that is in the relations between the aristocracy and the peasantry. In the first place, here as everywhere, the old rural slavery had disappeared. But this disappearance had as its corollary – and this is crucial – the entry into dependence of a large part of the old free peasantry. In fact, north-west Spain experienced during the eleventh century the establishment of what Spanish historians call jurisdictional lordship, manifestly closely related to the French or Catalan *seigneurie banale*: 'from the beginning of the eleventh century', writes García de Cortazar, 'the lords began to venture all sorts of exactions, and subjected their men, by virtue of a jurisdictional right (analogous to the French *ban*) which carried with it the right to command, compel and punish, and which appeared in forms as vague and widespread as disturbing'.[69] From this 'Castilo-Leonese ban' derived all sorts of new rents and services imposed on the peasantry: *facenderas, castellarias, anubdas, nuncios, mañerías, ossas, montazgos, herbazgos, infurciones*, etc.,[70] which were regarded by the peasantry as so many 'bad usages' but which, by dint of the new revenues they brought to the ruling class, were to constitute the economic base for the establishment of feudalism.

It was, in fact, in the organisation of power that radical modifications were still not visible. Until the reign of Alfonso VI, the monarchy continued to dominate from on high all the country's socio-political structures. Nothing shows this better – to use the example quoted by Hilda Grassotti[71] – than the treatment by Alfonso VI of the Cid: the king presumed to punish the Cid at will – almost at whim –, to exile, pardon and exile him anew, and the *Poema de mío Cid* shows us Rodrigo accepting the sovereign's decisions with a quite astonishing humility, prostrating himself on the ground in tears, attempting to kiss the monarch's feet, even eating the grass of the field where the scene was enacted.[72]

This attitude on the part of the nobility of Castile and León is in

[69] García de Cortazar, 'La época medieval', p. 228.
[70] *Ibid.*, pp. 228–30.
[71] Grassotti, *Las instituciones feudo-vasalláticas*, vol. 2, pp. 942–9.
[72] *Poema de mío Cid*, ed. Ramón Menéndez Pidal, 10th edn (Madrid, 1963), pp. 214–15, verses 2010–29.

marked contrast with that of the Catalan aristocracy, in revolt from the 1040s. The difference is easily explained by the political circumstances; while the counts of Barcelona deliberately adopted a policy of peace towards Islam, thus denying their nobility the pleasures and profits of external warfare (which could only provoke their discontent and heighten internal conflicts), the monarchy of Castile-León had, since Ferdinand I, embarked on the great age of raiding, and the bellicose sorties into Muslim territory acted as so many outlets for the aggression and the growing appetites of their nobility. The king, in any case, by means of the huge profits he drew from the *parias*, could encourage the loyalty of the barons by making them lavish payments and increasing his liberality towards them. This euphoria, which made possible the maintenance of the *status quo* between aristocracy and monarchy, and thus the long survival of the old order, came to a sudden end with the reverses experienced in the face of the Almoravid offensive. The defeat of Uclés (1108), followed by the death of Alfonso VI (1109), was traumatic. The crisis, long contained, exploded into conflagration.

No purpose would be served by giving here a detailed account of this crisis as it has been so well studied elsewhere.[73] But we should note that it was foretold by precursory signs, for example, the revolt in 1087 of the Galician magnate, Rodrigo Avaquiz, possibly supported by the bishop of Compostela.[74] But it was mainly between 1109 and 1126 that the worst violence raged, with a veritable paroxysm between 1110 and 1117. At this point, the rising pitted all social groups in chaotic conflict. At the top, the pretenders to the throne tore each other to pieces: Queen Urraca against her husband Alfonso the Battler, each of them separately against, first, Enrique of Portugal, then his widow, Teresa, and all of them, naturally, against the designated heir, the infant Alfonso, son of Urraca. But these dynastic struggles barely obscured a generalised confrontation of the aristocratic lineages, each opposing party in practice representing only a more or less coherent coalition of high noble families. Even more radically, the crisis was

---

[73] In particular by Reyna Pastor de Togneri, *Conflictos sociales y estancamiento económico en la España medieval* (Barcelona, 1973), pp. 15–101. See also, Grassotti, *Las instituciones feudo-vasalláticas*, vol. 2, pp. 952–5.

[74] Reyna Pastor de Togneri, *Conflictos sociales*, p. 43 and note 37. See also Victoria Armesto, *Galicia feudal*, vol. 1 (Vigo, 1969), p. 160.

expressed in a global assault by the aristocracy on the institution of
monarchy, which it hoped to bend to its will; highly significant in
this regard was the guardianship arrogated to himself by the Galician magnate Pedro Froilaz over the child-king Alfonso, as were
the insults and brutality inflicted on Queen Urraca before the very
portal of the church of Compostela. The picture is completed by
an uninterrupted sequence of urban revolts (Lugo, Sahagún, Car-
rión, Burgos, Santiago and Palencia) and, last but by no means
least, by the great revolt of the peasantry of the Sahagún region in
1111.

In sum, for a period of at least fifteen years, north-west Spain
experienced a total power vacuum; it is therefore hardly surprising
that new solidarities were forged at this time. They were
manifested in the *germanitates* (alliances of lineages) recorded in
the *Historia compostelana* and whose members themselves
declared that they were uniting to fight against their enemies.[75]
But these alliances were also based on the rendering of homages
and oaths of fealty. We should note here that the two oldest
unequivocal references to feudal homage that we possess for the
kingdom of Asturias and León date from the year 1109, just when
the troubles began.[76] In the following years, these references
multiply, to the point where Hilda Grassotti could speak of a
'crescendo of homages'.[77] And these entries into vassalage are all
the more significant in that they often concerned all the members
of a *germanitas*, united in placing themselves in the service of a
leader who, in return, granted them payments and *prestimonios*.[78]
Thus, as in Catalonia and Languedoc, though at a much later date,
it was against the background of clashing arms and the rending of
the social fabric that feudo-vassalic structures were born.

We come, finally, to the third phase, that of the reconstitution of
authority. It is clear that this could only happen on the basis of

---

[75] *Historia compostelana*, in *ES*, vol. 20, pp. 97–8. See Grassotti, *Las instituciones feudo-vasalláticas*, 1, pp. 164, 174, 225 and note 292.

[76] Shortly before his death (30 June 1109), Alfonso VI, foreseeing the disputes which his succession would provoke, convoked the nobles of Galicia and León and made them render *hominium et juramentum* to his grandson, the future Alfonso VII (*ES*, vol. 20, p. 209; Grassotti, *Las instituciones feudo-vasalláticas*, vol. 1, p. 202). Shortly after the death of Alfonso VI, Diego Gelmírez, Bishop of Santiago, received the homage of the members of a *germanitas* of Galician magnates (*ES*, vol. 20, pp. 97–8; Grassotti, *Las instituciones feudo-vasalláticas*, vol. 1, p. 225).

[77] *Ibid.*, vol. 1, p. 174.   [78] *Ibid.*, vol. 1, p. 225 and note 292.

elements which emerged during the time of troubles. We need first therefore to examine what these were. They were three in number: the vassalic engagement, the fief and, crucial to the whole, the feudo-vassalic pact, the *convenientia*.

Vassalic engagement: throughout the length of the crisis, the most striking phenomenon was the formation of armed clienteles, grouped around a leader and composed of *milites* who owed him fealty and military service. In Languedoc, these bands, which we can now describe as vassalic bands, emerged with the onset of violence. This was made plain, for example, during the lawsuit in 1013 already mentioned, by the composition of the escorts with which each party was accompanied: that of the abbot of Conques was described as *nobilis beneficiatorum militum caterva* and that of Countess Garsinde as *valida vassorum manus*.[79] It would not be difficult to trace the growth in number of these vassals during the course of the century. In north-west Spain, the phenomenon was very similar. It was during the civil wars which followed the death of Alfonso VI that there was a transition from simple 'natural' loyalty to vassalic fidelity.[80]

The fief: the transition from the public *fevum* to the private fief seems to have taken place in Languedoc in the same conditions and at the same time as in Catalonia, that is in the decades 1030-60 (or 1040-80?); this, at least, is what I assume Mme Gramain is saying when she describes the wave of infeudations visible in lay aristocratic circles at this period.[81] North-west Spain, for its part, though not adopting the hereditary fief, closely associated the award of payments and *prestimonios* and the rendering of homage.

The *convenientia*: its history in Languedoc and Catalonia is now fairly well known.[82] It is clear that the term was at first applied to many different types of agreement, but that when, in the period 1020-60, it began to be used to define the respective obligations of lord and vassal, it also became the keystone of the feudo-vassalic

---

[79] *Liber miraculorum sancte Fidis,* I, 12. For this case, see above, pp. 118–19.

[80] Till the reign of Alfonso VI, in fact, the use of the word *vassus* (very common in the sources) did not imply an engagement of the vassalic type; the word remained, in fact, very vague. Grassotti, *Las instituciones feudo-vasalláticas,* vol. 1, p. 166: 'se importó el nombre *vassus* pero no la institución del vasallaje'.

[81] Monique Gramain, '"Castrum", structures féodales et peuplement en Biterrois an XIe siècle', *Structures féodales,* pp. 124–8.

[82] P. Ourliac, 'La convenientia' in *Etudes . . . offertes à P. Petot* (Paris, 1959); Chapter 6 below; also Bonnassie, *La Catalogne,* vol. 2, pp. 736–9.

system. What has hitherto not been realised is that such pacts were also known in the kingdom of Asturias and León, first with the name *placitum*, then *placitum et convenientia*. The oldest of these agreements known to us date from the years 1109, 1114, 1115, 1120 and 1121.[83] They are thus clearly an institutional product of the disturbances which here marked the advent of feudalism.

Vassalage, fief and *convenientia* were the three instruments at the disposal of princes and kings desirous of re-establishing their power. We must now consider how they were employed.

In north-west Spain, the restoration of authority was achieved during the reign of Alfonso VII, between 1126 and 1157. This reign was decisive for the history of feudalism in Castile though it is unfortunately as yet little studied. What is known, however, is that the young king had extreme difficulty in pacifying his domain; not only had he to reconquer the castles sword in hand, but he was on occasion forced to engage in hand-to-hand combat with some of his barons. The foundations on which he chose to base the restoration of his authority were precisely those we have discussed above.

Vassalage: it was by imposing a collective homage on the rebellious barons of Galicia in 1126 that he could receive their submission yet leave to them the royal honours which they held.[84]

The fief: whilst it is true that the word was not yet in current use under Alfonso VII, the two words *prestimonium* and *feudum*, as is shown by the acts of the Council of Burgos in 1117, were already regarded as synonymous (*feudum quod in Ispaniam prestimonium vocant*).[85] It seems that Alfonso VII was the first Castilo-Leonese monarch to link the grant of a *prestimonium* closely to the rendering of homage and vassalic services.[86] But the most characteristic

---

[83] Grassotti, *Las instituciones feudo-vasalláticas*, vol. 1, pp. 220–9. Hilda Grassotti does not seem to have accorded these pacts, which she calls *pleitos-homenajes*, as much importance as they deserve; she sees them only as a 'strange and unusual application of trans-Pyrenean *hominium*', and even calls them 'bastard forms of homage'. On the contrary, they constitute the very essence of the feudo-vassalic contract.

[84] *ES*, vol. 20, p. 443; Grassotti, *Las instituciones feudo-vasalláticas*, vol. 1, p. 203.

[85] F. Fita, 'El Concilio nacional de Burgos', *Boletín de la Real Academia de Historia* 48 (1957), 297; Grassotti, *Las instituciones feudo-vasalláticas*, 2, p. 759 and note 106.

[86] This feudalisation of the kingdom under Alfonso VII was clearly perceived by A. Ubieto Arteta, 'Navarra-Aragón y la idea imperial de Alfonso VII de Castilla', *Estudios de Edad Media de la Corona de Aragón*, 6 (1956), 41–82 (especially 76ff.).

type of remuneration of his reign was certainly the money-fief and, in this respect, the similarity with the practice of the counts of Barcelona is very striking. Not only did the use of this method of payment permit Alfonso to reward the services of many of his Castilian and Leonese vassals, but he attracted to Spain a mass of *milites* from the French Midi who became royal vassals: 'From the whole of Gascony and all the land stretching as far as the river Rhône', said the *Chronica Adefonsi imperatoris*, 'came many barons, and amongst them Guillem de Montpellier; they accepted silver and gold as well as valuable and diverse payments from the king, and they submitted to him and obeyed him in everything.'[87]

Lastly, the *convenientia*: it was during the reign of Alfonso VII that this practice was at its height in the kingdom of León and Asturias, and it was through it that the monarch extended his empire to other regions of the peninsula; in 1135 to Navarre, whose king, García Ramirez, declared himself his man, and in 1137 to Portugal, where the prince Afonso Enríquez promised him fealty and services. The texts recording these agreements are explicitly given the name of *convenientiae*.[88]

The study of the reconstitution of authority in Languedoc[89] is more difficult. The almost total loss of the archives of the counts of Toulouse seriously obscures the process by which feudal structures were systematised; one can only suppose that it was under the close control of the dynastic Raymonds. We have to make do with the documents – *convenientiae* and oaths of fealty, luckily quite numerous – concerning the territories under other lordships. First amongst these figure those of the great rivals of the dynasty of Toulouse, the counts of Barcelona, who were also, at different times, counts of Carcassonne and Razès, counts of Provence and viscounts of Millau and Carlat.[90] For Provence, J.-P. Poly has

---

[87] *Chronica Adefonsi imperatoris*, ed. Z. Sánchez Belda (Madrid, 1950), 68, p. 54; Grassotti, *Las instituciones feudo-vasalláticas*, vol. 2, p. 760, note 110.

[88] H. Grassotti, 'Homenaje de García Ramirez a Alfonso VII: dos documentos inéditos', *Cuadernos de Historia de España* (1963), pp. 319–29; *idem, Las instituciones feudo-vasalláticas*, vol. 1, pp. 234–7 and notes 301, 305.

[89] I will not deal here with south-west Aquitaine, which has, in any case, been studied by Ch. Higouet; the region beyond the Garonne seems not to have experienced a similar reconstitution of authority, which instead remained disseminated between many castellans.

[90] For the policy of the counts of Barcelona in the French Midi, Abadal, 'A propos de la domination de la maison de Barcelone sur le Midi de la France' and Bonnassie, *La Catalogne*, vol. 2, pp. 859–64.

shown how, after Ramon Berenguer III, the house of Barcelona
worked to extend to its benefit the use of homage and fealty and to
construct a veritable feudal hierarchy analogous to that known in
the Catalan counties.[91] The same is true of Carcassonne and Razès, at an even earlier
period. During the years 1067-9 alone, the period of the acquisi-
tion of the two counties, at least forty-four oaths of fealty – in
reality, certainly many more – were demanded by Ramon
Berenguer I from the castellans of the region;[92] which meant, of
course, that as many castles were taken back as fiefs of the count of
Barcelona by his new vassals. This assumption of control of
fortresses by the system of the *fief de reprise*, typical of Barcelona,
also happened in the Carladès in the twelfth century. It meant, as
we have seen, leaving to the feudatory the free disposition of his
castle, imposing on him only the obligation to return it on request
to his lord. This was the sole obligation, but one which was critical,
and the violation of it was regarded as a felony.[93] This, it seems,
was how the practice of 'free fiefs' spread in the Occitanian
countries; we should note, in this connection, that H. Richardot's
classic study of this institution was mainly based on documentation
concerning Carladès, geographically part of the Auvergne, but
politically attached to Barcelona.[94]

We can carry this study of the reconstitution of authority even
further if we examine the case of the lesser lordships whose
emergence in the twelfth century was nurtured by the conflict
between Barcelona and Toulouse. In addition to the one which the
lords of Les Baux attempted to build in Provence, discussed by
J.-P. Poly,[95] we should note, for Languedoc, those of Guillem de
Montpellier and of the Trencavel of Béziers-Albi-Carcassonne. In
the former case, over thirty lineages of castellans can be seen to

---

[91] J-P. Poly, *La Provence et la société féodale (859–1166)* (Paris, 1976), pp. 318ff.

[92] These oaths, often, unfortunately, in the form of abstracts, are given in the last
part of the *LFM*, 2, nos. 826–31, 834–6, 838.

[93] See above, p. 110. For the free fief in Catalonia and the obligation to surrender
fortresses, see Bonnassie, *La Catalogne*, vol. 2, pp. 765–7.

[94] H. Richardot, 'Francs-fiefs: essai sur l'exemption totale ou partielle des services
de fief', *Revue Historique de Droit Française et Etranger*, 27 (1949), 28–63, 229–
73. The documents for Carladès can be consulted in *Documents historiques
relatifs à la vicomté de Carlat*, ed. G. Saige and Cte de Dienne, 2 vols. (Monaco,
1900).

[95] Poly, *La Provence*, p. 358. See also the sections devoted to the principality of
Orange, pp. 355–7.

have become his vassals.[96] As for the Trencavel, it suffices to say that there have survived over three hundred oaths of fealty to them made between the end of the eleventh and the end of the twelfth centuries.[97]

Finally, we should not overlook the ecclesiastical lords and the networks of dependence which they were able to construct about them. The case of the bishops of Agde, studied by André Castaldo, is significant in this regard: 'in the cartularies of the bishopric and chapter', he writes, 'the acts betwen 1150 and 1200 have a profound unity as to their common aim: to strengthen or create feudo-vassalic ties to the benefit of the church of Agde, ties, that is, which were properly political and in conformity with the primary character of the grant of a fief, the lord bestowing it in return for political and military services on the part of the vassal'.[98] In practice, the acts referred to were almost all renewals of investitures, proof that the feudo-vassalic system established round Agde antedated 1150.

It remains to mention one last objection concerning the feudalisation of the Languedocian Midi. A view which is fairly widespread, and no doubt strengthened by the assertions of Robert Boutrouche,[99] holds that it was not a true feudalism: it had fealty without homage, vassalage without fief and fiefs without services. This, I think, is to rely on too literal a reading of the documents; that some oaths of fealty did not include mention of homage was only natural when homage had been done only a few moments before and the fact very firmly imprinted in the memory; that some vassals were not rewarded with fiefs was common from one end of the feudal world to the other; that the fief, finally, often took the form of the 'free fief' proves not so much weakness of the feudal order but, on the contrary, its extension by means of the transformation of allods into *fiefs de reprise*. On the other hand, examples of the opposite – of fealty with homage, of vassalage with fief, of fief with services – are so unequivocal as to carry conviction, in my view.

[96] J. Baumel, *Historie d'une seigneurie du Midi de la France: naissance de Montpellier (985–1213)* vol. 1 (Montpellier, 1969), p. 45. Source: *Liber instrumentorum memorialium: cartulaire des Guillems de Montpellier*, ed. A. Germain (Montpellier, 1884–6).   [97] Cheyette, 'The castles of the Trencavel', p. 271.
[98] A. Castaldo, *L' Eglise d'Agde (Xe–XIIIe siècle)* (Paris, 1970), p. 61.
[99] R. Boutruche, *Seigneurie et féodalité*, 2 vols. (Paris, 1968–70), vol. 2, p. 313, note 1: 'We will not dwell on the skin-deep feudalities.'

Fealty with homage: *fidelis ero . . . sicut esse debet homo suo seniori cui manibus se est commendatus.*[100] Homage implying vassalic service: *ero vobis adiutor a tenere et ad habere et ad guerreiare per directam fidem.*[101] Link between vassalage and the fief: *archiepiscopus donavit ei fevum . . . et vicecomes accepit fevum . . . et fecit ei hominium et iuravit ei fidelitatem et sacramenta.*[102] Such examples abound and many others could be found to testify to a considerable familiarity with the most diverse and the most characteristic feudo-vassalic practices: 'solid' homage,[103] the promise by vassals to respond to summonses from lords,[104] recourse to the judicial duel in legal disputes,[105] vassalic services of castle custody, garrison watch and host,[106] the institution of the *castlania*,[107] the money fief,[108] etc. All things considered, it is my view that these feudo-vassalic usages appear in Languedoc at the end of the eleventh and in the twelfth centuries in a very pure form.

In these circumstances, we may draw two conclusions. The first is that there was a sharp rupture in the history of the Hispano-Occitanian societies, a rupture which is precisely that which marks the advent of feudalism. Such a rupture in tenth-century Latium has been described by Pierre Toubert who has gone so far as to use the word 'revolution' to depict it ('the great revolution of the tenth century').[109] I believe we should accept this term, since we can see a radical change in both the material framework of people's lives and in socio-political systems. That the dates of this revolution

---

[100] *HGL*, 5, no. 363, col. 692 (1084); no. 364, col. 694 (c. 1084).
[101] *LFM*, 2, no. 831 (1067).
[102] *HGL*, 5, no. 427, col. 427 (c. 1107): *convenientia* between the viscount Bernard Aton and the archbishop of Narbonne.
[103] Guillem de Montpellier swears to the bishop of Maguelonne that he will be his *melior homo* (*HGL*, 5, no. 377, col. 719).
[104] The ritual formula: *et istum adiutorium sine tuo engan lo farei et comunir no m en devedarei par quantas vices tu m en comonras* (numerous examples).
[105] *LFM*, 2, no. 821 (1070): *convenientia* between Raymond Trencavel and Ramon Berenguer I.
[106] Numerous examples for the Carcassès in *Cartulaire et archives des communes de l'ancien diocèse . . . de Carcassonne* ed. M. Mahul, 6 vols. in 7 (Paris, 1857–82), vol. 5, especially pp. 257ff.
[107] *HGL*, 5, no. 390, col. 740 (oath of the direct feudatory followed by that of the castellan); and also Mahul, *Cartulaire et archives des communes, loc. cit.*
[108] Mahul, *Cartulaire et archives des communes*, vol. 5, p. 261 (1126).
[109] Toubert, *Les structures de Latium*, vol. 1, p. 320.

varied from one region to another does not affect the fundamental point.

The second conclusion concerns the feudal structures established after the rupture. They have, hitherto, too often been treated with disdain, by the application to them of terms such as 'incomplete', 'unfinished', 'skin-deep', 'bastard' etc. It is absolutely essential that we abandon once and for all such qualifications. The best proof of the non 'incomplete' character of these southern feudalisms is perhaps to be found in the extraordinary diffusion of the feudal vocabulary into popular language, by which I mean the language of the peasantry. It seems clear that feudal usages penetrated very deeply. In Spain, for example, we see the generalisation of the word 'vassal' to describe all sorts of dependants of diverse conditions, including the *vasallos de behetría*, or peasants subject to the seigneurial *ban*;[110] similarly, in southern France, the word 'fief' was used in the sense of rented property, and this in towns as well as in the countryside;[111] and in both Catalonia and Languedoc, lastly, we see the adaptation of homage to relations of dependence entered into at the lowest levels and even by serfs.[112] Thus, far from affecting only the nobility, feudal mentality and customs affected the whole of society. Finally, one may wonder if it is not time to reverse the assumption which, on the basis of a so-called northern model, declares southern feudalisms to be 'incomplete'; should not 'incompleteness' be sought instead between the Loire and the Rhine?

---

[110] Grassotti, *Las instituciones vasalláticas*, vol. 1, pp. 83ff.

[111] H. Richardot, 'Le fief roturier à Toulouse aux XIe–XIIe siècles', *Revue Historique de Droit Française et Etranger*, 4th series, 14 (1935), 307, 59, 495–569.

[112] As early as 1045/6, a Catalan castellan called all the inhabitants of his castellany *omines de meo ominatico* (Bonnassie, *La Catalogne*, vol. 2, p. 582). For Languedoc, P. Ourliac, 'L'hommage servile dans la région toulousaine' in *Mélanges Louis Halphen* (Paris, 1951), pp. 551–6. See also the examples quoted by Boutruche, *Seigneurie et féodalité*, vol. 2, pp. 170–2.

4. Descriptions of fortresses in the Book of Miracles of Sainte-Foy of Conques*

Saints' lives are one of those sources least exploited by historians of fortresses. They may well, however, in their own way, provide information which it is difficult to find elsewhere. Of this immense literature, the works which probably most merit our attention are the Books of Miracles.[1] Amongst their other admirable practices, saints were in the habit of delivering innocent prisoners, imprisoned, for the most part, in fortresses. Thus the story of their liberation and flight often involved the hagiographer in describing the disposition, of the site of the miracle of deliverance, that is, in describing, or at least suggesting, the location and the plan of the castle buildings, as well as enumerating the obstacles surmounted during the course of the escape. The information of a technical nature which can be garnered in this way cannot, of course, be accepted unquestioningly; hagiographical sources are, in fact, amongst the least reliable of those available to historians, and the traps they set are too well known to need emphasis here (uncertain dating of the stories, their constant rewriting, endless recourse to commonplaces drawn from models of the genre etc.). These faults are not, however, general and there exist works whose authors and dates of composition are precisely known; amongst them is the Book of Miracles of Sainte-Foy, which will be discussed here.

The *Liber miraculorum sancte Fidis*[2] consists of two quite separate sections written by different authors. The first (books I and II) is the work of Bernard of Angers, pupil of Fulbert of Chartres, and

---

* This article first appeared in *Mélanges d'archéologie et d'histoire médiévales en l'honneur du Doyen Michel de Boüard*, Mémoires et documents publiés par la Société de l'Ecole des Chartes, 27 (Geneva–Paris, 1982).
[1] There is an excellent discussion of Books of Miracles in P.-A. Sigal, 'Histoire et hagiographie: les *Miracula* aux XIe et XIIe siècles' in *L'historiographie en Occident du Ve au XVe siècle* (Actes du Congrès des Historiens Médiévistes de l'Enseignement Supérieur, Tours, 1977), special edn of *Annales de Bretagne*, 87 (1980), 237–57.
[2] Ed. A. Bouillet (Paris, 1897).

was composed in three stages at Conques: in 1012 or 1013, at some unspecified date between 1013 and 1020, and in 1020. The first journey gave rise to thirty-four accounts of miracles (which form book I), the second to six (book II, 1 to 6) and the third to nine (book II, 7 to 15). The second section is the work of an anonymous monk of Conques and everything tends to suggest that it was composed partly about 1030 (book III, twenty-four stories) and partly in the decade 1040–50 (book IV, twenty-eight stories).[3]

Overall, in all the accounts, thirty castles are mentioned, some simply referred to, others described at some length. Twenty-five of them can be identified,[4] see table 4.

Table 4. *Castles mentioned in the Book of Miracles of Sainte-Foy*

Location	Description	Reference
Aveyron:[5]		
Aubin (arr. Villefranche, cant.)	Albineum castrum	I, 5; IV, 4
Belfort (arr. Villefranche, cant. Décazeville, comm. Almon)	Castrum quod Belloforte dicitur	III, 5; IV, 16
Cassagnes (arr. Rodez, cant. Rignac)	castrum Casannas	I, 6
Castelpers (arr. Rodez, cant. Naucelle, comm. Saint-Just)	castrum Persum	I, 33
Conques (arr. Rodez, cant.)	Conchacense castrum	III, 4, 5, 17
Entraygues (arr. Rodez, cant.)	castrum vulgari opinione Inter Aquas vocatum	IV, 2
Servières (arr. Rodez, cant. Estaing, comm. Villecomtal)	Cerverium castrum	III, 15

[3] It would be impossible here to attempt to discuss in detail the problems posed by the dating of the two sections of the Book of Miracles. I will say only that all research to date supports more or less the chronology proposed here (Bouillet, *Liber miraculorum*, introd. pp. x–xxx; J. Bousquet, *La sculpture à Conques aux XIe et XIIe siècles: essai de chronologie comparée* (Lille, Service de reproduction des thèses, 1973, vol. 2, pp. 426–35; most recently, Sigal, 'Histoire et hagiographie').

[4] Five castles are not named. Three were in Rouergue: one was *vico Conchensi contiguum* (*Liber miraculorum*, I, 22), the second *non a Conchis longius quam sedecim millibus* (I, 1); no details are given for the third (III, 4). A fourth was situated in the region of Nîmes (*in partibus Nemausensium*, III, 18). The fifth, the most interesting since described in some detail, was near Montpezat-de-Quercy (IV, 8); for this, see below, note 7.

[5] For the castles of Aveyron, see R. Noël, *Dictionnaire des châteaux de l'Aveyron*, 2 vols. (Rodez, 1971); it is not, however, very informative for the period discussed here.

Table 4. (cont)

Location	Description	Reference
Cantal: Aurouze (arr. Saint-Flour, cant. Massiac, comm. Molompise)	castrum Aurosa nomine	III, 10
Broussadel (arr. and cant. Saint- Flour, comm. Saint-Georges)	castrum Brucciadul vocatum	I, 31
Carlat (arr. Aurillac, cant. Vic-sur-Cère)	castrum quod Carlatum dicitur	IV, 14
Châteauneuf (arr. Saint-Flour, cant. Chaudesaigues, comm. Sarrus)	castrum quoddam nomine Castellum novum vocitatum	III, 3
Gransoux (arr. Saint-Flour, cant. Ruynes, comm. Faverolles)	Gravissonis oppidum	III, 7
Valeilles (arr. and cant. Saint-Flour, comm. Neuvéglise)	castrum Vallilicis nomine	III, 3
Corrèze: Turenne (arr. Brive, cant. Meyssac)	castellum quod dicitur Torenna	II, 6
Dordogne: Montagrier (arr. Ribérac, cant.)	castrum Montagrerium	III, 9
Salignac (arr. Sarlat, cant.)	castrum Saliniacum	IV, 9
Haute-Garonne: Le Bousquet (arr. Toulouse, cant. Lanta, comm. Saint-Pierre-de- Lages)	municipium quod Bochittum rustici vocant	II, 2
Hérault: Loupian (arr. Montpellier, cant. Mèze)	castrum ex nomine Lupianum	III, 21
Haute-Loire: Le Monastier (arr. Le Puy, cant.)	castrum vocabulo Calmilliacum	I, 2
Lot: Castelnau-Bretenoux (arr. Figeac, cant. Bretenoux, comm. Prudhommat)	municipium quod Castellum novum nominant	I, 11
Gourdon (arr.)	castrum cui Gordonum nomen est	II, 5
Puy-de-Dôme: Miermont (arr. Riom, cant. Saint- Gervais, comm. Espinasse)	Murmontis castrum	III, 11
Roche d'Agoux (arr. Riom, cant. Pionsat)	castrum Roca Dafulgi (for: Dagulfi)	IV, 7
Tarn: Penne (arr. Albi, cant. Vaour)	castrum vocabulo Penne nuncupatum	I, 11

Location	Description	Reference
Turiès (arr. Albi, cant. and comm. Pampelonne)	Turusia castrum	III, 24
Tarn-et-Garonne: Montpezat (arr. Montauban, cant.)	castrum quod Mons Pensatus dicitur	IV, 8
Catalonia:[6] Calonge (province Barcelona, judicial district Igualada)	oppidum quod vocatur Colonicum; Colonicum castrum	IV, 6

(arr.: *arrondissement*, cant.: canton, comm.: commune)

The descriptions of these fortresses should not, obviously, be taken literally. The story-tellers, in particular Bernard of Angers, had for the most part never seen them. But, though second hand, their accounts do not entirely lack interest. On the one hand, in certain specific instances (Castelpers, Servières and, of course, Conques), the accumulation of concrete detail seems convincing evidence that the accounts of eye witnesses had been faithfully transcribed.[7] On the other hand, even (perhaps especially) when they reproduce a stereotype, the descriptions deserve attention; they give us the picture of a castle which came spontaneously to mind when, in their reflections or discussions, the men of the first half of the eleventh century thought of this type of construction.

The terminology

Five terms are employed to designate a fortified place: *castrum* (thirty-two mentions), *castellum* (eight), *municipium* (eight), *oppidum* (seven) and *phala* (one).[8]

---

[6] For Catalonia, the Book of Miracles also mentions the *castrum de Balaguer* (IV, 6: *quidam Sarracenus ex castro Balagario*). But the word *castrum* here applies to a town, and, what is more, a Muslim one.

[7] This is most marked in the case of a castle which is unfortunately not named (IV, 8). It may be Castelnau (today Castelnau-Montratier, Lot). The reference puts it close to the castle of Montpezat-de-Quercy and in the possession of a certain Gauzbert. There is an act of the *Cartulaire de l'abbaye de Conques* (ed. Desjardins, no. 347), unfortunately undated, which quotes a *Gauzbertus de Castello novo* as witness to a donation *in pago Caturcinio*; this could well be our Gauzbert. This would put the foundation of Castelnau-Montratier as early as the beginning of the ninth century. There are, however, other castles close to Montpezat, such as Flaujac, Mondemard and Montcuq. Room for speculation is all the greater in that documentation for this region is almost non-existent before 1250.

[8] The number of references is greater than the number of castles, the same castle sometimes cropping up in different stories or several times in one story.

Castrum, the classical Latin word, is by far the preferred choice of our authors, who both prided themselves on their fine language. The meaning of the word varies. It usually very concretely indicates the fortified buildings themselves (it was said of one prisoner that he was imprisoned in a *castrum*).[9] But it can also take on a wider sense to designate the whole of the territory over which the castellan exercised power.[10] On the other hand, the sense of a fortified village, prevalent in Italy at this period,[11] and destined to prevail in Languedoc from the twelfth century on,[12] does not appear: no *incastellamento* in the Occitanian countries, it would appear, before 1050. At the very most, we can observe the existence of a *suburbium castri*, but at Calonge in Catalonia.[13]

Castellum is only, in this source, the vernacular equivalent (crudely Latinised) of *castrum*, for which it could be substituted in both its meanings: either fortified construction[14] or castellany.[15] The adjective *novum* applied to *castellum* looks interesting, suggesting the possibility of early *castelnaux*. But this was not the case; the two *castella nova* cited (Castelnau-Bretenoux and Châteauneuf-près-Malet) present none of the features of the future *castelnaux* of Aquitaine.[16] They were defensive works with no distinguishing features and the adjective *novum* – already joined to the noun to form a place-name – cannot even tell us the date of their construction.

Municipium raises no specific problems in that it is clearly

---

[9] II, 5: *tentus redactusque in captionem in castro cui Gordonum nomen est.*
[10] I, 2; I, 11.
[11] P. Toubert, *Les structures du Latium médiéval* (Rome, 1973), especially vol. 1, pp. xxii–xxiii and pp. 321ff.; A. Settia, 'La struttura materiale del castello nei secoli X e XI: elementi di morfologia castellana nelle fonti scritte dell'Italia settentrionale', *Bolletino Storico-Bibliografico Subalpino*, 77 (1979), 361–430.
[12] Monique Bourin-Derruau, *Villages médiévaux en Bas-Languedoc: genèse d'une sociabilité (X^e–XIVe siècle)*, 2 vols. (Paris, 1987), in particular vol. 1, *Du château au village.*
[13] IV, 6. The Muslim town of Balaguer was also described as a *castrum*, but this was a special case (see above, note 6).
[14] II, 5; III, 21.
[15] II, 6 (Turenne): the expression *fines castelli* meant the borders of the castellany.
[16] These characteristics are described by B. Cursente, *Les castelnaux de la Gascogne médiévale* (Bordeaux, 1980); see also his '*Castra* et castelnaux dans le Midi de la France' in *Chateaux et peuplements en Europe occidentale du Xe au XVIIIe siècle*, Flaran 1 (Auch, 1979).

employed as a synonym for both *castrum*[17] and *castellum*.[18] The word is used in its first sense of fortification and is also found associated in the same account, even in the same sentence, both with the verb *munire*, and the noun *munimen*.[19] Nor does *oppidum*, contrary to what one might expect, imply any special features. There are no echoes of the Celtic *oppida*. This word, too, was used as an equivalent for *castrum* and the *oppidani* are simply the castellans.[20]

There remains *phala*, an unusual word, one of those by which an author demonstrated the quality of his Latin culture. Found in Antiquity from Plautus to Juvenal, it had the meaning 'tower of wood'; in the early Middle Ages it recurs with the same meaning, from Abbo of Saint-Germain des Prés to Guibert of Nogent.[21] Used only once in this Book of Miracles, it referred to the *castrum* of Montagrier in Périgord. Was this, therefore, a castle on a motte? It seems likely.[22] The context in which the word is used shows that it had a wider meaning than just a wooden tower. The event described (leaping over a brazier) took place *media in phala*, before a large audience.[23] It could only have happened in the *basse cour*. The *phala* mentioned by the Anonymous Monk of Conques

[17] The castle of Cassagnes is successively described by the terms *castrum* and *municipium* (I, 6). The same is true of Castelnau-Bretenoux (I, 11), Le Bousquet (II, 2) and Belfort (III, 5 and IV, 16). Also: *Albineum castrum . . . aliud municipium* (IV, 4). This meaning of the word *municipium* is not unusual: Du Cange defines it as *castrum, castellum muris cinctum*, with references to Suger and the *Vita Norberti*. On the other hand, in Orderic Vitalis, *municipatus* is given as the equivalent of *castellania*.

[18] III, 21: *castellum invasit, ubi a filio ejusdem municipii latenter telo confossus, infelicem animam expiravit.*

[19] I, 1 (*municipium/munire*); III, 4 (*municipium/munimen*).

[20] I, 33 (Castelpers); also III, 10: *castrum Auroso . . . in memorato oppido* (Aurouze) and IV, 6: *oppidum quod vocatur Colonicum . . . seniores ejusdem castri* (Calonge).

[21] Du Cange; for classical Antiquity, references to Plautus, Vitruvius and Juvenal; for the early Middle Ages, to Abbo, Orderic Vitalis, Guibert of Nogent and to the *Miracula sancte Fidis*. There is a clear definition in Guibert, *Hist. Hieros*, VII, 9: *Duo jubentur institui lignea castra quae nos sumus soliti vocare phalas.*

[22] An investigation of the site would clearly be necessary. Montagrier does not figure in the only, and very old, list of mottes for Périgord: Marquis de Fayolle, 'Observations sur les mottes féodales du Périgord', *Bulletin de la Société Historique et Archéologique du Périgord*, 38 (1911), 104–25.

[23] III, 9: the wife of Elie, lord of Montagrier had been cured of sterility by Ste-Foy; two sons were born from this miracle, whom their father regarded as invulnerable. To prove this, he made them leap over a brazier: *et ut inde experimentum*

equates pretty well with what English students of castles call a 'motte and bailey'.[24]

The sites

Montagrier, it must be said, was an exception. Most of the castles described were built on sites such that there was no need to raise the ground. Nature had done the work: *eius municipium in ementi rupe situm erat ita natura rerum undique muniverat*.[25] Highly revealing in this regard was the astonishment of Bernard of Angers at the sites of the castles of Rouergue. Dedicating his book to Fulbert of Chartres, another inhabitant of the plains, and anxious to make himself understood, he was obliged to begin by describing the countryside. Thus when he wanted to tell of an escape effected from the fortress of Castelpers:

> But before telling this . . . I must say a few words about the sites and the features of this country. It is a particularly mountainous region, which is even in places surmounted by horrible rocks from the top of which the view extends over vast distances . . . This land, then, is very different from our own: from which it follows that the buildings of the said fortress were based on an absolutely solid rock, and raised to a very great height so that they seemed to float in the sky.[26]

And, throughout the rest of his story, the author never ceased to tremble with horror at the depth of the abysses (in fact, the gorges of Céor and Giffou) dominated by the castle; the rocky platform (*durissima rupes*) on which it was built overhung a first precipice, at the bottom of which were 'lower rocks' (*inferiores scropules*) which, in their turn, surmounted a yawning chasm.[27] This

---

daret, coram astantibus et instanter prohibentibus, media in ejus phala accenso rogo, nudis cruribus ac pedibus, per medios flammarum globos transire faciebat.

[24] M. de Boüard, 'La motte' in *Les fortifications de terre en Europe occidentale du Xe au XIIe siècle* (Colloque de Caen, October, 1980), forthcoming (p. 2 of typescript paper).

[25] I, 1 (unidentified castle near Conques).   [26] I, 33.

[27] This can be compared with the description given by R. Noël (*Dictionnaire des châteaux de l'Aveyron*, vol. 1, p. 272) of the remains of the primitive castle of Castelpers: 'Long before the fifteenth century, the castle of Castelpers had been abandoned; there remained only a few traces near the place of that name. These ruins were remarkable for the retrenchments cut into the rocks (tenth and fourteenth centuries).' There is a brief description of Castelpers drawn from the Book of Miracles in P. Ourliac, 'Le pays de la Selve à la fin du XIIe siècle', *Annales du Midi*, 80 (1968), 581 (reprinted in *Etudes de Droit Médiéval*, 1 (1979), 185–6).

insistence on recording the steepness of the sites of castles, constant in Bernard of Angers, was not entirely absent in his successor, even though the latter, coming from Rouergue, was more familiar with the local relief. For him, for example, the rock on which the castle of Servières was constructed was the Caucasus:[28] no fortress, it seems, without at its base an *immane precipitium*.

The type of fortress most often described in the Book of Miracles was, in fact, simply the *roca*, a type now pretty well defined by specialists in the castles of southern Europe, where the rocky infrastructure and the constructed superstructure combine to form one single defence.[29] The first quality of such castles was to be almost inaccessible ('inaccessible to machines' specified Bernard of Angers),[30] before being rendered impregnable by the construction of a tower. It is true that the word *rocca* – very common in Italian and Catalan charters of the tenth to eleventh centuries[31] – was not commonly employed by the authors of the Book of Miracles, who preferred the more classical *rupes*, but its use was already sanctioned by place-names: *quidam miles ex castro Roca Dagulfi*.[32]

The disposition of the buildings

Was the rocky plateau on which the fortress was generally built surrounded by an enclosure, even a wall, however sketchy? Nothing makes it possible to say. It is tempting to reply in the

---

[28] III, 15: *super enim Caucasam rupem turris illa sita est.*

[29] See, in particular, Settia, 'La struttura materiale del castello', pp. 366–9: 'dopo la metà del secolo X, la voce *rauca, roca* (rupa, altura rocciosa isolata) presto passa ad indicare direttamente il manufatto sorto su di essa, com se la rocca o la pietra formassero una sola cosa colla fortezza prestabilitia dalla natura stessa del sito arduo, inaccessibile' (p. 367). For Catalonia, Bonnassie, *La Catalogne*, vol. 1, pp. 123–6

[30] I, 1: *omnimodis machinis inaccessibile.*

[31] For northern Italy, many references in Settia, 'La struttura materiale del castello, including: *roca et castrum qui apellatur Querciola; roca Petra luizoni; Landasia cum castro et roca.* For Catalonia, for example: *ipsa Rocheta que vocabulum est ad Fontaned; ipsa roka cum ipsas parietes, cum ipsos superpositos*; and this nice definition of the rock: *estmons cum silice atque constructionibus suis que ibi apparent vel appueruerint* (ref. in Bonnassie, *La Catalogne*). For Provence: *cum ipso castro que dicunt roca; ipsum castrum de la Roca* (J.-P. Poly, *La Provence et la société féodale* (Paris, 1976), pp. 154, 324). In Latium, however, as a result of the precocious *incastellamento*, the phrase *roca castri* had a slightly different meaning (Toubert, *Les structures du Latium médiéval*, vol. 1, pp. 203ff.).   [32] IV, 7 (Roche d'Agoux).

negative, since not one of the prisoners glorified by our hagiographers had to surmount such an obstacle during the course of his escape. But the argument is not conclusive, since it was always by the steepest face that, supported in their vertiginous descent by the miraculous intervention of Sainte-Foy, her protégés fled from their prison. Clearly, no special protection was either necessary or conceivable on this side. As for elsewhere, it seems that even on the least steeply inclined side, the site in itself was considered an adequate defence. Access to the castle was never easy; at Cassagnes, for example, the fortress was reached by means of steps carved in the rock: 'a tortuous and crooked staircase', says the text. We may add 'dangerous' even for the inhabitants of the castle; descending one day from his eyrie, the owner himself missed a step and broke two ribs.[33]

The buildings themselves, as a result of the shortage of suitable ground, were few in number. We should note at once the absence of chapels. Though generally considered, along with the *aula* and the *camera*, as one of the essential elements of any seigneurial residence, the *capella* is never mentioned. And the silence of the texts must be significant; had a sacred place existed within the perimeter of the fortress, our hagiographers would not have failed to make one or other of their escaped prisoners visit it in thanksgiving. This absence is not, in fact, particularly surprising, considering, on the one hand, the reputation for impiety of the local castellans and, on the other, that in contemporary Catalonia the very concept of a castle chapel had not yet emerged.[34]

The only two noteworthy buildings constructed on the rock were the *mansio* and the *turris* (or *arx*). The first appears as the normal residence of the castellans (*oppidanorum mansio*); it was situated at the least steep and least disagreeable side of the summit platform (*de parte illa que planior habitabiliorque videtur*).[35] Should we see in this the *aula* and the *camera* of the fortress? The answer

---

[33] I, 6:

   Cumque per oblicos graduum descenderet idem
   Anfractus, ira turbatus, crura vacillant,
   Labunturque pedes, cadit in latus, atque gemelle
   Intereunt coste.

[34] The authors of the *Glossarium mediae latinitatis Cataloniae* note the infrequent use of the word *capella* up to the end of the eleventh century; and the few references recorded did not concern castle chapels (*Glossarium*, p. 375, note 2).

[35] I, 33 (Castelpers).

varies, no doubt, from castle to castle: at Cassagnes, where it was described as *exedrae*, it served as a reception room, thus equating more with the first function, but this may well not have been general.[36] Further, was there always a *mansio* close to the tower, or, conversely, was there only ever one? Here, too, it varied. Everything depended on the residential capacity of the interior of the tower. In many cases, it seems that there was nothing else; on the other hand, it is possible that the *milites* at Châteauneauf-de-Malet possessed their own *mansiones* alongside that of the castellan; the text referring to this castle records that in the course of a nocturnal attack, though certain *milites* were *intra turrim*, others slept *extra*.[37] Finally, we must not rule out the existence of other more rudimentary constructions serving, in particular, as stores for provisions; in a *castrum* near to Conques, a prisoner was shut up in an *obscura mansiuncula*, where he was chained to a *dolium*, also called a *frumentorum cumera* (corn chest).[38]

The tower itself, which overhung the chasm (*erecta in aditiore loco, ad illam videlicet plagam que altiore ruitur precipitio*), generally comprised three storeys. The lowest room, at ground level, was almost totally dark; it was, we are told, situated 'in the hideous depths of the tower' (*in tetra turris profunditas*) and its only access to fresh air was by a narrow slit (*artissinium foramen*) let into the defensive wall.[39] Whilst it usually consisted of one single room, it could also, on occasion, be divided into two cells communicating by a door fitted with bolts.[40] In any case, it had only one exit: an opening, which seems to have been a simple trap-door, let into the floor of the first storey, and which was reached by a ladder (Conques) or a staircase.[41] Only one of the uses of this

---

[36] Even for Cassagnes, the texts (I, 6, 22) are not entirely clear. Elsewhere, the reception room was situated on the first floor of the tower (see below). It is not impossible that the *mansio* served primarily as a residence for the lord's wife and children, the castellan himself usually sleeping in the *camera* on the second floor of the tower with the armed men and one or more concubines (Castelpers, see below). In Catalonia, during the course of the eleventh century, better conditions for the castellans came above all through the improvement of the *mansiones* situated alongside the donjons; they then often took the form of *solaria*, houses with an upper storey, sometimes equipped with a porch and not totally without comfort (Bonnassie, *La Catalogne*, vol. 1, p. 497).

[37] III, 3: *milites intra et extra somno indulgentes.*

[38] III, 4.   [39] III, 5 (Conques) and IV, 8.

[40] IV, 8. Unidentified castle in lower Quercy (see note 7).

[41] At Conques, once the ladder was raised, the first floor was inaccessible; the prisoner managed to reach it, nevertheless, with the help of a pole which he

dark room is indicated: that of serving, as at Doué-la-Fontaine, as a prison.[42] The unfortunates who languished there were attached to a chain which passed through the narrow *foramen* let into the wall to be fixed to an iron peg inserted into the ground outside; an interesting piece of information, since it demonstrates that the single slit made in the defensive wall at ground level was not on the cliff side, but opposite it, on the same side as the entrance. We should perhaps, therefore, see the *foramen* as a loophole for arrows situated below the first floor door and defending it.

The first floor was the floor of state. When a special term was employed for it, it was *exedrae*. If we regard *exedrae*, as I suggest we should, as equivalent to *aula*, we may assume that this was situated on the first floor of the tower in the case of buildings with two storeys and outside, in the *mansio*, when there was only one. It was this room which had the only external door, access to which from ground level was by a ladder or a stone staircase climbing round the wall.[43] The furniture of this room is never described, except for objects attached to the walls. Amongst these, we should note the presence of ballistas at Servières, and elsewhere a chess-board (*tabula scachorum*).[44] The former were only to be expected in a building with a military function, but to find the latter in a castle in Quercy round about 1050 may come as a surprise. In fact, the earliest reference to the penetration of the game of chess into a Christian country dates from 1010[45] and from that date its diffusion seems to have been fairly rapid in aristocratic circles in the South. The reference to this luxury item is a confirmation of the function

---

miraculously discovered (III, 5). Elsewhere, in contrast, we hear of the gaolers sleeping on the steps of a staircase (IV, 8).

[42] For the well-known excavation of Doué-la-Fontaine, see M. de Boüard, 'De l'aula au donjon: les fouilles de la motte de La Chapelle à Doué-la-Fontaine (Xe–XIe siècle)', *Archaéologie Médiévale*, 3–4 (1973–4).

[43] The existence of such staircases is by no means certain in the case of fortresses of the tenth to eleventh centuries (M. de Boüard, *Manuel d'archéologie médiévale*, pp. 117–18). The Book of Miracles never mentions one (unless, at Cassagnes, the phrase *per oblicos graduum anfractus* describes such a staircase; this seems unlikely, the word *anfractus* (winding or bends in a path) applying rather to the steps of a footpath carved in the rock, see above, note 33).

[44] III, 15 (Servières) and IV, 8 (unidentified castle in Quercy).

[45] Will of Ermengol I, count of Urgell, who bequeathed his game of chess to the Abbey of Saint-Gilles; also a reference in a letter from Peter Damien, around 1040 (Bonnassie, *La Catalogne*, vol. 1, pp. 499–500).

of reception room held by the *aula*; it even tells us what sort of diversion was proposed to distinguished visitors.[46]

The upper floor contained the private residence of the castellan, the *camera* (*herilis camera*).[47] This sometimes (as, for example, at Roche d'Agoux) occupied the whole floor. It might only take up a part; the upper storey at Castelpers was divided into two rooms: the largest, which had a window (*fenestra*) giving on to the precipice, was effectively the lord's chamber; the second, on the less steep side (*de parte reliqui municipii*), served as a prison. We should note that captives were not always held in the basement of the tower; in at least two cases, for reasons which are not explained – possibly because the ground floor served another purpose (kitchen?) – their prison was at the top of the building, either in a room set aside for this purpose (Castelpers) or in a wooden cage specially installed within the *camera* (Roche d'Agoux). Apart from this cage, no piece of furniture is mentioned; the bedding probably consisted, as was often the case in Catalonia at this period, of furs placed either on the floor itself or on improvised beds. Lastly, who slept in this upper chamber? The lord and his *familiares*, say the texts. Amongst the latter there were certainly some armed men. Did it include the castellan's wife and children? Their lodgings may have been in this vertiginous lair or in the *mansio* built outside. Only one thing is certain: a female servant (*cubicularia, pedissequa*) slept alongside the master and his men. At Castelpers, the lord woke her to send her for news as soon as he heard the prisoner moving. The nocturnal guard of the fortress was the responsibility in turn of the *milites* who surrounded the castellan and was effected from the window of the *camera* or, if this was accessible, the upper terrace of the tower.[48]

Building materials

The general aspect of these buildings can be gleaned from these various indications. The towers were massive, probably square or

---

[46] Was chess played in the *aula* of Duke William at Caen around 1060? Why not? This connection, quite common, between *aula* and chess might throw light on the origins of the Norman Exchequer.

[47] I, 33 (Castelpers).

[48] A *summe arcis* is mentioned at Châteauneuf (III, 3).

rectangular,[49] and usually of two storeys.[50] Two faces were completely blind, the others almost. On the access side, apart from the loophole at ground-floor level, there was only the door, at the level of the first floor; opposite (the cliff side), two windows, one above the other, lit the *aula* and the *camera*.

All this suggests that the castles were already of stone. This, if we except the special case of the motte of Montagrier, is confirmed by the texts: the towers were described as *saxee turres*.[51] But apart from this common feature, the quality of construction seems to have varied enormously. There were large and small castles; and castles which were either well or badly built. Some, too old or carelessly built, split or collapsed; this happened to the tower of the *castrum* of Conques, and the hagiographer saw in its collapse a sign of divine vengeance against a family of impious castellans.[52] In practice, such accidents seem likely to have been frequent, to judge by the precarious nature of some constructions. At Roche d'Agoux, the prisoner, having escaped from his cage and reached the ground floor of the tower, had little difficulty in opening up a passage through its wall. The latter was only, we are told, a 'collection of beams and stones, heaped up without cement'.[53]

Overall, the stories in the Book of Miracles warn us to exercise great caution when studying the military architecture of the eleventh century. The few buildings which have survived, even in a ruined state, were the best conceived, probably those built for the most powerful lords, and constructed, *a petra et calce*, by the most

---

[49] Though unlikely, the hypothesis of round towers cannot be ruled out, even for such an early date. In Catalonia, the construction of round towers is clearly demonstrated for the tenth century. See Ph. Araguas, 'Les châteaux des marches de Catalogne et de Ribagorce (950–1100)', *Bulletin Monumental*, 137 (1979), 205–24.

[50] The existence of two storeys is certain at Castelpers, and likely in most other cases.

[51] For example, IV, 8: *per foramen saxee turris.*

[52] The castellan and his four sons were struck dead one after the other. The tower fell down: *Turris vero, in qua hoc perniciosum succreverat concilium, a vento validissimo undique concutitur, ac sic cum ingenti precipitio obruta solo equatur* (III, 17). This collapse happened too conveniently for one not to be a little sceptical. Nevertheless, as the event is recorded as having taken place at Conques itself, how could the author have mentioned it unless it contained at least a grain of truth?

[53] IV, 7: *deinde perforata turris maceria, trabium ac lapidum commissura sine cementi glutinio congesta.*

expert masons.[54] Alongside them must have existed many less substantial buildings (*oppidula, castellucia, castelleta*, simple *turres* or *guardiae*), simple intermediate bases whose defence was entrusted to *milites* of the second rank.[55]

Functions

If we think only of the major fortresses, the castles appear to have been essentially centres of power. The verbs which define the functions of the castellans (*regere, presidere, praesse*) make this quite plain, as do the titles and qualifications applied to them (*dominus, senior, princeps, primus et maximus*).[56] This authority extended over an area, itself often called by the name of the *castrum*, whose bounds seem clearly defined; the lady castellan of Turenne had a liberated prisoner accompanied as far as the frontiers of her castellany (*fines castelli*).[57]

What was the origin of these territorial circumscriptions? To pose this question amounts to asking what was the origin of the power of the castellans. None of the castles mentioned is referred to as a comital fortress. Only two, Turenne and Carlat, belonged to viscounts;[58] for the rest, only the noble status of the castellans (*nobilissimus vir, eques nobilitate pollens, vir nobilitate clarissimus* etc.)[59] was remarked on by the authors. We are given one clue: the master of the castle of Conques was (in one account only) described as *vicarius*:[60] a fleeting hint suggesting that, as in Catalonia,[61] the castral dynasties of the eleventh century were descended from the families of Carolingian vicars.

---

[54] The expression *a petra et calce* is not found in the Book of Miracles, but is common for eleventh-century Catalonia in deeds of donation with the obligation to build, see ACA perg. RB I, no. 218 (1058), *turrem de petra et calc . . . muros de petra et calc*; see also Araguas, 'Les châteaux des marches de Catalogne et de Ribagorce', p. 223, note 8.

[55] I, 22: *Est quodam oppidum, vico Conchensi contiguum, quod sub ditione monachorum quidam Austrinus presidebat.*

[56] III, 10: *in memorato oppido princeps quidam Robertus preerat* (Aurouze); IV, 8: *Bernardus predicti castri primus et maximus* (Montpezat), etc.

[57] II, 6: Beatrice of Turenne was the sister of Richard II of Normandy.

[58] And the viscounts were not designated by their title: Eble of Turenne was called only *dominus Oebalus* (II, 6); and in the case of the viscount of Carlat, the author was content simply to emphasise his nobility: *genere clarus et milicia strenuus* (IV, 14).

[59] I, 33; III, 9; III, 18.   [60] IV, 3: *vicarius loci ejusdem.*

[61] Bonnassie, *La Catalogne*, vol. 1, pp. 173–7.

However that may be, the power based on possession of a castle seems to have been completely autonomous. There is no reference to any superior power. In this period of disintegrating public authority (1010–40: the years of the feudal revolution), all power seems *de facto* power. That of the castellans derived directly from their military power, represented on the one hand by the walls of their fortresses, and on the other by the bands of armed men they were able to gather: households, or, since we are in the *pays d'oc*, *manades* of five, fifteen, thirty or fifty *milites*.[62]

The sole function of the fortresses, therefore, to judge from our document alone, was war. They were the military bases for the private wars between the various noble families, which were essentially wars of plunder. These almost permanent conflicts form the subject of a very large number of the stories in the Book of Miracles. It is not part of our purpose here to describe them in detail; we will simply indicate their general pattern. First came ambushes (*insidiae*), intended to kill opponents or, more often, to capture them to hold for ransom. A second feature consisted of surprise attacks on the least protected parts of the enemy castellany (peasant dwellings, sometimes churches). Third came systematic ravaging (*vastatio, depopulatio*) of the countryside subject to the rival castle. Laying siege to castles was a last resort, since difficult and extremely hazardous. Only one such case is described, the siege of Loupian, in lower Languedoc, by the *milites* of Bernard of Anduze.[63] The military operations consisted essentially of razzias, accompanied by acts of intimidation. The victims were the *inermes*: mostly peasants, but also, on occasion, monks.

It follows that the picture of the fortress as a centre of power in the Book of Miracles is totally negative. The castle was a source of fear. It was a source of violence, not protection. The construction of a new fortress was seen not as a guarantee of security but as a deadly threat to the established order; it was a sin which would certainly call down divine punishment on its perpetrators.[64] The

---

[62] Five: III, 10; IV, 9. Fifteen: I, 10. Thirty: I, 5. Fifty: III, 14.
[63] III, 21.
[64] Raymond III of Rouergue was struck dead by Sainte-Foy because he planned to construct a castle on the crest dominating the monastery of Conques: *eo quod, ad destructionem predicte ville, supra sublimam cristam que monasterio imminet castellum facere minitaretur.* The author also refers to the disorder which would have resulted if the project had been carried out: *si id sibi fas fuisset efficere, graviter status locis atque ordo permutaretur* (II, 3).

castellans themselves were seen as at best trouble-makers, at worst savage beasts. *Erat quidam Vuigo, in pago Anciensium, regens castrum Calmilliacum, vir inhumanissimus, ingenioque ferocissimo*;[65] this is but one amongst many such examples. , Should we, in this general depreciation of the military class, assume an anti-noble clerical party? Perhaps, but only if we also note that the peasantry, even more exposed than the monks, cannot have failed to share their views on this subject. Fear of castles may well explain why they never appear, in the period we are interested in, as centres of settlement. It was elsewhere that the peasantry sought refuge; in particular in the sacred space surrounding churches, which continued to enjoy, in men's minds, the advantages of the right of asylum. It was a protected space by virtue of the saints, but it was also enclosed within walls (*ecclesie claustrum, murorum ecclesie ambitus*). It was to just such a space, close to the church of Pallas, on the shores of the Etang de Thau, that the peasants of the castellany of Loupian flocked, with their beasts and provisions, during the wars which ravaged the region.[66] It was an analogous phenomenon to that visible in Catalonia, with the creation of *sacrariae*,[67] and very similar to that which led to the foundation of the *sauvetés*,[68] and which shared the spirit which inspired the movement of the Peace of God.[69]

It was not till much later, when the lords of fortresses perceived that a rational management of their territories, associated with a systematic policy of settlement, was more productive than simple rapine, that peasant settlements came close to seigneurial castles, and together formed a new type of agglomeration. But the word

[65] I, 2. Calmillac is now Le Monastier (Haute-Loire).

[66] III, 21: *omnia sua intra murorum predicte ambitum coacervaverunt et nichil extra preter tuguria sua reliquerunt.*

[67] Bonnassie, *La Catalogne*, vol. 2, pp. 653–6. See also K. Kennelly, 'Sobre la paz de Dios y la sagrera en el condado de Barcelona (1030–1130)', *Anuario de estudios medievales*, 5 (1968), 107–36.

[68] The oldest known *sauveté*, that of Vieux in the Albigeois, dates from 987. In the eleventh century, Conques participated actively in the creation of *sauvetés* (Sainte-Foy de Peyrolières, Coueilles, Castelmaurou, Cépet etc.). For *sauvetés*, see Ch. Higouet, *Paysages et villages neufs d'Aquitaine* (Bordeaux, 1975), pp. 207–34, 373–400, especially p. 382.

[69] It should be noted that the region of Ste-Foy's miraculous interventions coincides pretty well with that of the beginnings of the movement of the Peace of God. The chronological coincidence is also remarkable. In Rouergue itself, the Book of Miracles records the holding of a synod at Rodez between 1004 and 1012, which there is every reason to think was a synod of peace (I, 28).

castrum then changed its meaning to designate, for example, the nucleated villages of Languedoc,[70] or the Gascon *castelnau*.[71]

[70] Bourin-Derruau, *Villages médiévaux en Bas Languedoc* and her "'Castrum", structures féodales et peuplement en Biterrois au XIe siècle' in *Structures féodales et féodalisme dans l'Occident méditerranéen (Xe–XIIIe siècles)*, Actes du Colloque de Rome, 1978 (Rome, 1980), pp. 119–34. See, in particular, p. 128: 'It is at this period [after 1080] that the idea of *castrum* and the configuration of habitation really changed. This semantic evolution was slow. It took more than a century before *castrum* came to mean the fortified village.'

[71] Cursente, *Les castelnaux*: also Ch. Higouet, 'Structures sociales, *castra* et castelnaux dans le Sud-Ouest Aquitain (Xe–XIIIe siècles)' in *Structures féodales et féodalisme*, pp. 109–17. The creation of the *castra populata* or 'castelnaux' ("fortified and organised villages, subordinate to castles") is found especially – if we except a first, relatively small-scale, flowering between 1050 and the middle of the twelfth century – between 1150 and 1270 (Higouet, pp. 113–15).

5. *The formation of Catalan feudalism and its early expansion (to c. 1150)**

It might perhaps be useful to begin by surveying developments during recent years in defining the concept of feudalism and, more particularly, of Catalan feudalism.

Only fifteen or twenty years ago, when historians spoke of *féodalisme*, or rather of *féodalité*,[1] they meant, for the most part, a juridical system based on vassalage and the fief. The study of this system belonged, therefore, to institutional rather than to social history. Even when such studies extended to society, its upper strata was almost all that was considered; no other 'feudal' relations, in fact, were conceived of than those which bound vassals (indeed, only noble vassals) to their lords.[2] When the history of the peasantry was addressed (which was rare), it was always outside the feudal context. The research of the last twenty years, associated with a more interdisciplinary approach, has discredited

---

* This paper was delivered at the international conference on *La formació expansió del feudalisme català* held in Girona in 1985, and first published in the Actes del col. loqui organitzat pel col. legi universitari de Girona (8–11 January 1985), under the direction of J. Portella i Comas, Autonomous University of Barcelona, *Estudi General*, no. 5–6 (1985–6), pp. 7–21.

[1] The scholastic dispute raging amongst French medievalists over the use of these two terms is well known. The word *féodalisme* was long shunned because of its Marxist connotations; certain historians, such as Robert Fossier, still refuse to use it (*Enfance de l'Europe* (Paris, 1982), vol. 1, p. 69). It is clear that this battle of words has become so virulent only as a result of ideological differences (see, on this subject, Alain Guerreau, *Le féodalisme: un horizon théorique* (Paris, 1980); and, in even more detail, Youssef Ngadi, *Les concepts de féodalité et de féodalisme dans l'historiographie de langue française depuis Marc Bloch*, thèse de 3e Cycle (Toulouse, 1984). Happy are those countries which have only one word for the two concepts – for example, 'feudalism' (England) and *feudalismus* (Germany). Catalan distinguishes between *feudalitat* and *feudalisme*, but by assigning different, and, indeed, extremely sensible, definitions to the two terms (Feudalitat: condició del feu; Feudalisme: sistema feudal de govern i d'organització de la propietat. E. Vallès, *Diccionari català illustrat* (Barcelona, new edn 1962)).

[2] For an ultra-classical example of this conception: F-L. Ganshof, *Qu'est-ce que la féodalité?* (Brussels, 1944), translated by P. Grierson as *Feudalism*, 2nd edn (New York, 1961).

this excessively narrow juridical conception of the feudal order.[3] As early as 1978 the conference at Rome on the feudal structures of the Mediterranean West,[4] despite reservations on the part of some participants, proposed a wide definition of feudalism, seen both as a 'system of institutions' and as a 'structure of production and profit'.[5] It is this definition which will be used here, and without reservation.

As for Catalan feudalism, twenty years ago it was hardly perceived except as a marginal and imperfect variant of a feudal order designated as classic, that of the region between the Loire and the Rhine. On this point, too, radical revisions have been effected. Recent research has brought out the great originality of southern feudalisms, amongst which Catalan feudalism appears as one of the most structured. Catalan feudalism has, in its turn, assumed the role of model, and it is as such that we must consider it here. How, then, was this model worked out, and to what extent and by what means was it imposed outside Catalonia? For the period before 1150, it is, of course, the first of these problems which is more important; I shall try to establish what is known, emphasising both those points on which there is general agreement and those on which further research is needed. But the expansion of Catalan feudalism began before the mid twelfth century; we need also, therefore, to establish what were the first manifestations of this phenomenon. Lastly, a third question cannot be avoided; that of the relations between the genesis of feudalism and that, contemporary with it, of the Catalan nation.

Before feudalism

What was the situation at the beginning? What mode of production and what types of social relations characterised Catalonia before the appearance of feudal structures?

[3] Just as this process is tending, on a more general plane, to devalue the idea of a 'history of law' distinct from social history (see, on this subject, the critical analysis of a contemporary legal historian: Jacques Poumarede, 'Pavane pour une histoire du droit défunte' in *Procès, cahiers d'analyse politique et juridique*, 6 (1980), 91–102.
[4] *Structures féodales et féodalisme dans l'Occident méditerranéen (Xe–XIIIe siècles)*, Colloque de Rome, 1978 (Rome, 1980).
[5] P. Toubert, 'Discours inaugural: les féodalités méditerranéennes, un problème d'historie comparée' in *Structures féodales*, p. 3.

Can we speak of a slave system? And if so, till when? For the Visigothic period, the existence of a large slave population is not in doubt;[6] there were as many – perhaps even more – slaves in Spain in the sixth and seventh centuries as in the Roman period, and the north-east of the peninsula was no exception. For the period of the Muslim occupation, information is almost totally lacking. At the beginning of the Frankish period and up to the first years of the tenth century, slaves seem still to have been numerous.[7] I use the word 'seem' because no count of references to them has as yet been made for the ninth century; it is vital that this information be established, with dates and locations as precise as possible. In any case, to quote just one example, the act of *sponsalitium* executed around 900 by Count Sunyer in favour of his wife, Aimildis, shows that the fiscal demesnes still included numerous troops of *mancipia*, and this even in the frontier zone (for instance, at Cervelló).[8]

But this situation changed very quickly, from late in the ninth century, definitively in the tenth century. Mentions of *servi* and *ancillae* become rarer, and disappear completely after the year 1000.[9] How are we to explain the extinction of rural slavery? Clearly, this phenomenon must be related to the very marked economic growth which Catalonia experienced at this period. The colonisation of frontier lands offered obvious possibilities of escape to the slaves of the hinterland. The demand for labour was such that flight was tolerated, even facilitated and legalised, by the authorities (as shown by the foundation charter of Cardona).[10] Further, the process of assarting required not only many workers, but that they should be mobile, a mobility which was obviously incompatible with the maintenance of the slave system. Land-owners who wished to participate in the process of land clearance had no option but to enfranchise the last of their slaves and install

---

[6] P. D. King, *Law and Society in the Visigothic Kingdom* (Cambridge, 1972) pp. 160–79; chapter 2 above, 'Society and mentalities in Visigothic Spain'; chapter 1 above, 'Survival and extinction of the slave system in the early medieval West'.

[7] There is an abstract of these references for the tenth century in Bonnassie, *La Catalogne*, vol. 1, p. 301.

[8] F. Udina Martorell, *El archivo condal de Barcelona en los siglos IX y X* (Barcelona, 1951), no. 9 (898–917).

[9] Last mention in 1035 (in the will of Count Guifred of Cerdanya: *LFM*, 2, no. 693).

[10] Font Rius, *CPC*, 1, no. 9.

them on colonising tenures which were usually remote from estate centres. We may perhaps apply to Catalonia the concept formulated by Pierre Toubert with regard to the Sabina, that is that the phenomenon of agrarian expansion was, to a large extent, the achievement of the 'small proletariat of the enfranchised'.[11]

To the extent that slavery became a residual phenomenon, Catalan society at the end of the tenth and in the early years of the eleventh centuries may be characterised as a society of free men. This peasant liberty emerges from many documents of the period and can be defined on the basis of four principal criteria:

1 judicial criteria: peasants attended public courts and could, individually or collectively, bring judicial actions before the comital courts, which sometimes decided in their favour.[12]

2 military criteria: in such a frontier region as Catalonia, the peasants were often armed and sometimes participated, up to the early eleventh century, in public expeditions into Islamic territory.[13]

3 economic criteria: the peasant allod based, for the most part, on the *aprisio* was the predominant form of landholding in the tenth century. This hegemony was particularly marked in some places, where it might account for as many as 80 per cent of the plots of land.[14]

4 lastly, this peasantry possessed its own forms of organisation, within the framework of the village communities. The latter often benefitted from a charter of franchise (Vallès, Penedès etc.); they often owned the parish church, even, as at Ribes, the *castrum*.[15]

In the second half of the tenth and the first quarter of the

---

[11] P. Toubert, *Les structures du Latium médiéval* (Rome, 1973), vol. 1, pp. 465-87.

[12] Examples: *HGL*, 2, no. 185 (874); Udina, *El archivo condal de Barcelona*, App. 2, Docs. A (913) and no. 181 (977); ACA, perg. Ramon Borrel, no. 104 (1013).

[13] Expeditions which, we are told by a document dating from 1013, included *maximi* and *minimi* (AC Vic, Episcopologi I, perg. no. 98; ed. A. Udina Abelló, *La successió testada a la Catalunya altomedieval* (Barcelona, 1984), no. 93, p. 258).

[14] For example, in the district of Montpeytà (Pla de Bages), as revealed by the 109 documents from before 1020 which refer to this (Bonnassie, *La Catalogne*, vol. 1, pp. 224-8).

[15] For Ribes, *CPC*, 1, no. 10. For the more general problem of the village communities, P. Bonnassie and P. Guichard, 'Rural communities in Catalonia and Valencia (from the ninth to the mid-fourteenth centuries)' see below, chapter 8. For the franchises, most recently, Font Rius, *CPC, 2*.

eleventh centuries, then, Catalonia experienced a situation which was quite exceptional: slavery was dead, feudalism was not yet born. It was an intermediate phase, a period of hiatus, of rupture, a phase during which social changes were in suspense and which saw the development of an increasingly free society. This was paradoxical in a Europe in which the majority of people lived in conditions of dependence, sometimes servitude. But the paradox can be explained by the decisive role played by the independent peasantry, whether in the defence of the country or in undertaking the conquest of new land. Such a situation was not destined to last, however, since it was unacceptable to the ruling class.

For if society of the late tenth and early eleventh centuries was effectively a society of free men, it was also characterised by extreme inequality. The disequilibrium between the *potentes* (a handful of great families) and the *pauperes* (the mass of peasants) was as flagrant there as elsewhere in Europe. The peasantry had been able to retain its independence, but it was very poor. The peasant allod predominated numerically, but only as an extremely fragile micro-property, at the mercy of every adverse circumstance. After each bad harvest and during every period of shortage the small allod-owner was obliged to sell or borrow to survive: of this phenomenon the mass of deeds of sale and mortgage preserved in the Catalan archives are eloquent testimony. And to these 'voluntary' alienations must be added the frequent judicial confiscations pronounced by the courts, usually to the benefit of the great landowners, lay and, above all, ecclesiastical.[16] There was, therefore, from the tenth century, a process of continuous erosion of the peasant allod which was the basis of the liberty of the poor. The peasantry was weakened, and its independence became increasingly illusory. It could not resist the onslaught it faced in the eleventh century at the hands of an aristocracy determined to seize for itself alone the fruits of expansion, and it could not effectively oppose the establishment of those seigneurial and feudal structures from which its enserfment sprang.

[16] Hence the interest of Ramon Marti's paper, which clearly demonstrates this phenomenon on the basis of examples from Bàscara and Ullà, 'La integració a l'"allou feudal" de la seu de Girona de les terres beneficiades pel "règim dels hispans". Els casas de Bàscara i Ullà, segles IX-XI', *Formació i expansió del feudalisme català*, pp. 49-62. See also Bonnassie, *La Catalogne*, vol. 1, pp. 197-202.

Factors in the establishment of feudalism

Economic factors are the most obvious, by which I mean, simplifying hugely, the development of the productive forces.[17] This point, today generally accepted, needs little emphasis. Let us note simply that, around 1000, growth accelerated, changing its rhythm and nature. Effort was devoted less to the conquest of agricultural land (already almost totally completed by the mid tenth century) than to the diversification and intensification of production. Progress (in particular, technical progress) was, at all events, more and more rapid. In direct consequence, investment was increasingly heavy; it could no longer be undertaken by the allod-owning peasantry and became the prerogative of the great landed proprietors, lay and ecclesiastical.

The example of mills is significant in this regard. The mills of the early Middle Ages were still very simple, of an archaic type (probably with horizontal wheels) and requiring only inexpensive materials; for the most part, they were constructed by small groups of peasant allod-owners who shared in their ownership.[18] From the eleventh century, the power of mills increased; they were now modern installations (probably with vertical wheels), fitted with extremely heavy *ferramenta*, and their construction was a major operation. They were now built by counts, castellans and monasteries and they offered formidable competition to peasant mills. In practice, the peasantry had no possibility of meeting the demands of technical and economic progress except by operating in groups and undertaking collective investments. This sometimes happened; let us remember, for example, those villagers of Corró d'Amunt, in the Upper Vallès, who went as a group to the comital palace of Barcelona to buy the water of a stream from the countess Ermessend in order, they said, to dig an irrigation channel to water their fields.[19] But such initiatives were insufficient and, in general, the control of economic growth passed, in the eleventh century, into the hands of the aristocracy.

---

[17] The concept of productive forces extends, in fact, well beyond the economic domain, and encompasses an essential part of the 'ideal'; see the recent analysis of Maurice Godelier, *L'idéel et le matériel* (Paris, 1984), especially pp. 175-82.

[18] Hence the frequent sales or donations of parts of mills (*hebdomadas de molino, dies et noctes molentes*, etc.) which are found in the documents of the second half of the tenth century and the first years of the eleventh (examples in Bonnassie, *La Catalogne*, vol. 1, p. 461).   [19] ACA, perg. BR I, no. 30.

It is equally important to consider the military factors, though these have hitherto been neglected by historians. As a consequence of the development of metallurgy and technical progress in iron working, arms improved and became increasingly heavy, thus increasingly expensive. It was now often beyond the material possibilities of the peasantry to acquire them – hence the growing disparity between the military equipment of the rich and the poor. This can be seen in testamentary bequests; it is particularly clearly revealed by iconography. The miniatures of the Bible of Sant Pere de Roda, for example, show us mounted men equipped with both offensive and defensive equipment of high quality (hauberk, helmet, shield, lance and sword), foot-soldiers provided with casque and javelin but neither sword nor coat of mail, and, lastly, 'fighting men' lacking any weapons, able only to throw stones at knights, whether by hand or by sling.[20]

This distance between *equites* and *pedites* was further increased by the progress made in rearing horses, decisive in the development of the feudal cavalry. Selective breeding resulted in the development of a specialised war-horse, the destrier. To this end, studs were set up, as is shown as early as 1010 by a charter from Pallars which refers to the 'curial' and 'private' places where it was the practice to rear horses.[21] The development of the cultivation of oats, clearly visible in the proliferation of rents in *cibades* throughout the eleventh century, was a relevant factor, as was the establishment of numerous *ferragenalia* which, often located on the edges of towns, were primarily designed to cater for the horses of the urban *milites*. There is a history of the Catalan horse yet to be written!

Last but by no means least, castles became the ultimate weapon of the aristocracy. We need, therefore, to know how these fortresses, originally built to defend the population against the Islamic threat, were transformed into instruments for their oppression. Research into the geography of castles, and changes in it between the ninth and eleventh centuries is, in this respect, essential. How

---

[20] BN, Latin MS. 8 (Bible de Sant Pere de Roda, called 'the Maréchal de Noailles'), 3; see, in particular, fols. 19v, 134, 144. For arms, see Victoria Cirlot, *El armamento catalan de los siglos XI al XIV* (summary of doctoral thesis), Autonomous University of Barcelona (1980).

[21] Document published by E. Magnou, 'Note sur le sens de mot *fevum* en Septimanie et dans la Marche d'Espagne à la fin du Xe et au début du XIe siècle', *Annales du Midi*, 76 (1964), 151.

many new castles were built? How were the old castles altered (alterations explicable as much by the evolution of techniques of construction as by changes of function)? How, lastly, was the link between fortress and village established? This brings us to the major problem of *incastellamento*, a problem about which, it seems to me, we would be well advised to exercise extreme caution in the case of Catalonia. On all these points, history cannot progress alone; despite the exceptional abundance of written documentation for Catalonia, there is a pressing need for the assistance of archaeology.[22]

The specific features of the genesis of Catalan feudalism

What is most striking is the speed and the violence of the transformations which affected Catalan society in the eleventh century. The feudal order, which elsewhere sometimes took a century to impose itself, was here dominant within the space of a generation, in twenty or thirty years (between 1030/40 and 1060). Anyone at all familiar with the eleventh-century archives is aware how abruptly the documents change at this period. Everything changes: the nature of the acts (with the appearance and rapid proliferation of *convenientiae* and oaths of fealty),[23] their form, content, vocabulary, syntax, contractual and judicial procedures etc. The reader has the impression of witnessing an earthquake.

This is because feudalism was here the product of a veritable insurrection, of a civil war which raged in the county of Barcelona (with the revolt, now well-known, of Mir Geribert and his barons), but also in Pallars, in the county of Urgell and in Cerdanya.[24]

---

[22] I would stress the importance of the very rich and original paper of Manuel Riu reviewing archaeological research in this area and its contribution to social history: L'aportació de l'arqueologia a l'estudi de la formació i expansió del feudalisme català', *Formació i expansió del feudalisme català*, pp. 27–45.

[23] Oaths analysed by Michel Zimmerman, 'Aux origines de la Catalogne féodale: les serments non datés du règne de Ramon Berenguer Ier', *Formació i expansió del feudalisme català*, pp. 109–49. This extremely detailed paper raises a number of questions. For the moment, I will say only that the formula of these oaths in itself frequently testifies to a situation of crisis. The insistence laid by Ramon Berenguer I on demanding from his followers both respect for his sovereignty over Penedès (and the 'city of Olérdola') and recognition of the legitimacy of the dower of Almodis is explained by the fact that violent disputes – including resort to arms – had arisen over these two points.

[24] For these events, most recently, Bonnassie, *La Catalogne*, vol. 2, pp. 611–46. See also, for the revolt of Mir Géribert, S. Sobrequés Vidal, *Els grans comtes de Barcelona* (Barcelona, 1961), pp. 56–73.

Violence was everywhere, and it was this which the promoters and participants in the movement of the Peace and Truce of God attempted, with the energy born of despair, to combat.

Why was there such a sudden eruption? It was probably because the traditional structures, inherited from a more or less remote past (Carolingian, Visigothic, Roman, even pre-Roman), were here maintained more strongly and longer than elsewhere. These structures were complex in origin but solidly based on certain very simple principles: scrupulous respect for the written law (the *Liber iudiciorum*),[25] the public character of the exercise of justice, and recognition of peasant franchises and communal usages. When these principles ceased to be recognised, the social contract which they defined was destroyed. The structures disintegrated – at one go.

How did this disintegration come about? Its most striking feature was the split which appeared within the rural communities, the 'peasant neighbourhoods'.[26] A section of the peasantry changed sides, to join the camp of the castle-owning nobility, to become their armed auxiliaries. Which section of the peasantry was involved? It is difficult to be certain, but it seems likely to have been its upper ranks, that is, the last allod-owners, still rich enough to possess horses and weapons.[27] It was the sons of the well-off peasant families (the strongest, the most agile in combat, and the best equipped) who, singled out by the castellans, were to compose the retinues (*maisnatas*) of *cavallarii* attached to the castles, to form the redoubtable and homogeneous group of the *milites castri*. It was they who were to impose, to the benefit of the nobility, but also to their own, the regime of the seigneurial (or castral) *ban* on the class from which they themselves had originated. They would be generously rewarded – with fiefs.

The diffusion and transformation of the concept of the fief was directly related to these social upheavals and, in particular, to the massive recruitment of these troops of mounted warriors. The fief, which had remained an institution of a strictly public character up

---

[25] Anscari M. Mundó, 'Els manuscrits del "Liber Iudiciorum" de les comarques gironines' *Formació i expansió del feudalisme català*, pp. 77–86.

[26] More generally, the importance of this phenomenon has been emphasised by J.-P. Poly and E. Bournazel, *La mutation féodale* (Paris, 1980), pp. 81–103.

[27] The social origin of certain *milites* can similarly be deduced from their wills: examples in chapter 7 below, pp. 208–11. See also Poly and Bournazel, *La mutation féodale*, pp. 129–36.

to the period 1030/40 (*fevum sive fiscum*), was privatised in the years 1040–50 (at the height of the troubles), as the number of infeudations multiplied with frenzied speed. Castellans vied with each other to endow the largest possible number of *milites*; they made grants of land, but even more of parts of seigneurial revenues (or those new revenues which derived from the imposition of the *ban* on the peasantry: *toltas*, *questias*, profits of justice etc.).[28] The *milites castri* in receipt of such fiefs (*cavallarias* for the simple horsemen, *castlanias* for those whose service was such that they were entrusted with custody of a fortress) thus found themselves indissolubly linked to a new social order. This was an order which they had to impose by force of arms, and which can equally well be described as seigneurial (because based on the profits of the *ban*) or feudal (because these profits were redistributed through the system of the fief).

What was the attitude of the counts faced with these changes? They adapted, and very rapidly, to the new realities. Until the middle of the eleventh century, the counts, guarantors of the social equilibrium, held the balance between the interests of their nobility (which provided them with almost all the personnel of government) and those of their peasantry (who constituted an indispensable force in the resistance to Islamic pressure). The count of Barcelona, in particular, showed himself to be a punctilious defender of village franchises. This was still the attitude of Ramon Berenguer I in 1052, during the first legal action he brought against Mir Geribert, the contumacious leader of the rebellious barons. The first demand made on Mir was that he should redress the wrongs he had done the peasantry of the Vallès, restore their franchises and compensate them for the *albergas* and *forcias* he had imposed. Six or seven years later, at the beginning of 1059, during the second sentence pronounced on Mir, this time in his presence and after negotiation, the violation of franchises was passed over in silence; the count neither demanded compensation for the peasants nor the restoration of their rights.[29] In other

---

[28] The composition of these fiefs is analysed in Bonnassie, *La Catalogne*, vol. 2, pp. 600–8, 749–55.

[29] The text of the two sentences appears in the same document (ACA, perg. sense data, RB I, no. 38). This has been published by J. Carreres Candi, 'Lo Montjuich de Barcelona', in *Memorias de la Real Academia de Buenas Letras de Barcelona* 8 (1903), app. 19, pp. 403–13 (ignore the incorrect date attributed by the author).

words, he tacitly accepted the establishment of the *seigneurie banale* in those old regions of liberty, the Vallès and the Penedès. This was a crucial date, which can be regarded as that of the recognition of the seigneurial regime in Catalonia, and of the legitimation of nascent feudalism.[30]

The structures of the first Catalan feudalism

These structures have to be considered at two levels: that of relations between nobility and peasantry and that of the internal organisation of the noble class.

The study of the relations between nobles and peasants raises the question of the definition of lordship and of the imposition, within a seigneurial framework, of new forms of servitude. It is an immense problem, only certain aspects of which can be mentioned here.

As far as the forms of peasant dependence are concerned, we should note to what extent they were, in Catalonia, modelled on usages which were properly feudo-vassalic. The peasants were the 'men' of their lords and even, in many cases, their 'solid' men (*homines solidi*, an expression synonymous with *homines proprii*).[31] The use of such a vocabulary assumes the swearing of an oath of allegiance and even the doing of homage, though obviously of servile nature. That peasants submitted to such rites is attested very early: Alamany de Cervelló and his wife Sicards called their peasants *homines de nostro hominatico* in 1045/6.[32] At the end of the eleventh and the beginning of the twelfth centuries, the engagement of fealty (coupled with associated obligations) was regularly demanded in many regions when holdings were granted. The lord of the land was described as *melior senior* (an expression which, in feudo-vassalic relations, implied the concept of liege

---

[30] We should here pay especial homage to Santiago Sobrequés Vidal. It was he who, in *Els grans comtes de Barcelona*, established for the first time a correct date for the two sentences against Mir Geribert, thus also making intelligible the progress of the revolt. It was also Sobrequés who first grasped the importance of this crisis. His work therefore enables us to study from a sound basis one of the crucial moments in the history of Catalan society.

[31] The expression *homines solidi* was first applied to peasants in 1114 (ACA, Monacales, perg. Sant Benet, no. 380). The description *homines proprii et solidi* became common at the end of the twelfth and in the thirteenth centuries (J. Vicens Vives, *Historia de los remensas en el siglo XV* (Barcelona, 1945), p. 30).

[32] AC Barcelona, Diversorum C-c, no. 473.

lordship), the tenant was his *solidus habitator*.[33] Similarly, the peasant tenure was often – at least in the region of Vic – designated by the term 'fief': it was the *terra fevale*.[34] This is clear evidence of the strength of the movement of feudalisation in Catalonia, which affected not only the upper layers of society (as, for example, in northern France), but spread right down to the very bottom.[35]

As far as the nature of peasant servitude is concerned, the crucial problem is that of the origin and definition of the *mals usos*.[36] I believe that the latter emerged along with the exactions of the *ban* in the eleventh century. But they remained for a long time extremely diverse, varying from one lordship to another. If we take the example of the restrictions imposed on peasant freedom of marriage, we see that, in the eleventh century and for much of the twelfth, they were confused with the right of *presentalias* or *presentalges* exercised by the lord.[37] The exercise of this right took forms which varied according to place: here an imposed choice of spouse, there the demand for favours of the young bride (the sinister *dret de cuixa* which survived in the collective memory of the peasantry) and, elsewhere again, the levy of a tax on the occasion of the wedding. It was only later that the practice was codified to become the *ferma de spoli*, a tax on the marital dowry, or, more accurately, the price of seigneurial consent to the contract of *sponsalitium*. The studies of Thomas Bisson and Paul Freedman show that it was at the end of the twelfth and in the thirteenth century that these *mals usos* were, essentially, defined and systematised.[38] It was then, too, that they were regularly asso-

---

[33] The tenant undertook to behave towards the master of the soil *sicut homo debet esse de suum meliorem seniorem* (AC Vic, perg. no. 1821 (1129). Similarly: *fiam vestrum solidum abitator* (AHN, Clero, perg. Poblet, carp. 1997, no. 1: 1126).

[34] Examples: AC Vic, perg. 928 (1035), 1058 (1071), 1893 (1086).

[35] On this theme, see chapter 3 above, p. 131; also Poly and Bournazel, *La mutation féodale*, pp. 134-6.

[36] For the *mals usos*, the essential work of reference remains W. Piskorski, *El problema de la significación y del origen de los seis 'malos usos' en Cataluña* (Barcelona, 1929), a remarkable work, given the period in which it was written (original Russian edn Kiev, 1899). More recently, chapter 7 below, pp. 217–21; P. Freedman, 'The enserfment process in medieval Catalonia: evidence from ecclesiastical sources', *Viator*, 13 (1982), 225–44.

[37] *Presentalias de ipsos aut ipsas qui duxerint maritos aut uxores*: ACA, perg. RB I, no. 383 (1067); *presentalias*: AHN, Clero, Poblet, carp. 1997, perg. no. 6 (1127); *persentalges: ibid.*, carp. 1997, perg. no. 14 (1130).

[38] P. Freedman, 'The enserfment process in medieval Catalonia'; also his 'Peasant

ciated with the attachment to the land which constituted the *remença* (whose antecedents can also be traced to the end of the eleventh century).[39] How this servitude spread is still very difficult to follow. Certainly not all the peasantry was enserfed at the end of the eleventh century. Areas of freedom existed – but where, and how important, were they? Did they coincide with those zones best protected by the Peace of God? Put another way, were the peasants who remained free the inhabitants of the *sagreres*, as claimed by J.-P. Cuvillier for the plain of Vic?[40] Or did the areas of liberty coincide with the comital demesne? This would show that the count, at least on his own land, resisted the feudal contagion and that rather than behave like a vulgar *seigneur banal*, he preferred to preserve certain forms of peasant freedom.[41]

Finally, were these privileged zones tending to expand or contract in the twelfth and thirteenth centuries? One might well tend to the conclusion that they were expanding, to judge simply by the number of franchises granted at this period. But Thomas Bisson puts us on our guard; these franchises experienced a new crisis in the middle of the twelfth century. Already before 1200, 'the franchisal communities were like clearings in a thickening jungle of seigneurial violence'.[42]

The internal structures of the noble class were, for their part, shaken and battered by the accession to the nobility of a host of new arrivals, sprung from the *militia* (*castlans, cavallarii*) who were five, ten, even twenty (?) times more numerous than the nobles of old stock.[43] This produced two major problems: the

---

servitude in the thirteenth century', *Formació i expansió del feudalisme català*, pp. 437–45; T. N. Bisson, 'The crisis of Catalonian franchises (1150–1200)', *ibid.*, pp. 153–72.

[39] Attachment to the land is already implied (in practice, if not in law) in the agrarian contracts of the end of the eleventh century which stipulate very heavy penalties in the case of a tenant who left his tenure (chapter 7 below, pp. 229–30, 236–7).

[40] J.-P. Cuvillier, 'Les communautés rurales de la plaine de Vich (Catalogne) aux XIIIe et XIVe siècles' in *Mélanges de la Casa de Velázquez*, 4 (1968), 73–103.

[41] At least till the new crisis of the middle of the twelfth century (Bisson, 'The crisis of Catalonian franchises').

[42] *Ibid.*, p. 168.

[43] The increase in size of the noble class through the absorption of the body of *milites* has never been precisely measured. It is, nevertheless, a crucial phenomenon in the history of feudalism. Georges Duby has hazarded an estimate: the *milites*, he says, were from twenty to thirty times more numerous

integration of all these warriors (*milites*) of humble extraction, and the cohesion of the new class which was constituted. On the former point, we have to bemoan a grave lack of documents. Charters, whose sole purpose was to make a record of contractual acts, tell us almost nothing about the occasion of dubbing, clearly an initiation ceremony. But this rite was crucial: a rite of passage involving entrance tests intended to sort the mass of castle knights (*milites castri*) into those judged worthy to share the aristocratic way of life (and thus accede to noble status) and those who remained relegated to the subordinate role of auxiliary fighting men. When was the practice of dubbing established in Catalonia? We may never know.[44]

On the other hand, we have an exemplary text for the juridical recognition of this new nobility: the *Usatges of Barcelona*, one early clause of which (article 5)[45] was intended specifically to define a new hierarchy of persons and, in consequence, the new noble categories (viscounts, *comtors*, vavasours i.e. castellans, and *milites* i.e. *cavallarii*), with their respective tariffs of composition for murder and injury. We here come up against the very difficult

than the nobility of ancient stock (*Les Trois Ordres ou l'imaginaire du féodalisme* (Paris, 1984), p. 192 (translated by A. Goldhammer as *The Three Orders: Feudal Society Imagined* (Chicago, 1980)). This is certainly an exaggeration. How can we progress beyond guesswork? The best method might be to make a systematic record, whenever possible, of the number of *milites* attached to a castle. Assuming one noble family (of ancient origin) per castellany, one could then deduce the number of families of *milites* attached to the lineage. Such a method is, however, far from totally reliable: 1) many barons possessed several castles, thus there was less than one ancient noble family per castellany; 2) all *milites* (some settled on holdings, but others simple prebendaries in a precarious situation) did not found families: the number of families of *milites* is therefore fewer than the number of individuals recorded; 3) the baronial families, which often had several collateral branches, were certainly larger than the new families of the *milites*. With these reservations, however, here are some figures: in 1039, seven *milites* for the two castles of Linyà and Cambrils, in Solsonès (AC Urgell, Cart. I, no. 523, fo. 174); twelve at Reus in 1045 (AHN, Clero, perg. Poblet, carp. 1992, no. 4); five *milites* not settled on tenures (and an unknown number enfeoffed) at Mediona in 1057 (ACA, perg. RB I, no. 204). Manuel Riu records ten knights at Tàrrega, four at Taradell, and twenty for the two castles of Cervià and Pùbol. These figures tally; it seems to me not unreasonable to argue that in Catalonia, at the time of the first feudal generation (1030–60), the *milites* were between five and ten times as numerous as the nobles of ancient lineage. This proportion certainly increased later.

[44] It is attested for the years 1080–90 at least, chapter 7 below, p. 214, but was certainly older.

[45] More exactly, the second paragraph of article 4 (*Ut qui interfecerit*) and article 5 (*De vasvassore*) which must originally have formed one single article.

problem of the dating of the *Usatges*, which Frederic and Antoni Udina have been brave enough to tackle and on which they both shed new light and offer valuable comments.[46]

As for the cohesion of the new noble group, it was far from being acquired in advance. It could only be assured by two means. The first was a very extensive development of feudo-vassalic relations, which resulted in a dense network of ties between man and man from top to bottom of society (the *convenientiae* concluded between lineages and indefinitely renewed, completed and complicated in the second half of the eleventh and in the twelfth centuries, provide the best evidence of this overlapping network of dependencies).

The second method was a regrouping of all the nobility, old and new, round the count of Barcelona. The latter, after his definitive victory in 1059 over the aristocratic rebels, was instituted as supreme arbiter of the internal relations of the noble group (and the exercise of this arbitration led him almost inevitably to define new rules of conduct, a new code of relations, that is, to enunciate and legalise new usages). Also – and this was the counterpart of the recognition of his authority, his *potestas* – he was invested by his nobility with the mission of procuring for it glory and prosperity. Hence the necessity for a politics of expansion, whose first expression can be seen in the war waged from 1058 to 1062 against Muqtadir of Saragossa, which ended in the conquest of the castles of lower Ribagorza.[47]

The early expansion of Catalan feudalism

I will deal briefly with this point, since I am discussing only the period prior to 1150, a period during which the expansion remained, in spite of everything, limited. Territorial progress was achieved in two directions: towards the west and south-west, at the expense of the emirates of Lleida and Tortosa, and to the north into Occitania. The problem is to establish to what extent this expansion, in either case, was accompanied by the export of the feudal model worked out in 'Old Catalonia'.

---

[46] F. Udina i Martorell and A. M. Udina i Abelló, 'Consideracions a l'entorn del nucli originari dels "Usatici Barchinonae"', *Formació i expansió del feudalisme català*, pp. 87–104.

[47] Purroy, Estopinyà and Canyelles (*LFM*, 1, nos. 148, 39).

The conquest westwards took place from the start within a feudal framework. In fact, the lands of the western frontier (Lower Penedès, the Conca de Barberà, Lower Urgell) appear, from the mid-eleventh century, as amongst the most feudalised of Catalonia; one might even surmise that they constituted the cradle of Catalan feudalism. It was here (Lower Penedès), for example, that the typically feudal revolt of Mir Geribert against Ramon Berenguer I started.[48] It was here, too, that the terms of the *convenientiae* relating to fiefs and pacts for the custody of castles were defined both most precociously and with the greatest precision. The oldest documents in the Poblet archive (drawn up between 1045 and 1055)[49] are particularly significant in this regard; the words *castlania* and *cavallaria* with their technical meanings of fief of *castlà* and fief of *cavaller* appear here.[50] The first reference to 'solid' homage is found here;[51] and also the oldest acts of the donation of 'men', which constitute the earliest evidence of the enserfment of free peasants.[52] And it is, lastly, in these western castellanies that the first *mals usos* were established: the oldest references to *cugucias* (as seigneurial taxes on peasant adultery) date from 1058 and 1068 and concern the lordships of Forès and Barberà.[53]

It was, therefore, quite natural for the process of colonisation to continue to take place within a feudal framework. This can be seen around 1100 in the reconquest of Balaguer and the many infeudations to which it gave rise.[54] It is equally visible after 1150, in the

---

[48] Mir Geribert was lord of Subirats, La Vid, Sant Martí Sarroca; he also held Ribes and Olérdola and had not renounced his family rights to Albinyana and Caldars.

[49] Substantially earlier than the date of the foundation of the abbey, they come from exclusively lay archives. They represent the records of the frontier seigneurial families and are, accordingly, of exceptional interest.

[50] AHN, Clero, Poblet, carp. 1992, no. 7 (1047).

[51] *Ibid.*, no. 4 (1045).

[52] *Ibid.*, carp. 1993, no. 5 (1063).

[53] For Forès, Font Rius, *CPC*, 1, no. 20; for Barberà, ACA, perg. RB I, no. 405. The charter concerning Forès is wrongly dated to 1038. The correction of 1058 was proposed by S. Sobreques (*Els grans comtes de Barcelona*, p. 103, note 68) and accepted by Font Rius (*CPC*, 1, p. 39); it is clearly correct.

[54] See, in particular, the deeds of infeudation subscribed by Bishop Ot of Urgell in favour of Mir Arnal de Concabella (Cart. Urgell, I, no. 535, fols. 176–176v) and Bernard Berenguer Babot (*ibid.*, no. 536, fols. 176v–177); the last deed is particularly interesting because it contains the first mention of *vasvassores* in a Catalan charter and also because it provides for the division of the fief into fourteen *cavalarias de feu* (two retained by the feudatory for his own use and

aftermath of the occupation of Lleida and Tortosa; the paper of Antoni Virgili, which destroys numerous myths, is particularly illuminating on this score.[55]

Still further afield, it appears that feudal practices penetrated into the countryside of New Catalonia much more strongly than is generally thought. What confuses the issue here is that the natural propensity of the barons towards the enserfment of the peasantry was to some extent counteracted by the specific circumstances resulting from the necessities of resettlement and the need for labour. This conjuncture forced a contrary attitude: the concession of franchises to attract colonists. But this was not enough to prevent the spread of the *mals usos*. This explains the irregular geography of the bad customs in New Catalonia, clearly shown by the work of Agusti Altisent and Paul Freedman.[56] Hence the sort of dialectic of enfranchisement/enserfment, enserfment/enfranchisement which characterises the history of these regions.

The problems posed by the expansion into Occitania are difficult to resolve by reason of the deficiencies of the documentation, which is infinitely poorer here than for Catalonia, even, on some subjects almost nonexistent.

To measure the influence which Catalan feudalism was able to exert on Languedocian and Provencal societies, we must first know the degree of feudalisation of these societies before the installation of the house of Barcelona. But on this point, nothing is certain; the most widely divergent opinions have been expressed by specialists,[57] the disagreements explicable by the paucity of

twelve subinfeudated). See also the *Rememoracio de ipsas cavallarias de Bala-guer* (*ibid.*, no. 537, fo. 177), which lists fourteen fiefs of vavasours and thirty-four fiefs of knights.

[55] Antoni Virgili, 'Conquesta, colonització i feudalització de Tortosa (segle XII)', *Formació i expansió del feudalisme català*, pp. 275–89. The author's research contradicts at every point the traditional ideas on the regime of 'quasi-democracy' or 'mitigated feudalism' from which the town and its territory benefitted after their supposed 'liberation', actually their conquest.

[56] The situation was quite different, for example, in two villages only six kilometres apart in the Conca de Barberà: the peasants of Espluga de Francoli were mostly free, those of La Guardia dels Prats were all serfs (A. Altisent, 'L'Espluga de Francoli de 1079 a 1200: un poble de la Catalunya nova els segles XI i XII', *Anuario de Estudios Medievales*, 3 (1966), 131–209; P. Freedman, 'La condition des paysans dans un village catalan du XIIIe siècle', *Annales du Midi*, 94 (1982), 231–44. More generally, Freedman, 'The Enserfment Process', and Bonnassie and Guichard, 'Rural Communities'.

[57] It has long (though not always) been traditional to see the *pays d'oc* as only slightly, if at all, feudalised. This view is generally that of northern historians,

sources (especially of lay origin, the only really reliable ones on this question) which leaves the field wide open to speculation. My own opinion is that, in both Provence and Languedoc, the appearance of structures of feudal character antedates the arrival of the Catalans. To take only one example, the major institution of southern feudalism, the *caslania*, existed in Provence by the mid-eleventh century;[58] it is therefore as old as the Catalan *castlania* and presents exactly the same features.[59]

In these circumstances, it would be natural for the counts of Barcelona to try to make use of these local feudal customs in establishing their domination. The best evidence of this is the thirty-five oaths of fealty sworn by the nobles of Carcassès and Razès to Ramon Berenguer I, in 1067, immediately after his acquisition of these counties;[60] or the eighty-nine oaths sworn to Ramon Berenguer III in 1113 by the castellans of Provence.[61] These *sacramentalia* are identical in their terms to the oaths demanded of Catalan vassals; on the one hand they imply

often rather scornful of southern feudalisms. It is also, paradoxically, shared by some southern historians who, anxious to highlight the specificity of the social evolution of the Midi, make it out to be a bastion of resistance to the 'penetration' of feudal practices. This attitude is as prevalent at the level of scholarly research (for example, E. Magnou-Nortier, *La société laïque et l'Eglise dans la province écclésiastique de Narbonne de la fin du VIIIe à la fin de XIe siècle* (Toulouse, 1974)) as at the level of popularising works of 'Occitanist' inspiration (for example, Ph. Martel, 'Naissance d'une société' and 'L'espace occitan au coeur du Moyen Age' in *Histoire de l'Occitanie*, under the direction of A. Armengaud and R. Lafont (Paris, 1979), pp. 161–255). But another trend has recently emerged which, rejecting the assumption of a northern model, sees in the southern feudalisms indigenous and original structures, at least as coherent as those of northern Europe, perhaps even more complete. For this point of view, see above, chapter 3, 'From the Rhône to Galicia'; Monique Bourin-Derruau, *Villages médiévaux en bas-Languedoc: genèse d'une sociabilité (Xe-XIVe siècle)*, 2 vols. (Paris, 1987), especially Part I, chapter 3, 'La crise de la société biterroise vers 1030–1060', vol. 1, pp. 175–202; Poly and Bournazel, *La mutation féodale*, pp. 123–7, 134–6 and *passim*.

58 J.-P. Poly, *La Provence et la société féodale (879–1166)* (Paris, 1976), pp. 152–3 and notes 126–7, 131–4.

59 It is worth remembering, given that the concept of *castlania* is not always fully understood by northern historians, that the *castlania* is not the castellany (which is usually described by the term *castrum*); it is a fief, composed of lands sited within the castellany and, above all, of revenues (*banal*, from land or parish) belonging to it, a fief granted as remuneration for custody of the castles. By definition, the *castlania* never included the fortress.

60 *LFM*, II, no. 838. The oaths are, unfortunately, only listed.

61 *Ibid.*, no. 878. Here, too, we have only the list, not even complete in this case (the total number of oaths must thus have exceeded eighty-nine).

homage,[62] on the other, they refer to the positive obligations of the fealty: *tenere, aiudare, defendere, guerreiare*.[63] This in no way necessarily signifies an import. The formula of the vassalic oaths may have been, from the beginning, the same all along the Mediterranean shores, from Provence to Catalonia.

Occitanian feudalism, though sister to Catalan feudalism, was thus born independently of it. It was as it developed that it was opened to Catalan influence. It remains, however, to determine in what circumstances this influence was exercised. Were feudal structures, in Provence in particular, strengthened under the influence of the counts of Barcelona?[64] It seems more likely, if we are to believe Martin Aurell, that in many cases they served rather to cement the resistance of the Provencal nobility in the face of Catalan intervention.[65]

Catalonia, daughter of feudalism?

Whether influence was exerted or not, the social structures in the Occitanian and the Catalan countries in the eleventh and twelfth centuries were strikingly similar. These similarities are such as to make me pose one last question: that of the birth of a properly Catalan identity (differentiated, that is, from the Occitanian context) and its relations to the development of feudalism.

I am not, on this subject, in total agreement with my colleague, Thomas Bisson, when, in his recent article, he declares that in Catalonia the nation preceded the state.[66] I am far from convinced of the oft-asserted 'precocity'[67] of the birth of the Catalan nation.

---

[62] Where the text of the *convenientiae* has been preserved, it is clear that homage and oath were inseparable. For example, *ibid.*, no. 839: *ipse vicecomes fiat homo de predicto vicecomite Raimundo et iuret ei fidelitatem* (Carcassonne, 1068); no. 885: *facio inde tibi hominium et fidelitatem et iuro tibi mea propria manu* (Provence, 1154).

[63] Examples taken from the *LFM*: for Languedoc, nos. 827, 830, 831, 837; for Provence, nos. 879, 881, 884.

[64] This is the thesis put forward by Poly, *La Provence*, pp. 318–59.

[65] M. Aurell i Cardona, 'L'expansion catalane en Provence au XII siècle', *Formació i expansió del feudalisme català*, pp. 175–95.

[66] T. N. Bisson, 'L'essor de la Catalogne: identité, pouvoir et idéologie dans une société du XIIe siècle', *Annales*, 39 (1984), 454–79, especially p. 455. (English version in Bisson, *Medieval France and her Pyrenean Neighbours*, London, 1989, chapter 6).

[67] Asserted, in particular, by Joseph Calmette ('Le sentiment national dans la Marche d'Espagne' in *Mélanges F. Lot* (Paris, 1925) and 'Origines légendaires

It seems to me very dubious to claim to detect the assertion of some 'national identity', whether in Catalonia or elsewhere, before the twelfth century at the earliest. It is true that we find in the tenth and eleventh centuries, in all those counties composing Catalonia (ten or a dozen, depending on the period), a perfect community of language and way of life. But it was a community which extended far beyond this particular area; the dialects spoken from Nice to Ribagorza differed little, and the mentality, behaviour, traditions and heritage were the same. What was it then which produced, at the heart of this grouping, which, for want of a better term, can be called Catalo-Occitanian, the differentiation of Catalonia in the strict sense of the word?

In reply, let us consider the etymology of the word 'Catalonia'.[68] This has given rise to much controversy, but it appears, nevertheless, to be increasingly certain that at the origin of Catalonia are to be found the *castlans*.[69] During the course of the expedition to Majorca in 1114, when the Italians (the Pisans, in particular) questioned the warriors of Ramon Berenguer III as to their identity, they replied: 'We are *castlans*.' They thus identified themselves with a feudal institution, the *castlania*. The first identification of Catalonia was feudal in nature.

But it is still too general, since the *castlania* also existed elsewhere, in particular in Provence. For the emergence of a true Catalonia, it was necesesary for all the castellanies which were properly Catalan, *and them only*, to be united under a single regime; hence the importance of that 'custom of the castles' rightly evoked by Thomas Bisson,[70] a custom first elaborated in the *convenientiae*, then codified in the *Usatges of Barcelona* and applied to all the counties of Catalonia, and to them alone. It was necessary also for all these castellanies to be brought together under one same power, that of the counts of Barcelona. Hence the decisive

---

et historiques de la Catalogne' in *L'amitié franco-espagnole*, 4 (1921)) and later by numerous Catalan historians of the pre-war generation.

[68] We should remember that the word appears for the first time in an unequivocal manner in the *Liber Maiolichinus de gestis Pisanorum illustribus* in connection with the proposed Catalo-Pisan expedition against Majorca in 1113–15.

[69] The Catalans/Castlans identification was made for the first time by J. Balari Jovany, *Orígenes históricos de Cataluña* (Barcelona, 1899, in 2 vols. re-ed. Sant Cugat del Vallès, 1964, in 3 vols.) It seems to be increasingly frequently accepted today (chapter 7 below, p. 212, note 47; Bisson, 'L'essor de la Catalogne', p. 456).   [70] *Ibid.*, pp. 455–6.

role of the construction of the Catalan state (or, if preferred, the Catalan monarchy)[71] from Ramon Berenguer I to Ramon Berenguer IV,[72] something which to me appears not the consequence of, but one of the conditions for, the birth of the Catalan nation.

In other words, if the fact of Catalonia is a cultural fact (and who would think of denying this?), it was and is, as much and perhaps more, yesterday as today, a political fact.

[71] The use of the term state to designate the politico-social *dominium* of Ramon Berenguer I is unacceptable to both Thomas Bisson (L'essor de la Catalogne', p. 457) and Michel Zimmermann ('Aux origines de la Catalogne féodale', p. 120, note 470). I grant that if, with the latter, we mean by state an organism implying both 'an administrative structure and a sense of the public interest', the appearance of such an organism as early as the eleventh century is difficult to conceive (though Ramon Berenguer I was not entirely devoid of some sense of the public interest). Let us say, so as to avoid pointless debate, that Ramon Berenguer I created the conditions for the emergence of a state, which was more clearly defined, as shown by Thomas Bisson, in the reign of Ramon Berenguer IV.

[72] That is, from 1059 (the date of Ramon Berenguer I's victory over noble sedition and of the first *convenientiae* incontestably establishing his supremacy) to 1162, the date of the death of Ramon Berenguer IV.

6. Feudal conventions in eleventh-century Catalonia*

In 1959, in an important article which remains the only thing written on the subject, Paul Ourliac drew historians' attention to a type of act still little known, even though absolutely characteristic of the history of southern societies between the tenth and the twelfth centuries: the *convenientiae*.[1] These agreements or 'covenants',[2] common throughout Lombardy, Provence, Languedoc and Catalonia, and occasionally found as far afield as Aragon and the Loire valley,[3] can be defined as contracts by which two parties agreed between them, freely and without the intervention of any public or private jurisdiction, the definition of the obligations binding one to the other, and guaranteed their execution by a solemn engagement. Highly original in their form, and without antecedents in Roman or barbarian law, these contracts were employed for a wide variety of purposes. In Catalonia, in particular, the range of the *convenientiae* is enormous; they can be seen variously applying to, for example, a promise of marriage,[4]

---

* This paper was first published in *Annales du Midi*, 80, no. 89 (Oct.–Dec., 1968), pp. 529–50, also in *Les structures sociales de l'Aquitaine, du Languedoc et de l'Espagne au premier âge féodal*, Colloque international de Toulouse, mars 1968 (Paris, 1969), pp. 187–219.

[1] P. Ourliac, 'La "convenientia" ' in *Etudes d'histoire du droit privé offertes à Pierre Petot* (Paris, 1959), pp. 413–22. Previously, the existence of such documents for Languedoc had been noticed by A. de Boüard, *Manuel de diplomatique*, 2 vols. (Paris, 1929–48), vol. 2, pp. 96–7 and F. L. Ganshof, *Qu'est-ce que la féodalité* (Brussels, 1944, 3rd edn, New York, 1961).

[2] Writing in French, Ourliac translated *convenientia* as *convenance*, and recalled the old French proverbs 'Convenance loi vault' and 'Covenant vainc' ('La "convenientia" ', p. 419).

[3] The majority come either from Lombardy or from Languedoc and Catalonia. For Provence, there are allusions to *convenensas* or *covinensas* in twelfth-century charters. For Aragon, there are later references in the *For de Teruel*. For the Loire valley, there is an example of a *convenientia* in the *Cartulaire blésois de Marmoutier* (Ourliac, 'La "convenientia" ', p. 417 and notes 29, 36).

[4] ACA, perg. sense data, RB I, no. 11. Guillem, count of Besalú, engages to marry Lucia, sister of the countess of Barcelona, Almodis.

170

the investiture of an abbey by the count,[5] the farming of revenues[6] and even settling a problem of succession.[7]

Once having entered into contemporary practices, it was natural for this type of contract to be applied to feudo-vassalic relations, and, in fact, the largest and most homogeneous group of *convenientiae* to have survived concerns the definition of the ties binding lords and vassals.[8] The oldest of these documents dates from the period 1018–26, and records the homage done by Ermengol II, count of Urgell, to the count of Barcelona, Berenguer Ramon I.[9] From this date on, they proliferate, to the point where the archives of the Crown of Aragon contain over a hundred – in their original form – for the reign of Ramon Berenguer I (1035–76) alone. There can be no doubt about their importance in the eyes of contemporaries; the conventions made by Ramon Berenguer I retained enough significance at the time of his great-great-grandson, Alfons I, for the latter to put them at the beginning of the comital cartulary whose compilation he ordered, the *Liber Feudorum Maior*.[10]

---

[5] ACA, perg., RB I, no. 107. The abbot Andreu receives from Count Ramon Berenguer I and the countess Elizabeth the abbey of Sant Cugat and promises them obedience and fealty (1050).

[6] *Ibid.*, no. 99, a *convenientia* dealing with the mills of Barcelona (1048).

[7] *Ibid.*, no. 110. After the renunciation by Sans, son of Count Berenguer Ramon I, of the inheritance of his father, Count Ramon Berenguer I gave him, in compensation, two of his own vassals.

[8] The word vassal is used here for convenience, though the term does not, in fact, appear in Catalan charters of the eleventh century, where only the words *fidelis* and *homo* are used to indicate the vassal.

[9] *LFM*, 1, no. 157, pp. 158–64. We cannot take into account an agreement concluded between the viscounts of Urgell and Cerdanya with regard to their castles of Miralles and Queralt, supposedly dated by the historians of Languedoc to 1 March 954 (*HGL*, 2, no. 209, cols. 421–3). Numerous other anomalies apart, the single fact that this act is almost entirely in Catalan is enough to date it to the twelfth century. In fact, the date (*anno XVIII regnante Ledovico rege*) must apply to the reign of Louis VI and not to that of Louis IV of Outremer.

[10] The *Liber Feudorum Maior* includes some sixty feudal agreements from the eleventh century. Apart from the originals of these, about a hundred others, unpublished, are to be found in the 'Pergaminos' and 'Pergaminos sense data' series in the ACA. Acts of the same type are also included in various collections (*Cartulario de sant Cugat del Vallés*, ed. J. Rius Serra, 3 vols. (Barcelona, 1945–7), nos. 553, 571, 612, 619 etc.; *Cartulaire roussillonnais*, ed. B. Alart (Perpignan, 1880), nos. 56, 62 etc.). There is also a splendid series of *convenientiae* in the archive of the monastery of Poblet (AHN, Clero, perg., carpetas 1992ff.). For the most part, only unpublished documents will be quoted as examples here.

General characteristics of the feudal conventions

THE CONTRACTING PARTIES AND THE LENGTH OF THE CONTRACT

Haec est convenientia quae facta est inter . . . et inter . . . It is immediately apparent that the feudal covenant is a bipartite pact – on one side, the lord or lords, on the other, the vassal or vassals. Lord or lords: we should understand by this the lord himself and certain members of his family regarded as co-lords. It might be a brother, though this was rare; Catalonia was not a land of *frérêche*.[11] It was usually the wife of the lord who sat at his side during the conclusion of the agreement, and this female intervention into the world of feudo-vassalic relations is less surprising if we remember the role played by women in all other areas of social life in Catalonia at that time. When the woman in question was the countess (*nutu Dei comitissa*),[12] she occupied this place by right; oaths of fealty were always sworn jointly to the count and countess, and – in Barcelona, at least – no case is recorded of a countess being excluded from the negotiation of a *convenientia*. Further, she could herself conclude agreements of this type on her own, in the absence of her husband, for the lands composing her dower.[13] Lastly, if there were sons who were of age, they too participated in the conclusion of the pact. Thus we have the splendid family scene presented by Bernard Sinfre de Conesa, his wife, his son and his daughter-in-law together receiving the liege homage of one of their vassals and entrusting to him the custody of a castle.[14]

On the side of the vassals, the situation was more complicated. Firstly, the *convenientia* was sometimes concluded collectively by a group; we might remember, for example, the dozen knights who, as their service to Ramon Berenguer I and Almodis, engaged

[11] This despite a famous exception, that of Ramon Berenguer II and Berenguer Ramon II, who shared the government of the county of Barcelona from 1076 to 1082; throughout this period, the two brothers received the engagements of their feudatories jointly. But this was, it must be said, an isolated case, and, indeed, this co-government ended tragically.

[12] ACA, perg. sense data, RB I, no. 8.

[13] ACA, perg., RB I, no. 434 (1071). See also the numerous oaths of vassalage sworn to Almodis alone by the magnates of the county of Girona (ACA, perg. sense data, RB I, nos. 151–69, 196).

[14] AHN, Clero, perg., carp. 1994, no. 19 (undated – second half of eleventh century).

themselves to guard the castle of Palau for one month each in the year, and further promised not to make war during the remaining eleven months on whichever one was then on duty.[15] Or, as was most often the case, the vassal might act alone and contract an engagement which concerned only himself, and not his family. Or finally, like his lord, he might be surrounded by his family for the conclusion of the pact, in which case it created a link between two lineages.[16]

The duration of the contract varied. Some *convenientiae* were for fixed periods of time; the twelve knights of Palau mentioned above were engaged by the count and countess for only three years. Sometimes the contract might be terminated if there was a change in the condition of the vassal; this was the case, for example, with the pacts made between the count and the sons of his great feudatories, which were *ipso facto* annulled when the latter entered into possession of their paternal honours.[17] Most agreements, however, were drawn up without any temporal limit, which does not mean – far from it – that the absence of set date of expiry had the same significance for the vassal and his lord.

The obligations of the vassal were not, as a general rule, terminated by the death of the lord; since most often they were contracted not only towards the latter, but towards his wife and sons, they were naturally transferred to them. Thus in 1061, Gauzfred Bastón, rendering homage to Ramon Berenguer I and Almodis, engaged, on the death of either one, to renew his engagements towards the survivor, then towards whichever of their sons had been bequeathed the county of Girona by the count and countess, whether verbally or by written testament.[18]

If the lord was thus assured of seeing his descendants benefit from the services due to him in his lifetime, the situation of the

---

[15] ACA, perg. sense data, RB I, no. 7. Another case of a *convenientia* concluded collectively by a group of vassals: *ibid.*, no. 26.

[16] For example: ACA, perg., RB I, no. 147 (1055), 220 (1058); AHN, Clero, carps. 1993, no. 9 (1079), 1994, no. 4 (1088), no. 11 (1090), etc.

[17] For example: ACA, perg. sense data, RB I, no. 9; ACA, perg., RB I, no. 407.

[18] Item . . . convenit ut, post mortem de iamdictis comite et comitissa, si ipse Gaucfredus vivus fuerit, attendat et adimpleat omnes supradictas convenientias eorum filio vel filiis cui vel quibus comes et comitissa, aut unus ex eis si alter mortuus fuerit, relinquerit Gerundam et comitatem, Gerundensem, verbis aut scripto (ACA, perg., RB I, no. 269). We should note, once again, the power exercised by the countess – equal to that of her husband – in transmitting the comital patrimony.

vassal was often less secure. The imprecision of the terms of the contract as far as duration was concerned might mean for him, in the eleventh century at least, the threat of being expelled from his fief or of seeing his heir so expelled.[19] Especially when the covenant had been drawn up by the vassal himself personally, his son was never absolutely sure of being able to renew it (and renewal was all the more unlikely if the son was not yet of age at the death of his father). The problem was very different when the vassal had agreed the pact in the company of his family; it then united two lineages and detailed clauses governed the future. These clauses might even end up constituting the major part of the document; every conceivable possibility was envisaged as to the succession of the vassal and his lord and the bonds linking the respective heirs were defined in advance.[20] Sometimes the agreement was said to have been concluded once and for all, and engaged, with no possible remedy, the posterity of the contracting parties. Sometimes, in contrast, it was agreed that it should be renewed with each generation, but, which came to the same thing, in terms which were defined forevermore:

et istas conveniencias suprascriptas sic faciat posteritas Guilelmi ad posteritas Bernardi et posteritas Bernardi ad posteritas Guilelmi et hoc siat firmum omnique tempore. (1054)[21]

Was the vassalic contract, in short, for life, or was it hereditary? This is an old problem, to which it is impossible, for eleventh-century Catalonia, to give a simple reply. In effect, the duration of the agreements varied essentially according to the status of the vassal and the means he possessed to make his rights respected. The more powerful he was, the more chance he had of preserving his fief indefinitely and of bequeathing it to his descendants.

THE NATURE OF THE ENGAGEMENTS

These might be unilateral or reciprocal. The *convenientia* was very often confined to recording only the promise of fidelity to the lord, without any equivalent engagement on the part of the latter. Does this imply an unconditional engagement? Definitely not, because –

---

[19] For this problem, see below, p. 179.
[20] ACA, perg., RB I, no. 449 (transcribed in appendix).
[21] *Ibid.*, no. 153.

make no mistake – the agreement was then completed by a second document, the charter drawn up by the lord which granted a fief.[22] But, just as often, the agreement itself contained the two parts of the contract; in which case, it might even take the form of a chirograph.[23]

The vassalic engagement, as it was defined by the pact, was first of all a promise of homage. This was directly consequent on the *convenientia*:

Convenientia talis est ut Odolardus et uxori sue et illorum filiis stent in hominaticum et fidelitatem domni Guislabertus episcopi.[24]

And it followed immediately on the conclusion of the contract.[25]

But, without in any way diminishing the symbolic value of homage, the *convenientia* went far beyond it in its juridical implications. In the first place, as we have seen, it often involved not only one homage, but a chain of them. When an agreement was concluded between two lineages, the heirs of the vassal were no longer free to choose their lord; the act of homage became for them a duty, the first of their vassalic obligations. Secondly, the *convenientia* determined the nature of the homage: liege homage – 'solid', as it was more precisely called in Catalonia - or simple homage. A crucial point, when we remember the gulf which here separated these two types of engagement by the eleventh century. Finally, as a written document, the agreement had greater weight than homage if a vassalic contract was disputed before a feudal court. In a civilisation as deeply imbued with the written word as was Catalan civilisation at this period, it brought direct and decisive proof of the reality of the contract. In contrast, in the absence of *convenientia* (if, for example, the document had been lost), the act of homage had to be proved by the complicated and risky procedure of the *averamentum*.[26]

As well as defining the homage, the convention also governed the oath of fealty. The relations between these two types of act

---

[22] Charters of this type are numerous in contemporary records: for example, *ibid.*, nos. 90 (1047), 92 (1047), 205 (1057) etc.

[23] ACA, perg. sense data, no. 5.   [24] ACA, perg., RB I, no. 220 (1058).

[25] *Ibid.*, no. 446: *et super hoc mitimus vobis, domnos suprascriptas, nostras manus infra vestras, sic quod nullus homo debet facere ad domno suo* (1072).

[26] Affirmation under oath by the interested party and his witnesses to the reality of the homage, then, if the oath was contested, a judicial duel (ACA, perg., RB IV, nos. 154 (1143).

were, however, rather more complex, with the oath (*sacramentum, sagrament*) being a written act like the *convenientia*, or, more exactly, an act requiring that a written document (the *sacramentalis*) be drawn up. There were, in fact, two possibilities; either the oath was integrated into the covenant (sworn *convenientia*),[27] or it was transcribed in a different document.[28] In any case, the fact that it was put into writing did not dispense with the drawing up of an agreement; more flexible than homage, certainly, since it could specify the nature of the engagement (*fidelis ero* or *solidus ero*), it was nevertheless no less set in its stereotyped formulas and was not in itself enough to define vassalic service. At the very most, some oaths, amongst the least schematic, repeated certain clauses of the pact.[29] More often, they were content with a general reference to the *convenientia*.[30]

The service which derived from the agreement was extremely variable, depending both on the condition of the vassal and the nature of the engagement entered into. Certain *convenientiae* did not even include any sort of service. But, when it existed, as it did in the vast majority of cases, it was always spelled out in the most minute detail.

Overall, if we consider the conclusion of the *convenientia* within the context of the vassalic engagement, it would be wrong to see it only as a supplementary ceremony, a third rite, additional to the classic rites of the homage and the oath. Certainly, it, too, presented a solemn aspect; the pact might be drawn up in a church,[31] and ratified in the presence of numerous and powerful witnesses.[32] But the external forms hardly counted; what mattered was the negotiated content of the act, which, in itself and beyond a more or less fixed ceremonial, constituted the contract. A little later, towards

---

[27] For example: ACA, perg., RB I, nos. 105, 220. Other examples in *LFM*.

[28] The ACA has, in the 'Pergaminos sin fecha' series, nearly two hundred oaths of fealty (mostly unpublished) for the reign of Ramon Berenguer I alone.

[29] The clauses most often repeated are those referring to the surrender of control of the castles held as fiefs, or the clauses about breaches of the contract.

[30] For example: ACA, perg. sense data, RB I, no. 55: *sic superius scriptum est si o tenré et o atendré . . . si tu atenderis mihi ipsam convenientiam que est facta inter me et te.*

[31] AHN, Clero, perg., carp. 1994, no. 4 (1087).

[32] Three viscounts, an abbot and twenty-three *proceres* subscribed the covenant concluded between Ramon Berenguer I and Almodis on the one hand, and the count Guillem de Besalú on the other. The lists of witnesses to the *convenientiae* constitute a sort of 'Who's Who' of eleventh-century Catalonia.

the middle of the twelfth century, when a feudal court, at the end of a hearing, decided to order a knight to enter into dependence, it could forget homage and oath, and retain only the *convenientia* and the service in its prescriptions.[33] This was what mattered.

We must now consider the engagement of the lord, in other words, the grant of the fief. Here the covenant took the form of a charter of donation: *donatio ad fevum* or *per fevum*. But, remarkably, the infeudation invariably preceded the promise of fealty. According to the form of the contract, homage was a function of investiture; a man became a vassal when, by means of a written charter, he received a fief:

sub ista conveniencia donat prefatus Guilelmus cum iamdicta Ermengards ad prefatum Bernardum suprascripta omnia [i.e. the fief] ut se comendet Bernardus iamdictus ad Guilelmum prefatum et ad Ermengards iamdicta et iuret illis fidelitatem sine enganno.[34]

The pact finished with a series of clauses dealing with breach of contract: any breach by the vassal was punishable by the confiscation of the fief, subject to reparation for the harm done in the twenty, thirty or sixty days after the customary summons, in some cases with provision for a commission of arbiters (*boni homines*) to judge the value of the reparation.[35] Certain more mistrustful lords, such as the abbot of Sant Joan de Besalú, even made their vassals, at the time of the investiture, draw up a charter establishing a security for the land being granted![36] Further, some felonious vassals might be penalised by the confiscation of part of their allod, in addition to the loss of their fief.[37] But one law for the rich, another for the poor: the possibility of default by the lord was not usually mentioned, which gave a rather arbitrary character to the contract and rendered problematical the rights of the more humble vassals in their fiefs.

---

[33] ACA, perg., RB IV, no. 154.
[34] ACA, perg., RB I, no. 153 (1054).
[35] ACA, perg. sense data, RB I, no. 3 (*convenientia* between Ramon Berenguer I and Bishop Guislabert of Barcelona): si supradictus episcopus non tenuerit prefato comiti et comitissae omnia que eis iuravit, infra primos XX dies quod comes et comitissa . . . ad predictum episcopum se querelaverint, faciat eis directum ad iudicium de baronis hominibus qui per directum iudicent.
[36] ACA, perg., RB I, no. 265 (1061).
[37] AHN, Clero, carp. 1994, no. 2 (1087).

Different types of feudal convention

FROM CASTELLAN TO *CASTLÀ:* CONVENTIONS FOR THE CUSTODY OF CASTLES

Amongst the least well-protected vassals were certainly the *castlans*. These custodians of castles were both numerous and situated right at the bottom of the feudal hierarchy; they were numerous because fortresses had sprung up everywhere in Catalonia, a frontier region, and a class of specialists was necessary for their defence; they were relatively despised, because they did not belong to the old aristocracy of the *proceres* but had come, without it being possible to be more precise, from the lower ranks of society. The *convenientiae* concerning them are abundant and simple enough in principle: the lord of the castle – of, if preferred, the castellan – a high personage who did not normally live in his fortress, entrusted it to a *castlà* who was made leader of the garrison. In return, the latter received a fief.

This fief was the *castlania*. This was not the same as the castellany, and, in any case, never included the castle, over which the *castlà* had no rights. It consisted of a defined group of lands and, above all, of powers and revenues within the bounds of the castellany. The powers of the *castlà* consisted of that part of the *districtum* and the *mandamentum* which he received, by delegation from his lord, over the peasants who were dependent on the castle, a large part, since only high justice was, as a rule, excluded.[38] The *castlá* thus became the holder of the seigneurial *ban*, and the revenues allocated to him derived from the *seigneurie banale*: for example, a quarter of the rights of justice, the profits of the seigneurial forge, half of the *trobas*, half of the joints of pork owed by the local peasants, a quarter of the 'new usages' etc.[39] Taking charge, in the name of the castellan, of the exploitation of the peasantry, he had an interest in its profits.

His service, properly speaking, was extremely onerous: permanent supervision of the castle – *die cotidie*, escort for the lord, host and cavalcade, at every summons and without limits to duration and distance, in either Christian or Islamic territory.

---

[38] For example: ACA, perg., RB I, no. 405 (transcribed in appendix); only cases of homicide and adultery escaped the jurisdiction of the *castlá*.

[39] *Ibid*. See also nos. 204 (1057), 278 (1062), 383 (1067) etc.

His engagement, therefore, was total, and the *convenientiae* specified in detail every aspect of his dependence: he was the *solidus* of the castellan, who disposed of him more or less at will, who could, for example, transfer his service to another lord,[40] make him (literally, command him to) do homage to someone else, without his being able to object,[41] who could even mortgage the *castlania*, with the *castlà*, of course, thrown in.[42] His chances of being able to retain his fief, or even bequeath it to his children, were extremely variable. The strongest guarantees could be obtained in the frontier zone, where the danger was great and candidates for the position, consequently, thin on the ground; he might, for example, receive assurances that he would retain his position if the castle was sold,[43] or he might even, on occasion, be granted part of the *castlania* as an allod, no longer only as a fief.[44] Elsewhere, the covenants bring out very clearly the non-hereditary nature of the office, and some transactions completed between castellans bluntly allow for the *castlà* to be dismissed (literally, thrown out) without further formality:

et ipso kastellano que i metra, si no sen contenet ad sua guisa de Petro Mir, aquel en geten e altre ni meten (1045)[45]

– a clause on which comment would be superfluous!

BETWEEN MAGNATES: AGREEMENTS NEGOTIATED BETWEEN THE POWERFUL

If we climb further up the hierarchy, and examine the pacts concluded in the upper echelons of the aristocracy, the tone changes. The distance between lord and vassal shrinks, and *convenientiae* often brought together men of the same rank: castellans, viscounts and counts.

The function of the covenant itself changes: what was principally

---

[40] *Ibid.*, no. 105 (1049): *et propter hoc convenit ei Raimundus suprascriptus oste de ipso kastellano quod predictus Raimundus misit aut mitterit in predicto kastro.*
[41] *Ibid.*, no. 225 (1058): convenit . . . Udalardus ut chomendet ipsum chastellanum quem ibi miserit ad chomitem et chomitissam . . . ut ipse chastellanus iuret fidelitatem . . . comiti et comitissa. See also nos. 153, 281.
[42] ACA, perg. sense data, RB I, no. 31: mitto in pignoras duos chastros de Fenestres cum illorum castellanias et cum Remundo Ademari qui eos tenet, in potestatem Remundi senioris mei.
[43] AHN, Clero, carp. 1994, no. 4.   [44] *Ibid.*, carp. 1993, no. 9
[45] *Ibid.*, carp. 1992, no. 4. See also ACA, perg. sense data, RB I, no. 4.

at issue was no longer the service of the vassal but the fief, often a substantial collection of landed estates and fortresses. The *convenientia* was then tantamount to a treaty between territorial powers. It might be negotiated amicably, a simple arrangement between one lord and another: as, for example, in 1058, when the bishop of Barcelona, Guislabert, enfeoffed the viscount Udalard, his nephew, the viscountess Guisla and their son with the castle of La Guardia, receiving from them in return, as a life allod, the castle of Piera.[46] But in many cases the treaty concluded a conflict, often armed. The battle waged between Ermengol III of Urgell and Ramon III of Pallars Jussà for the fortress of Llimiana, for example, terminated in 1040 with a division of the rights: the castle would belong to Ermengol, but Ramon would receive it as a fief, receiving in addition an annual rent of forty ounces of gold.[47] The battle in which Ramon Berenguer I and Almodis opposed Guillem II of Besalú ended with a similar covenant.[48] On occasion, it was no longer clear who was the victor and who the vanquished; Artau I of Pallars Sobirà rendered homage to his cousin Ramon IV of Pallars Jussà and handed over to him the dozen fortresses he had won in the fierce war which had raged between them, but, at the same time, he acquired vast territories and numerous castles in exchange, as fiefs or allods, and the homage he rendered was balanced by the oath he received from Ramon IV.[49]

But war led to *convenientiae* in another way – through the coalitions it produced. A close analysis of the clauses of these treaties would amount to a political history of eleventh-century Catalonia. We need only cite here those which united Ramon Berenguer I and Ermengol III of Urgell against the Muslims of Spain or against Ramon Guifred of Cerdanya, and by which Ermengol became the man of the count of Barcelona.[50] We might also mention the way in which, by concluding *convenientiae* and granting fiefs, the same Ramon Berenguer I enticed away the vassals of his grandmother, the acrimonious dowager countess of Girona, Ermessend.[51] In general, the proliferation of feudal agreements was related to the climate of violence experienced by Catalonia in the years 1040–60.

[46] ACA, perg., RB I, nos. 220, 221.   [47] *Ibid.*, no. 48.
[48] ACA, perg. sense data, RB I, nos. 5, 31.
[49] ACA, perg., RB I, no. 449 (transcribed in appendix).
[50] *Ibid.*, no. 120, and perg. sense data, RB I, no. 1.
[51] ACA, perg., RB I, no. 80 (1045).

The public courts themselves, outflanked by this development, ended up by terminating their debates with the conclusion of *convenientiae*! The engagements so contracted were, as one would expect, a function of the circumstances. They were usually very limited in their purpose. In high aristocratic circles, 'solid' homage was rare – or dearly bought: the three castles of Barberà, Prenafeta and Piera, plus an annual rent of twenty ounces of gold, for such homage in 1071.[52] More normal in these contracts seems to have been a clause reserving fealty: a promise of aid and counsel against whomsoever, except for such and such.[53] Service was restricted in space as in time.[54] It might even disappear completely, especially in Pallars, where the counts, often less powerful than their vassals, could hardly make demands on them: Arnau Mir de Tost in 1053, Ramon Mir d'Orcau in 1056 and Ficapal of Vallfarrera in 1076 obliged Count Ramon IV not only to release them from all service, but even to prohibit himself, by written charter, from entering the castles they held of him as fiefs, except following an abuse for which they could not make reparation.[55] Arnau Mir de Tost even had himself exempted from the oath of fealty for three of his fortresses.[56]

The ties created in this way were often very tenuous and some lords were not averse to demanding guarantees on the part of their vassals, extending even, in some cases, to hostages; in 1045, Ramon Mir of Hóstoles handed over two of his sons to Ramon Berenguer I as a pledge for the fealty he had just sworn,[57] while Guerau Alemany of Cervelló surrendered four sons, representing a total value of eight million *sous*.[58] The sureties were sometimes in land, as, for example, in the agreements concluded between the counts of Barcelona and Besalú,[59] and between the counts of Pallars Jussà and Sobirà.[60] The provision of pledges or guarantees

---

[52] *Ibid.*, no. 438 (1071).

[53] A lord might even accept, in a *convenientia*, that his vassal might fight against him, if he himself waged war on another of his vassal's lords. The contract was confined, in this case, to specifying the number of warriors that the vassal might bring with him on campaign (*ibid.*, no. 482 (1075)).

[54] For example: AHN, Clero, carp. 1993, no. 3: *et vos non faciatis alium servicium ost neque cavalcatum, exceptus quod iscatis ad So et ipsum die tornetis ibi* (1063).

[55] ACA. perg., RB I, nos. 141 (1053), 208 (1056), RB II, no. 1 (1076).

[56] ACA. perg., RB I, no. 141.   [57] *Ibid.*, no. 80.

[58] *Ibid.*, nos. 337, 337 duplicate.   [59] ACA. perg., sense data, RB I, no. 209.

[60] ACA. perg., RB I, no. 449 (transcribed in appendix).

eventually became an integral part of the *convenientiae*: strange agreements, where *fides* might come to mean distrust, and the fealty sworn by the vassal hardly went beyond a fealty of convenience, in other respects almost always entirely negative. There remained, nevertheless, one obligation which the vassal could almost never escape,[61] that is, to surrender to his lord the command of the castles he had received as fief whenever he was summoned. The formula here was ritual, and of such importance that it was often given in full in oaths of fealty:

et dabo vobis ipsam potestam de iam dictis chastris sine vestro engan per quantas vices requisieritis ipsam potestatem, vos ambo aut unus ex vestris, per vos ipsos aut per vestros missos vel missum et comonir no men devedaré.[62]

What did this surrender of power consist of? For the lord, it was the right to install his vassal in the castle, enter and leave it at will and, above all, to use it as a base for his military operations:

et que abeat prefatus Guillelmus et prefata Ermengards in ipso castro de Arraona introire et exire et guerreiare et stare, quantum illi voluerint.[63]

The importance of the clause is obvious; it was the sole remedy at the disposal of the lord against the complete appropriation of the fief by his vassal and it alone often distinguished infeudation from simple alienation. Its violation by the vassal constituted the offence *par excellence*, common enough, it appears, and source of innumerable feudal skirmishes.

But its importance was even greater if it concerned a *fief de reprise*; by voluntarily submitting to such an arrangement, the holder of an allodial fortress agreed to put it at the disposal of his new lord. The clause for the surrender of the *potestas* then usually became the sole purpose of the *convenientia*. Its role was crucial, and the counts of Barcelona showed a clear grasp of this, when, by systematically imposing such agreements on the magnates of their counties, they succeeded, in the second half of the eleventh century, in gaining access to the majority of the allodial castles of Catalonia. This policy, initiated by Ramon Berenguer I, would suffice to establish their authority over the whole aristocracy of the

---

[61] Except in exceptional cases, such as those mentioned earlier in connection with Pallars.
[62] ACA, perg. sense data, RB I, no. 105.
[63] ACA. perg., RB I, no. 153 (1054).

country.[64] It was still necessary for them to have the means to achieve this.

THE COUNT OF BARCELONA AND HIS SALARIED VASSALS: CONVENTIONS BASED ON THE MONEY FIEF

If the counts of Barcelona were able to impose themselves in this way on the great Catalan families, it was because they disposed of a host capable of keeping in check even the most ambitious. This military power derived from their financial power.

By 1052, and perhaps earlier, Ramon Berenguer I, possibly one of the richest men of his time,[65] made use of the money fief.[66] His example was soon copied by other Catalan notables, such as Ramon IV of Pallars,[67] and the bishop of Girona.[68] Systematic recourse to the money fief remained, nevertheless, a characteristic of the house of Barcelona, which alone, in the second half of the eleventh century, disposed of the necessary means.

The vassal's payment consisted of an annual rent payable at Easter or Michaelmas, of up to twenty, exceptionally as many as a hundred, ounces of gold.[69] This method of remuneration might be only temporary, intended to keep the vassal happy while he waited till it was possible for him to take effective possession of a promised fief,[70] or until he inherited his paternal honours.[71] Sometimes it was only a supplement, when, for example, a fief situated in a recently reconquered region still produced too little to constitute an adequate recompense for the vassal's service.[72]

---

[64] For the development of this policy and its results, see S. Sobrequés Vidal, *Els grans comtes de Barcelona* (Barcelona, 1961), pp. 73–7.

[65] Sobrequés Vidal (*Els grans comtes de Barcelona*, pp. 80–1) has calculated that Ramon Berenguer I and Almodis, in the ten years from 1062 to 1071, invested more than ten thousand ounces of gold in the purchase of castles or the acquisition of the counties of Carcassonne and Razès.

[66] On 15 March 1052, Ramon Berenguer I and his wife, the countess Blanca, promised an annual payment of ten ounces of gold to their vassals Guillem Seniofred and Berenguer Seniofred who held for them the castle of Santa Perpetua (ACA, perg., RB I, no. 122).

[67] ACA, perg. sense data, RB I, no. 29.

[68] AC Girona, Llibre vert, fol. 145 (1085).

[69] Twenty ounces of gold: ACA. perg., RB I, no. 387; perg. sense data, RB I, nos. 9, 10, 14; one hundred ounces of gold: perg., RB I, no. 460.

[70] ACA. perg., RB I, no. 80.

[71] ACA, perg. sense data, RB I, no. 9.

[72] ACA. perg., RB I, no. 405.

Nevertheless, in most cases the payment was sufficient in itself and the contract was of no fixed duration. It was also unconditional. The homage was always 'solid' homage, accompanied by absolute fealty. Not only did the vassal have no right to enter into new engagements, but, and on this point all such agreements are absolutely categoric, he must also break off his previous ties, repudiating all oaths sworn to former lords. His service (host, cavalcade, escort, court service etc.) was, like that of the *castlà*, continuous, and amongst the most binding which existed. The large-scale recruitment of such vassals probably constituted the most effective instrument of the hegemony exercised by Ramon Berenguer I over the whole of Catalonia at the end of his reign, all the more so in that it applied in particular among the young knights and the still unenfeoffed heirs of the great families, and thus attached to the count, by very strict ties, a whole new generation.

The place of the feudal conventions in the history of Catalan society in the eleventh century

The system of the *convenientia* thus emerges as the basis of social relations, and especially of feudo-vassalic relations, in eleventh-century Catalonia. It seems reasonable, therefore, to postulate that a period which saw agreements of this type multiply was also a period of rapid 'feudalisation' of society. This raises the problem of chronology: at which precise moment was it felt necessary to formalise in contracts of this type the new power relations which were beginning to emerge?

For the period prior to 1040, only one feudal convention is to be found in the comital archives of Barcelona, that, already quoted, which bound Count Ermengol II of Urgell to Berenguer Ramon I, and which can be dated to the years 1018–26.[73] The first substantial group of documents of this type comes from the decade 1040–50: nine *convenientiae*, six of which involve the count of Barcelona, two involve the count of Urgell and the bishop of Vic, and two were drawn up between private persons.[74] Similar acts appear at

[73] *LFM*, no. 157.
[74] ACA. perg., RB I, nos. 80, 107, 110; perg. sense data, RB I, nos. 1, 3; *LFM*, no. 433 (Barcelona); ACA, perg., RB I, nos. 92 (Vic), 48 (Urgell), 90 and 105 (covenants between private persons).

the same period in other archival deposits, unconnected with the comital archive: there are two *convenientiae*, from 1040 and 1044, in the Cartulary of Sant Cugat,[75] and two others, from 1045 and 1047, among the parchments of Poblet.[76] This first flowering is confirmed in the following decade, for which the comital archive alone has thirty or so feudal contracts.

The middle of the eleventh century, then, was clearly the period of the diffusion of the *convenientiae*; it was also a time when the county of Barcelona, vital centre of the country, went through a period of serious upheaval. Threatened by the Muslims of Saragossa and attacked by Ramon Guifred of Cerdanya, Ramon Berenguer I saw, at the start of his personal rule, a coalition of magnates rise against him. The civil wars began in 1041; Guislabert, bishop of Barcelona, the viscount Udalard, the dowager countess Ermessend and, above all, the man who quickly became the inspiration of the revolt, Mir Geribert, the most powerful of the frontier barons, all participated in their turn. Briefly pacified in 1044, the conflict broke out with renewed vigour in 1049, only ending in 1058, and then by a compromise.[77] Should we see a relation of cause and effect between the outbreak of violence and the proliferation of feudal covenants? The two parties, driven by circumstances, were no doubt compelled to seek allies and recruit warriors, thus to grant fiefs, and the *convenientia* lent itself naturally to such transactions.

But it is difficult to see the covenants as no more than the product of a temporary crisis. Nor is there anything to prove that such agreements were uncommon before 1040; oral pacts almost certainly preceded the written acts. By the time that it emerges from the shadows in the reign of Ramon Berenguer I, the feudal agreement seems already to be endowed with all its attributes and its own technical vocabulary, and the formulas which it employs seem already polished by use. The *convenientiae* of 1040–60 are surely the heirs of a first generation of feudal pacts, of which we have a vestige in the single document surviving from 1018–26.

If we thus push back in time the date of the birth of the feudal covenants, the question remains: to what politico-social context should we attribute the phenomenon of their appearance? It is

---

[75] *Cartulario de Sant Cugat del Vallès*, 2, nos. 553, 571.
[76] AHN, Clero, carp. 1992, nos. 4, 7.
[77] See Sobrequés Vidal, *Els grans comtes de Barcelona*, pp. 56–65, 71–3.

surely to the process of the disintegration of public authority which did not wait for the crisis of 1041–58 to be made manifest. With the death of Ramon Borrell in 1018, the vast territorial grouping which constituted the counties of Barcelona, Osona and Girona entered a long phase of weakening central power; two minorities, those of Berenguer Ramon I from 1018 to 1023, and Ramon Berenguer I from 1035 to 1041, during which the regency was exercised by a woman, the countess Ermessend, separated by the rule of a weak and even openly despised prince, Berenguer Ramon I, sufficed to emancipate the great Catalan families.[78] It is hardly surprising that, given this deficiency in public authority, these same families developed the system of the *convenientiae*, a system, that is, which enabled them to settle their problems amongst themselves, without reference to a superior authority. The example was provided by Languedoc, near at hand, where the collapse of public institutions had been both earlier and more complete, and where the habit of concluding private pacts between families was formed as early as the tenth century.[79] The Languedocian *convenientiae* were not yet feudal conventions, it is true, but the form existed, and the Catalan aristocracy had no difficulty in adapting it to new social conditions.

In sum, we may now propose – as a provisional conclusion, or rather as a working hypothesis – the following schema. Firstly, prior to 1020, the *convenientia* was unknown in Catalonia. The regular exercise of a public justice entrusted to a group of highly qualified, professional judges who were appointed by the count, and the subjection of all alike to the same written law, the Visigothic law, so frequently cited in contemporary documents,

---

[78] For the reign of Berenguer Ramon I, we can refer to the opinion of the *Gesta comitum Barcinonensium*, which, though compiled in the twelfth century, transmit the memories of this count held amongst the aristocracy: Post Raimundum vero Borrelli, Berengarius filius eius tenuit comitatum Barchinonae, nihilque ibi boni gessit, immo in omni vita sua parentelae probitate fuit inferior (*Gesta*, cap. IX, ed. L. Barrau Dihigo i J. Massó Torrents (Barcelona, 1925), p. 30). The attempts of certain Catalan historians, in particular Bofarull, to rehabilitate Berenguer Ramon I are not very convincing.

[79] Archibald R. Lewis dates the weakness of comital authority in the domains of the house of Toulouse-Rouergue to the period 950–75 (*The development of Southern French and Catalan Society (718–1050)* (Austin, 1965), pp. 204–7). This was also the period when the first *convenientiae* appeared in southern France: acts of 961, 960, 989 etc. (Ourliac, 'La "convenientia" ', pp. 415–18).

enabled the disputes arising between the great families to be satisfactorily settled and rendered recourse to procedures of a private nature unnecessary. These same families readily submitted to the authority of a count, in this case Ramon Borrell, who, by his expeditions into Islamic territory, showed himself capable of procuring for them both glory and booty: so there were no cabals, no conspiracies, no pacts. Nor, in fact, true feudalism: the fief remained a strictly public institution, a public property granted by the count to reward public service.[80] Finally, though it is impossible to speak with absolute confidence on this point, the vassalic network seems to have been confined to the count's own followers; there are, at least, very few tenth-century examples of the epithet *senior meus* being applied to anyone other than him.

Secondly, from about 1020, Catalan society experienced a rapid development – even a veritable revolution – of which the *convenientiae* constitute one of the most spectacular evidences. This took place under the impetus of two factors.

The first, already discussed, was the temporary weakening of comital power. For the space of a generation, from 1018 (death of Ramon Borrell) to 1041 (majority of Ramon Berenguer I), the count of Barcelona, whether due to extreme youth or physical or moral defects, was incapable of exercising his traditional function as war-lord. This was a serious matter in a frontier region where the danger was constant and where, what is more, the razzia into Islamic territory remained the aristocracy's most lucrative activity. The magnates thus acquired the habit of acting alone and on their own account, and this, for them unprecedented, situation impelled them to new measures: the quest for new leaders, the natural leader having defaulted, engagement of warriors, with fiefs of a new type (now of private origin) as payment and the search for alliances between families. Thus were born the first of those pacts which, because they now stipulated a bond between man and man, and were sanctioned by the surrender of fiefs, merit the term feudal convention. They were simple oral contracts to begin with,

---

[80] On this point, we should remember the statement of Elisabeth Magnou, 'Note sur le sens du mot "fevum" en Septimanie et dans la Marche d'Espagne à la fin du Xe et au début du XIe siècle', *Annales du Midi*, 76 (1964), 141–52: 'As far back as one can go and up to 1020–1030, [the fief] appears as a life tenure granted in a piece of land subject to the public authority, by the public authority, to an agent of this authority.' I believe this conclusion to be absolutely correct.

and confined to the high aristocracy. Born of the necessities of war, such private accords proliferated with the decline of a public justice whose decisions the count was often unable to make respected, and it is typical to see, in the documentation from the years 1030–50, the number of references to law-suits steadily diminish while those to *convenientiae* increase; the compromise negotiated between families little by little replaced the sentence of the judge.

If the relative eclipse of comital power had the effect of permitting the spread of the system of the *convenientiae* amongst the *proceres*, another phenomenon indirectly favoured its diffusion amongst the lower ranks of the aristocracy: the unusually precocious economic growth experienced by eleventh-century Catalonia. There was a spectacular increase in trade, certainly, as a result of the massive entry of Muslim gold, but even more, though less visible, an increase of agricultural production. Assarting, irrigation, arboriculture – all this human labour enabled the production, at least in the richest lands, the Pla of Barcelona, the Vallès and the plain of Vic, of a surplus. The appropriation of this surplus value of peasant labour constituted, of course, one of the major concerns of the high aristocracy, which was extremely successful, by means of the well-known process of establishing the *seigneurie banale* and imposing the 'new customs'. The lynch-pin of this policy was the *castlà*, whose essential function was to put pressure on the peasants dependent on the castle, defend the revenues from this exploitation against the activities of neighbouring lords and, lastly, with his knights, launch pillaging raids (*cavalcatas*) into adjacent castellanies. Given the importance of the profits at stake, it was necessary to spell them out in due form in contracts: hence a second series of *convenientiae* concluded between the lords of castles and their castellans, relating to the custody of the castles and regulating the service of the garrisons.

But, in the end, in the midst of all this confusion, it was economic growth which saved comital power. In practice, the count, through the privileged position he occupied, through the vastness of his landed estates, through the control he exercised over foreign trade (principally with Islam) and through the quasi-monopoly he enjoyed over the issue of money,[81] was the one who, by far, drew

---

[81] An effective monopoly in the counties of Barcelona and Girona. In the county of Osona, the bishops of Vic and the viscounts of Cardona also possessed mints. For the monetary problems of Catalonia in the eleventh century, J. Botet i Siso, *Les monedes catalanes*, vol. 1 (Barcelona, 1905) remains today the most valuable study.

the greatest profit from the new resources. And it was the count who introduced the power of cash into the world of feudo- vassalic relations. This was accomplished under Ramon Berenguer I: by 1052, he had concluded the first agreements providing for the engagement of paid knights. This was a first step, but a decisive one: the policy seemed to bear rapid fruit and the count of Barcelona recovered a dominant place in the Catalonia of his time. His gold and his host impressed the *proceres* of his counties, who, one by one, in the middle of the feudal crisis, approached him to negotiate *convenientiae*. These were fairly loose pacts, which specified hardly any service and almost never 'solid' homage, but which, by the clause for the surrender of *potestas*, opened up the fortresses of his vassals to Ramon Berenguer I. The revolt of the feudatories was cut short, and with the coalition dissolving, its leader, Mir Geribert, came, in his turn, in 1058, to seek from the count a negotiated compromise.[82]

From this point on, the way was clear: the *convenientiae*, increasingly numerous and more and more detailed, would be the instrument by which the count of Barcelona attached to himself the members of his aristocracy, and systematised, within his counties and beyond, and always very much to his own benefit, feudo-vassalic relations. Thus Catalonia, a country in which, at the beginning of the eleventh century, vassalage and the fief enjoyed only a marginal role, would become, less than three-quarters of a century later, and by means of the *convenientia*, one of the most 'feudalised' countries in Europe.

Appendix: Three types of feudal convention

1. From castellan to *castlà*: type of convention concluded for the custody of a castle

25 August 1068

Arnau Pere entrusts to Berenguer Ramon his castle of Barberà, grants him as a fief various defined revenues within the castellany, delegates to him his right of ban *and promises him an annual pension in cash: in return, Berenguer Ramon engages himself to be the 'solid' man of Arnau Pere and to perform the service attached to the custody of the castle.*

---

[82] For this negotiation, Sobrequés Vidal, *Els grans comtes de Barcelona*, pp. 72–3, who uses the documents published in the *LFM*.

Original: ACA, perg. RB I, no. 405. Twelfth- century copy: perg., no. 405 duplicate.

Hec est conveniencia que est inter Arnallus Petri et Berengarius Raimondi de ipsum castrum de Barbera. Comendo tibi ipsum castrum iamdictum e dono tibi ipso fevo medietatem de ipsas decimas et ipsas estacamentum et quartam partem de ipsos placitos, e pledeg ipsos placitos exceptus qugucia et umedii [*omicidium* in twelfth century copy] que pledeg Arnal Pere cum suo bale. Et dono tibi ego Arnaldus Petri ad te Berengarii Raimundo mandamentum et districtum et senioraticum super ipsos homines. Et dono tibi ipsas iovas et tragins cum ipsa ferreria et medietatem de ipsas trobas et medietatem de ipsos quarters qui inde exierint. Et dono tibi ipsas gautas et civadas et de totos alios usaticos ipsam quartam partem, exceptus dominicaturas de comite. Et dono tibi alaudio ad tuum dominicum a tres parels de bous in ipsa coma de Col qui pergit ad Apiera. Et dono tibi, per unoquoque anno, de una festa resurrectione ad aliam, X uncias de auro. Et per ista donacione qui est superscripta, cove Berenguer Ramond ad Arnalus Petri que sia suo solido contra cunctos homines et feminas et que sia estadant de Barbera die cotide si terc de cavalers et faciatis ostes e cavalcades e cortes e pleds e segies et sitis adiutor et valedor contra cunctos homines et femines de ipsa onore que habeo vel in antea acaptare potuero cum tuo consilio.

Actum est hoc VII kal. september, anno VIIII regnante Filipo rege.

Sig+num Arnalus Petri qui ista conveniencia mandavi scribere et ad testes firmare rogavi.

Sig+num Raimondus Gonbaldi.

Sig+num Giem Raimondus que vocant Botet.

Sig+num Giem Mir.

Bernardus sacer qui ista conveniencia scripsit die et anno quod supra.

2. Between magnates: type of convention concluded between men of the same rank and power

9 December 1072

Ramon [IV], count of Pallars [Jussà] gives as allod or fief to Artau [I], count [of Pallars Sobirà], a certain number of fortresses and villae, *pledges others and swears not to attack his life, members or honours; in return, Artau restores to Ramon other castles, other* villae *and the monastery of Lavaix, promises to do homage and take an oath, and to his son, and to surrender to him, on request, the castles received as fief, in witness to which he also pledges a castle; the contracting parties agree, lastly, on the conduct to be followed in case of the death of one or the other or their heirs.*

Original: ACA, perg. RB I, no. 449. Twelfth-century copy: perg. no. 449 duplicate.

Haec est conveniencia que facta est inter Raimundum comitem Paliarensem et Artallum comitem. Convenit namque prefatus comes Raimundus que donet ad predictum Artallum ipsas valles de Anavo, hoc quod fuit de Guilelmo Suniario, pater Artallo, per alodem siat de prefato Artallo similiter per alodem. Et hoc quod fuit et est de prenominato comite Raimundo teneat Artallo comite per fevum de predictum comitem Raimundum. Item convenit ei quod donet ei ipso Vallato cum suas pertinencias per fevum et quod donet ei ipso castro de Monterosso per alodem cum suis pertinenciis. Et item convenit ei que comandet ei Petro Raimundo cum ipso castro de Claverolo que donat ad eum per fevum, salvam suam fidelitatem. Item comendat ad eum Rodger Umberto aut filium suum cum ipso castro de Valle Senniz cum suas pertinencias, que donat ad eum per fevum, salvam suam fidelitatem. Et istos supradictos duos castros Claverol et Valle Senniz in tale conventu que non tollet nec mutet inde ipsos castellanos qui ibi sunt nec illorum posterita, nisi per forisfactura que non posseant emendare aut noleant. Et si ipsos castellanos aut illorum posterita de hoc seculo hobierint aut perdiderint per predictas forisfacturas, fiant illos castellanos qui ibi missuri sunt ad lodamentum et voluntatem de prenominato comite Raimundo. Item convenit ei Raimundus prescriptus que donet ei ipsa villa de Boi et ipsa de Eril et comendet ad eum Mironi Guerreta, et donet ad eum per fevum. Item convenit ei que dimittat ad eum ipsa honore de Sanctum Petrum de Malezas. Item convenit Raimundo, prenominato comite, que iuret ad Artallo prescripto sua vita et sua membra et suum honorem et que unquam non aprehendat eum. Item namque mitit in pignora Raimundo prenominato ad Artallum prescriptum ipsum castrum de Speluncha Rotunda, cum ipsa valle de Badanui, cum suis pertinenciis, in tale conveniencia que teneat Bernard et fiat per hoc suo homine de Artallo et iuret ei que si Raimundo comite non tenia ista fine qui erat facta inter eos et foresfactura fazia Raimundo comite prescripto ad Artallo prenominato et inter centum dies que Artallum prescriptum querellasset ei per se aut per suum nuncium ad Raimundo comite, Raimundus iamdictus fecisset directum ad Artallum prescriptum, et si non faciebat ad illum directum aut facere non voluerit inter centum dies iamdictos, tendat Bernardus prenominatus ad prescripto Artallo cum ipso kastro de Spelunca Rotunda, sive cum ipsa valle de Badanui et sine engan de prescripto Artallo. Et si ad Bernard mors venerit, similiter faciat aut faciant ipsos castellanos aut castellanum que Raimundus comes prescriptus metra in supradictum kastrum, similiter tendat aut tendant ad Artallo prescripto et siant suos homines et iurant ad Artallo isto sacramento prescripto sine suo engan. Et si Bernardus obierit, tantum teneant sui homines istum castrum donec ipsi kastellani que Raimundus comes ibi miserit abeat afidatum ad Artallum prenominatum per sacramento et per hominatico, ita sicut Bernardus prescriptus fecit. Et propter hoc quos superius scriptum est, convenit Artallus prescriptus ad Raimundo comite prelibato que fenescat illi kastrum de Toralla, cum suis terminis et pertinenciis, et ipso chastro de Eril, cum suis terminis et pertinenciis, et ipsas valles de Bovi et de valle Orzera, simul cum ipsas villas que detenet Raimundus comes et simul cum ipso cenobio de Sancta Maria de Lavais, cum suis terminis et pertinenciis, et ipsum kastrum de Enrense et de Adonce, cum illorum terminis et pertinenciis, et ipsum kastrum de Castelaz, similiter cum suis terminis et pertinenciis, et ipsos kastros de Puimannos et de Tenrui et de la Petra et de Tormeda, cum illorum terminis et pertinenciis, similiter castro de Charcho, cum suis terminis et pertinenciis, et ipso termino qui fuit de Castelo, qui est de Gordia usque ad Puio Alto et ipsos terminos de Arin et de Orrid, quomodo illorum directum est, hoc totum quod superius est scriptum, convenit Artallus prescriptus ad Raimundo comite prenominato que ei fenescat et iachescat per fide, et sine engan. Item convenit ei Artallus prescriptus ad Raimundum iamdictum que siat suo homine comendato et de suo filio et iuret ei fidelitatem et suam vitam et suis membris et suam honorem et que iam no aprehendat eum. Iterum convenit que de istos kastros prescriptos que donat comite Raimundo ad Artallum per fevo, Artallus prescriptus donet potestatem ad Raimundo prenominato per quantas vices ille requisierit per se ipse ipsum aut per suos misos vel misum. Et si Raimundus obierit et Artallus vivus fuerit, similiter donet potestatem de supradictos castellos ad Valencia comitissa, coniux prenominato Raimundo, et ad Petro filio suo, et tales conveniencias faciat ad Petro suo filio et tales sacramentos et tales pignoras mittat sicut modo facit ad Raimundo prenominato. Et propter hoc quod superius scriptum est, mittit in pignore Artallo prescriptus ad Raimundus prenominatum ipsum castrum de Vivo, cum suis terminis et pertinenciis, in tale conventu que Bertrandus Atoni teneat supradictum castrum de Vivalavata et fiat suo homine de Raimundo comite et iuret ei que si Artallo comes no tenia ista conveniencia et ista fine qui erat inter eos et foresfactura fazia Artallus prescriptus ad Raimundum prenominatum, que ei emendet inter centum dies que ille querallaverit per se aut per suos nuncios et si emendare non voluerit aut non emendat inter istos centum dies, atendat prefatus Bertrando ad Raimundo comite prescripto, cum ipso chastro de Vivalavata, cum suis pertinenciis, sine engan de Raimundo prescripto. Et si Bertrandus hobierit, similiter faciat filius suus, cui ille dubitaverit supradictum castrum in suo testamento vel verbis, de hominatico et de pignora et de sacramento ad Raimundo comite. Et si Raimundus obierit, similiter faciat Bertrandus aut filius suus qui ipsum castrum tenuerit ad Valenciam comitissam et ad filium vel ad filios, filiam vel filias ad cui

Raimundus comes dubitaverit suam honorem in suo testamento vel verbis, et similiter apreendat per suam manum sive per illorum manus, sicut
modo apreendit per manu de Raimundo prescripto omnem fevum quod
suprascriptum est, et donet eis potestatem de supradictos castros Claverol
et Cheralto. Et conveniunt inter se ipsos ut si unusquisque voluerit edifi-
care chastros infra terminos de illorum kastros, licenciam habeant sine
querela ex utraque parte. Et si Artallus obierit et Raimundus prescriptus
vivus fuerit, aut unum de filiis vel filiabus suis ad cui ille suam honorem
dimiserit, similiter tendant et atendant ista conveniencia ad ipsum vel ad
ipsos, ad ipsa vel ad ipsas cui Artallus dubitaverit vel dimiserit suam
honorem, de conveniencias et sacramentos vel pignoras.

Hactum est hoc V idus december, in anno XIII regni Philipo.

Sig+num Raimundus comitis, signum Valencia comitissa, signum
Sunarius que vocant Artallo, qui ista conveniencia mandavimus scribere
testesque firmare rogavimus.

Sig+num Bertran Ato.

Sig+num Rodger Umbert.

Sig+num Oliver Bernard.

Sig+num Petro Folco.

3. Engagement by the count and countess of Barcelona of a paid knight (1052–71)[1]

*Berenguer Riculf engages to be the 'solid' man of the count Ramon
[Berenguer I] and the countess Almodis and to perform the service
attached to this position; the count and countess promise him in return
an annual payment of twenty ounces of gold.*

Original: ACA, perg. sense data, RB I, no. 14.

Haec est convenientia que facta est inter domnum Remundum, Barch-
inonensem comitem, et domnam Almodem comitissam et Berengarium
Riculfi, filium Adalaizis.

Convenit iamdictus Berengarius Riculfi predictis comiti et comitisse ut
ab hac hora et deincebs sit solidus illorum, sine engan, et non fatiat ullum
seniorem sine illorum licentia et absolutione et de ipsos quos habet non
retineat ullum set desfidet eos, sine engan, si predicti comes et comitissa
velint. Et stet assidue cum iamdictis comite et comitissa et faciat eis hostes
et cavalgadas et curtes et placitos et seguimentum, sine illorum engan, et
faciat guerram per illos et teneat pacem illis hominibus quibus ipsi
voluerint, et fatiat directum et iusticiam per eos, et amet amantibus illos et

---

[1] Undated, but after the marriage of Ramon Berenguer I and Almodis (1052)
and the death of Almodis (1071).

voleat malum sine engan ad illos inimicos. Et faciat per eos hoc totum quod homo debet facere per suum meliorem seniorem.

Et ut predictus Berengarius bene et sinceriter attendat et teneat totas istas supradictas convenientias iamdicti comiti et comitisse, conveniunt ei ad dare per unumquemque annum XX uncias auri monete Barchinone de mancusos atalis, excepto alio bene et honore quod illi fecerint si bene servit eis.

7. The noble and the ignoble: a new nobility and a new servitude in Catalonia at the end of the eleventh century*

Catalan society was already, towards the year 1000, divided by barriers of blood into two quite distinct classes: above were the *maximi*, the *majores*, the *nobiles* (the words were synonymous), below, the *minimi*, the *minores*, the *inferiores*. The *maximi*, of illustrious birth, enjoyed a monopoly of power, under the superior authority of the count. The *minimi* obeyed. This antithesis was tempered, however, by a number of factors, amongst them, most importantly, respect for the law – and the limits it imposed on the arbitrary actions of the great – and the protection accorded by the counts to village franchises. The lesser people, then, a few residual pockets of servitude apart, were free, and their liberty was based on the allodial nature of most peasant holdings and on the capacity to bear arms.[1]

A century later, the gulf not only still existed, but was far wider. The harsh realities of economic growth had had the effect of accentuating the disparities. At the same time, in the fever of violence provoked by the lure of new wealth, the liberties of the peasants had been destroyed. The degradation of their condition was apparent in all areas of life. Vocabulary itself bears witness to it: while the terms *minimi* and *minores* were in no way pejorative, the term *ignobiles* which replaced them was redolent of contempt. Even before 1100, *ignobilis* had become a synonym for *vilis*.[2]

But it is not enough to show that the gulf separating noble and

* This text comprises chapter 15 (pp. 781–829) of my thesis, *La Catalogne du milieu du Xe à la fin du XIe siècle: croissance et mutations d'une société*, vol. 2 (Toulouse, 1976).
[1] *La Catalogne*, vol. 1, pp. 282–4, 307–16.
[2] *Nobili et vili homines*: Cart. Urgell 1, no. 755 (1059); *Nobilis vel ignobilis: ibid.*, no. 504 (1083); *Nobili aut vili persona; ibid.*, no. 302 (1084); *Nobilis aut vilis: ibid.*, no. 459 (1094) etc.

ignoble had increased; we need also to ask whether the composition of these two social groups had changed. We need to pay particular attention to the study of the nobility at the end of the eleventh century in view of the divergences of opinion which have split historians on this question.[3] Was the new nobility descended from the old aristocracy of the early Middle Ages or had the nobility as a body been radically renewed by an influx of new blood? This raises the major problem of the relationship between nobility and knighthood, associated with the no less important, though less often discussed, problem of changes in the size of the noble class. As far as the peasantry is concerned, the fierceness of the debates between specialists about the origins and forms of the 'new servitude' is too well known for its importance to need emphasis.

The new nobility

Whoever kills a viscount or wounds or dishonours him in any fashion, should make reparation as for two *comtors*; for one *comtor*, the reparation should be as for two vavassors. (*Usatges* 4)

In the case of the vavassor who has five *milites*, his murder carries a reparation of 60 ounces of refined gold; for wounding, 30. If he has more *milites*, the composition will increase in proportion to their number. Whoever kills a *miles* will give a composition of 12 ounces of gold. Whoever injures one, inflicting one or more wounds, owes him 6 ounces of gold in reparation. (*Usatges* 5)

These dispositions from articles 4 and 5 of the *Usatges of Barcelona* are amongst the oldest – even, perhaps, the oldest – in the Code.[4] They establish a noble hierarchy with four levels (viscounts, *comtors*, vavassors and *milites*), to which we should add one higher level, that of the counts. We need to ask how the men of the eleventh century had come to define this stratification of levels within the aristocracy and how it corresponded to reality. We should note at once, since it is not simply by chance, that the authors of the document established a distance between viscounts

---

[3] There are surveys of the debate in G. Duby, 'The nobility in medieval France' in *The Chivalrous Society*, trans. C. Postan (London, 1977), pp. 94–111 and L. Genicot, 'La noblesse au Moyen âge dans l'ancienne Francie: continuité, rupture ou évolution?', *Annales*, 17 (1962).

[4] They can thus be dated to the period 1060–70 and attributed to Ramon Berenguer I and Almodis.

and *comtors* on the one hand, and vavassors and *milites* on the other, the clauses relating to each group being divided between two separate articles.

COUNTS, VISCOUNTS AND *COMTORS*: SURVIVAL AND PRE-EMINENCE OF THE OLD LINEAGES

The comital and viscomital lineages

From 1060–70, all the attributes of sovereign power in Catalonia were in the hands of the house of Barcelona. The majority of the other comital families (Urgell, Pallars, Cerdanya, Besalú, Empúries (Ampurias) and Rosselló (Roussillon)) were resigned to this state of affairs, and confined their ambitions to the pursuit of glory and riches in the wake of the prince of Barcelona.[5] Or, seeing their prospects blocked within Catalonia, they went off to try their chances in foreign fields: in Castile and Provence in the case of the Ermengols of Urgell.[6] Of the Catalan counts, only Pons Hug II of Empúries attempted to fight to retain the last vestiges of his independence; a vain attempt, totally defeated by the military reprisals carried out against him by Ramon Berenguer III in 1128.[7]

But, for all that they had lost their ancient power, the comital families remained at the top of the social hierarchy. Able to boast of ancestors already famous at the time of Charlemagne, the counts were, through their blood and their renown, the first among the vassals. This rank remained theirs until the extinction of their lineages, which happened during the course of the twelfth century in most cases, at the beginning of the thirteenth century in the case of the counts of Urgell, and only in the fourteenth century for the counts of Empúries. Their inheritance was then claimed either by the house of Barcelona or, in the case of Urgell and Empúries, by the viscomital families to which they were related.

The fate of the viscomital lineages was little different. By the end of the eleventh century, the viscounts had lost all their attributes of public office; they had long ceased to be the devoted lieutenants of the counts in the administration of their counties.

---

[5] Like Hug II of Empúries, who actively supported Ramon Berenguer III in the expedition to Majorca in 1116.
[6] *La Catalogne*, vol. 2, pp. 863, 865.
[7] For these events, S. Sobrequés Vidal, *Els barons de Catalunya* (Barcelona, 1957), pp. 16–19.

Table 5. *Members of the court of the counts of Urgell in the eleventh century (the dates are those of the different sessions known)*

Families	1024	1028	1036	1048	1057	1077	1087	1094	1100	1102
Benavent	—	—	—	—	Bernard Trasver	Bernard Trasver	—	—	—	Guillem Bernard
Caboet	Isarn	Isarn	Isarn	Isarn	Dalmaz Isarn	—	—	Guitard Isarn Ramon Mir	—	Guitard Isarn
Capolat	—	Trasver	—	—	—	—	—	—	—	—
Clara	Ricard	—	—	—	—	—	—	—	—	—
Concabella (?)	—	—	—	—	—	Guillem Arnau	—	—	—	Mir
Conques	—	—	—	—	—	—	—	—	—	Arnau Guillem Guitard
Florejacs	—	—	—	Eriman	—	—	Mir & Pons Eriman	Mir Eriman	—	—
La Fabrica	Mir	—	—	—	—	—	—	—	—	—
La Vansa	Guillem	Guillem	Guillem	—	—	—	—	—	Guillem Gauzbert	Guillem Gauzbert
Mediano	Guillem	—	—	—	—	—	—	Ramon Guitard	—	—
Montferrer	Daco	—	—	—	—	—	Arnau Daco	—	Pere Arnau	Tedbal Arnau Pere
Pinell	Guitard	—	—	—	—	—	—	—	—	Ramon
Ponts	Mir	Mir	—	—	Pere Mir	—	—	—	—	Pere Arnau

Puigvert	—	—	—	—	—	—	—	—	—	—	—	Berenguer Ramon	Berenguer Ramon
Ribelles	—	—	—	—	—	—	—	—	—	—	—	—	—
Solsona	Mir	—	—	—	—	—	—	—	Ramon Gombal	—	Ramon Gombal	Ramon Gombal	—
Taravall	Borrell	Ramon Borrell	Borrell	Borrell	—	—	—	—	Ramon Geral	—	Ramon Geral	Ramon Geral	Ramon Geral Bernard Ecard
Tarrega	—	—	—	—	—	—	—	—	Ecard Mir	Ecard Mir	—	—	—
Tartareu	—	—	—	—	—	—	—	—	—	—	—	—	—
Taus	—	—	—	—	—	—	—	—	—	—	Guillem Guitard	—	—
Tolo	Maior	—	—	—	—	—	—	—	—	—	Ramon Guillem	Ramon Guillem	Ramon Guillem
Tost	Arnau Mir	Arnau Mir	Arnau Mir	Arnau Mir	Arnau Mir	—	Arnau Mir	Arnau Mir	—	—	—	—	—
Unidentified	Ricard Altemir Guadal Domnuz Bonfill Sans	Ricard Altemir	Berenger Altemir	Ricard Altemir	Ramon Bonfill	Ramon Bonfill	Berenguer Ricard	Berenguer Ricard	—	—	—	—	Sans Eribal Ramon Barnard
				Ramon Bonfill Hug Guillem Ramon Guerruz			Arnau Bonfill	Arnau Bonfill					

References: AC Urgell, Cart. I, nos. 228, 197, 44, 42, 176, 473, 33, 31, 485, 32.

Table 6. *Dates of extinction of the comital and viscomital families of the early Middle Ages (male lines)*

Comital families		Viscomital families	
Besalú	1111	Besalú (Bas)	1127
Cerdanya	1118	Cerdanya (Urtg)	1134
Rosselló	1172	Barcelona	1207
Lower Pallars	1177	Urgell (Castellbò)	1226
Upper Pallars	1199	Girona (Cabrera)	1477
Urgell	1209	Empúries (Rocaberti) ⎱ early modern	
Empúries	1322	Osona (Cardona) ⎰ period	
Barcelona	1410		

They became *seigneurs banaux* – the first such – and their power lay in their tenure of a number of important castellanies. The evolution of their titles reflects this transformation; they ceased to be called by the name of the county they were deemed to administer under the direction of the count and assumed the name of their patrimonial castellany. First, by 1057, the viscounts of Vallespir called themselves viscounts of Castellnou, followed by the viscounts of Besalú (viscounts of Bas), Urgell (Castellbò), Rosselló (Tatzó), Empúries (Rocaberti) and Girona (Cabrera).[8] Only the viscounts of Barcelona failed to conform, but, crushed and reduced to inactivity by the power of the counts of Barcelona, they left Catalonia; Reverter Guislabert (1124–46) and his son, Berenguer Reverter, spent their lives in Morocco.[9]

Some of these viscomital houses, all originating in the ninth or tenth centuries, died out soon after 1100. The others survived and succeeded to those which had disappeared; they then embarked on a period of growth which continued unchecked till the end of the Middle Ages, sometimes even into the early modern period.[10] Drawing strength from their territorial powers and landed wealth, connected to the highest comital and soon royal families, they

---

[8] The evolution of the viscomital title has been briefly studied by J. Miret i Sans, *Investigación histórica sobre el vizcondado de Castellbó* (Barcelona, 1900), pp. 34–6.

[9] Their adventures are described by F. Carreras Candi, 'Relaciones de los vizcondes de Barcelona con los Arabes' in *Homenaje a Codera* (1904), pp. 207–15. See also *La Catalogne*, vol. 2, p. 865.

[10] The story of this rise constitutes the principal theme of Sobrequés Vidal's *Els barons de Catalunya*, a remarkable achievement of dynastic history.

accumulated titles and honours. Thus the Cabrera viscounts of Girona acquired by 1066, through marriage, the new viscounty of Ager, in the county of Urgell; in 1220, they themselves became counts of Urgell, in 1335 counts of Osona and in 1394 counts of Modica in Sicily. The Cardona provided, in the late Middle Ages, constables of Aragon and viceroys of Catalonia, Sicily and Naples. The destiny of the Rocaberti, descendants of the early Baró, viscount of Empúries before 989,[11] was no less elevated.

It is, therefore, immediately apparent that it is a mistake to pose – as so many historians tend to do – the question of the survival of the old nobility of function of the early Middle Ages only in terms of 'decadence' or 'impoverishment'. In Catalonia, all the major lineages entered the twelfth century with their brilliance undimmed, and those who survived the twelfth century concentrated in their hands an increasing amount of riches and power. This phenomenon, apparent at the level of the counts and viscounts, can also be seen at the level of the castellans.

The *comtors*

The term *comtor* (or *comitor*) appears for the first time in a document of 1045: Alamany de Cervelló and his wife, Sicards, when selling a vineyard and a piece of uncultivated land in their castellany of Cervelló to a couple of peasants, prohibited the resale of this property *ad comite nec ad comitore*.[12] From 1060 on, the word became common and, used in the plural, described, within each county, a distinct social group: *ipsos comdors de Gerunda*,[13] *comtores de Urgello*.[14]

The *comtors* constituted, in fact, the high aristocracy of the late eleventh century: those who were close to the count, formed his court and held their fiefs only from him.[15] A *comtoria* (the word was coined at the very end of the century) was a group of honours (fiefs) held directly from the count by a magnate.[16] Comital favour thus played a not unimportant role in the power and wealth of this

---

[11] *La Catalogne*, vol. 1, p. 171.
[12] AC Barcelona, Divers. B, perg. no. 1446.
[13] *LFM*, 1, no. 403 (1061).   [14] *LFM*, 1, no. 147 (*c.* 1067).
[15] See, in particular, *LFM*, 1, no. 265 (1072) where Ramon Berenguer I uses the term to denote a direct feudatory.
[16] First use in 1097, J. Miret i Sans, 'Documents en langue catalane', *Revue hispanique*, 19 (1908), 12–13.

group, but was not in itself a sufficient explanation; it was from their ancestors that the *comtors* derived their glory and their wealth.

They were the grandsons and great-grandsons of the *proceres*, the *optimates* and the *preclarissimi viri* who were already witnessing comital charters around the year 1000. They can therefore be seen, absolutely unequivocally, as the descendents of the old curial nobility of the early Middle Ages. Their names are those of the castellanies which their ancestors administered as vicars. Whenever it is possible to reconstruct genealogies, they go directly back to the dominant families of the tenth century: the Caboets and the La Vansas, mentioned as *comtors* towards 1067, already figured at the court of Ermengol I in 997,[17] Gerau Alamany of Cervelló, who fought the Cid alongside Berenguer Ramon II, was the grandson of Hug of Cervelló, counsellor at the court of Count Ramon Borrell, and great-nephew of the vicar Enneg Bonfill, leader of the embassy despatched to Cordova in 971 and, even further back, descended in direct line from the vicars of Gurb (Ansulf and Sindered) who directed the movement of repopulation in the region of Vic.[18]

The study of the subscriptions to comital acts confirms this remarkable continuity in recruitment to the high nobility. In the county of Urgell, for example, some twenty families provided the totality of the ruling personnel from the beginning of the eleventh century (it is impossible to go further back without risk of errors of identification) to the beginning of the twelfth century;[19] soundings in the documents of a later period show that this monopoly was even preserved much later.[20] It is the same for the other counties, where the same names recur, decade after decade, at the foot of official documents.

It is true that some families died out, at least in the male line: the Besora-Montbuy, for example, in the county of Osona.[21] But, conversely, some lineages split into autonomous branches, starting

---

[17] *LFM*, 1, no. 147 (*c*. 1067); AC Urgell, Cart. 1, no. 230 (997).
[18] For the Gurb-Cervelló family, see *La Catalogne*, vol. 1, pp. 290–1 and note 146.
[19] See table 6.
[20] AC Urgell, Cart. 1, nos. 149 (1104), 411 (1116), 412 (1126), 87 (1137), 5 (1149).
[21] Gombal of Besora died not long after 1050, without male heir; his inheritance was acquired by his son-in-law, Mir Geribert, in well-known and dramatic circumstances (*La Catalogne*, vol. 2, p. 643).

Table 7. *Castles bequeathed in magnates' wills (1060–1110)*

Reference	Date	Testator	Castles bequeathed
AHN, Poblet, carp. 1992, no. 2	1061	Pere Mir de Ponts	Ponts, Solsona, Agramunt, Almenara, Puigverd, Oliola. Unidentified: *Baiona*
AHN, Poblet, carp. 1995, no. 19	1069	Bernard Pere (called Vidian) de Ponts	Ponts, Solsona, Agramunt, Almenara, Oliola, Clariana de Cardener, Barberà, Piera, Prenafeta, Puigverd. Unidentified: *Baiona, Castellans subirans et sutirans*
Cart. Urgell, I, no. 585	1071	Ramon Mir d'Orcau	Orcau, Basturs, Claverol, Figuerola, Peralba Unidentified: *Neslia, Mesons, Bescarbo*
ACA, RB II, no. 26	1077	Folc Ermengol d'Oló	Oló, Aquiló, Corbera, in part: Odena
Cart. Urgell, no. 59	1092	Bernard Trasver de Benavent	Benavent, la Guardia, Figuera, Castelló de Farfanyà
Cart. Urgell, I, no. 70	1094	Gaucerand Eriman	Ager, Estopanyà, Peralba, Suterranya, Pennelles, Florejacs, Santalinya, Trago, Corçà Unidentified: Petra, Fabregada, Camporells
AC Vic, perg. 1554	1105	Guillem Ramon de Calders	Calders, Segur, La Granada, Gelida, Rubí, Fals, Castellfullit del Boix Unidentified: Soris, Valle Lordo, Colonge

new dynasties.[22] Overall, the numbers of the high nobility (of families, that is, the number of individuals proving impossible to count) seem to have remained fairly stable. The *comtors*, like the tenth-century *proceres*, represented only a tiny layer at the top of the social hierarchy.

Their small number made them rich, their wealth being measured primarily in the number of fortresses they possessed, either as allods or fiefs (often 'free fiefs') held of the counts. To their patrimonial castles they had often added castles inherited from those families which had disappeared without direct heirs.

[22] Like the Gurb-Cervelló, from whom derived the Gurb-Queralt and the Cervelló-Montagut, themselves the founders of numerous lines of descendants (for this family, see *La Catalogne*, vol. 1, pp. 290–1).

Above all, they had been the chief beneficiaries of the many new fortresses built in western and south-western Catalonia, either unbeknown to the counts (between 1020/30 and 1060) or with their agreement or even at their instigation. In these circumstances, every family of *comtors* held two or three castles at least. In some cases, the number could rise to a dozen, even fifteen. Exceptionally, one *comtor*, Arnau Mir de Tost, alone controlled over thirty castles scattered through the counties of Urgell and Pallars and the kingdom of Aragon.

The castles of Arnau Mir de Tost [23]

Allodial castles: Tost, Selvanyà, Biscarri, Tolo, Ager, Artesa

Allodial castles given in 1067 to the collegiate church of Ager: Castelló de Llordà, Malagastre, Cas, La Régola, Corçà, Sant Llorenç, Anyà

Castles held as fiefs of Ramon Berenguer I of Barcelona: Camarasa, Cubells, Puigroig, Pilçà

Castles held as fiefs of Ermengol IV of Urgell: Alós, Comiols, Gavarra, Peramola, Sant Jaume

Castle held half allodially, half as a fief (of Ermengol IV of Urgell): Santalinya

Castles held as fiefs of Ramon IV of Pallars (free fiefs): Llimiana, Mur, Areu, Montanyana

Castles held as fiefs of king Sancho Ramirez of Aragon: Falcs, Vicamp, Luzas, Capella, Lascuarre

Castles of uncertain status: Lordà, Castellserà, Besora de Navès

This was exceptional; it shows, nevertheless, to what heights the fortunes of Catalan magnates of the second half of the eleventh century could rise. Arnau Mir de Tost came, in fact, from a relatively modest family, that of the vicar-castellans of Tost, whose tower dominated the Sègre river gorge below Urgell. His rise was owed both to his personal qualities (his adventures foreshadowed, though on a smaller scale, those of the Cid) and to the period of exceptionally weak comital power, between about 1030 and 1060, in the western parts of Catalonia. Profiting from the permanent rivalry between the Ermengols of Urgell and Ramon IV of Pallars, he emerged as war-leader, fought the Muslims on his own account,

---

[23] The documents have been published by P. Sanahuja, *Historia de la villa de Ager* (Barcelona, 1961), apps. 3–26, pp. 316–47.

or, on occasion, offered them his services, and allied himself now with Ramon Berenguer I of Barcelona, now with the king of Aragon (both of them happy to find such support in these parts) and finished up by creating, around the Tremp basin and on the flanks of the Sierra of Montsec, a quasi-independent power which the local counts, whether they liked it or not, were obliged to recognise. He married one of his daughters to Ramon IV of Pallars, the other to the viscount Pons Geral of Girona, and created for the latter the new viscounty of Ager.[24]

Arnau Mir represented, in a sense, the model towards which most of the Catalan *comtors* were moving. The model was social, rather than political. What must have attracted them was not so much his independence vis-à-vis comital authority (no one, after 1060, any longer questioned the supremacy of the house of Barcelona) as the splendour of his way of life. We can still today, by chance, get a very clear impression of this, thanks to two unusually rich documents – the inventory of his moveable possessions which Arnau had drawn up before his departure for St James of Compostela in 1071, and the will dictated three years earlier by his wife, Arsendis.[25]

One cannot but be astonished by the extraordinary luxury – tinged by what was, for the period, wild exoticism – revealed by these two sources. I repeat: all magnates in 1070 were not as rich as this. All the same, by its style of life, by the number of its castles, and by the extent of its clienteles, the ancient nobility of the early Middle Ages continued to exist, throughout the eleventh century and beyond, at a level far above that of every other strata of the Catalan population.[26]

---

[24] P. Sanahuja, 'Arnau Mir de Tost, caudillo de la Reconquista en tierras de Lérida' in *Ilerda*, 1 (1943), 11–27, 155–69, 2 (1944), 2–21, 53–147, 4 (1946), 25–55. See also his *Historia de la villa de Ager*, pp. 31–75. Father Sanahuja used for these two works documents since lost (destroyed during the bombardment of Lérida in 1939) and published the most important of them in the appendices of the second (app. 1–26, pp. 315–47).

[25] See Appendix.

[26] These observations do not, of course, apply only to Catalonia. They are in line with the research carried out over the last forty years by both Belgian (L. Genicot, L. Verriest) and French historians; among the latter, we may quote G. Duby: 'We may now consider it to be established as axiomatic that the Carolingian nobility was transmitted by blood to large numbers of feudal descendants' ('The nobility in medieval France', p. 98).

VAVASSORS AND *MILITES:* THE EMERGENCE OF NEW STRATA
WITHIN THE NOBILITY

If, around the year 1000, the illustrious lineages of the counts, the
viscounts and vicar-castellans between them constituted the whole
nobility, things had changed sixty or seventy years later. In this
sense, article 5 of the *Usatges of Barcelona,* which defines two new
noble levels below the *comtors,* represents the culmination of a
period of change. Vavassors and *milites* were accorded an exceptional status – that is, tariffs of composition higher than the norm –
which distinguished them from the mass of the peasantry. Who
were they?

To identify them with precision, we need in the first place to
consider their role within the seigneurial system on which the new
society was based. They were of necessity situated in the space
separating the great families who were masters of the castle *ban*
(the *nobiles* of ancient stock) from the peasants on whom it bore
(the *ignobiles*). They were neither the masters of the new lordships, nor its subjects; they were the lords' delegates, entrusted
with the power of the *ban.*

The *vasvessores*

We can, without too much difficulty, detect in the vavassors, the
castlans (the custodians of castles, or leaders of castle garrisons).
Article 5 of the *Usatges* itself suggests this identification; the
vasvessor is there defined as the lord of a household of five or more
milites, which corresponds exactly to the normal size of a castle
garrison (five or six *cavalers* on average).[27] If confirmation is
needed, it can be found in certain *convenientiae* which clearly
establish a hierarchy *comtores/castellani/milites* which is very
similar to that (*comtores/vasvessores/milites*) given in the *Usatges.*[28] Finally, a charter of infeudation of 1117, issued by Bishop
Odo of Urgell, describes the same men – that is, the guardians of
the castles the bishop owned in Balaguer – as both *castellani* and
vasvessores.[29] In effect, the *castlans* (except for those guarding the
comital fortresses) were always, in relation to the counts, vassals

[27] See below, p. 211 and note 46.
[28] *LFM,* 1, nos. 471 (1064), 451 (1065), 119 (1079).
[29] AC Urgell, Cart. 1, no. 536.

of vassals. So we can understand why the authors of the *Usatges* chose, to describe them, the term of vavassor (a word only recently introduced into Catalonia) which had the advantage of naming them not after their function, but after their place in the feudal hierarchy.[30]

From which social milieu did they come? This raises the whole question of the origins of the 'new lesser nobility'.[31] If we confine ourselves for the moment to the vavassors, we can distinguish quite clearly two different levels of recruitment. The highest in rank were the *vasvessores de paradge*, who were put immediately after, and almost on a level with, the *comtors* in a convention from around 1078.[32] We should probably see in them members of the lateral branches of the great families, in somewhat reduced circumstances. We should include in this category, for example, Borrell de Tost, who received from his cousin (?), Arnau Mir, custody of the castle of Artesa,[33] and the *castlans* of the Espluga de Francoli who, in the twelfth century, bore the illustrious name of Queralt.[34] We are witnessing, in a sense, the birth of a 'lesser nobility of blood', very similar to that which appeared, at the same period or a little later, in the Mâconnais and the Germanic countries.[35]

There is, however, little doubt that the majority of vavassors came from the lower category of the *milites*. It was from amongst the garrison knights – from amongst the ablest and richest of them – that the *castlans* were generally chosen. Ultimately, therefore, we have to examine the origin and status of those *milites castri* who, in the second half of the eleventh century, managed to prise

---

[30] In this connection, we should note that the word *vasvessor* appeared in Catalonia before the word *vassus*, which had fallen into complete disuse since the Carolingian period and which did not reappear in the documents until towards the middle of the twelfth century. *Fidelis* or *homo* might denote a vassal, but there was no word to indicate the vassal of a vassal, hence the necessity to resort to a loan-word.

[31] On this problem, see Duby, 'The nobility in medieval France', pp. 97ff.

[32] ACA, perg. RB II, no. 69: Ramon Berenguer II guaranteed to carry out an engagement he had just made with Ermengol IV *per sacramentum per unum comptor aut per unum vasvessor de paradge.*

[33] AHN, Clero, perg. Poblet, carp. 1992, no. 7 (1047).

[34] A. Altisent, 'Un poble de la Catalunya nova els segles XI i XII: L'Espluga de Francoli de 1079 a 1200' in *Anuario de estudios medievales*, 3 (1966), 151–3.

[35] Duby, 'The nobility in medieval France', p. 97 (referring to the works of A. Hagemann and K. Bosl); also his *La société aux XIe et XIIe siècles dans la région mâconnaise* (Paris, 1953), pp. 411–18.

open the doors of the nobility and make themselves into its lowest, and easily its most numerous, layer.

The *milites*

Some of their wills survive.[36] They reveal men of very modest wealth, but all, nevertheless, enjoying from the outset some small inheritance of land. Their parents had left them, as their personal property, at least two or three, at most fifteen, manses; they thus possessed allods which were often scattered over various neighbouring territories.

Table 8. *The landed property of some* milites *(based on their wills)*[37]

Date	Name	Place where will drawn up	Patrimonial allods[a]	Acquisitions Allods	Fiefs	Rented properties
1085	Ardmann	Bagà (Cerdanya)	2	4	3	1
1088	Ademar	Taradell (Vic)	3	0	?	0
1092	Roland Guillem	Figuerola (Urgell)	2	0	2	0
1105	Ramon Arnau	Alp (Cerdanya)	14	4	5	1
1119	Jordà	Tuixén (Urgell)	8	0	1	1
1122	Ramon Enard	Montardit (Pallars)	5	?	?	?
1126	Pere Oliver	Viladecavals (Osona)	2	0	3	2
1134	Bertrand	(Urgell)	4	?	?	?

(a) Number of agricultural units inherited.

Their way of life remained, nevertheless, fairly basic (the finest moveable possession in one case was a cauldron, bequeathed to the chapter of Urgell)[38] and they possessed little in the way of cash

[36] ACA, Monacales, perg. Bagà, no. 350 (1085); AC Vic, perg. no. 322 (1088); AC Urgell, Cart. 1, nos. 164 (1092), 710 (1105), 49 (1119), 610 (1122), 151 (1134); Arch. Montserrat, perg. Bages, no. 1666 (1126). The bequests of land in these wills are analysed in table 8.

[37] Based on references cited in note 36 above.

[38] AC Urgell, Cart. 1, no. 710.

(from 0 to 7 *sous*, though one had 44 *mancusos*). Their principal wealth lay in their military equipment (swords, hauberks and *sellas caballericias*) which appears to have been fairly complete,[39] and was the subject of detailed testamentary dispositions. Most important of all, they owned a horse (sometimes a horse and a mare, in one single case, several mares and foals). These *milites* were, in fact, the sons or grandsons of peasants; their origins are to be found in the upper ranks of the allodial peasantry, among well-off farmers who not only owned the land which they worked but could rent land out to other villagers, and who already, towards the year 1000, possessed a horse and arms and participated in the military expeditions organised by the counts.[40]

But by 1080 or 1090 their status was no longer that of their fathers or grandfathers. What distinguished them, above all, was the specialised expertise they had acquired in the profession of arms. This was not, in practice, evenly developed, and, in this regard, several types of *milites* can be distinguished at the end of the eleventh century.

Some seem still to perpetuate the ancient tradition of the *coloni*-soldiers, living off their own resources and free from all vassalic ties. This might explain the position of those *milites aloders* who, in an inventory which is undated (but datable to the years 1078–95), are mentioned by Count Guillem-Ramon of Cerdanya, along with the vines, fields, and comital pleas, as amongst the attributes of the *dominicatura* he had retained in the frontier castellany of Les Oluges; these men, he said, owed him only host and cavalcade.[41]

Attachment to the land remained equally strong amongst others of these knights, who were not above renting some fields or entering into precarious contracts with monasteries. In 1078, for example, a certain Bertrand, dignified by the monks of Sant Benet with the name of *miles*, received from them a holding comprising a house, lands, vines and gardens, *in tali tenore ut ipsa omnia supras-cripta bene laboret et excolat et condrigat*; he further engaged to live on the holding granted to him and to pay a rent in wine, round-cakes, oats and pigs.[42] Similarly, the *milites* Ardmann (of

---

[39] Complete, but often only just adequate; the *miles* Ardmann left 'a part' of his hauberk to each of his three sons (ACA, Monacales, perg. Bagà, no. 350).
[40] *La Catalogne*, vol. 1, pp. 304–6.
[41] ACA, perg. RB II, no. 68.   [42] Arch. Montserrat, perg. Bages, no. 1554.

Bagà), Ramon Arnau (of Alp) and Jordà (of Tuixén), though fairly well-off allod-holders, held lands *a laboratione* from the abbey of Bagà and the chapter of Urgell.[43] But mostly they held fiefs, and were thus vassals. Ardmann, in 1085, had three lords; Ramon Arnau, in 1105, had five. It is not difficult to picture the lives and habits of these men; the allods and military equipment received from their fathers assured them material independence, but in order to increase their patrimony, they offered their services to the local castellans. Rather than engage themselves too strictly to one master, they multiplied their homage. The fiefs they obtained were very modest, but in return imposed only light obligations (a few days' fighting per year for each lord?). They invested the profits derived from this service in the purchase of allods; Ardmann and Ramon Arnau each acquired four manses. Thus they rapidly rose above their original class (they had their own *homines*: the tenants who worked their land) without being wholly assimilated into the feudo-vassalic system. Within the military profession, they were, in a sense, like independent artisans.

But they were few. Lords had, in fact, no need of such dilettante vassals. They preferred to engage fully professional fighting men, grouped in households under strict control, able to respond to any call and to defend their castles at all times. The bulk of the *milites* therefore consisted of the *milites castri*, that is, the garrison knights of the fortified towers. These were men who had left their villages with no hope of return, except at the onset of old age. Bound by 'solid' (that is, liege) homage to the *castlà* who directed them, subject through him to every wish of the *comtor* who owned the fortress, their role was to be perpetually available for whatever war or more humdrum police operations devolved to them. They lost, as a result, almost all connection with the land. The *milites* of Mediona enjoyed an exceptional leave (that is, an exemption from the service of cavalcade) for ten days at the time of the grain and wine harvests, but they could not, even then, leave the castellany; it was on the *cavallerias terre* granted to them as fiefs that they supervised the harvest.[44] They were *milites*, and *milites* only; the

---

[43] ACA, Monacales, perg. Bagà, no. 350 (1085); AC Urgell, Cart. 1, nos. 710 (1105), 49 (1119). See also table 8.

[44] ACA, perg. RB I, no. 204 (1057). The *cavalleria terre* was a feudal unit (an agricultural holding intended to assure the subsistence of one garrison *miles*).

texts also call them *cavalers*. We can now translate this word as knight.

KNIGHTHOOD AND THE DEFINITION OF A NEW NOBLE ORDER

From horsemen to knights

One of the most important developments of the second half of the eleventh century was the massive accession to noble status of those who specialised in fighting on horseback. This was a development which changed, in a truly revolutionary manner, the nature and the composition of the aristocracy, and which threatened the very concept of nobility.

In the ninth and tenth centuries, the nobility existed, but the noble remained a rare being. The body of the *nobiles*, from which were recruited all public officers and all the followers of the count, consisted of no more than ten or fifteen families in each county.[45] Within a castellany, only the vicar-castellan was noble. The men who, as and when required, fought under his orders, had no claim to this dignity, even when they fought on horseback. They were only performing their service as free men; they remained peasant-soldiers. From about 1050, when war had definitively become an affair of professionals, it was waged by the household of the castle. The *castlà* and the *cavalers* who composed the castellan's host, and who were increasingly clearly distinguished from the mass of the peasantry by their function, aspired to nobility. To accede to their wishes would mean a massive increase in the number of nobles; no longer one noble per castellany, but five or six. This was, nevertheless, what happened; the integration of the mass of the *milites* – *milites aloders* or mounted vassals – into the nobility had the result of increasing its numbers to an almost unimaginable degree: it multiplied it at least fivefold, perhaps tenfold.[46]

Such a change could not take place peacefully. It was a product of the climate of violence which characterised eleventh-century

---

[45] *La Catalogne*, vol. 1, pp. 284–6.

[46] To measure this progress exactly, we would need to know precisely the number of *cavalers* in each garrison: more than five at Mediona in 1057, ten at Tarrega in 1058 and twenty in the same castle in 1069, ten at Estopanyà in 1064 (ACA, perg. RB I, no. 204; *LFM*, 1, nos. 171, 174, 40). It is hardly necessary to emphasise the very approximate nature of the figures provided by these documents. We also need to take into account those *milites* who were not part of regular households, but served several lords in turn.

Europe. More precisely, it was in Catalonia the direct consequence – one of the most dramatic consequences – of the crisis of the years 1020–60. It seems hardly likely, indeed, that the *nobiles*, so imbued with their superiority and so proud of their ancestors, welcomed with open arms this host of parvenus thrown up by the war, still not wholly purged of their rustic origins, which constituted the bands of mounted warriors. Their hand was forced.

Castlans and *cavalers* represented, in fact, in mid eleventh-century Catalonia, a social force in constant ascent. They constituted in themselves the whole military force of the country; those foreigners who, making contact with Catalonia through the intermediary of its warriors, called the country after its *castlans* were not in error. In the mouths of men from Languedoc or Italy, *Castlà* would become *Català* from which would come Catalunya.[47] Here, as in Castile and for the same reasons, the name of the custodians of the castles (*castlans*, *castellanos*) would eventually apply to the whole population. In any case, for the counts, viscounts and *comtors*, it had become impossible to manage without the services of the castle garrisons; how, without them, could they defend themselves against the operations of neighbouring castellans, and how, in addition, could they contain the discontent of peasants crushed by the weight of impositions of the *ban*? In practice, the function of control assured by the *castlans* in the fortresses quickly made them arbiters in the wars waged between the counts and magnates.

[47] The origin of the word Catalunya has aroused much controversy. There is a survey in the short work devoted to this question by F. Udina Martorell: *El nom de Catalunya* (Barcelona, 1961). The hypothesis of J. Calmette, who derives the word from *Gotholonia*, is untenable, as is that of J. Coromines, who links it to the name of the Iberian people of the *Laketani*; if the word had such remote origins, it must surely have appeared in the documents before the end of the eleventh century. Aebischer's idea of making Catalonia the country of the castle of Montcada is based on a mis-reading: the form *Mont Catlan* never existed to denote this castle. We have, therefore, to return to the old theory of Balari, who, in 1899, proposed the etymology *castlà*; this has never really been contested by Catalan historians. The oldest reference to the anthroponym *Catala* is found in a charter drawn up in Carcassonne in 1105; the names Arnal Catalan, Ramon Catalan and Geral de Cataluing are borne by three inhabitants of this town. The first use of the word 'Catalonia' to denote the whole country appears in the *Liber Maiolichinus de gestis Pisanorum illustribus* compiled by the poet, Henry of Pisa, after 1115. The word *Taluniya* which J. Vernet has found in the writings of Al Udri (before 1100) and in which he claimed to see the name of Catalonia ('La mas antigua cita de Catalunya?' in *Al Andalus*, 32 (1967), 231–2) seems in fact rather to apply to a simple site located on the road from Huesca to Lérida.

On a still wider plane, their role was decisive in all the relations between the great families; if their lord did not fulfil the engagements of a *convenientia* he had entered into, it was for them to hand over to the opposing party the fortresses promised as guarantee.[48] In these circumstances, *castlans* and *cavalers* disposed of the means to exert considerable pressure on the high aristocracy. The powerful house of Caboet learned this to its cost, when, between 1080 and 1095, it suffered countless insults on the part of its *castlans* of Cabó, and proved powerless to bring them to their senses.[49]

Whether they liked it or not, the nobles of old stock had to make room at their side for men of base extraction. But some limit had to be put on the number; inflation threatened. A choice had to be made from amongst the mass of rustics who aspired to fight on horseback and thus escape the customs of the *ban*. One criterion for access to the nobility was certainly economic; it was impossible to admit men who did not dispose of the resources necessary to maintain their status. Highly revealing from this point of view, despite the uncertainty surrounding the date of its promulgation, is article 12 of the *Usatges of Barcelona*, which stipulates clearly that only those who ate wheaten bread everyday could be regarded as noble.[50] At a period when wheat was still a luxury grain, this clause was fairly selective, but it left too large a margin for interpretation. It was necessary to establish a stricter barrier; this, in the event, took the form of an initiation ceremony, dubbing.

It is impossible to know with any precision exactly when the rite of dubbing appeared in Catalonia; the verb *adobar* does not appear in the charters. This omission is quite natural; it was no part of the purpose of contracts dealing with land or *convenientiae*, any more than of wills or oaths, to refer to such a practice. In these circumstances, and if we still prefer not to relegate the question to total obscurity, the best method seems to be to study the evolution

[48] *LFM*, nos. 37 (*c.* 1057); 269 (1059), 112 (*c.* 1066).

[49] According to the *memoria de ipsas rencurias* dictated by Guitard Isarn de Caboet, which contains a long list of his grievances (published by Miret i Sans, 'Documents en langue catalane', pp. 10–11).

[50] The article refers to bailiffs, and distinguishes between noble and non-noble bailiffs: *Bajulus interfectus vel debilitatus sive cessus vel captus, si nobilis est et panem frumenti comedit cotidie et equitat, emenditur sicut miles.* This article is often accepted as having been part of the original nucleus of the *Usatges*, but this is not certain. On the question of the bailiffs, see also below, p. 217.

of the two words which came to be used to designate a dubbed knight: *miles* and *cavallarius*. They were more or less synonymous – the former belonging to scholarly language, the latter to everyday speech – but they could also at the same time have very different meanings:

1. *Miles* retained in the eleventh century the meaning it had always – with very rare exceptions – held in the previous century: the classic sense of 'fighting man'. Similarly, *cavallarius* often indicated, without further precision, a mounted fighter. The participants in judicial duels, for example, were frequently referred to as *cavallarios*.

2. *Miles* (but never *cavallarius*), followed by a personal name in the genitive or preceded by the preposition *de*, could be synonymous with *fidelis* or *homo*, in which case it meant vassal.

3. In the *convenientiae*, the two terms *milites* and *cavallarius* almost always mean the garrison knights who composed the household of a castle.

4. The sense of 'dubbed knight' appears for the first time in a will of 1086:

I leave my honour to my wife for her to hold as I have held it; but if she remarries, it should revert to my son Pere under the tutelage of my brother Berenguer, who should hold it until Pere is a knight (*tantum usque sit kavallarius*) when he should hand it to him.[51]

This same meaning recurs in 1092, applied to the word *miles*:

He ordains that Guillem Durand should take charge of this hauberk until Guillem Pons is a knight (*usque dum fuisset militem*).[52]

These examples, we should note, are few and late.[53]

5. In the *Usatges of Barcelona*, *miles* indicates nobles of the lowest category. The *milites* are classed in rank after the *vasvessores* (Us. 5). The term *milites* may also be opposed to that of *magnates* (Us. 29).

6. Lastly, in certain documents from the end of the eleventh (first example in 1085)[54] and the beginning of the twelfth centuries, the word *milites* serves to describe all the members of the new

[51] ACA, Monacales, perg. Bagà, no. 348.
[52] ACA, perg. BR II, no. 77.
[53] We should also note their formulation: *usque sit kavallarius* and not *usque fiat kavallarius*. The rite of passage was not formally attested, it is, nevertheless, implied by the context.   [54] AC Vic, perg. no. 1502.

noble order, as opposed to *pagenses*, or *clerici* and *negociatores*.[55] The word *cavallarius* took on the same meaning; when Guillem Guitard of Caboet instructed his family to provide his daughters with *maritos cavallarios*, he cannot have been thinking of garrison knights.[56]

This analysis reveals that by entry into vassalage and then, above all, by dubbing, simple mounted fighting men, despite the obscurity of their extraction, acquired a sufficient degree of honour for the doors of *nobilitas* to be opened to them. But their integration was not without its problems.

One nobility or two?

It is clear that knighthood conferred nobility at the end of the eleventh century. But can we go further and say that it was eventually confounded with it? Or, put another way, did the *nobiles* of old stock follow this example and have themselves dubbed? This is an important question, but a very difficult one, for lack of evidence. We may think that some of them, for example the Caboet, did so.[57] It is not impossible that Ramon Berenguer III himself was dubbed as a knight; a text of around 1170 claims that he was, on the basis of oral tradition,[58] but can we believe it? There is nothing to stop us from thinking that the castellans, even the viscounts and counts, inspired by the companionship of arms, imitated their vassals and underwent dubbing. The hypothesis is all the more probable in that this rite, by its rather mysterious formalism, and by the sacred character the Church was doubtless beginning to confer on it (though on this point the Catalan documents are silent), was in itself not without its attractions. However that may be, old and new nobles shared the same passion for the profession of arms. This was a powerful psychological factor contributing to the cohesion of the new noble order. A 'chivalric' mentality was in the process of being born, and its first manifestations were as visible amongst the greatest magnates as the simple

---

[55] AC Barcelona, Divers. B, perg. no. 136 (1089); AC Urgell, Cart 1, nos. 536 (1117), 528 (1117).

[56] AC Urgell, Cart. 1, no. 509.

[57] According to the will of Guillem Guitard de Caboet, cited above.

[58] *HGL*, V, no. 6, col. 32. The authors of this account themselves state: *sed quia nondum nati erimus quando haec facta sunt, utrum vera sint nescimus* (col. 33).

Table 9. *Tariffs of composition for murder and injury (in ounces of gold)*

	Death	Injury
Viscounts	160	120
Comtors	80	60
Vavassors	40	30
Milites	12	6
Peasants	6	2

milites. It was already finding expression at the very end of the eleventh century in an ardent quest for military glory.[59] We are already on the path leading to that ideal of prowess which was to find, in the second half of the twelfth century, one of its most striking illustrations in the Catalan romance of *Jaufre.*[60]

But psychological rapprochement does not imply social fusion. Old and new nobility co-existed, but did not merge. The magnates, to use a phrase of 1093, remained the *tellure primi ac domini.*[61] They may have been dubbed, but they had no need of this to be noble; their nobility derived from their ancestors. Dubbing served only as a 'decoration'.[62] Between them and those for whom entry to knighthood was a necessity there yawned a chasm which was clearly demonstrated in the tariffs of composition promulgated by the *Usatges*: a *comtor* was worth ten times more, a viscount twenty times more, than a simple knight.

So if the noble class was opened up to upstart knights, the latter remained confined to a very subordinate position. This strict hierarchy persisted; as late as the fourteenth century, when the Catalan Corts met, different summonses were issued to the barons

---

[59] In 1085, the canons of Urgell lauded the 'military glory' of Arnau Daco, one of the first barons of the county, who, in old age, retired to their cathedral (AC Urgell, Cart. 1, no. 364).

[60] Edited by R. Nelli and R. Lavaud, *Les troubadours*, vol. 1, *L'oeuvre épique* (Paris, 1960). It was dedicated to a king of Aragon, in whom Rita Lejeune has recognised Alfonso the Chaste.

[61] AC Urgell, Cart. 1, no. 310.

[62] I refer here to a text from Namur which could just as well apply to a Catalan magnate: *decoravit nobilitatem suam militari studio* (quoted by L. Genicot, *L'économie rurale namuroise au bas Moyen âge*, vol. 2, *Les hommes, la noblesse* (Namur, 1960), p. 7, note 5).

and to the simple knights: *pro nobilibus, magnatibus seu barones* for the former, *pro militibus* for the latter.[63] It is true that Catalonia never had two noble orders, like late medieval Aragon; it kept only one, but one split into two almost watertight compartments.[64]

It remains to establish the lower limit of this nobility. The answer to this question is simple; the cut-off point came in the group of servants. Some of the bailiffs had been able to follow in the footsteps of the *castlans* and *cabalers*, with whom they collaborated in the imposition of the charges of the *ban*; article 12 of the *Usatges* gives them the rank of *milites*. The rest, who were probably only domanial agents and did not have the honour of accomplishing their service on horseback, were described as *ignobiles* in the same text, and relegated to the status of peasants.

A new peasantry, a new servitude

Since the liberation of the last rural slaves (round about 1035),[65] there had no longer been any non-free amongst the Christian population of Catalonia. The development of the *seigneurie banale* had already, it is true, before 1060, considerably restricted the independence and aggravated the lot of the free peasantry; but they could still regard themselves as masters of their own bodies and, in the case of the allod-holders, of their land. By 1100, this illusion had, for most of them, disappeared.

FROM THE EXACTIONS OF THE *BAN* TO PERSONAL SERVITUDE

From *banal* obligations to the *mals usos*

The return to civil peace during the 1060s did not mean the end of the exactions. On the contrary, documents from the end of the eleventh and the beginning of the twelfth centuries show that they continued to spread, now unimpeded. Further, they were increasingly to be seen as a normal practice which the clergy, nobility and counts were of one mind in accepting without qualms. Certainly, the peasants still occasionally baulked; such a one was the Albert

---

[63] *Historia de España y América*, under the direction of J. Vicens Vives, vol. 2 (2nd edn 1961), p. 111.
[64] *Ibid.*, pp. 111–51.   [65] *La Catalogne*, vol. 1, pp. 298–302.

Salomon who, on 28 May 1100, before the crowd gathered in the village square after mass, agreed to submit to trial by boiling water to prove that the lord and *castlans* of Taradell had no rights over his person or his possessions.[66] Vain attempts, we may be sure! The only disturbances now provoked by the levy of *toltas* arose from conflicts between ecclesiastics and castellans when the latter imposed unwarranted *banal* charges on the tenants of the Church. It often took two or three generations before the protests of chapters and monasteries were heard and many deeds of renunciation made by magnates around 1120, even 1150, applied to exactions already regularly practised by their fathers and grandfathers.[67]

In these circumstances, it is hardly surprising to observe that the first purpose of the *convenientiae* remained, as in the past, the establishment of an equitable division of the profits of the *ban* between the castle-owning barons, their *castlans* and their *milites*; here they shared the *presentalias* and the *pregueras de blad* (1127), there it was the *lexivos*, the *exorchias* and the *trobas* (1132), elsewhere it was the *questias*, the *lexivos*, the *estacaments* and the *guaitas* (1148).[68] Little would be gained by multiplying these examples. What matters more is that the counts themselves now participated in this movement. Pons Hug I of Empúries, even before 1078, imposed *forcias*, *toltas* and 'bad customs' on the people of his castellanies.[69] Ermengol IV and Ermengol V of Urgell disposed quite arbitrarily of both the persons and possessions of the allodial peasants who depended on their castles.[70] And in neither Urgell nor Barcelona, lastly, did the counts respect the franchises

---

[66] AC Vic, perg. no. 2213.

[67] References in table 10. The *tolta* or *questia* was the Catalan equivalent of *taille* or tallage: it was originally (mid-eleventh century) a payment in kind levied arbitrarily on a peasant's resources (*tollere*: to take, carry away by force).

[68] AHN, Clero, perg. Poblet, carp. 1997, nos. 6 (1127), 19 (1132), carp 2000, no. 5 (1148). The *presentalias* were the dues levied by lords on peasant marriage. The *lexivos* and *exorchias* were taxes on inheritance. *Pregueras*, *questias*, *toltas* and *forcias* are synonymous words; they denote arbitrary seigneurial levies on peasant resources (*preguera* and *questia* imply a simple 'request' or 'entreaty' on the part of the lord; *tolta* and *forcia* openly imply the use of force). The *trobas* were the equivalent of the *droit d'aubaine* (the right of the lord to objects 'found' within his castellany). The *estacaments* were the deposits demanded from plaintiffs before any law-suit by the lord possessing the rights of justice. The *guaitas* were the taxes replacing watch service. For the *presentalias*, *exorchias*, *cugucias* and *arsinas*, which were later legalised as 'bad customs', see below, pp. 234–5. See also *La Catalogne*, vol. 1, pp. 587–93.

[69] AC Girona, Llibre verd. fo. 183v.

[70] AC Urgell, Cart. 1, nos. 473 (1077), 33 (1087), 412 (1126).

which their ancestors had granted and of which they were the guarantors.

The lot of the peasantry in the old franchisal zones deserves particular attention. We know that their liberties had already suffered during the noble troubles of the years 1040–60; *seigneuries banales* had been created, quite illegally, by Mir Geribert and his men and, in both Vallès and Penedès, these had survived the end of the rebellion.[71] Some islands of liberty persisted, nevertheless, within the county of Barcelona, and also in the county of Urgell, under the theoretical protection of the counts. But the latter no longer felt any reluctance about alienating franchises when they thought this of any material or spiritual benefit; in 1077, Ermengol IV gave the church of Urgell, for the salvation of his soul, the free lands of Nabiners, Ortóns, Fontelles and la Freyta, with the peasants who lived there;[72] in 1083, the countess Mahaut, widow of Ramon Berenguer II, pledged to the seneschal Guillem Ramon of Montcada, for one thousand *mancusos* of Valencia, the *franchedas* of Sant Minat, in the Vallès, with the *usaticos* and the *servicios* levied on the 'free men'.[73] We see from this last example that, even before being alienated, the franchises had been violated by the counts themselves. Once they had passed, by an act of sale or by being constituted a pledge, into the hands of the barons, the free territories inevitably lost all their privileges. It was little different, despite the hesitations of certain prelates, when the beneficiary of the alienation was a church. The history of the franchises of Bescarán, in the county of Urgell, is revealing in this regard; instituted long before by Count Borrell, they were abused by Bishops Guillem Guifred and Bernard Guillem; in 1085, the latter recognised his error and restored them. The respite was temporary; in 1095, Bishop Odo, in exchange for his protection, imposed an *alberga* on the inhabitants and, in 1097, pledged it to three of his creditors, along with the *cugucias* and the *arsinas*, that is the 'bad usages' to which the free men were now subject.[74]

---

[71] *La Catalogne*, vol. 1, pp. 628–30, 640; pp. 677–8, 680–1.

[72] AC Urgell, Cart. 1, no. 492.

[73] ACA, perg. BR II, no. 2.

[74] AC Urgell, Cart. 1, nos. 925 (1085), 924 (1095), 926 (1097). Another instance of the evolution of a free community has been studied by J. M. Font Rius, *Notas sobre la evolución juridico-pública de una comunidad local en el Pirineo catalan: Ager* (Saragossa, 1950). The inhabitants of Ager-La Régola obtained a charter of franchise in 1084; during the second half of the eleventh century, this was

Table 10. *'Usages' and 'bad usages' improperly imposed by lay lords on tenants of the church*

References	Date of deed of renun- ciation	Places concerned	Nature of the 'usages'
AC Girona, Llibre verd, fo. 182v	1062	Foixà Creixell	*appellationes, acclamaments, baiulias, servitia, acaptes, adempraments, toltas*
Ibid., fo. 183v	1091	Castelló of Empúries	*fortias, toltas, malas presones, malos usaticos*
AC Barcelona, Divers, C–b, 308	1091	Taradell	*paleas, erbas, ligna et alia servicia, civadas, locid*
Ibid., 342	1092	Castellterçol	*acaptes*
AC Girona, Llibre verd. fo. 183	1099	Navata	*fortiar, acaptes exactiones*
Montserrat, perg. Bages, 1630	1111	Les Preses	*fortias, usus*
ACA, Mon., perg. S. Benet, 404	1122	Les Preses	*malas prisiones, toltas, forças, achaptes placita, iusticias, iniusticias, iovas, albergas, ququcias, omicidios*
ACA, Mon., perg. Bagà, 453	1129	various places	*forças, toltas, malos usaticos, homicidium cuguciam*
AC Vic. perg. 1653	1142	Gaià	*toltas, usaticos*
ACA, Mon., perg. Amer, 16	1152	Les Olives?	*acaptes, toltas, forces, alberga*

Thus the *banal* charges, which had first appeared in the castellanies in the possession of lay magnates, spread to all lordships, the comital and episcopal castellanies included, between about 1060 and 1100. The inhabitants of the ancient franchisal zones did

violated by the imposition of *questias, toltas, pregueras* and *servicia*. These charges were abolished by the viscount Pons Geral, who granted a new franchise in 1094. The process of enserfment recommenced in the twelfth century, and a third charter of enfranchisement was needed in 1228 to liberate the peasants from the *mals usos*.

not escape, except those living in towns. Consisting initially of a host of diverse and unconnected dues and services, they tended, as they spread geographically, to become more systematic and to assume a quasi-institutional character. The vocabulary which increasingly grouped them under the global title of *usaticos* or *malos usaticos* was quite correct; these were already the *mals usos* which, right up to the end of the fifteenth century, were to represent the characteristic obligations of servitude in Catalonia.

Personal servitude

But did not possessing rights over a man mean, for a magnate, possessing that man? There was a difference of degree, not of kind, between the two types of possession, and the boundary was soon passed. It was permissible for a magnate to give (to a church or to an individual) the service owed by a peasant; why could he not give the peasant? By 1063, the castellans of Granyena had ceased to make such a distinction:

Donamus nos vobis . . . II homines, Arnal Pere et Arnal Iover, ab lur servidi . . . et servidi asi com la acapte de Geral de Graiena . . . et l'acapta d'en Selvan.[75]

It was in north-west Catalonia – in the county of Urgell and above all in Pallars – that this evolution was most rapid. There, as a result of the almost complete breakdown of public authority, the castellans had become the absolute masters of the men who lived in the shadow of their fortresses; as for the counts, they were now hardly more, at least in Pallars, than lords of the *ban* like the rest. Charters bear witness to the extreme dependence into which the peasantry had fallen, by revealing with what ease not only lands but men were now given or exchanged. The transaction sometimes applied to all the inhabitants of a castellany, parish or village – all the men of Cellers (1054), of Tremp (1109), of Cerchsent (1126) and of Llarvén (1129).[76] Sometimes it applied only to some of them; half the dependants of the castellanies of Montalbà (1092) and Sersui (1118), three-quarters of the inhabitants of Vilagrassa (1109), a sixth of those of Claravalls (1089).[77]

[75] AHN, Clero, perg. Poblet, carp. 1993, no. 5. The *acapte* was, in the eleventh century, an ill-defined seigneurial tribute; it may be identified with the *tolta* and the *questia*.   [76] AC Urgell, Cart. 1, nos. 577–8, 580, 618, 604.
[77] *Ibid.*, nos. 35, 596, 67, 38.

But donations might equally well involve isolated individuals – one peasant at Coscó (1041–71), one at Castellet (1080), three others *in castro Gavase* (1087).[78] In 1126, Ermengol VI even offered the chapter of Urgell one man from each of his castellanies.[79] The church of Urgell, was, in any case, to our knowledge, the principal beneficiary of such alms:

But it would be a mistake to think that such reductions to servitude were to be found only in the mountainous regions of the north-west. They also affected lower Catalonia and even the pioneer lands of the south-west; in the county of Urgell, the castellanies of Claravalls, Vilagrassa and Montalbà, where we have already observed donations or exchanges of 'own men' (*homines proprii*), were situated on the frontier, on the edge of the plain of Lleida. The situation was similar in the county of Osona (at Granyena and at Verdu)[80] and also in the county of Barcelona where, for example, in 1071, Arnau Pere of Barberà gave *alaudio a II parilios de bovis et I omine a domenge per badle* to his *castlà*.[81]

The state of dependence into which these men had fallen, to be given or exchanged like things, originated, in all the cases cited, in their residence within the boundaries of a castellany; they were the *omines qui ad ipsum castrum pertinet* (Vilagrassa), the *homines qui in prescripta villa habitant* (Cellers), or the *homines infra prefatos terminos habitantes* (Tremp). Here and there, they began to be given the generic name of *homines commanentes*[82] or *homines commorantes*.[83] Whether they were tenants of the castellan (or of one of his agents) or allod-holders mattered little; they were subjects and, as such, men owing loyalty and service (*homines commanentes et servicium facientes*).[84] Initially, according to the logic of the *banal* system, only the obligations bearing on them could be alienated. By a progressive shift, which constitutes the very essence of the process of enserfment, they were themselves given with these charges. Eventually, and this was the end of the road, they were given with their services and their allods:

donamus vobis tres pagenses cum illorum decimis et serviciis . . . cum illorum alodiis et domibus.[85]

[78] *Ibid.*, nos. 551, 587, 33.   [79] *Ibid.*, no. 412.
[80] AHN Clero, perg. Poblet, carp. 1993, no. 5 (1063); carp. 1997, no. 19 (1132).
[81] ACA, perg. RB I, no. 438.
[82] AC Urgell, Cart. 1, no. 405 (1064).   [83] *Ibid.*, no. 35 (1092).
[84] *Ibid.*, no. 405 (1064).   [85] *Ibid.*, no. 33 (1087).

Table 11. *The earliest donations of* homines proprii *to the chapter of Urgell (before 1110)*

Reference (Cart. Urgell)	Dates	Donator	Description of peasants	Place of residence
551	1041/7	Fruga Bonfill	unum hominem cum omnem censum quod donare debet	Cosco (Urgell)
577–8	1054	Ramon IV	ipsos homines qui in prescribta villa habitant	Cellers (Pallars)
587	1080	Ramon Arnau de Castellet	unum hominem	Castellet (Pallars)
631	1087	Artau II	quendam obtimum hominem cum omni eius funcío	Lleret (Pallars)
33	1087	Ermengol IV	tres pagenses cum illorum decimis et serviciis	*castro Gavase* (Urgell)
579	1106	Pere Ramon Count	meos quos habeo homines	Cellers (Pallars)
67	1109	Pere Gauzbert de Vilagrassa	homines qui ad ipsum castrum pertinent	Vilagrassa (Urgell)
580	1109	Pere Ramon Count	homines infra prefatos terminos habitantes	Tremp (Pallars)

They could be enfeoffed.[86] In the majority of cases known to us – when given to a church or a relative – they were granted as personal property – *ad vestrum dominicum*,[87] *a domenge*,[88] even *per alodium*.[89] With this degree of servitude, we can no longer assume that residence alone sufficed to establish dependence. The *homines commanentes* had become *homines proprii*,[90] whose attachment to their master was unbroken even if they left their village of origin; one act of restitution tells us, for example, that the monks of Cervià owned a family of smiths in Besalú, though they had no power over that village.[91] How are we to explain this change in the nature of the tie of dependence? Its origin may be found in the oath demanded by the barons from the subjects of

[86] *Laboratores* held in fief: *ibid.*, no. 536 (1117).
[87] AHN, Clero, perg. Poblet, carp. 1997, no. 19 (1132).
[88] ACA, perg. RB I, no. 438 (1071).
[89] AC Urgell, Cart. 1, no. 587 (1080).
[90] The term first appears, to my knowledge, in 1119 (*ibid.*, no. 555). It is subsequently used very frequently.
[91] ACA, Monacales, perg. Cervià, no. 472 (1132).

their castellanies. This very likely derived from the oath sworn by all free men to the public authority, and which was thus a proof of liberty. Appropriated by the lords of the *ban*, it engendered a dependence so strict that it was transformed into servitude. It could, lastly, be accompanied by homage of the type called servile: Alamany of Cervelló and his wife Sicards, for example, referring to the peasants subject to their *ban*, called them *omines de nostro ominatico* as early as 1045/6.[92] This entry by peasants into commendation was effected by various methods. Some peasants had to 'give' themselves with their families in reparation for a deed injurious to their lord;[93] others did so voluntarily, to protect themselves against some danger.[94] Mostly, however, it seems that lords imposed the oath of allegiance on whole communities.

Having thus become virtually the *homines solidi*[95] of their lords, the subject peasants had ceased to depend on them by the sole fact of residence; they had become their *hommes de corps* or bondsmen. In fact, from one type of subjection to the other, the distance was very much less great than one might think, as is shown by this statement of Count Pere Ramon of Pallars, who, when he granted his possessions of Tremp to the church of Urgell, added that he gave them:

with the men who live within the said bounds, whether they are within or without and wherever they can go. (1109)[96]

Attached by such a tie to his lord, the peasant now belonged to him, like the Ramon Oriol and Guillem Muliner mentioned in a deed of 1076:

with his comings and goings, with all he has and may have . . . with all he may acquire, plant, assart . . . without any reservation, and with any posterity he may have.[97]

---

[92] *La Catalogne*, vol. 2, p. 582 and note 32.

[93] AC Urgell, Cart. 1, no. 555 (self-donation, 1119). *Ibid.*, no. 556 (oath).

[94] ACA, perg. RB II, no. 10 (1076); ACA, Monacales, perg. S. Benet, no. 372 (1098); *ibid.* perg. Cervià, no. 445 (1126).

[95] This expression appears for the first time applied to peasants in 1114 (ACA, Monacales, perg. S. Benet, no. 380). Associated with the expression *homines proprii* (*homines proprii et solidi*), it became common, especially at the end of the twelfth and in the thirteenth centuries (J. Vicens Vives, *Historia de los remensas en el siglo XV* (Barcelona, 1945), p. 30).

[96] AC Urgell, Cart. 1, no. 580: *cum hominibus infra prefatos terminos habitantibus, intus vel extra, ubi longius ire possint.*

[97] ACA, perg. RB II, no. 8: *Donamus tibi . . . uno homine in Sanctum Petrum,*

THE EVOLUTION OF LAND-LORDSHIP AND SERVITUDE 'OF THE SOIL'

The evolution of lordship over land

By 1100–20, the peasant allod – a century earlier the dominant structure in the agrarian geography of Catalonia – existed only in name. The allod-holder had ceased, in effect, to be the real master of his property. He could no longer alienate it without the consent of his lord, who tended to authorise such transactions only between his own subjects, to exclude any purchaser from too elevated a social level who might escape his *ban*.[98] No longer able to dispose freely of his land, the allod-holder himself, as we have seen, might be given bodily or exchanged, in which case his allod suffered the same fate. Can we still, in these conditions, speak of allods? The small peasant property had expired under the weight of the obligations loaded on it.

It also disappeared as a result of the process of concentration of land which had continued for two centuries. Nothing is more significant in this regard than the graph of the sales of land. The deeds of sale which represent 75% of the original documentation for the year 1000, constituted no more than 55% in 1050, less than 25% in 1100 and only 6% in 1150.[99] Further, the average value of these transactions rose steadily; in the course of the years 1040–80 alone, it passed from 39 to 239 *sous*.[100] Even allowing for the rapid inflation characterising this period, the conclusion is inescapable; the small allods which formed the vast majority of lands sold in the year 1000, had been, to a very large extent, swallowed up by the large estates.

It becomes all the more important to observe the fate of tenants. It ought not, in principle, to have differed from that of the allod-

cum suo exio et regressio et cum omnia quod hodie habet et in antea habere potuerit, nomine Ramon Oriol, et alium, in ipsa Torre, nomine Guillem Muliner, cum suo exio et regressio et cum omnia quod hodie habet et in antea habere potuerit; et istos homines iam suprascriptos, sic donamus vobis . . . et ad vestra posterita, sine enganno, per fidem, cum compras, cum plantas, cum conderzimens, cum scalidis, cum aprisiones, cum rupturas ubicumque facere potuerint illi vel sua posteritas, sine ulla reservacione, sicut superius scriptum est, ipsos homines iamdictos aut eius posteritas qui eorum omnia tenuerint.

[98] Examples: AC Vic, perg. nos. 1478 (1074), 1479 (1076), 1082 (1083).
[99] *La Catalogne*, vol. 2, diagram 6, p. 893.
[100] *Ibid.*, pp. 913, 914.

holders; the castle *ban* extended in theory over all those subject to the castellany, whatever the status of their land. In practice, it seems that, at the end of the eleventh century, the authority of masters of castles and their agents often stopped at the boundaries of certain landed properties, though still within the perimeter of the *castrum*. Churches and monasteries, in particular, had by this date succeeded in freeing many of their possessions from the *toltas*, *questias* and usages originally imposed on them by local magnates.[101] We can be sure, even though the documents are less forthcoming on this point, that some large and medium land-owners had managed to do the same. Does this mean that the lot of the tenants, in these circumstances, was better than that of the allod-holders, abandoned without defence to the exactions of the castellans? Some deeds of self-donation entered into by allod-holders in favour of churches and abbeys might suggest this.[102]

But we should not exaggerate the difference in their condition. Though some (but not all, or even, probably, most) tenants might escape the dues and services owed to the castle, they were not, for all that, free. Their master, albeit not a castellan, could himself subject them to certain lesser forms of the *ban*. There took place, at the end of the eleventh and the beginning of the twelfth centuries, an ultimate dissemination of the powers of command and constraint (*mandamentum et districtum*), which sometimes passed – whether by acts of 'restitution' (if the beneficiary was a church) or by *convenientiae* – from the hands of the castellans into those of lesser lords. The rights thus 'restored' or abandoned by the master of men (the castellan) to the masters of the soil remained, all the same, of fairly minor importance. When it came into the possession of an owner who was not a castellan, the *ban* was reduced to the imposition of *guaitas*, *civadas* and *fogassas*,[103] or even more often *albergas* called in this case *receptiones*.[104] To which were

---

[101] See, for example, the acts of restitution cited in table 10.

[102] ACA, perg. RB II, no. 10 (1076); ACA, Monacales, perg. S. Benet, no. 372 (1098); *ibid.*, perg. Cervià, no. 445 (1126).

[103] *Ibid.*, perg. S. Benet, no. 340; a certain Sendred and his wife enfranchised two manses from all land rent, specifying that they would continue to impose *guaitas*, *civadas*, *porcos annales* and *fogassas* (1066). (*Civadas* were rents in oats, *fogassas* were round-cakes.)

[104] On monastic estates, the *receptio* consisted of the tenant lodging the abbot or the prior of the abbey, accompanied by three or four monks or *milites*, once a year and providing enough oats for their horses: *et insuper donent receptum per unumquemque annum domno abbati vel priori ad quatuor inter monachos et*

added, in rare cases, the levy of *questias* or *acaptes* (like those which the monks of Sant Llorenc de Bagà imposed in some years on their tenants)[105] and the demand for 'services' whose nature was not spelled out;[106] probably *iovas*, periodic ploughing services.[107] Overall, these charges do not seem very heavy, but they were superimposed on dues on land which were, for their part, constantly on the increase at this period.

Up to 1050/60, the *tasca* (one eleventh of the crop) remained the most widespread type of share-cropping levy. From then on, it was regarded only as a preferential rent reserved for land which was particularly unproductive or difficult to cultivate. At the end of the eleventh century, the tenant had, in most cases, to render a quarter of the grain he produced and half the wine. The harvest rent might even rise to a half, in which case the owner usually (but not, it seems, always) provided part of the seed.[108] Around 1130, there was a fresh increase in the rent on land; if he provided the tenant not only with half the seed but also plough-beasts, the lessor might demand three-quarters of the corn harvested;[109] he sometimes also claimed three-quarters of the wine.[110] Lastly, to the usual share-cropping rents were increasingly often added additional rents such as the *braçatge* (one-sixteenth of the crop) on the harvest, or the *vignogolia* (level unknown) on the wine harvest.[111]

---

caballarii et civada ad IIII caballos (1075, Arch. Montserrat, perg. Bages, no. 1541). Other examples: AC Barcelona, Divers. A, no. 580 (1072); Arch. Montserrat, perg. Bages, nos. 1546–7 (1067); *Cart. S. Cugat*, 2, no. 749 (1093). The *albergas* owed by the tenants of the abbey of Tabernoles were converted into rents in kind: a half-barrel of wheat, four cheeses, a hundred eggs and a hundred trout (1084, *Cart. Tabernoles*, no. 42).

[105] Arch. Montserrat, perg. Bagà, no. 17: *et quomodo fecimus kesta sive acapta in alia nostra honore, vos similiter secundum honorem quem vobis damus similiter faciatis* (1130).

[106] Examples: AC Urgell, Cart. 1, nos. 46 (1090), 58 (1106).

[107] The *iova*, originally a *banal* payment (*La Catalogne*, vol. 2, pp. 593–4), was often classed as a rent on land in the twelfth and thirteenth centuries (Hinojosa, *El regimén señorial y la cuestión agraria en Cataluña* (Madrid, 1905), p. 189; Vicens Vives, *Historia de los remensas*, p. 32). It was a service due on the *iou*, the yoke of oxen.

[108] AC Vic, perg. nos. 1506 (1085), 1946 (1118), 1593 (1134); AC Urgell, Cart. 1, no. 277 (1106); *Cart. Tabernoles*, no. 46 (1090): in all these cases, the lessor promised an (unspecified) part of the seed. In some cases there was no such undertaking: AC Vic, C9, Episcop. II, no. 67 (1075); AC Vic, perg. 1548 (1100).

[109] AC Vic, perg. no. 1821 (1129).   [110] *Ibid.*, perg. 1593 (1134).

[111] For the *braçatge* (*braciacitum*), *La Catalogne*, vol. 2, p. 579; see also table 12; for the *vignogolia*, ACA Monacales, perg. Cervià, no. 463 (1131).

Table 12. *The level of harvest rents, based on rent contracts in the archives of Vic and Sant Benet of Bages (1020–1140)*

1025	SB	$\frac{1}{11}$	1100	V	$\frac{1}{4}+\frac{1}{11}$ or $\frac{1}{2}+\frac{1}{11}$
1026	SB	$\frac{1}{11}$	1101	V	$\frac{1}{11}$
1043	SB	$\frac{1}{11}$	1105	SB	$\frac{1}{11}+\frac{1}{16}$
1056	SB	$\frac{1}{4}$	1105	SB	$\frac{1}{4}$
1065	V	$\frac{1}{11}$	1105	SB	$\frac{1}{4}+\frac{1}{11}+\frac{1}{16}$
1065	V	$\frac{1}{11}$	1110	SB	$\frac{1}{11}+\frac{1}{16}$
1069	SB	$\frac{1}{11}$	1111	SB	$\frac{1}{4}+\frac{1}{16}$
1073	V	$\frac{1}{4}+\frac{1}{16}$	1114	SB	$\frac{1}{11}$
1075	V	$\frac{1}{4}+\frac{1}{16}$ or $\frac{1}{2}+\frac{1}{16}$	1116	SB	$\frac{1}{11}$
1075	SB	$\frac{1}{11}$	1116	V	$\frac{1}{4}+\frac{1}{11}$
1076	SB	$\frac{1}{11}$	1117	SB	$\frac{1}{11}$ or $\frac{1}{4}$
1076	SB	$\frac{1}{4}$	1118	V	$\frac{1}{4}+\frac{1}{16}$ or $\frac{1}{2}+\frac{1}{16}$ (s)
1077	SB	$\frac{1}{4}$	1118	SB	$\frac{1}{4}+\frac{1}{16}$
1078	SB	$\frac{1}{4}$	1120	SB	$\frac{1}{4}$
1079	SB	$\frac{1}{4}$	1120	V	$\frac{1}{4}+\frac{1}{16}$
1080	V	$\frac{1}{11}$	1128	V	$\frac{1}{11}+\frac{1}{16}$
1085	V	$\frac{1}{4}$ or $\frac{1}{2}$ (s)	1129	V	$\frac{3}{4}$ (s)
1096	SB	$\frac{1}{4}$	1133	V	$\frac{1}{4}+\frac{1}{16}$
1096	V	$\frac{1}{4}$	1134	V	$\frac{1}{4}$ or $\frac{1}{2}$ (s)
1098	SB	$\frac{1}{4}$ or $\frac{1}{2}$	1135	SB	$\frac{1}{5}+\frac{1}{16}$
			1135	V	$\frac{1}{4}+\frac{1}{16}$

S: the landowner engaged to provide part of the seed corn.
SB: Sant Benet; V: Vic.

Such increases in rent worsened the position of the tenants. But this also deteriorated for another reason, that is the strengthening of the tie which bound them to the master of the soil. Formerly, the majority of tenants had also been allod-holders; the great estates, in fact, were often no more than aggregates of dispersed parcels which their owners leased to the local peasantry.[112] This type of holding gradually disappeared in the second half of the eleventh century, the result, no doubt, of a policy of rationalisation of the exploitation of their land on the part of the great landowners. Fields and vineyards were regrouped into units of cultivation which were then the subject of rental contracts; at the same time, many allods were transformed into rent-paying tenures. Consequently, the number of holdings considerably

[112] *La Catalogne*, vol. 2, pp. 222, 235–6, 246–7.

increased, especially in the old pioneering zones.[113] To describe them, a word which was relatively new in this region was increasingly employed: manse. This term, characteristic of the agrarian vocabulary only of Pyrenean Catalonia till around 1050,[114] spread rapidly in the lowland regions from that date. Certainly, its meaning here was far from what it had been in ninth-century Gaul; the manse of Bages, Vallès or the Penedès around 1100 has to be defined both as share-cropping tenure and as a unit for the imposition of the *ban*. As such, it was still a powerful element for structuring the tenant peasantry. It was also one of the instruments of its enserfment.

Serfs bound to the soil

Whereas in the past, a free allod-holder who had leased some parcel situated on the border of his own property from a monastery or rich landowner could cease to work it one day if he chose, without thereby incurring any sort of culpability, the tenant of a manse no longer had the right to leave his holding. On this point, the rent contracts are quite clear; there was an obligation on the lessee to reside 'all the days of his life' on the land leased to him (*ibi semper stetis dum vixeretis*)[115] and this constraint extended, explicitly or implicitly, to his heirs. The attachment to the soil was thus very strict and the fact that it had been, at the time the contract was concluded, freely (?) accepted by the tenant of the manse hardly altered his situation. Tied to his holding, he nevertheless had few rights in it. He could not alienate it without the formal authorisation of the lord. On his death, he could bequeath it only to one of his sons; the right of succession to manses, inspired by, but much stricter than, that for fiefs, recognised, at the end of the eleventh century, only the direct line. Nor was it certain that daughters could inherit without problems; in 1134, a

---

[113] For example, here is a list of contracts of lease contained in the original series alone of AC Barcelona: Divers. C-b, 239 (1066), Divers. A, 2254 (1070), 480 (1072), 1436 (1072), 2300 (1073), 1437 (1073), Divers. B, 812 (1074), Divers. A, 518 (1079), Divers. B, 747 (1084), Divers. C-b, 304 (1090), Divers. B, 1225 (1091), Divers. A, 588 (1097), 313 (1098). For the beginning of the twelfth century: Divers. B, 1279 (1110), 1496 (1111), 541 (1117), 1421 (1120), 1372 (1121), 546 (1121), 805 (1128), 1490 (1128), 572 (1131), 649 (1134), 789 (1135), 120 (1136), 742 (1138), 1496 (1140) etc.

[114] *La Catalogne*, vol. 1, pp. 246–7.

[115] AC Vic, C9, Episcop. II, no. 67 (1075) – and many other examples.

tenant's son-in-law had to pay inheritance dues to the monks of Cervià so that his wife could enter into possession of the paternal manse.[116] And whilst the tenant was generally permitted to designate which of his sons should succeed him, certain lords of land – the abbey of Tabernoles,[117] for example – reserved this choice to themselves.

Any infraction of these rules was treated as a breach of contract and incurred the application of whatever penal clauses had been provided. The tenant had to compensate his master and the indemnities to be paid were heavy: 2 ounces of gold (1070), 6 ounces of gold (1072), a pound of silver (1105).[118] They sometimes far exceeded the possibilities of peasants: 2 pounds of gold (1079), 5 pounds of gold (1090).[119] Such penalties applied, in particular, when the tenant wanted to discontinue his service and leave the manse. Even if he was able to pay the sum demanded of him, it would appear to him all the more scandalously heavy in that he (or his father or his grandfather) had had to pay, when the contract was drawn up, for the right to settle on the holding. From 1035–40, in fact, it became customary for the masters of the soil, to 'sell' manses to their future tenants;[120] this custom became widespread at the end of the eleventh and the beginning of the twelfth centuries.[121] The price demanded might be symbolic (a few *sous*), but was sometimes heavy (many pieces of gold); the fact remained that the tenant, in paying this newly established due, bought his land, then paid a rent of a quarter or a half of the crop throughout his life, but was nevertheless, if he wished to withdraw, obliged to pay once more.

This economic subjection inevitably engendered, for the inhabitant of the manse, a situation of strict dependence with regard to the master of the land. This was given concrete form by a tie between man and man. *Fidelis nobis sitis*,[122] ordained the les-

---

[116] ACA Monacales, perg. Cervià, no. 481.

[117] *Cart. Tabernoles*, no. 46 (1090).

[118] AC Barcelona, Divers. A, nos. 2254, 1436; Arch. Montserrat, perg. Bages, no. 1628.

[119] AC Barcelona, Divers. A, no. 518; Divers. C-b. no. 304.

[120] *La Catalogne*, vol. 2, p. 579 and note 18.

[121] Examples: AC Vic, perg. nos. 1072 (1080), 1506 (1085), 1607 (1101), 1141 (1116), 1574 and 1636 (1120), 1575 (1120); AC Barcelona, Divers. B, perg. no. 747 (1084), Divers. C-b, no. 304 (1090); AHN, Clero, perg. Poblet, carp. 1995, no. 11 (1116), carp. 1996, no. 17 (1122).

[122] Arch. Montserrat, perg. Bagà, no. 17 (1130). *Ibid.*, perg. Bages, 395 (1116).

sors when they drew up contracts. To this injunction the tenants responded with the promise: *Convenimus ad vos donatores ut fiamus vobis fidelis*,[123] or, even better: *Convenio vobis ut fiam vestrum solidum abitator.*'[124]

The demand for 'solid', or liege, fealty was increasingly frequently repeated in charters leasing land from about 1100.[125] An oath by the peasant sealed this dependence, for him and his heirs; it might be accompanied by homage.[126] Thus engaged, the tenant was required to comport himself towards the master of the land he tilled *sicut homo debet esse de suum meliorem seniorem*.[127] Every default on his part became, in consequence, a felony and could be punished as such. At the limit, some landowners, like the chapter of Urgell and the abbey of Tabernoles, obliged the men they established on their lands to promise not to take before anyone else the legal disputes which might arise in connection with the manse.[128]

At this point, servitude 'of the soil' merged with personal servitude. *Homines solidi*, the tenants became, like the allod-holders, subject to the castle *ban* and even when they escaped this, *homines proprii*; subjected to a master by reason of their manse, they were subject also by reason of their person. Many of them could thus already by 1100 or 1120 be assimilated to those *serfs de corps et de biens* soon to be found in many other parts of Europe.[129] Like them, they were given, sold and exchanged along with the land they worked:

I give you the third of all I possess at Gra, that is, a third of my manses, the men who live there, their rents and services.[130]

Such grants of *manses vêtus* had existed in Catalonia in the ninth and tenth centuries – at least in the Pyrenean regions – just as vestiges of rural slavery had survived. Since the year 1000 at the latest, they had completely disappeared from the documents. The

[123] AHN, Clero, perg. Poblet, carp. 1997, no. 1 (1126).
[124] *Ibid.*
[125] ACA Monacales, perg. S. Benet, nos. 389 (1114), 397 (1117), 422 (1141); AC Vic, perg. no. 1821 (1129).
[126] *Ibid.*, perg. no. 1478: *possideatis vos et posteritas vestra in servicio Sancti Petri Vici et nostri aut posteritas nostra et fiat in nostrum hominaticum* (1074).
[127] *Ibid.*, perg. no. 1821 (1129).
[128] *Cart. Tabernoles*, no. 46 (1090); AC Urgell, Cart. 1, no. 691 (1127).
[129] R. Boutruche, *Seigneurie et féodalité* (Paris, 1959), vol. 2, pp. 70–1.
[130] AC Urgell, Cart. 1, no. 58 (1106).

end of the eleventh century witnessed their reappearance in ever-increasing numbers.[131] The men who were thus alienated with their holdings were no longer the same; formerly, they were *mancipia*, now they were *homines proprii*, that is, former free peasants. But a new servitude had truly been born.

We might ask, finally, what happened to the condition of the tenant who was subject to the *ban* of a lord other than the lord of his holding. Jurisdictional conflicts certainly arose, which were solved in different ways, depending on the relative power of the two lords. But whatever compromises were reached in no way diminished the dependence of the peasant. Here is what a rich allod-holder of Guissona said when alienating manses subject to the *ban* of the bishop of Urgell:

I give you the allod which I bought from Mir Guifred, that is the houses with the men who live there, their tithes, their services and their rents, with the exception of the aid and the *alberga* which they customarily pay to the bishop.[132]

Let the rich fall out or agree, the losers were always the peasants.

THE ORIGINS OF THE *REMENÇA* PEASANTRY

The problem of the origins of the *remença* peasantry – the name given in Catalonia to the enserfed peasantry of the later Middle Ages – has long given rise to debate. The old Catalan historians, it must be said, experienced little difficulty with it. During the course of the Carolingian reconquest, they said, one section of the population revolted against the Arabs and attached themselves to the Franks; they were, in recompense, liberated from all obligations. Another section, out of fear, chose to remain under Muslim domination; as a punishment, they were condemned to live under the yoke of the 'bad usages' established by the Saracens.[133]

Already questioned in the eighteenth century, this legend was

---

[131] *Ibid.*, nos. 72 (1056), 405 (1064), 291 (1089), 311 (1090), 46 (1090), 63 (1100), 333 (1105), 58 (1106) etc.

[132] *Ibid.*, no. 46 (1090).

[133] This was the thesis put forward in the fifteenth century by the jurist Socarrats, and adopted by, amongst others, Pujades, *Coronica universal del Principat de cathalunya* (1609).

destroyed, towards 1900, by Brutails[134] and Hinojosa;[135] the former, in fact, against all evidence, denied the existence of any form of serfdom in medieval Rosselló; the latter, on the other hand, saw serfs in the *remença* peasantry, and made them into the distant successors of the *coloni* of the Late Roman Empire and the *mancipia* of the Visigothic kingdom. It was with Piskorski[136] and then Vicens Vives,[137] that the issue was at last clarified; both defined the *remença* as a new servitude, whose origins it was vain to seek in the early Middle Ages, a period of peasant liberty. It was imposed on the Catalan peasantry at a later date. As to precisely when, there was some hesitation on the part of both authors. They both opted, provisionally, for the thirteenth century, commenting, to quote Vicens Vives, 'that at that period the problem was posed of retaining on their holdings the peasants who cultivated them, who might emigrate to the lands of liberty; that is, either to the towns or to the newly conquered regions of the New Catalonia'.[138] This argument is irrefutable; it is quite clear that, from 1150 on, the pushing back of the frontiers of colonisation towards the west and the south – with the conquest of Lérida and Tortosa, then Valencia – changed the social climate by opening up significant possibilities of escape to the peasants of 'Old Catalonia'.

That a sharp seigneurial reaction ensued, which had the result of strengthening even further the ties which bound the peasants to their tenures and their masters, seems unquestionable. It was certainly in the thirteenth century that the juridical texts (Constitutions of the Corts of Cervera (1202), Barcelona (1283) and Monzón (1298),[139] *Commemoracions de Pere Albert*[140] and *Con-*

---

[134] *Etude sur la condition des populations rurales du Roussillon au Moyen âge* (Paris, 1891).

[135] *La pagesia de remensa en Cataluña* (Barcelona, 1902); *Le servage en Catalogne* (Paris, 1902); *El regimen señorial*.

[136] *El problema de la significación y del origen de los seis 'malos usos' en Cataluña* (Barcelona, 1929) (Spanish translation of the original Russian edition which appeared in Kiev in 1899).

[137] *Historia de los remensas*. See, in particular, chapter 1 'Importancia, gravedad y complejidad del hecho remensa' (pp. 17–41).

[138] *Ibid.*, p. 29.

[139] Quoted by Piskorski (pp. 54–6) and Vicens Vives (pp. 33–4 and notes 66–7). The acts of the Corts of Cervera are published in the *Marca hisp*, app. 493, col. 1394.

[140] Ed. J. Rovira i Ermengol (Barcelona, 1933).

suetudines diocesis Gerundensis)[141] defined the *remença* and form-
alised the new serfdom. But did the fact not to a large extent
precede the law? Perhaps the nobles of the thirteenth century were
simply content to claim (and obtain) legal recognition of a state of
affairs which was already in existence before 1200, even before
1150. Neither Piskorski nor Vicens Vives excluded the possibility
that the antecedents of the *remença* might be found in the twelfth
and even the eleventh century; let us take advantage of the
latitude they allowed.

The Catalan *remença* of the late Middle Ages can be defined by
the coming together of two subjections: on the one hand, submission to the *mals usos*, henceforward seen as degrading charges,
characteristic of servitude; on the other, hereditary attachment to
the tenure, linked to the obligation of repurchase (of himself and
his manse) for any tenant wishing to quit his condition.[142] It is not
difficult to find references to similar constraints around the year
1100. This needs, however, to be spelt out.

The classic *mals usos* (those of the thirteenth to fifteenth centuries) are five in number: *exorquia, intestia, cugucia, arsina* and
ferma de spoli.[143] *Exorquia* and *intestia* represent the rights of the
lord over the inheritance of peasants who had died either without
heirs or intestate. In the former case, the levy was equal to that
part which the children would have had if they had existed or
survived[144] (that is, four-fifths of the inheritance, if we refer to the
relevant clauses of the Visigothic code which were still in force); in
the latter case, the lord confiscated one-third of the estate if the
dead tenant left a widow and orphans, half if he left only a widow
or orphans.[145] Such rights clearly had their origin in the *causas
lexivas* and *lexivos* which had regularly figured amongst the
revenues of *banal* lordships since 1053 at the latest, and which
were no less often shared between castellans and *castlans*.[146]

---

[141] Ed. J. Rovira i Ermengol, in *Anuario de historia del derecho español* (1928),
pp. 450–85.
[142] As defined by Vicens Vives, *Historia de los remensas*, p. 30.
[143] Piskorski makes it six, but he includes the *remença* itself in the *mals usos*.
[144] *Usatges* 109: *De rebus* (a late article: thirteenth century?).
[145] *Usatges* 138: *De intestatis* (*id.*).
[146] *La Catalogne*, vol. 2, p. 592 and note 78. To the references given there should
be added, for the twelfth century: AHN, Clero, perg. Poblet, carp. 1997, no. 19
(1132), carp. 2000, no. 5 (1148).

Whilst the word *intestia* did not appear before 1156,[147] *exorquia* is attested in 1126; at this date, the seneschal Guillem Ramon of Montcada and his wife sold two allods which had come to them, they said, *per exorchia* or *propter exorchia* of two inhabitants of their castellany of Oris who had died without heirs.[148] The word is also found in 1132 in the list of revenues of the lordship of Sant Martí de Maldà.[149]

Cugucia and *arsina* were rights of justice already attributed to castellans possessed of the *ban* by the mid-eleventh century. The former, mentioned as early as 1058,[150] would consist in the thirteenth century of the confiscation of half the possessions of an adulterous woman (when the adultery was committed without the husband's consent) or of the whole of these possessions (when the husband had acquiesced in his misfortune).[151] The latter, mentioned as early as 1071,[152] represented a levy of a third of the patrimony of a peasant whose house had been burned down and who was thus punished for his negligence.

The *ferma de spoli*, which the old authors confused (not without some justification) with the *ius primae noctis*, represented the price of the consent given by the lord to the marriage of his subjects, or, more precisely – in the fourteenth and fifteenth centuries – the price of his subscription at the foot of the contract of *sponsalitium*; until its abolition at the end of the Middle Ages, it amounted to an arbitrary tax on the marital dowry. Its antecedents are clearly to be found in the eleventh century in the form of the *presentalias de ipsos aut ipsas qui duxerint maritos vel uxores* imposed on the inhabitants of Aramprunyà by 1067,[153] and are subsequently found, under the abbreviated title of *presentalias* or *presentalges*, in two agreements concluded for the custody of castles from the first half of the twelfth century.[154]

The *mals usos* of the thirteenth to fifteenth centuries thus quite clearly derived from the *banal* charges imposed on the Catalan

---

[147] B. Alart, *Privilèges et titres de Roussillon et de Cerdagne*, vol. 1, p. 47 (act quoted by Piskorski, p. 22).
[148] AC Vic, perg. nos. 1165, 1166.
[149] AHN, Clero, perg. Poblet, carp. 1997, no. 19.
[150] *LFM*, 1, no. 257. *La Catalogne*, vol. 2, p. 589 and note 63.
[151] *Usatges* 110: *Similiter de rebus*.
[152] *Marca hisp.*, app. 281. *La Catalogne*, vol. 2, pp. 589–90 and note 64.
[153] *Ibid.*, p. 592 and note 77.
[154] AHN, Clero, perg. Poblet, carp. 1997, nos. 6 (1127), 14 (1130).

peasantry from 1040/50. They represented, however, only a part of them. From 1050 to 1200 there was a process of sifting and simplification. The jungle of primitive 'bad usages' had been cleared away and only five had survived, but they sufficed to define the new servile condition; they affected the peasants subjected to them with the two taints characteristic of unfreedom throughout the West: *mainmorte* (in the form of *exorquia*) and the limitation on the right to marry.

In these circumstances, it is clear that the *remença* itself (attachment to the holding) only completed the process of enserfment. But, even if we continue to see it as one of the essential elements of the new servitude, there is still no justification for placing its birth in the thirteenth century. The formulas for specifying residence to which Vicens Vives drew attention, for example, in leases of 1243, 1255 and 1258,[155] were already to be found – sometimes in very similar terms – in contracts from 1075, 1098, 1126 and 1129.[156] Furthermore, the expression *redemptiones mansorum et hominum* which was, amongst others (*redemptio*, *redimentia>remensa*), to designate the dues to be paid by the tenant to recover his liberty, appeared – and this is no new discovery – as early as 1126.[157] In fact, the obligation on the holder of the manse to buy back both himself and his tenure derived directly from the penal clauses in leases. Certainly, it was the arbitrary way in which the lord fixed the amount of the redemption which would make the *remença* into an abuse intolerable to the peasantry. But the arbitrariness was equally great when, before 1100, lessors of land imposed on their tenants the contractual obligation to pay, if they left, indemnities which far exceeded their capabilities.[158]

From the end of the eleventh to the thirteenth centuries, the definition of the servile condition was constantly being refined and it was in the thirteenth century that, under the influence of conditions so well described by Vicens Vives, the regime of the *remença* was institutionalised. But its features were all already in existence

[155] Vicens Vives, *Historia de los remensas*, pp. 30–1.
[156] AC Vic, C9, Episc. II, perg. no. 67; Arch. Montserrat, perg. Bages, no. 1616; AHN, Clero, perg. Poblet, carp. 1997, no. 1; AC Vic, perg. no. 1821.
[157] ACA, perg. RB III, no. 246. This reference was known to Balari Jovany in 1899 (*Origenes Históricos de Cataluña* (Barcelona, 1899, reed. Sant Cugat del Vallès, 1964 in 3 vols.), vol. 2, p. 535). It was quoted anew by Hinojosa (*El regimen señorial*, p. 213 and note 1) and Vicens Vives (*Historia de los remensas*, p. 30).
[158] See above, pp. 229–30.

by 1100: personal servitude (*mals usos*), attachment to the land (*remença*) and also the link between the two:

I promise, my lords, that I will reside on this land of Cocola and that I will be yours, as a man ought to be to his best lord.[159]

Conclusion

Launched for some pages now into historical controversy, let us persist for a moment, and try to widen the debate. Reflecting on the work of Georges Duby, Robert Boutruche expressed surprise at the break Duby established between the old and the new servitudes.[160] It is, indeed, surprising, and even a little daunting to the spirit, to admit the existence, between the disappearance of the last rural slaves (descendants of the *mancipia* of the early Middle Ages) and the definition of the new forms of peasant dependence, of a 'period of transition' during which certain regions knew, at least in law, no form of servitude. But the facts are stubborn and show that such a period did exist; it is clear to see in mid-eleventh-century Catalonia.

The phenomenon is perfectly explicable; it appears even an imperative requirement of the global history of the societies in which it occurred. Technical progress, the conquest of new land, the corresponding increase in agricultural production, the first signs of which appear here particularly precociously, all naturally tended to alleviate the constraints weighing on the peasantry; the emancipation of the last *servi* on the one hand, and a momentary amelioration of the lot of the mass of country dwellers (easily visible in Catalonia around 1020) on the other, were their direct effects. But the social context of the period was such as to make it impossible for the peasantry to benefit for long from the new riches born of their labour. Even before the old slavery had totally disappeared, new chains were forged that would soon bind the peasant class. The establishment of the powers of the *ban* prepared the new servitude, which was all the harsher in that the peasants had, for a short span, been able to believe themselves, within their village communities, to be all, and wholly, free.

The generalisation of the 'bad usages' and the increase in obli-

---

[159] AC Vic, perg. 1821 (1129).
[160] *Seigneurie et féodalité*, vol. 2, pp. 75–6.

gations on land permitted, conversely, an idle group to prosper. In the social evolution of the period, the birth of chivalry corresponded to the new servitude; the two phenomena are contemporary and inseparable. It was because an increasing part of their production could be extorted from the peasantry that the size of the aristocratic class swelled in the proportions which still astonish us today. The old families maintained themselves at the top of the tree, sometimes increasing their fortunes to a considerable degree. But, in their shadow, the numerous troop of new specialists in war and the maintenance of order (custodians of castles, salaried or enfeoffed horsemen) could accede to the noble way of life, and then, through dubbing, to nobility itself.

At the end of the eleventh century, a new society was born.

Appendix. *The moveable wealth of Arnau Mir de Tost and his wife Arsendis (1068–71)*

		Numbers	
Name of items	Identification (partial)	Arnau	Arsendis
1. Wardrobe			
vestimentos de ciclato	clothes of brocade		2
vestimentos de pallio	clothes of silk		2
vestimentos de oztorin			3
vestimentos de oved		1	1
vestimentos de cafalbafal		1	
vestimentos de almoncharac		1	
vestimentos de margmed		1	
indumentos laneos et lineos	clothes of wool and linen	?	?
capas de ciclato	cloaks of brocade		2
capas de tirez	cloaks of brocade		15
capas de pallio	cloaks of silk		1
capas de oztorin			3
(tota facta cum auro)	cloak of cloth of gold	1	
capas de berraga	cloaks of camlet	2	
capas coopertas de berraga		1	
capas de oved			3
capas de castanea			1
capas de remlias			1
mantas de pallio	mantles of silk	6	
bamben de ciclato	tunic of brocade	1	
bamben de tirez	tunic of brocade	1	
pelles grisas qui sunt mantellos	fur mantles (gris)	3	
pellicias armelinas	pelisses of ermine	1	1
pellicias de alfanech			
copertas de ciclato		2	

Appendix (*cont*)

Name of items	Identification (partial)	Numbers Arnau	Arsendis
copertas de tirez		4	
copertas de fres			1
pellicones armelinos	pelisses of ermine	2	
pellicones vair	pelisses of vair	1	
pellicones gris	pelisses of gris		
pels matrinas copertas de oved	skins of marten	6	
pels veras	skins of vair	4	
manegas armelinas et grisas in alias pellicias	pelisses with sleeves of ermine and gris		
canlzas de auxtori	hose of ?	unas	
parilios de calza de pallii	hose of silk	4	
parilios de braga cum alfiuvianos	breeches	3	
kamisas de arrides ad guisa de Spania	shirts in the Spanish style	7	
kamisia de arrides ad guisa de Xipra	shirts in the Cyprus style	1	
stola de pallii	stoles of silk	1	
brisal de pallii	tunic of silk	1	
brisal purpura feminile	purple tunic for a woman	1	
velosos de capite	head veils		2
capels de feltro	felt hats	6	
capels gris	hats of gris	1	
capel de yanetas	hat of civet cat	1	
calota	skullcap	1	
capel de fres	hat of Frisian cloth	1	
parilios de guais de Luca	pairs of gloves of Lucca	14	
parilios de guais de Podio	pairs of gloves of Le Puy	5	
2. Materials			
telas de ciclato	cloths of brocade		1
telas de tirez	cloths of brocade	2	
telas de pallio	cloths of silk	2	2
telas de oztorin			1
telas de ezceni			1
telas de oved		4	
sasa alcot	bag containing cotton	1	
saccots aput seda	bags containing silk	2	
sacot cum pecias de pallii, alias pacias et chammalegas	bag containing silk and camlet	1	
saccet cum multas pecias de pallii et alias chausas	bag containing silk and other cloths	1	
ligatures cum pecias de pallii		3	
3. Jewellery			
anulos ex auro	gold rings	multos	

Appendix (*cont*)

Name of items	Identification (partial)	Numbers Arnau	Arsendis
annulos cum iemis et gegonciis et nudellis de auro	gold rings with precious stones	plurimos	
ornamentum de capite de auro	gold ? diadem		1
chapud ligamine de auro	gold chain	1	
parilios de bogs de auro	pairs of gold earrings	4	
aflivallos auri maiores	gold fibulas		unos
aflivallos auri minores	gold fibulas		unos
botons de auro	gold buttons	plurimos	
pumbo de auro	gold pommel	1	1
pumbo de argento	silver pommel		1
pumbo de olores	pommel		1
4. Toilet articles			
concas de loto	brass bowls	6	
arachias de loto	brass ?	5	
orcols	toilet jugs	7	
pintines de vivorii	ivory combs	2	
speculum indium cum argento	mirror from the Indes		1
speculum indium coperto argen	mirror from the Indes	1	
5. Furniture and hangings			
kandelers argentos	silver chandeliers	5	
kandelers de ferro coberts de argen	silvered iron chandeliers	18	
kandelers de loto	brass chandeliers	2	
bancals de tapid	bench covers	22	
bancals de Cordues	bench covers of Cordova	5	
dossales de ciclato	bed-head covers of brocade	1	
dossales de pallio	bed-head covers of silk	2	1
dossales de fres	bed-head covers of Frisian cloth	1	1
dossales de Alamania	bed-head covers of German cloth	1	
cortinas de seda	curtains of silk	1	
cortinas de lino apud listas	curtains of linen	3	
parapsides de fust oltramari	? of wood from Outremer	2	
6. Beds and bedlinen			
lectum de almocelia			1
almocelias de palii	? of silk	5	
almocelias de castanea		3	
cobtos de alfanech copertos de pallii		3	
cobtos martrinos copertos de pallii	featherbeds of marten covered in silk	1	

Appendix (*cont*)

Name of items	Identification (partial)	Numbers Arnau	Arsendis
cobtos martrinos copertos de castanea	featherbeds of marten covered in ?	2	
feltros de pallii	draw-sheets of felt covered in silk	2	
feltros inter banbeizals et lana	drawsheets of felt covered in silk or wool	6	
superlectos de pallii	bedcovers of silk	7	
superlectos ex brosdei cum attocs de auctauri		2	
superlecto vulpino	bedcover of fox		1
cobertors	coverlets		13
cobertors de fres	coverlets of Frisian cloth		2
cobertos de lupo cervario coperts de palli	coverlets of lynx covered in silk	2	
lencols	sheets	3	8
lencio Bocari	sheets of Bokhara	1	
sabanas de seda	sheets of silk	1	
sabanas de zofia	sheets of ?	1	
plumacios de pallii	pillows of silk	12	
plumacios de castanea	pillows of ?	1	
plumacios de lana	pillows of wool	15	
coxins aput plumba	feather cushions	15	
ganabs de seda	? of silk	2	
brecals de lecto		3	
velosos	covers (for beds?)	4	
colcedras		10	
beragas		2	
tapids de Kastella et alios	covers from Castile and elsewhere	11	

7. Tableware

vexella ex argento	silver vessels		composi-tion not specified
anapos planos	goblets	14	
anapos paucos (cum opera de copasal cobretados)		10	
anaps de madre		10	
copas de madre	cups	10	
ampullas arachias		6	
gradails argenteos	silver platters	2	
gradails salamonenc	platters	1	
naves salamoneches	plates	1	
eschudelas grandes	large plates	4	
eschudelas paucas	small plates	9	
coclearas argenteas	silver spoons	43	

Appendix (*cont*)

Name of items	Identification (partial)	Numbers	
		Arnau	Arsendis
cocleara argentea maxima	silver ladle	1	
cifo aureo	gold vase	1	
ciphfo salamonec	vase ?	1	
ramos argenteos	? of silver	8	
molto argenteo becer	? of silver	1	
mapos apud tovalas	table covers with serviettes	15	
mapas de castella (apud tovalas)	table covers and serviettes of Castile	3	
8. Kitchen utensils			
morters apud illorum pisones	pestles and mortars	3	
calleres	cauldrons	20	
ollas ereas	bronze cooking pots	6	
alchomcoms de aram	? of bronze	3	
patellas	frying pans	5	
bufadors	bellows	2	
9. Chess sets and table games			
tabulas argenteas cum illorum tabulers	silver tables	13	
parilios escachs vivoril	ivory chess sets	3	
parilios excachs de cristallo	crystal chess sets	3	
10. Equipment for travel and war			
sellas de argento	silver saddles	2	
frenos de argento	silver bits	2	
spatas	swords	number not specified	
alspergos	hauberks	11	
alchoba cum suos feltros	felt tent	1	
alcovas	tents	12	

Sources: will of Arsendis (22 May 1068), inventory of legacies made by Arnau for the repose of the soul of his wife (1068) and inventory of Arnau's moveables at the time of his departure for Saint James of Galicia (1071): documents published by P. Sanahuja, *Historia de la villa de Ager*, apps. 25, 27, 28, pp. 339–49.

8. *Rural communities in Catalonia and Valencia (from the ninth to the mid-fourteenth centuries)**

It might seem strange to discuss rural communities in Catalonia and Valencia in a single paper. In the first place, the documentation is different in the two regions; whilst charters from the ninth and tenth, and even more for the eleventh and twelfth, centuries, abound in the Catalan archives, the history of Valencia at this period is dependent on brief references in chronicles and the meagre information provided by toponymy and archaeology. Further, the two societies themselves appear dissimilar: one Christian, the other Muslim. Even after the conquest of Valencia, the problems were by no means the same in the two countries; that of the future of the subject Muslim communities, for example, crucial in Valencia, was only marginal in Catalonia. It seems, nevertheless, that a link exists between these two histories. One major problem, in fact, was common to both; that of the consequences of the establishment of an order of the feudal – or, if one prefers, the 'seigneurial' – type on the life of the communities which predated it. This system appeared earlier in Catalonia, by the eleventh century, consequent upon a period of internal evolution – or rather revolution; in Valencia, it was imported in the thirteenth century by the Christian conquest.

Catalan village communities

BEFORE FEUDALISM (NINTH, TENTH AND EARLY ELEVENTH CENTURIES

The mountain communities

To reach as far back as possible into the past of the Catalan rural communities, we have to look to the mountains, to those high

* This paper, presented to the fourth Flaran Colloquium in 1982 (*Les communautés villageoises en Europe occidentale du Moyen Age aux Temps modernes* (Auch, 1984), pp. 79–115) was jointly prepared with Pierre Guichard. I would like to thank him for permitting me to reproduce his contribution, 'The rural

243

Pyrenean valleys which, from time immemorial, seem – I say 'seem' advisedly – to have experienced a stable history. There, in villages whose names (pre-Indo-European, for the most part) testify to their great antiquity,[1] and whose sites remained unchanged from when they were first recorded at the beginning of the ninth century,[2] lived populations amongst whom it is clearly possible to discern developed habits of collective life. Some light is thrown on these communities by the documentation, in particular that of the rich archives of La Seu d'Urgell.

The acts through which the village communities appear most clearly are the acts of consecration of parish churches; ten have survived for the diocese of Urgell for the ninth century, twenty-eight for the tenth.[3] It is clear that the construction of the sanctuary was in many cases the collective labour of the local peasantry, called *fundatores* or *edificatores* by the texts, and that the dedication itself took place at their initiative alone.[4] It was from them that the bishop received the church, it was they who endowed it, and it was they who subscribed the act of consecration: six heads of family at Lillet and Campelles, nine at Ardovol, fourteen at Saldes and Frontanyà, sixteen at Greixer, eighteen at Estoll, twenty-two at Canalda and thirty-one at La Quar.[5] The list of local founders is sometimes not given, but – which is equally interesting – the community was denoted by one word: the *plebs* or the *populus*. At Saillagouse, for example, the *plebs abitancium in Salagosa*,[6] at Corbera, the *populus habitancium in dicta parrochia, ecclesiam fundatores*.[7] In return for its work of devotion, the community might itself receive the patronage of the church, in particular the

communities of the kingdom of Valencia', which I believe to be, from every point of view, of the greatest importance.

[1] For the place-names of the high Catalan valleys, see the numerous and important works of J. Coromines, collected in *Estudis de toponimía catalana*, 2 vols. (Barcelona, 1966–70), especially vol. 1, pp. 83–91, 112–41, 153–217.

[2] Bonnassie, *La Catalogne*, vol. 1, pp. 86–9.

[3] These acts have now been published: C. Baraut, 'Les actes de consagracions d'esglésies del bisbat d'Urgell (segles IX–XII)' in *Urgellia*, 1 (1978), 11–182.

[4] For example, Baraut 'Les actes de consagracions', no. 13: Veniens venerabilis Nantigisus pontifex in villa vocitata Kanativa, rogatus a populo ibidem abitancium qui aeclesiam ibi edificaverunt et ad culmen sacrationis perduxerunt . . .' (Sant Julià de Canalda, 900).

[5] Baraut, 'Les actes de consagracions', nos. 1 (Lillet, 833), 4 (Campelles, 857), 5 (Saldes, 857), 6 (Greixer, 871), 7 (Ardovol, 890), 9 (La Quar, 899), 12 (Canalda, 900), 19 (Frontanyà, 905) and 25 (Estoll, 913).

[6] *Ibid.*, no. 26 (913).   [7] *Ibid.*, no. 12 (899).

right to choose the priest: *abeant potestam ipsi homines qui ipsa ecclesia edificaverunt ad clericum elegendum.*[8] In this case, the village community received the tithes, which it also disbursed; it was only obliged by the bishop to distribute the income according to canonical rules.[9]

Joint ownership of the parish church thus appears as an early form of communal possession; the church, it was sometimes expressly stated, was the allod of the inhabitants.[10] Can other forms of collective property be discerned? They clearly can, and the acts of consecration offer further interesting evidence on this point; in the endowment of the parish church, they occasionally distinguish goods given individually by certain local landowners and goods granted collectively: *nos omnes donamus, nos circummanentes donamus.*[11] The existence of communal property is also shown by other types of document, in particular by some accounts of legal proceedings.[12] It would be wrong, however, to generalise and assume that collective ownership of land predominated;[13] by the ninth and tenth centuries (and no doubt much earlier), individual ownership, in its Roman definition, was by far the most common form of land holding, at least in areas of habitation and cultivation. What, on the other hand, the communities held jointly were rights over the uncultivated land – woods, wastes and summer pastures – which, in these mountainous regions, represented a considerable area. This was part of the public domain, hence of the sovereignty of the count, but the communities generally enjoyed the use of them or, more precisely, to use the Catalan term, the 'appropriation' (*adimparamentum, ademprivum, empriu*: rights of passage, to gather, to cut wood and to pasture

---

[8] *Ibid.*, no. 4 (Campelles, 857).

[9] Exceptionally, this situation could last till the beginning of the twelfth century; as at Santa Eugenia d'Ollà (Cerdanya), where, in 1122–3, the inhabitants restored the tithes to bishop Ot of Urgell, and engaged no longer to nominate themselves the priest to their church, but to accept whoever the bishop sent them (AC Urgell, Cart. 1, no. 829, fo. 241).

[10] ACA, perg. BR I, no. 22 (1019).

[11] Baraut, 'Les actes de consagracions', nos. 9, 10, 21.

[12] R. d'Abadal, *Catalunya carolingia*, vol. 3, *Els comtats de Pallars i Ribagorça* (Barcelona, 1955), 2, no. 297, pp. 441–2 (995); B. Alart, *Cartulaire roussillonnais* (Perpignan, 1880), no. 32, pp. 49–51 (1027).

[13] This is the mistake made by A. Barbero and M. Vigil, *La formación del feudalismo en la Península ibérica* (Barcelona, 1978), pp. 354–62, who generalise on the basis of examples which are too few and insufficiently significant.

animals).[14] And when, on occasion, such rights were contested, for example by a monastery, the communities did not hesitate to defend themselves before the public courts.[15]

With these judicial interventions on the part of the village collectively, we touch on another problem: that of their juridical identity and their place in the socio-political structures. It is extremely difficult to know to what extent they enjoyed – and from what period, and how many of them – a status in derogation of public law. In these regions of upper Catalonia, the franchises are known only from allusion and later documents, at any rate later than 1000: those of the inhabitants of Andorra, for example, are referred to in just one word in a text of 1003,[16] and those of other communities, much smaller in size, are known only from various acts dating from the eleventh century.[17] It seems, however, that the vast majority of villages were subject to the normal rules governing free men, and thus were responsible either directly to the count (in the domains of the fisc), or to his agents – viscounts and vicars – or to abbeys possessing immunities. This obedience might be signalled by the swearing of an oath of collective fealty.[18] It took concrete form in the payment of a rent – analagous to the Aragonese *tributum soli* or the Italian *fodrum* – and, above all, in the performance of military service.[19] For these peasants were also fighting men who participated actively, it seems, in the defence of the counties. In return for these obligations, the communities enjoyed a large degree of self-government. Their internal affairs were the province of the village notables, the *boni homines* whose presence is attested in the earliest documents to have survived:

[14] For a juridical and ethnological study of these rights, based on the example of Capcir: L. Assier-Andrieu, *Coutume et rapports sociaux: étude anthropologique des communautés paysannes du Capcir* (Toulouse, 1981), especially pp. 23–7.

[15] For example: law-suit in 987 between the villagers of Gombreny and the monastery of Sant Joan de les Abadeses before the court of the count of Cerdanya (F. Udina Martorell, *El archivo condal de Barcelona en los siglos IX–X. Estudio crítico de sus fondos* (Barcelona, 1951), App. 1, Doc. D. pp. 446–7.

[16] C. Baraut, 'Els documents dels anys 981–1010 de l'Arxiu Capitular de la Seu d'Urgell' in *Urgellia*, 3 (1980), no. 286, 117–18: *ex franceda de homines de valle Andorra*.

[17] AC Urgell, Cart. 1, nos. 492, 924, 925, and Bonnassie, *La Catalogne*, vol. 1, pp. 311–12.

[18] ACA, perg. sense data, RB I, nos. 183, 185. Text of two oaths sworn by two communities of upper Pallars in Bonnassie, *La Catalogne*, vol. 1, p. 140, note 32.

[19] Bonnassie, *La Catalogne*, vol. 1, pp. 158–60.

judicial auxiliaries, arbiters, experts, they appear as the regulators of social relations within the peasant communities.[20] These early communities should not, however, be seen as little Arcadias or as egalitarian republics. From the ninth century, social cleavages, chiefly differentiating the families of the *boni homines* from the rest of the peasantry, were very marked.[21] Moreover, the communities had to face increasingly severe attacks, from both the lay and the ecclesiastical aristocracy, on their property and their rights.[22] These encroachments grew increasingly serious, especially in the tenth century, and could amount to complete dispossession. Hence already a vigorous reaction on the part of certain communities, to the extent, on occasion, of open rebellion; this was the case with the inhabitants of Andorra, against whom Count Borrell defended himself by building a castle, which the Andorrans took by brute force and occupied for many years[23] – a foretaste of the social strife of the eleventh century.

Finally, though these communities give ample evidence of dynamism, it should not be assumed that they escaped hardship. On the contrary, most of them seem to have been sunk into the most abject poverty, the result of over-population, isolation, the shortage of cultivable land and the poverty of agricultural equipment. It was this distress, in fact, which impelled the inhabitants of the high valleys to undertake, at great risk, the colonisation of the lowlands, which was primarily an exodus of the hungry.

Expansion to the beginning of the eleventh century: the first age of the franchises

A priori, the movement of colonisation hardly lent itself, at least initially, to the constitution of village communities in the repopulated zones. It took place, for the most part, in a very

---

[20] *Ibid.*, vol. 1, pp. 309–10. The role of the *boni homines* is already referred to in Visigothic law (V, 6, 3).

[21] In 905, for example, the act of consecration of the church of Frontanyà used the expression *boni homines* for those of the parishioners who contributed to the endowment of the church from their patrimonial property, thus implicitly contrasting them to the *cetera plebs* who could only offer their labour (Baraut, 'Les actes de consagracions', no. 19).

[22] Examples of complete dispossession: Udina, *El archivo condal*, no. 38 (913); *ibid.*, App. 1, Doc. D (987); d'Abadal, *Els comtats de Pallars i Ribagorça*, no. 297 (995).

[23] Baraut, 'Els documents dels anys 981–1010', no. 286.

scattered fashion; it was mostly the work of young men or young couples leaving their native villages, alone or in tiny groups, to try their chances on the almost deserted lands stretching along the foot of the mountains. As far as agrarian structures were concerned, the outcome was the hegemony of the peasant smallholding, itself born of the right of *aprision* which accorded free disposal of the soil to whoever occupied it, brought it under cultivation and assured its continued exploitation for thirty years. As far as settlement was concerned, this movement quite as frequently took the form of dispersal into hamlets and isolated farms as the creation of true villages.

The need, however, to cope with the Muslim threat (very pressing till the end of the tenth century), the extreme harshness of life and the multitude of obstacles encountered in the struggle against difficult natural conditions encouraged people to cluster together and help each other.

The organisation of collective defences is attested by certain documents from the end of the tenth century. In 954, for example, at Freixà, on the western frontier, fifteen heads of family undertook together – *in communo*, says the document – the construction of a tower.[24] In 990, it was the associated inhabitants of Ribes, in Penedès, who received possession of the local *castrum* from the bishop and responsibility for its defence: *donamus namque vobis predictum castrum.*[25] There can be no doubt that, right up to the early years of the eleventh century, the village communities – like the Castilo–Leonese *concejos*[26] – played a key role in the country's military protection, sometimes by assuming it in a practically autonomous fashion (as in the two cases cited above), sometimes – most often – by combining under the direction of the regular authorities.

But it was in the economic sphere that the activities of the communities of colonists were most clearly revealed. They can be seen in certain collective assarting enterprises which, though they remained few, are nevertheless significant. They were very

---

[24] Font Rius, *CPC*, vol. 1, no. 5.   [25] *Ibid.*, no. 10.

[26] M. del C. Carlé, *Del concejo medieval castellano-leonés* (Buenos Aires, 1968), pp. 33–42; Cl. Sánchez Albornoz, 'Conséquences de la reconquête et du repeuplement sur les institutions féodovassaliques de León et Castille', *Annales du Midi*, 80 (1968). See also J. A. García de Cortazar, 'Les communautés villageoises du nord de la Péninsule ibérique au Moyen Age', *Les communautés villageoises en Europe occidentale*, pp. 55–77.

apparent in the creation of the technical infrastructures necessary to the process of bringing new land into cultivation. In particular, their role was decisive in building the hydraulic mechanisms which alone could make possible a growth of agricultural production. The first mills were certainly of peasant construction, and many of them were still, towards 1000, owned jointly by groups of peasant allod-holders.[27] The same was true of the conduits fed by these mill ponds, which watered the cultivated fields downstream. Some village communities went further, to the extent of creating veritable networks of irrigation. This is revealed, for example, by a contract of 1020, by which a group of eight heads of families from a hamlet of Vallès bought from the countess Ermessend the water of several mountain streams intended to feed a channel they were proposing to dig.[28] This document alone shows that the village communities, far from being content with unvarying routine, as is so often alleged, were capable not only of inventing progressive solutions, but of saving from the fruits of their labour and investing their joint savings in productive enterprises.

The key role the peasant communities played in the development of productive forces is shown, lastly, in the way power was organised. The counts – and particularly the counts of Barcelona – relied on them both to resist the Muslim threat and to contain the ambitions of the aristocracy. They were extremely heedful both of their petitions and their grievances and freely received their representatives in audiences in the comital palace. One count – Ramon Borrell – is even to be seen accepting defeat in an action brought against him by the peasants of the Vallès and magnanimously agreeing, before his own court, that right was on their side.[29] So, at least until the first third of the eleventh century, there was a close alliance between comital power and the village communities, which found its most striking expression in the charters of franchise.

For the Catalan lowlands, that is chiefly the county of Barcelona, these have survived. Recently edited, they are still being studied;[30] there is little point, therefore, in enlarging on them here. Let us say simply that their origins date back to the

[27] Bonnassie, *La Catalogne*, vol. 1, p. 461.
[28] *Ibid.*, pp. 466–9; ACA, perg. BR I, no. 30.
[29] ACA, perg. Ramon Borrell, no. 104.
[30] This research has since been published as volume 2 of Font Rius, *CPC*.

beginning of the occupation of the country and that the liberties which they stipulate were steadfastly maintained throughout the ninth and tenth centuries. Their content was only made more precise and expanded with the passage of time. Many of their clauses, it is true, were addressed specifically to townsmen, but others were primarily relevant to the countryside. Amongst the latter we should note in particular the solemn guarantees of the collective rights to the use of assets regarded as public: 'the pastures and the woods, the running waters and springs, the entries and exits to all the places which properly derive from the said franchises, enjoy them freely and for this perform no service, and pay no rent, either to us or to any other'.[31] The underlying principle of these privileges, in short, was to place the free communities under the direct authority of the count, without intermediaries, particularly in judicial matters. This immunity – the word is expressly employed in the charter of Montmell in 974[32] – accorded to the villages collectively removed them, in theory, from all seigneurial constraints.

The communities in the feudal crisis

THE ASSAULT ON THE FRANCHISES

It was inevitable, therefore, that the advent of the feudal regime in Catalonia would assume the form of a generalised assault by the aristocracy on the village franchises and, more broadly, on all peasant liberties.

This assault, the major event in the social history of the eleventh century, had, in fact, been long in preparation. It was prefaced by the process of concentration of land ownership which had, throughout the tenth century, resulted in the transfer of a large number of peasant allods into the patrimony of the monasteries and noble families. It was also doubtless implicit in the transformation of the techniques of combat which henceforward increasingly privileged the mounted warrior as opposed to the foot-soldier and tended to render derisory the paltry arms of the peasantry. Thus, in spite of the prime role they played in the economic development of the country, the village communities found themselves increas-

---

[31] Font Rius, *CPC*, vol. 1, no. 15. See also *Cartulario de Sant Cugat del Vallès*, ed. J. Rius Serra (Barcelona, 1946), 2, no. 436.
[32] Font Rius, *CPC*, vol. 1, no. 7.

ingly weakened. Their enfeebled condition is apparent by the end of the tenth century. If we take once again the example of the consecration of churches in the diocese of Urgell, we find that out of ten churches newly consecrated in the ninth century, nine were of village foundation; in the first half of the tenth century, six out of eighteen; in the second half, one out of ten. In less than two centuries, the places of worship had thus passed almost entirely out of the control of the village communities into that of the great families and abbeys.

Was this decline general? Not quite; in the free zones of the south and west the communities resisted better and even, as late as the beginning of the eleventh century, still held their heads high. But they owed this respite to the jealous protection provided by the counts. This only had to falter to spell doom for their powers and their liberties.

The feudal revolution – let us so call, for simplicity's sake, the brutal and general seizure of power by the castle-owning aristocracy – which raged in Catalonia during the years 1030–60 thus comprised two major and closely interlinked elements. On the one hand, armed challenge to the power of the counts; on the other, the destruction of the village franchises. These two aspects are particularly clearly revealed by the solemn legal proceedings brought in 1052 or 1053 by Count Ramon Berenguer I of Barcelona against the leader of the revolting barons, Mir Geribert; a trial *in absentia*, since the accused, who at that date controlled the whole western part of the county, was clearly out of reach. What was primarily held against the rebellious magnate and his men were the misdeeds perpetrated against the free communities (*omnia malefacta que predictus Miro et sui homines fecerunt in iamdictis franchedis*), misdeeds which the documents spell out: the Vallès and the Penedès were subjected to a regime of terror, in which villages were burned and their inhabitants put to the sword.[33] At the same time or a little later, Pallars endured similar atrocities: there, too, the documents record a long litany of slaughter, pillage and arson.[34]

These noble insurrections, which, in one form or another, lasted

---

[33] ACA, perg. sense data, RB I, no. 38 (act edited by F. Carreras Candi, 'Lo Montjuich de Barcelona' in *Memorias de la Real Academia de Buenas Letras de Barcelona*, 8 (1903), App. 19). For these events, Bonnassie, *La Catalogne*, vol. 2, pp. 641–4, 677–8.

[34] ACA, perg. sense data, RB I, nos. 33, 34; Bonnassie, *La Catalogne*, vol. 2, pp. 612–18.

for several decades, resulted in a complete transformation of social relations. In practice, they invariably ended in a compromise with the count. The authority of the latter was recognised anew, but on a different footing, of a frankly feudo-vassalic character. The destruction of the village franchises, however, was never called into question. The village was everywhere subordinated to the castle. The seigneurial *ban* bore down on the ancient free communities, with its accompanying exactions, 'bad customs', *toltas*, *acaptas*, restrictions on the freedom of marriage and the right of free disposal of property. A process of enserfment began, which was to mark the history of a large part of the Catalan rural population for four centuries.

Attempts at resistance and their results

In the face of these assaults, the peasantry did not remain passive, and their reactions are all the more interesting in that the structures of resistance then established contributed, to a very large degree, to shaping the future form of the village communities.

To noble violence the inevitable response, at least sporadically, was peasant counter-violence. This was the case in Andorra where the communities managed, by resorting to armed struggle, to escape the servitude with which they were threatened.[35] It was very probably the case in Vallès and Penedès since nothing else could explain the bloody repression to which these regions were subjected.

But peasant resistance more often took the path of non-violence. For the most part, it was assimilated into the movement of the Peace and Truce of God, of which it was here one of the prime movers. Among the many forms assumed by this movement, one deserves closer examination since it had a strong influence on the history of Catalan villages, on their social organisation and topography alike. This was the creation of the *sagreres*.[36] The word *sagrera* (Latin *sacraria*) was used for the protected space immediately adjacent to the parish church: a circular area with a radius of thirty, or exceptionally sixty, paces. This area enjoyed the privi-

---

[35] AC Urgell, Cart. 1, no. 504.
[36] K. Kennelly, 'Sobre la paz de Dios y la sagrera en el condado de Barcelona' in *Anuario de Estudios Medievales,* 5 (1968), 107–38; Bonnassie, *La Catalogne,* vol. 2, pp. 653–6.

leges attached to the church: right of asylum and inviolability. It enjoyed, in particular, and absolutely explicitly, all the protection which the Assemblies of Peace afforded to the property of the church. They were, in a sense, *sauvetés* before the fact: minuscule in size, but densely populated, even over-populated. The creation of the *sagreres* had as a consequence a dramatic contraction of village settlement which now huddled up against the church. This phenomenon, which had its exact parallel in the establishment of inhabited cemeteries in western France,[37] can be precisely dated; whilst a few (dubious) references to *sagreres* appear in the tenth century in the region of Vic, the vast majority were created at the time of, and in response to, the troubles (it was in 1034, for example, that the movement took off in the county of Barcelona).[38]

How effective was this protection? In many cases it was illusory. The threat of spiritual sanctions did not stop the exactions. Worse, some barons chose from preference the days consecrated to the Truce to carry out their assaults so as to enjoy the advantage of surprise. The favoured objectives of pillage where the *sagreres* in which the peasants crammed their provisions. Thus, for example, Artau de Pallars and his horsemen, whose deeds are, quite by chance, described in a document:

fregit tregua Domini ad Mala, ad Enesses . . . ad Corroncui, ad Adonz
. . . fregit tregua Domini ad Puio Manions, que suas manus proprias occisit ibi homines; ad Torella, per tregua Domini, fregit ipsos sacrarios; ad Agremont, in tregua Domini, fregit sacrarios; fregit tregua Domini ad Claverol; fregit tregua Domini et sacrarios ad Segun; fregit tregua Domini et sacrarios ad ipsa serra de Claverols; fregit tregua Domini et occisit homines ad ipsa Petra; fregit tregua Domini ad Espillos, ad Clareto, ad Anuu, per multas vices; fregit tregua Domini et sacrarios ad illo Midiano; ad Olb, accepit homines et preda; cavalcavit ad Siarp et fregit sacrarios; ad Saort fregit sacrarios; ad Badanui occisit homines at fregit sacrarios; ad Ssars aprehendit preda multas vices . . . ad Gramened occisit homines

---

[37] L. Musset, 'Cimiterium ad refugium tantum vivorum non ad sepulturam mortuorum', *Revue du Moyen Age latin* (Jan.–April, 1948), pp. 56–60; L. Musset, 'Le cimitière dans la vie paroissiale en Basse-Normandie (XIe–XIIIe siècles)', *Cahiers Léopold Delisle*, 12 (1963), 7–27; P. Duparc, 'Le cimitière séjour des vivants (XIe–XIIIe siècles), *Actes du 89e Congrès national des Sociétés Savantes (1964)* (Paris, 1967), pp. 483–504. Lastly, E. Zadora-Rio, 'Les cimitières habités en Anjou (XI–XIIe siècles)', in *105e Congrès national des Sociétés Savantes* (Caen 1980).

[38] Kennelly, 'Sobre la paz de Dios', pp. 133–5.

suas proprias manus; sui homines aprehenderunt uno homine de Sancta
Maria de Mur et tulerunt ei omnia et fecit illum redimere . . . fregit tregua
Domini de Castellaz et sui homines occiserunt uno homine in tregua
Domini . . . in tregua Domini aprehendit captivos et preda ad Liminiana
. . . etc., etc.[39]

This was not an isolated example. In Vallès and Penedès, for
example, Mir Geribert and his men were equally ready to attack
the *sagreres*, which they pillaged and burned.[40]

Nevertheless, even if it could in no case prevent the advent of
feudalism and the imposition of the 'bad usages', the movement of
peasant resistance was not entirely negative. The Peace of God,
once institutionalised, became the peace of the count. And the
sagreres survived, even becoming from the end of the eleventh to
the thirteenth centuries, the basic structure of many communities.

THE VILLAGE COMMUNITIES IN THE PERIOD OF TRIUMPHANT
FEUDALISM (LATE ELEVENTH TO LATE THIRTEENTH
CENTURIES)[41]

Before embarking on the history of the village communities in the
twelfth and thirteenth centuries, it might be useful to clear away

[39] ACA, perg. sense data, RB I, no. 34.
[40] Carreras Candi, 'Lo Montjuic de Barcelona', App. 19.
[41] To the references given below should be added the important communication
presented by T. N. Bisson to the international conference at Girona in 1985:
'The Crisis of the Catalonian Franchises (1150–1200)' in *La formació i expansió
del feudalisme català*, Actes del col. loqui organitzat pel col. legi universitari de
Girona (8–11 January, 1985), Universitat Autónoma de Barcelona, *Estudi
General* 5–6 (1985–6), 153–74. Bisson has discovered a series of documents of
exceptional interest: complaints (*querimoniae*) formulated, between about 1150
and 1190, by the inhabitants of a dozen free villages of the comital demesne,
denouncing the abuses perpetrated against them by castellans, vicars and
bailiffs. These documents, addressed to the court of the count-kings, appear as
'memorials of rural violence'. They demonstrate, on the part of the peasantry
who are their authors, 'nostalgia for a better past' (the former times when the
count effectively protected the village communities and saw that their franchises
were respected). These appeals to comital justice were not entirely ineffective;
some abuses were checked, though others persisted. The *mals usos*, in fact,
increasingly tended to be absorbed into the ranks of customs. One of the most
interesting aspects of Bisson's discovery is to show that the enserfment of the
Catalan peasantry (at least of a large part of it, especially in 'Old Catalonia')
could only be achieved through a succession of crises; the first, mentioned
above, was certainly in the mid eleventh century; a second, described by Bisson,
occurred around the middle and the second half of the twelfth century. This
tends to show that the Catalan peasantry was never passive in the face of the

one historiographical obstacle. For a very long time (since, indeed, the fifteenth century), Catalan historians and jurists have liked to contrast two types of peasantry corresponding to two different geographical areas: an enserfed peasantry in Old Catalonia, a free peasantry in New Catalonia.[42] This conception, already attacked at the end of the last century, should now be rejected as false, at least in the extreme form in which it is generally presented.[43] That it has been influential for so long is because it is based on a conception which is essentially correct, that is that the rural populations of Catalonia were subject in the twelfth and thirteenth centuries to two contradictory processes of evolution: enserfment linked to the establishment of one of the harshest forms of feudalism known to Europe, and enfranchisement resulting from the particular conjuncture produced by the reconquest and resettlement. The most that we can allow the old Catalan historians is that the pressures generating servitude were more marked in Old Catalonia, whilst aspirations to freedom had a greater chance of success in New Catalonia.

The village communities during the process of enserfment

The enserfment of a large part of the Catalan peasantry was the direct consequence of the feudal revolution of the eleventh century. When the upheavals characterising this had died down, and

attempts to impose constraints on them, but that it was necessary, on successive occasions, to break their resistance by the harshest repression. In this sense, as the author points out, the crisis of the second half of the twelfth century, though to be located in the aftermath of the crisis of a century earlier, also prefigured the crises provoked by the *remença* revolts in the fourteenth and fifteenth centuries.

[42] This thesis was first put forward by the jurisconsul Socarrats (*Ioannis de Socarratis Iuriconsulti Cathalani in Tactatum Petri Alberti* (Barcelona, 1551), p. 501). It was repeated almost unchanged up to the end of the nineteenth century and is still widely believed. (Old Catalonia is used of the part of Catalonia, largely to the north and north-east of Barcelona, which was reconquered by the Christians at the beginning of the ninth century. New Catalonia (south-west Catalonia) was not conquered till the middle of the twelfth century, at the time of Ramon Berenguer IV's campaigns against Lérida and Tortosa).

[43] Objections were first formulated by the Russian historian Piskorski (W. Piskorski, *El problema de la significación y del origen de los seis 'malos usos' en Cataluña* (translation, Barcelona, 1929)). For the position today, see P. Freedman, 'La condition des paysans dans un village catalan du XIIIe siècle', *Annales du Midi*, 94 (1982), 231–44; also his 'The enserfment process in medieval Catalonia: evidence from ecclesiastical sources', *Viator*, 13 (1982), 225–44.

the imposition of the seigneurial regime was definitively established, the situation was normalised – a normalisation which, as usual, boded ill. The exactions became institutionalised, first in the form of regular levies on peasant resources (*toltas*, *questias*, *forcias* etc.), then and above all in the form of the five 'bad customs' (*mals usos*) which defined personal servitude in Catalonia.[44] To this was added a servitude which bound the peasant to his holding, that is to say, very often, to the ancient allod of his ancestors, now assimilated into a lordship. Attachment to the land took concrete form in the *remença*, that is in the obligation on the peasant to redeem his tenure in case of departure. From the beginning of the twelfth century to the end of the fifteenth, men and women subject to the *remença* and the *mals usos* could thus be given or sold quite arbitrarily by their lord, with or without their manse, but always with the obligations – legal and illegal, say the texts – weighing on them: *cum questiis debitis vel indebitis et omnibus exactionibus, licitis vel illicitis, gratis vel vi, iuste vel iniuste.*[45] During the course of the thirteenth century, this situation, doctrinally justified by the jurists, was legalised by the Catalan Corts which clearly confirmed the practice of the *ius maletractandi* exercised by lords over their peasants.[46]

How did the village communities evolve in this new climate of servitude? Firstly, what proportion of communities were enserfed? This is a difficult question. For the end of the fourteenth century, J. Vicens Vives estimated that the *remença* peasantry represented at least a quarter of the total population of Catalonia.[47] It is prob-

---

[44] For the *mals usos*: Piskorski, *El problema*; J. Vicens Vives, *Historia de los remensas (en el siglo XV)* (Barcelona, 1945, 2nd edn 1978); chapter 7 above, pp. 232–7; Freedman, 'The enserfment process in medieval Catalonia'.

[45] E. de Hinojosa, *El regimen senorial y la cuestión agraria en Cataluña durante la Edad media* (Madrid, 1905), pp. 251, note 3, 252, note 1.

[46] Corts de Cervera of 1202: 'Ibidem eciam constitut inviolabiliter quod si domini suous rusticos male tractaverint vel sua abstulerint, tam ea que sunt in pace et treuga quam alia, nullo modo teneantur Domino Regi in aliquo, nisi sint de feudo Domini Regis vel religiosorum locorum . . .' On this subject, Hinojosa, *El regimen señorial*, pp. 95ff.; Vicens Vives, *Historia de los remensas*, pp. 30–4; Manuel Riu, 'La feudalització del camp català' in *Cuadernos de Historia económica de Cataluna*, 19 (1978), 29–46; Freedman, 'The enserfment process in medieval Catalonia'. See also his more recent article, 'The Catalan *ius maletractandi*' in *Recueil de mémoires et travaux publié par la société d'Histoire du Droit et des Institutions des Anciens Pays de droit écrit*, 13 (Montpellier, 1985), pp. 39–53.

[47] Vicens Vives, *Historia de los remensas*, p. 23.

able that the proportion was higher in the thirteenth century, without it being possible to proffer even an approximate percentage. In any case, enserfed and free communities coexisted at this period in every region of Catalonia. In the plain of Vic, for example, in the heart of Old Catalonia, there were great differences between the villages dependent on the church of Vic, which were at least partly free, and those subject to lay lords, which were very strictly enserfed.[48] In the Conca de Barberà, in New Catalonia, the villagers of Espluga de Francoli (studied by Agusti Altisent) seem to have been for the most part free,[49] whilst, six kilometres away, those of La Guardia dels Prats (studied by Paul Freedman) were all serfs.[50]

How are we to explain these differing degrees of liberty and servitude between neighbouring communities and even within the same community? A study by J. P. Cuvillier of the villages of the plain of Vic goes some way towards a reply.[51] It appears that in this region – very typical since it constituted the historic heart of Catalonia – two types of rural dweller can be distinguished: on the one hand, the inhabitants of small farms (*mas*), isolated on their holdings and subject (especially in lay lordships) to the harshest regimes; on the other, those who were concentrated into villages, especially within the sacral perimeter of the churches, whose lot was much less harsh. The *sagreres*, in fact, descended from the movement of the Peace of God, had not disappeared. Rather, they had grown stronger, and they constituted, in the thirteenth century, 'the keystones of the village communities'. They helped to structure 'a sort of village aristocracy accumulating privileges and franchises' which can be estimated, in some cases, at a quarter of the parish population. Placed under the protection of a bishop and chapter, the inhabitants of the *sagreres* were endowed with certain forms of autonomous administration (they nominated representatives who, for example, had sovereign power to arbitrate in conflicts relating to the employment of water) and above all they appeared as the most dynamic elements in both the economic

---

[48] J. P. Cuvillier, 'Les communautés rurales de la plaine de Vich aux XIIIe–XIVe siècles' in *Mélanges de la Casa de Velazquez*, 4 (1968), 73–103.
[49] A. Altisent, 'L'Espluga de Francoli de 1079 a 1200: un poble de la Catalunya nova els segles XI i XII' in *Anuario de Estudios Medievales*, 3 (1966), 131–209.
[50] Freedman, 'La condition des paysans dans un village catalan'.
[51] Cuvillier, 'Les communautés rurales de la plaine de Vich', especially pp. 80–2.

management (especially hydraulic) of the countryside and in resistance to the seigneurial regime. 'It was the *sagreres*', wrote Cuvillier, 'which, in general, up to the middle of the fourteenth century, inspired that attitude of resistance to lay feudalism which characterised the peasant mentality of this part of Catalonia.' It was they who were often the originators of what we may here call the second wave of franchises, from the mid-twelfth to the mid-fourteenth centuries.

The village communities during the process of enfranchisement

These new franchises present a very different character from those of the pre-feudal age.[52] The latter were always, by definition, granted by the public authority (count, bishop or viscount) and had as their main purpose to exempt the beneficiaries from rents and services of a public character; further, they often applied to very large areas (as, for example, the county of Barcelona, almost in its entirety). The franchises of the twelfth and thirteenth centuries might still, of course, emanate from the counts (or, more accurately, after 1162, from the count-kings), but the grantor might equally well be a lay or ecclesiastical lord; their principal purpose was exemption from the servitude linked with the seigneurial regime; and they applied to precisely defined communities. They were granted, in a sense, bit by bit, village by village, territory by territory.

In old Catalonia, liberties were won, as we have seen, by action of the inhabitants of the *sagreres*. This took place in various circumstances, differing primarily as a function of the relative strength of the ecclesiastical authority (which exercised a sort of tutelage over the *sagreres*) and the lay lordships. It might take violent forms: the inhabitants sometimes banded together in sworn associations, *conjurationes* or *confratriae*, against their lords.[53] Such struggles achieved only partial and often tardy success. To take a typical example, it was only in 1342–4 that the inhabitants of the *sagrera* of Sant Hilari Sacalm obtained from their lord, Bernard de Gurb, abolition of the '*questas, toltas*, voluntary or forced services, labour services, carting, errands, messages and

---

[52] Font Rius, *CPC*.
[53] As, for example, did the inhabitants of Banyoles (in the region of Girona) in 1236 (*ibid.*, vol. 1, second part, p. 624).

other servitudes', as also suit of oven. And the guarantee of individual liberties was confined to an engagement on the part of the lord not to seize the inhabitants within the free zone.[54] This was already something and makes it possible to draw a clear distinction between the condition of these villagers and that of the *remença* peasantry inhabiting the rest of the lordship.

In New Catalonia, the process of enfranchisement appears as a function of resettlement in a number of different ways.

In the first place, we can distinguish communities which were born free. These are the communities where the grant of the franchise preceded the resettlement (being intended to facilitate it) and where the land was not enfeoffed. Emanating directly from the count-king, the charter of liberty was thus addressed to the community of colonists itself, which was only answerable, therefore, to the representatives of royal authority (bailiffs or vicars). Receiving their lands either as allods or for a cash rent, the inhabitants escaped most or all of the usual obligations. We should note, however, that the number of communities of this type steadily diminished, as a result of the numerous infeudations to which the royal domain was subject from the second half of the twelfth century.[55]

Communities which developed within a seigneurial framework were thus more numerous. Here, it was to the lord that enfeoffed public rights devolved: *iura regalia, fiscalia, leuda, questias, placita*, fishing and hunting rights, and rights over the waste. Such rights, even in these new lands, might be exercised in an extremely coercive manner and involve certain forms of servitude for the peasantry. Nevertheless, the necessities of the colonising process and the shortage of labour both worked to the benefit of the rural communities which, in any case, were well aware of the liberties enjoyed by neighbouring towns (Lérida, Tortosa) and demanded that the benefits of urban franchises should be extended to them.[56]

Emancipation was achieved by two separate routes: the first was the recognition of the village collectively as a juridical personage, the second, liberation from the 'bad customs'. These two

---

[54] *Ibid.*, vol. 1, no. 374, pp. 556–8.

[55] J. M. Font Rius, 'La comarca de Tortosa a raiz de la reconquista cristiana (1148). Notas sobre su fisionomía politico-social' in *Cuadernos de Historia de España*, 19 (1953), 104–28.

[56] Font Rius, 'La comarca de Tortosa', also his *La reconquista de Lérida y su proyección en el orden juridico* (Lérida, 1949).

types of privilege were quite distinct. Paul Freedman has shown that certain villages were able to achieve recognition of a veritable collective identity whilst their inhabitants remained firmly subject to the most characteristic aspects of servitude.[57] Conversely, many communities obtained exemption from the *exorquias*, *intestias*, *cugucias* and other 'bad customs' without, for all that, acquiring even the most embryonic autonomous administration.[58]

In the nature of things, nevertheless, these two forms of emancipation tended to coalesce. Thus, at least in the thirteenth century, we may assume that the majority (though not all) of the peasants of New Catalonia enjoyed both individual and collective liberties. The former were characterised by suppression of the labour services and degrading customs, the latter by recognition of the free use of water and forests, the abolition of at least some of the *banalités* and the transfer to the village collectively of certain judicial powers. As regards the latter, the lord usually accorded the inhabitants the power to settle amongst themselves certain disputes before taking them to his court. The *probi homines* might also be permitted to sit in his court alongside the seigneurial bailiff. This village justice seems primarily to have concerned matters relating to irrigation or apportionment of running water; at any rate, in the region of Tortosa in 1165, the first public communal agent whose title is known to us was the *cavacequia*, the water-bailiff of the community of Horta.[59]

One might, to complete this discussion of Catalan rural communities, also examine the case of the rare Muslim *aljamas* which survived the conquest. The documentation relating to them is meagre and has been little studied. As their fate differed little from that of the Muslim communities in Valencia, it seems sensible to pass them over here.[60]

---

[57] Freedman, 'La condition des paysans dans un village catalan'.

[58] Very many examples in the charters published by Font Rius, *CPC*.

[59] *Ibid.*, vol. 1, no. 185, p. 185; 'et ut abeatis ibi cavacequia viccinaliter per manum vestra'.

[60] An up-to-date bibliography and an excellent study of the resistance of the Muslim communities of the Lower Ebro to seigneurial power are to be found in J. M. Font Rius,, 'La carta de seguridad de Ramon Berenguer IV a las morerias de Asco y Ribera del Ebro (siglo XII)', *Homenaje a don José Maria Lacarra*, vol. 1 (Saragossa, 1977), pp. 261–83.

The rural communities of the kingdom of Valencia

Linguistically, and, up to a certain point, geographically, the region of Valencia constitutes the southern prolongation of Catalonia. The coastal *huertas* of Castellón, Valencia and Gandia and a large part of the mountainous zones which surround and contrast strongly with them (the Maestrazgo and the Alcoy) received, after the 'reconquest' of the thirteenth century, a largely Catalan Christian population; this, coupled with a superior economic and cultural dynamism, explains the linguistic attachment of the kingdom of Valencia to the Catalan grouping rather than to Aragon, and the fact that Catalan is now spoken – in its Valencian version – in most of the three provinces, Castellón, Valencia and Alicante, which correspond to the ancient kingdom of Valencia; Castilo-Aragonese is confined to a few internal regions of little economic and demographic importance.

Initially, however, at the time of its reconquest by King James I in the period 1230–45, the region seemed more likely to identify with Aragon. Whilst the conquest of Majorca (1228–30) had been an essentially Catalan enterprise, it was primarily the Aragonese who wished to orient the expansion of the Catalan–Aragonese nobility which participated most actively in the conquest and received the largest share of the lordships distributed by the king in the newly conquered regions. Consequently, and for more than a century, the Aragonese continued to claim their 'national' rights in the Levantine zone.[61] It was the personal wish of James I which was responsible for the creation of the 'kingdom of Valencia' as a new administrative and political entity, distinct both from Catalonia and the kingdom of Aragon, and contributing on an equal footing with the two original elements of the monarchy to the constitution of the new state which composed the Crown of Aragon. The new kingdom was endowed from the outset with its own law, very strongly influenced by the Romanising tendencies then predominant, the *furs* (*feuros*) of Valencia (1240).

Within this particular grouping, where Catalan and Aragonese influences mingled and, in so doing, were themselves subject to change, the Christian conquest coexisted with the survival of a large Muslim population, probably initially in a majority; they

[61] See on this subject, Luis Gonzales Anton, *Las Uniones aragonesas y las Cortes del reino (1283–1301)*, 2 vols. (Saragossa, 1975), *passim*.

were for the most part dispersed in the rural zones, with the majority of the Christian population concentrated into towns and large villages. We should note, indeed, that the word 'village', in the sense it is traditionally understood in the west, corresponds ill to the reality of medieval Valencia. The Muslim settlement rather took the form of dispersed hamlets (*alquerías*), whilst the Christians tended to gather in large centres of colonisation of almost urban character. This is why we have preferred for the title of this section the adjective 'rural' – since the land undoubtedly remained the economic base of both hamlets and villages – to that of 'village'.

THE MUSLIM COMMUNITIES

In the beginning

What appears in the Catalan social panorama as only a marginal sector is thus, in contrast, essential to an understanding of Valencian society. Throughout the whole of the centre and south of the kingdom, the Muslim element survived in large numbers after the Christian conquest. In many rural zones, no 'old Christian' population was to be found until the very end of the Moorish period. We need to know, then, what was the situation of these Muslim peasants before their integration into the Christian kingdom.

Those authors who have attempted to portray the rural society of Muslim Spain have usually given a rather pessimistic picture of the condition of the rural masses; these have generally been described as composed principally of poor tenants, economically exploited both by the fisc and by the great and middling landowners belonging to the ruling aristocracy or the urban bourgeoisie.[62] This being so, there is little encouragement to attach much weight to the possibility of rural communities. The brief passage devoted to this question by J. Gautier Dalché, relying on existing works, seems to me significant in this respect: 'Ill-informed though we may be about life in the Andalusian countryside,' he wrote, 'we can at no time distinguish there the

---

[62] See, for example, the references given in A.-L. de Premare and P. Guichard, 'Croissance urbaine et société rurale à Valence', *Revue de l'Occident musulman et de la Méditerranée*, 31 (1981), 29 note 34.

existence of significant rural communities. The factors of cohesion constituted in the West [of Spain] by the parish, common practices, and not only economic but also human relations between lords and peasants did not exist.[63]

This absence of evidence for the existence of rural communities derives, in fact, both from the nature of the sources and the perspective of historians perhaps too impressed by the glamour of the urban civilisation of Andalusia. The Arab texts throw little light on the life of the countryside, apart from some stereotypical lamentations by authors of the Taifa period (eleventh century) about fiscal oppression, and from model agrarian contrasts preserved in notarial formularies.[64] There is also a tendency to infer the situation prior to the Christian conquest from the dependent condition of the Muslims after it. The documentation for Valencia contemporary with the great Christian advance of the thirteenth century (chronicle of the conquering King James I and the texts of treaties made with the Muslims),[65] on the other hand, provides a veritable 'snapshot', very partial, no doubt, but remarkably illuminating, of very strong and coherent rural communities, the *aljamas* already referred to with regard to New Catalonia.

The word *aljama* itself probably evokes those councils of elders (*shuyûkh*, which Catalan texts translate as *vells*) or notables who ruled these communities and must have been somewhat analogous to the *djemaas* of the Maghreb bearing the same name. The *aljamas* revealed in the texts, whose representatives often negotiated the conditions of their surrender directly with the Aragonese sovereign, were not 'villages', as indicated above, but rather relatively large rural districts consisting of several hamlets (*alquerías*) grouped round a fortified refuge or fortified hilltop village.[66] It is clear from the texts at our disposal that these com-

---

[63] J. Gautier Dalché, *Historia urbana de León y Castilla en la Edad Media (siglos IX–XIII)* (Madrid, 1979), p. 7.

[64] Example of a text on fiscal oppression in de Premare and Guichard, 'Croissance urbaine et société rurale', p. 19; the forms of agrarian contract are analysed in E. Levi Provençal, *Histoire de l'Espagne musulmane*, vol. 3 (Paris, 1967), pp. 266–70.

[65] The *Llibre dels feyts* or *Cronica* of James I is published in the *Colleccio popular Barcino*, 2 vols. (Barcelona, 1926–62). Reference will be made later to some treaties from the period of the Conquest.

[66] See A. Bazzana and P. Guichard, 'Châteaux et peuplement dans la région

munities exercised a collective right over all the lands of the district, as well as, in most cases, over the fortification which constituted its centre. A large landowning sector certainly existed, especially near the towns, but it seems neither to have predominated nor to have occupied, in the truly rural zones, more than a tiny proportion of the cultivated area. It was only in the most important fortifications that an *alcaide*, an officer acting in the name of a central power, was found. Elsewhere, that is in most of the some hundred and fifty to two hundred castral districts into which the Valencian countryside was organisationally and no doubt fiscally organised, no authority of the 'seigneurial' type is visible, and the only authorities coexisting with the assemblies of elders or notables were of a juridico-religious nature: these were the *alcadis* (judges) and *alfaquis* (probably simultaneously jurists, arbiters and schoolmasters), who reveal the attachment of these peasant communities to the Islamic socio-juridical norms.

The relationship of these communities to the central Muslim power (*sultan*) does not seem, therefore, to have been mediated by anyone claiming rights of a 'feudal' nature. The principal demand of the state was the payment of a tax which should, in principle, have corresponded to the tithe laid down by the Koran. In practice, in the irrigated zones, this tax took the form of a land tax (*almagram*) which was based on a unit called *alfaba*, which took account of both the extent and the profitability of the land. Certain fiscal accounts from the beginning of the Christian period appear to indicate that each rural community paid annually to the state a number of silver *dirhems* equal to the number of *alfabas* for which it was entered in the tax registers, and this collectively. The inadequacy of the sources evidently prevents us from evaluating with any precision the real weight of this fiscality, but many indications support the hypothesis of a moderate taxation, not departing far from the theoretical model of the legal tithe which was all that could be required according to Muslim law.[67] In the areas most distant from the towns, such as the mountains and plains of the interior where dry farming was predominant, the communities

---

valencienne', *Châteux et peuplements en Europe occidentale du Xe au XVIIIe siècle* Flaran 1 (Auch, 1980), pp. 191–8.

[67] Information on this subject in the contribution by P. Guichard to the recent history of the Valencia region published under the title: *Nuestra historia* (Valencia, 1980), vol. 2, pp. 249, 273, vol. 3, pp. 75–6.

were probably even strong enough to impose on the state respect for the principles of taxation laid down in the Koran, since the treaties of capitulation which the *aljamas* of these regions concluded with the king of Aragon at the time of the conquest were on the basis of payment only of the tithe on harvests.[68]

The impression given by the study of the geography of the castral territories of the Valencian region on the eve of its integration into the Catalan–Aragonese state is of a relatively stable socio-administrative system, contrasting with the apparent anarchy and ephemeral character of the political structures associated with the disorganisation of the Almohad empire. It is clear from the abundant Christian documentation of the mid-thirteenth century that each of the little rural districts constituted by a territory scattered with *alquerías* depending on a refuge or a hilltop village, corresponded to a precise area whose limits had long been fixed in the collective memory. Whilst some adaptation to natural conditions can be observed, with each *aljama* occupying a territory fairly clearly defined by the relief (usually all or part of a valley), within this it was the social unit formed by the *aljama* which prevailed over the units of settlement constituted by the *alquerías*, hamlets of at most several dozen houses, generally not defended. At the level of the *alquerías*, whose distribution within the castral territory may have fluctuated, place-name study reveals an identical subordination of the spatial organisation of settlement with regard to social structure: many hamlets were in practice designated by names which derived from a family name (of the type Beniali, Benisa, that is 'the hamlet of the Banu Ali' or 'of the Banu Isa'), indicating that the residential unit was frequently identical with the family group. Contrary to what is often the case in the west, where the rural community appears to be born of the settlement (village), of common dependence (lordship), or of a unit of worship (parish), everything suggests that here, even more strongly than in the pre-feudal Catalan mountains discussed at the beginning of this paper, the community existed before the elements of administrative, religious, and even, in a sense, territorial organisation.

---

[68] This was especially the case with the charter of capitulation of the *aljama* of Eslida and the Sierra d'Espadan in 1242, published in A. Huici and M.-D. Cabanes, *Documentos de Jaime I de Aragon*, vol. 2 (Valencia, 1976), pp. 138–40.

The impact of the Christian conquest

Valencian historiography, influenced by a whole tradition of medieval Hispanic scholarship, has tended to an exaggerated insistence on the continuities, real or supposed, observable between the Muslim period and the Christian kingdom of Valencia.[69] With some qualifications, this also appears to be the historiographical line followed by the works of R. I. Burns on the Mudejar Valencian society of the thirteenth century.[70] It seems to me, however, that we should not let the survival in the new Christian state of a large number of Muslims mislead us. If it is true that, in the very early years, numerous urban and rural communities were integrated into the Catalan–Aragonese monarchy, while retaining the status which had been theirs before the conquest, on the basis of the treaties of capitulation mentioned above, the situation evolved very rapidly in a direction much less favourable to the existing community organisations. By 1247–8, only two years after the completion of the military and diplomatic occupation of the kingdom, a localised Muslim revolt in the Denia region served as a pretext for the king to break the existing pacts and decree a general expulsion of the Muslims; this was followed by an accelerated colonisation of the more important localities and of the strategically best situated *castra*, which were cleared of their Muslim population and repopulated with Christians, who were granted large tracts of land.

In fact, though some Muslims emigrated – probably principally the urban elites – many remained behind, and the expulsion often took the form of an expropriation rather than a real departure. We may assume that some former landowners remained in place as tenants, even though certain zones, such as the Burriana region, the centre of the Valencian Huerta and the lowlying plain of the Júcar, were almost completely abandoned by the Muslims, as also were, rather more consistently, all the urban enclosures, the large walled villages and the majority of the *castra* or fortified villages which served as centres for the rural *aljamas*. The large communal

---

[69] See Guichard, in *Nuestra Historia*, vol. 3, pp. 9–11, also, on the more general question of the 'traditionalist' tendencies of medieval Spanish historiography, *idem, Structures sociales 'orientales' et 'occidentales' dans l'Espagne musulmane* (Paris/The Hague, 1977), pp. 7–16.

[70] R. I. Burns, *Islam under the Crusaders: Colonial Survival in the Thirteenth-Century Kingdom of Valencia* (Princeton, 1973), also his *Medieval Colonialism: Postcrusade Exploitation of Islamic Valencia* (Princeton, 1975).

refuge-enclosures were sometimes dismantled, more often used as royal or seigneurial castles, which in some cases involved major structural changes.[71] The urban communities and, in many cases, the communities in the richest countryside found near the towns were reduced to miserable *morerías* confined to a town suburb or dispersed in *alquerías* on the urban fringes, and made up of artisans, agricultural labourers and tenants. With the near-destruction of the urban social elements, the whole political and cultural framework of the Muslim socio-political system disappeared, at the very time when, in many cases, the landed base on which the autonomy of the communities reposed was also removed. In the second half of the century, the repression of another major revolt in 1276–7 produced similar results in the south of the kingdom, where the indigenous rural communities were better preserved, the Christian colonisation having been less important there than in the centre.[72]

Another important factor in the disintegration of the Muslim communities needs to be considered: the progressive seigneurialisation of the kingdom during the course of the thirteenth and the first half of the fourteenth centuries. Initially, as we have seen, royal power was often simply substituted for Muslim state power (*sultan*) in the collection of taxes inherited from the earlier system (tithes, *almagram*), the first charters of capitulation leaving collective possession of the land to the *aljamas*. The Muslim state system of the *alcaidías* was similarly preserved for the castles, which were neither seigneurialised nor integrated into the feudal system, but held by salaried officials removable at the king's will (*alcaides*). Apart from the loss of control of the refuge-enclosures, this system therefore involved little change for the large rural *aljamas* of the centre and south of the kingdom. Without it ever being clearly expressed in contemporary documents, we may assume that the revolts and repressions of the thirteenth century destroyed the very basis of this system, called 'pactist' by one Valencian historian.[73] The monarchy no longer felt itself bound to respect the initial contract, and in particular no

---

[71] Bazzana and Guichard, 'Châteaux et peuplement', p. 197, also an article on the castle of Perpunchent in vol. 18 (1982) of *Mélanges de la Casa de Velazquez*, and A. Bazzana, 'Le château d'Alcada de Chivert', *Château-Gaillard*, 8 (1976), 21–46.

[72] For this chronology: *Nuestra Historia*, vol. 3, pp. 22–39.

[73] Francisco Roca Traver, 'Un siglo de vida mudejar en la Valencia medieval', *Estudios de Edad Media de la Corona de Aragon*, 5 (1952), 115–208.

longer recognised to the *aljamas* full ownership of the soil. The expulsions and expropriations linked to the settlement of the Christian population represented only the most brutal form of this dispossession. The seized lands were sometimes, in the absence of Christian colonists, restored to the Muslims, but on the basis of individual or collective grants involving, in addition to the old state taxes, payment of a rent; this gave concrete expression to the establishment of an overriding system of landlordship previously totally unknown.

Nothing better illustrates the transition from the earlier state and community structure to the seigneurial system imposed by the conquerors than the evolution of the *sofras* or personal taxes. These seem originally to have consisted of labour services imposed on the members of the *aljama* by the state or by the community itself, and linked to the provision of supplies and upkeep of the collective or public fortifications (carrying water and wood, repair of walls), thus without economic value and probably light. In the Christian period, these taxes, at first simply continued, tended to be altered either into a rent in cash or into labour services due to the lord in return for a low wage, sometimes at will.[74] The transformation of the state relations which bound the Muslims to the Christian authority into relations of a seigneurial character was the prelude to a profound and general evolution of the whole system in a feudal and seigneurial direction, a transformation already almost complete by the beginning of the fourteenth century. At an early stage, we see the formation of small landed lordships based on an *alquería* granted or sold by the king, generally to a member of the lesser nobility or the urban bourgeoisie. Then, yielding to aristocratic pressure, the king abandoned, for the most part, the system of *alcaidías* in favour of grants – in this case in the form of fiefs – not only of the small residential and economic units represented by the *alquerías*, but of the castles themselves with their territories. Finally, during the course of the fourteenth century, we see that the crown alienated to the benefit of the seigneurial class, which was in this way progressively constituted, the last 'regalian' rights which it had been able to preserve, in particular high justice or *merimperi*.

The question of justice is without doubt one of the most import-

[74] P. Guichard, 'Le problème de la *sofra* dans le royaume de Valence au XIIIe siècle', *Awraq* (Madrid, 1979), vol. 2, pp. 64–71.

ant as well as least well known. In principle, the Muslim communities continued to exercise their own justice through the intermediary of the *alcadis*, who passed judgement according to Muslim law (*asuna*) and who seem to have been nominated without the intervention of the Christian power, at least initially. In cases opposing Muslims and Christians, however, as in cases of adultery involving Christians, or actions arising from insults to the Christian religion or royal authority – which must have happened fairly easily in an atmosphere of frequent tension between communities – it was the Christian courts which were competent. The royal bailiffs rapidly came to assume the role of court of appeal in cases arising from the *cadi*. Very soon, too, a system of compositions developed which enabled the king or whoever possessed the *merimperi* to commute death penalties, mutilation and flogging into fines or sometimes the sale of the condemned person into slavery, which represented a substantial potential profit. It seems, moreover, that the increasing manorialisation led to the multiplication of seigneurial courts competent to deal with minor offences against public order, agrarian disputes etc. The details of this evolution remain obscure, but it seems that, from the beginning of the fourteenth century, judicial rights over Muslims were the source of considerable profits which were fiercely coveted and disputed. Particularly significant, of the movement of manorialisation as much as of the economic importance represented by possession of such rights, were the provisions decreed by Alfonso IV in 1328–9 and known as the 'Alfonsine jurisdiction'. The new jurisdictional system recognised to all the lords who did not already exercise the *merimperi* a right of civil and criminal justice over their dependants, on condition that they possessed at least three *casas de moros* in Valencia and in the royal lands and seven in those of the great lay lords. Cases which might involve the death penalty or mutilation were excluded, but not those punishable by flogging or sale into slavery.[75]

The transformation of the condition of the Muslims was thus achieved progressively, though relatively rapidly, and, above all, unevenly. In the coastal *huertas*, the communities were generally physically destroyed, or so divided into little lordships of *alquerías* that the surviving Muslim population, united only by religious

[75] Sylvia Romeu Alfaro, 'Los fueros de Valencia y los fueros de Aragon: jurisdicción alfonsina', *Anuario de historia del derecho español* (1972), pp. 75–115.

solidarity or common subjection to a lord, preserved almost nothing of what had given strength to the collective organisations of the Muslim period. In the mountainous regions of the interior, in contrast, less favourable to Christian colonisation, large *aljamas* which were vassals of one single lord, having retained the use of their lands, and subject only to relatively light impositions derived from the original Muslim fiscality, were able to maintain, in a less altered context, forms of organisation and community life more reminiscent of those they had known before the conquest. It does not seem that, before the mid-fourteenth century at least, these still relatively well-preserved communities were subject to an economic exploitation comparable to that imposed on them at the end of the Middle Ages and in the early modern period.[76] One may wonder, nevertheless, whether, in spite of the apparently fairly favourable conditions which they had retained, they were truly and unreservedly integrated into the Christian state to which they formally belonged. The fourteenth-century documents show that these *aljamas*, like those of New Catalonia, supported with difficulty the new royal, seigneurial and ecclesiastical demands (tithes and first fruits claimed by the Church, *sofras* linked to the provisioning of castles or the transport of goods on behalf of the lord, provision of eggs and hens at a low price to the lord or his representatives), which tended to increase, gradually and often arbitrarily, the charges to which they had originally been subject.[77] These demands, the constant friction with the Christians in the areas where the two populations coexisted, and the frequent judicial abuses all tended to nourish a feeling of oppression on the part of the Muslims,[78] and a tension whose effects were given dramatic expression at the time of the mid-century wars between Aragon and Castile, during which numerous Valencian *aljamas* rose against the Crown and allied with the Castilians.[79]

[76] An exploitation often denounced, which should perhaps not be exaggerated as regards its economic burden. Good study in Eugenio Ciscar Pallares, *Tierra y señorio en el País valenciano (1570–1620)* (Valencia, 1977).

[77] See on this increase in charges imposed on the Muslims: Miguel Gual Camarena, 'Mudejares valencianos. Aportaciones a su estudio', *Saitabi*, 7 (1949), 165–99

[78] This aspect has been emphasised by John Boswell in his study of the *mudejares* of the Crown of Aragon in the years 1355–66, entitled *The Royal Treasure: Muslim Communities under the Crown of Aragon in the Fourteenth Century* (Yale University Press, 1977), pp. 324–69, chapter entitled 'The oppression of Mudejares'.

[79] *Ibid.*, pp. 391ff.

THE CHRISTIAN COMMUNITIES

It might seem paradoxical that it is more difficult to discuss the Christian than the Muslim communities of the kingdom of Valencia, even though the documentation concerning the former is infinitely more abundant than that concerning the latter. This disparity can primarily be attributed to a difference in the nature of the documentation, itself resulting from the inequality of status of the two communities. Like every ethno-religious 'minority', the Valencian Muslims were at first seen by the Christians as a mass or a collectivity distinguished by its beliefs, its way of life and the danger it represented, and not as a group of individuals with whom personal relationships might be formed. This was so at the level of each local community, large *aljama* of the interior or little group of inhabitants of a suburban *alquería*, in its relations with the Christian colonists, the king or the lord. We have no documentation regarding the internal life of the communities, only documents concerning the whole group, taken globally, in its relations with the Christian population or the authorities, for example the charters defining the relations of such and such an *aljama* with its lord. Conversely, the Christian documentation, here as throughout the Western world, is primarily constituted of royal charters or private contracts which reveal individuals in their relationships with each other or with authority. In the midst of this abundance of archives primarily emphasising relationships of an individual character, the reality of collective structures is not easily visible.

I am tempted to think, nevertheless, that the apparently greater consistency of the Muslim *aljama* results not only from the way they were viewed by the Christians, but also, and perhaps primarily, as I have tried to suggest above, from a different mode of politico-social organisation, inherited from the period before the Christian conquest. Of the rare notarial documents involving Muslims, for example, some are individual contracts between a Christian and a Muslim,[80] but others, significantly, are deeds

---

[80] I do not think contracts between Muslims are to be found in the registers of Christian notaries. The internal written documentation of the *aljamas* has almost completely disappeared, with the exception of a few fragments (see, for example, a contract of 1297 preserved in the ACA, published in W. Hoenerbach, *Spanisch-Islamische Urkunden aus der Zeit der Nasriden und Moriscos* (University of California Press, 1905), doc. no. 4).

involving a Muslim community as a whole, seen repurchasing a prisoner or selling its crop – a type of document unknown in Christian society. Also significant are the contracts made between the king or a lord and an *aljama* and corresponding to the purchase by the latter of royal or seigneurial rents for a period which might vary from one to several years. Here, too, this type of collective relationship appears not to have existed in Christian society, where royal, ecclesiastical and seigneurial rents were bought by rich individuals, sometimes in association, but not by the tax-paying communities themselves. The strength of collective relations seems to me less great in Christian society, and the relations between subjects or vassals and the royal or seigneurial power on the one hand, and between the different agents of social and economic life on the other, were more normally organised on the basis of charters and contracts of an individual character.

The origin of the Christian communities

More clearly, without doubt, than in New Catalonia, the reconquest being a century later, the need to attract people to assure the occupation and cultivation of the countryside created a conjuncture favourable to the constitution of a society of free men. The Catalan seigneurial 'bad customs' were unknown in Valencia[81] and personal dues in labour were exceptional.[82] Relations between lords and vassals[83] were always regulated by a sort of initial contract, the *carta puebla*, which clearly defined the latter's obligations; they were generally light in comparison with

[81] They were expressly excluded by many *cartas pueblas*, such as those of Burriana (1233), Villafamés (1241) and Puzol (1243); the first is published by P. Ramon de Maria, *Repartiment de Burriana y Villareal* (Valencia, 1935), p. 21, the second by M. Beti in the *Boletín de la Sociedad Castellonense de Cultura*, 3 (1922), 264, whilst the third is unpublished (Archives of the Cathedral of Valencia, perg. 2333).

[82] This was the case – exceptionally – for the *populatores* of Secha, an *alqueria* near Burriana, on which the Temple imposed a *jova* (labour service) once a year. Seigneurial demesnes (*dominicaturas*), though not unknown in the mid-thirteenth-century *cartas pueblas*, were relatively rare, and there no doubt existed a sufficiently numerous servile or salaried Muslim labour force for it not to be necessary to resort to labour services. (*La carta puebla* of Secha (1243) is in the Pergaminos particulares of Montesa, no. 73 P., AHN).

[83] The word is regularly used in Valencian documents to describe the dependants of the lordship who performed the oath of fealty and homage '*ore et manibus*' to the lord. Evidence of ceremonies for collective homage becomes frequent from the end of the thirteenth century.

those of the feudal period in most of Europe. The *populatores* were everywhere both colonists and soldiers. In the most exposed sectors, the king sometimes entrusted custody of a castle directly to the first Christian inhabitants,[84] and those in a position to equip themselves with a horse and knightly equipment were exempted from royal taxes and thus fiscally ranked with the nobility.[85] This situation was slow to change; for the whole of the thirteenth and most of the fourteenth centuries, the internal Muslim threat and possible Granadan invasions in the south meant that every Valencian Christian was necessary to the defence of the kingdom.

These communities of peasant-soldiers emerge more clearly in the seigneurial than in the royal zones. It is the northern part of the kingdom, the most strongly seigneurialised, which provides the largest number of *cartas peublas*, charters constituting rural communities. In this region, reconquered before the capital was taken, the king, his position vis-à-vis the aristocracy not yet sufficiently consolidated, had had, in practice, to grant vast lay and ecclesiastical *señoríos*. The general form of the charters of repopulation granted to the colonists by the new masters of the soil undeniably subjected them to a seigneurial regime, in particular in the judicial sphere, but seigneurial power operated within strict limits. On the one hand the charges imposed on the *populatores* were strictly defined and generally light (a tithe shared between the lay lord, if there was one, and the Church, sometimes a *tasca*, which cannot have been much heavier); on the other, the judicial system recognised to the inhabitants was that of a large town endowed with important franchises, usually either Saragossa or Lérida.[86]

---

[84] This was the case with the castle of Polop in 1257, during the war against the Muslim rebel Al-Azraq (Huici and Cabanes, *Documentos de Jaime I*, vol. 3, pp. 259–60), and those of Penáguila and Jijona, particularly exposed on the southern frontier, in the years 1268–78 (J. E. Martinez Ferrando, *Catálogo de los documentos del antiguo reino de Valencia* (Madrid, 1934), vol. 1, docs. nos. 792, 1998, and document of the ACA, Reg. Canc. no. 207, fos. 188v–189r (this document, which is the *carta puebla* of Penáguila, has recently been published by Ricardo Bano Arminyana in no. 33 of the *Revista de Estudios Alicantinos*, pp. 56–61, from a copy in the parish archives of Penáguila).

[85] Many privileges to various localities: Játiva (1265), Alcira (1266), Murviedro (1278, but repeating earlier dispositions); documents noted by Martinez Ferrando, *Catálogo*, vol. 1, nos. 627, 651, 2, no. 630.

[86] A collection of Valencian *cartas pueblas* was made by Miguel Gual Camarena, but not published. See, however, the same author's 'Contribución al estudio de la territorialidad de los fueros de Valencia', *Estudios de Edad Media de la Corona de Aragón*, 3 (1947–8), 262–89. Those of the present province of Castel-

Within this framework, the group of *populatores* was defined from the outset as a jointly responsible body, a *universitas*,[87] whose collective rights over those parts of the territory not granted in private *hereditates* were recognised,[88] and which was ruled by a *concilium* sometimes able to administer the first-fruits paid by the inhabitants.[89]

Further south, the Christian rural communities seem to present a rather different and less homogeneous aspect. In the plain of Burriana and the Valencian Huerta, zones which received a massive Christian settlement, the principal *señorios* were granted by the king to the military orders which appear to have sought to impose a more rigorous seigneurial regime on the colonists who settled their lands; this was particularly so in the economic sphere, where they sometimes demanded as much as a third of the crops, and occasionally introduced labour services.[90] Nevertheless, the benefits of an urban *fuero* were allowed to the inhabitants here, too, no longer by reference to the laws of an Aragonese or Catalan city, but to what had just been granted to the capital of the kingdom, the *furs* of Valencia; this led to the progressive adoption of Valencian institutions which, from the thirteenth century, characterised the towns and *bourgades* of the centre and south.[91]

What is visible, with more evidence, throughout the central and southern zone were communities of urban or semi-urban type. The Christian colonisation had first populated the large towns (Valencia, Alcira and Játiva) and the *bourgades* of an already almost urban character (Segorbe, Burriana, Liria and Cocen-

lón, mostly published in the *Boletin de la Sociedad Castellonense de Cultura*, have formed the basis of a useful study by Honorio García y García, *Estado económico social de los vasallos en la Gobernación foral de Castellón* (Vic, 1943).

[87] The term appears, for example, in the *carta puebla* of Cabanes (published by Font Rius, *CPC*, vol. 1, pp. 408–10).

[88] García, *Estado económico social*, pp. 44–52.

[89] This council is expressly mentioned in the *carta puebla* of Morella in 1233 (see the text in Roca Traver, *Justicia de Valencia*, pp. 406–7) and in others from the northern zone, for example Ares (1243) (*Boletin de la Sociedad Castellonense de Cultura*, 1 (1920), 187 and Alcolea (1245), where the text reads: 'et primicia sit de consilio, et quod expendat ad voluntatem domini et consilio in ecclesiis et in rebus que necessite sint in ecclesiis et in fortitudine castri' (AHN, Cod. 542 C., fos. 22v–23r).   [90] See note 82 above.

[91] See Gual Camarena, 'Contribución al estudio de la territorialidad de los fueros de Valencia', also the classic work of Roque Chabas, *Genesis del derecho foral Valenciano* (Valencia, 1902).

taina).[92] In many cases (Castellón, Villareal, Gandia), the Christians had created a veritable small town in a rural zone previously without it, and into which the Christian population was concentrated. This pattern has even been observed for less important centres of colonisation, like San Mateo, Nules, Albaida and Pego, where a *bourgade* populated by Christians was superimposed on the previous scatter of Muslim *alquerías*; these sometimes disappeared, but were sometimes, on the contrary, at least partly preserved within the dependency of the Christian settlement round which the old castral territory was now organised. The economic base of these centres, which varied in size but not, it seems, in essential function, was, in practice, land. Except in the largest towns, where nobles, clerics, notaries and merchants constituted a significant sector of the population, the majority of the inhabitants of these Christian *bourgades* were primarily landowners.

The questions of the mode of exploitation of the colonised plots distributed to the Christian *populatores*, and of the relationships, if any, established with the remaining Muslims, are extremely difficult to resolve for lack of adequate evidence. It seems, however, that the majority of the Christians cultivated their lands directly, alone or with the assistance of wage-earning Muslim or Christian labourers. However, the form of most of these new *poblas*, created out of nothing, often according to a regular plan round the central square and the church, and often enclosed, and the fact that there lived there clergy attached to local pious foundations or places of worship, knights endowed with landed property in the territory, a few notaries, agents responsible for managing the property of absentee landowners – burgesses, nobles or ecclesiastics from the capital or the larger towns – and the representatives of royal authority, *alcaide* or bailiff, produced in them conditions of social life of an already semi-urban character. It is important to emphasise that the institutional model which inspired the organisation and development of these *bourgades* was itself an urban one, since the king, by systematically granting them the *furs* of Valencia, extended the municipal law of the capital

[92] It is particularly the centres of colonisation of the modern province of Castellón (Nules, Almazora, Villareal and Castellón itself) which exhibit a characteristic grid-pattern plan; but traces of the initial nucleus and geometric plan can be detected elsewhere, for example, at Gandia.

throughout the kingdom and gave the new *poblas* the same institutions. With variations according to period, these were characterised by the presence of an elective administrative and judicial officer, the *justicia*, elected for one year, who dispensed justice in the name of the king and, with the assistance of *jurats* who were also elected, presided over the *consell* of the *prohoms*.[93]

Except in the north of the kingdom, where, as we have seen, the influence of Aragonese law was predominant, it was essentially within the context of these *municipios* of Valencian law, comparable perhaps to the fortified *bourgades* of other Mediterranean regions, that there developed communities to which one hesitates to apply the adjective 'village', and which were usually directly subject to royal authority. The foundation document was sometimes also a *carta puebla* granting the territory of an old Muslim *castrum* to a group of *populatores*, conditional on their sharing it out, with the size of the individual plots usually being specified in the documents. The group was often still not constituted at the time of the grant, and it was on several individuals, designated by name and invested with responsibility as *divisores*, that lay the responsibility to recruit colonists and divide out the land. But the communities formed in this way do not appear to have developed differently from those born, in a less autonomous and more '*dirigiste*' fashion, of the initiative of the royal bailiffs who distributed the colonising plots of one same territory direct to colonists assembled from various places. In all cases there was constituted, on the basis of ties of vicinity, relative equality of economic position and the institutions of Valencian law discussed above, a *universitas* endowed with a juridical personality and the capacity to act collectively.

---

[93] Valencian municipal institutions are the subject of a study by Francisco Roca Traver, *El justicia de Valencia (1238–1321)* (Valencia 1970). Its conclusions cannot all be accepted for the thirteenth century. Let us say only that at this period the *justicia* was normally elected by the *consell* (whose mode of nomination is unknown), or by the whole community in small places; particularly significant is the text of the *carta puebla* granted in 1278 to the *populatores* of Planes by its lord: 'Quod possitis eligere quolibet anno justiciam, juratos et mustaçafium, prout est quondam assuetum eligendi et ponendi in civitate valentina' (published by A. Dominguez Molto, *El señorio de la baronia de Planes* (Valencia, 1978), p. 272).

The limits to community action

I am very conscious of the rather theoretical and 'juridical' character of the preceding discussion, drawn, essentially, from the thirteenth-century *cartas pueblas*, whose texts, without ever having been systematically collected or studied as a whole,[94] have long been known.[95] It is more difficult to tackle the question of the concrete functioning of the Christian communities and the extent of their 'sphere of action'. Works on such problems are even less numerous,[96] and the documentation itself, as regards the thirteenth and early fourteenth centuries at least, is insufficient to approach these communities from the inside.[97] Their relations with the monarchy would no doubt be easier to study, but this remains to be done. As regards the lordships, we have primarily a certain amount of information about those belonging to the Church, but very little dealing with lay lordships.[98] What follows is thus fragmentary and put forward by way of provisional hypothesis.

The community instituted in the ways described was primarily a community of interests, sometimes strengthened by the fact that the colonists came from one same region or even the same town. An interesting case where we glimpse a collective act undertaken by a group of colonists even before they had embarked on bringing

[94] See note 86 above.

[95] See the works already cited by M. Gual Camarena, F. Roca Traver, H. Garcia etc. The tendency to use mainly the *cartas pueblas*, which are normative texts, gives a slightly ahistorical character to most studies of this period.

[96] There are, however, a few excellent recent studies, in particular: Antonio Furio, *Camperols del Pais Valencia: Sueca, una comunitat rural a la tardo de l'Edat Mitjana* (Valencia, 1982) and Ferran Garcia, 'La incorporació d'Almussafes al senyoriu del monestir de la Valldigna (1351)' in *Economica agraria i historia local, I Assemblea d'Historia de la Ribera* (Valencia, 1981), pp. 263–89. For the later period, Ciscar Pallarés, *Tierra y señorío* provides much information.

[97] The documentation is always seigneurial or royal, or notarial *protócolos*. Amongst the rare local archives preserved for the earliest period, we should, however, note the remarkable archive of the *Cort del Justicia* in the municipal archives of Cocentaina, which goes back to 1268. For the late Middle Ages, numerous local deposits remain to be used, as have been the archives of Sueca by Antoni Furio (*Camperols dels Pais Valencia*).

[98] Apart from the royal documents, very numerous but dispersed in the Chancellery registers of the ACA, there are chiefly ecclesiastical documents in the Archives of the Cathedral of Valencia and in the Clero archive of the AHN of Madrid. The seigneurial archives (Osuna, in AHN and Gandia, in the Archives of the Kingdom of Valencia) contain little material from the thirteenth and first half of the fourteenth centuries.

the land under cultivation, and before any real possibility of organising forms of communal life, is provided by Moncada, in the Huerta of Valencia. The king had granted the territory to one hundred *confratres* from Calatayud the very day after taking possession of the capital, in 1240. Since there were so many beneficiaries, it was necessary to apportion plots which were too small to form viable holdings, and the next few years saw an intense process of sales and purchases to the benefit of a smaller number of owners. Finally, and perhaps as a result of these difficulties, the king in 1246 offered these last a lump sum higher than the effective value of the land in order to persuade them to renounce their rights, after which he granted the territory as a lordship to the Order of the Temple.[99] The surviving documentation thus reveals an abortive village community, originally no more than a sort of grouping of interested parties, but one which was nevertheless capable of common action.

What emerge most clearly from the documents are the collective constraints bearing on the communities, in particular the royal fiscality of a more or less 'arbitrary' nature such as the *peytas*; these were additional to the fairly light charges laid down in the original *carta puebla*, and were imposed globally on all the non-noble landowners of a castral territory. The local authorities then apportioned the sum according to the property of each person who was liable. Conflicts were consequently frequent between the *universitates* who were taxed and the absentee landowners or the lay or ecclesiastical lords of entire *alquerías* situated on the locality's territory, but who claimed to escape taxation for a variety of reasons.[100] Another frequent occasion for collective action was provided by conflicts over the boundaries of old Muslim castral territories which had become districts dependent on a centre of Christian colonisation. The *universitas* then often clashed with the lord of a neighbouring locality, often populated by

---

[99] The original of the donation of Moncada to the *confratres* of Calatayud is preserved in AHN in the *pergaminos reales* of Montesa, no. 73r. A note on the back of the document indicates that it was handed over to the Preaching Friars of Valencia who were not to give it to the king until he had settled his debt of 18,000 *sous*.

[100] In some cases, as at Játiva, even the knights had to contribute to the communal charges. Sometimes the king, in granting an *alquería* to a non-noble, freed him from royal taxation. The very numerous members of the king's *familia* were also exempt.

Muslims, and it was necessary to resort to arbitration by a person nominated by the king.[101]

Forms of collective action in the economic sphere are less frequently revealed. Irrigation was, *par excellence*, susceptible to regulation of a communal character. But, especially in the Huerta of Valencia, the channels inherited from the Muslim period generally concerned several localities, and the forms of organisation therefore passed well beyond the municipal context. But when the irrigation system corresponded to the territory of the *vila*, responsibility for it rested with the municipal authorities, who appointed the *sobresequer* responsible for collecting the irrigation taxes and overseeing the water towers and the upkeep of the canals.[102] Several documents show that the communities were capable of initiative in the economic sphere. We see, for example, the *universitas* of Pego reach agreement with an entrepreneur for the digging of canals intended for new irrigation.[103] But the case is only known to us because the non-fulfilment of the contract led to a law-suit which went before the king. In general, the surviving documentation rather reveals the strict control exercised over economic activity by the king, who intervened directly in numerous aspects of local life relevant to the *regalias*: authorisation to hold a market or fair, construction of a bridge or a surrounding wall, even moving a place of worship.[104] Especially from the end of the thirteenth century, it seems that control of the traffic in grain, subject to a global prohibition and thus giving rise to individual royal licences, was also very strict, and it is rare for an export licence to be granted to a community as a whole.[105]

[101] Example of a conflict of this type in a document from ACA analysed at some length by R. I. Burns, 'Los limites interiores de la Valencia de la reconquista: Un genero de la tipologia documental', *Medievalia* (Barcelona, 1980), vol. 1, pp. 9–34.

[102] T. F. Glick, *Irrigation and Society in Medieval Valencia* (Cambridge, Mass.), p. 32) emphasises the distinction between the two ways of organising irrigation.

[103] Document of 10 kal. March 1292, ACA, reg. Canc. 94, fo. 114r.

[104] Documents of this type are numerous in the Chancery registers of the ACA, especially in the series *Gratiarum* from the time of James II. For the years 1290–1304, an index of the Valencian documents in this series has been published by Rafael Conde Delgado, in the first volume of the First Historical Congress of the Valencian countries already cited, pp. 220–32. For the earlier period, more detailed analyses are found in the catalogues of documents in the same Chancery registers by Martinez Ferrando and in Rafael Gallofre Guinovart, *Documentos del reinado de Alfonso III de Aragón relativos al antiguo reino de Valencia* (Valencia, 1968).

[105] For a fine study of the importance of this trade and the social groups who

In assessing the degree of freedom of economic action allowed to the *universitates* of Valencia, we need to remember that even if the obligations bearing on subjects and vassals were relatively light, the socio-economic system as a whole remained seigneurial. The allod was far from unknown, but it principally concerned the upper classes: the high urban bourgeoisie and the lay aristocracy, in particular. The small landowners were much less often in possession of allods since the grants of colonising plots at this level at the time of the conquest had usually been long-term leases which allowed for revocation in case of non-residence, failure to cultivate the plot, or non-payment of the light rent to which it was usually liable. Further, the king retained rights over the still uncultivated parts of the territory, thus limiting the possibilities for extending the cultivated area on the initiative of the communities. These seem hardly to have played a part, in particular, in the major enterprise of assarting the marshy zones or *marjales* which marked the beginning of the fourteenth century. Or at least they are not to be seen as such, all the royal grants of plots of land of this sort having an individual character, mostly to the benefit of the urban bourgeoisie or persons in the royal entourage.[106]

The question of the *aemprius*, or common rights, especially in natural pastures and woods, is one on which it is difficult to throw much light. The forests, *garrigues*, pastures and wastes always figured amongst the rights of the chief lord, whether this was the king in the zones called of *realenco* or the lay or ecclesiastical lords in the other parts of the kingdom. King and lords also collected the *herbatge* on the flocks using these uncultivated zones. However, most of the seigneurial *cartas pueblas* of the north of the kingdom – usually subject to Aragonese law – expressly included these areas in the grant of the whole of the territory made to the *populatores*, without reserving any specific right, except the tithe on cattle, mentioned along with that on crops; it is clear that, in these regions, where stock farming was important, the communities must have been responsible for managing the communal zones.[107]

In the centre and south, in contrast, regions where tillage

---

benefited from it, see Jean-Pierre Cuvillier, 'La noblesse catalane et le commerce des blés aragonais au début du XIVe siècle (1316–1318)', *Mélanges de la Casa de Velàzquez*, 6 (1970), 113–30.

[106] The very many documents of this type are also found in the *Gratiarum* series of registers in the ACA, especially for the years 1310–20.

[107] García, *Estado económico social*, pp. 44–52.

predominated, the commons were not usually conveyed in such an explicit manner. At Puzol, for example, the lay lord granted the use of the pastures, woods, chases, *aemprius* in return for an annual payment of five *sous* from each cultivator.[108] In general, the *carta puebla*, which precisely defined the extent of the land allocated to the colonists, did not mention these rights, but later agreements establishing a *bovalar* or a *dehesa*, where the cattle of the local inhabitants were admitted freely, appear to indicate that the lord exercised fairly strict control over the use of the uncultivated parts of the territory.[109] It is clear that in the royal zones the community of inhabitants exercised no perpetual right over these areas, since grants of colonising plots to new arrivals were always possible, as seen during the clearing of the *marjales*.

These problems did not arise with any urgency at the time of the conquest, when land was abundant and men few. But they acquired great importance later, and by the fourteenth century, in the context of a consolidated seigneurial regime, the question of the *aemprius* was the source of constant legal disputes between lords and communities.[110] Though it concerns the rural economy of an urban territory, one document can provide us with an interesting point of chronological reference: this is a deliberation of the town council of the town of Valencia in November 1325, where the jury and *prohoms consellers* made arrangements to regulate the pasturing of the citizens' cattle on the *dehesa* of Albufera, bearing in mind the difficulties created by widespread assarting of the uplands (*muntanyes*) and marshes (*marjales*) surrounding the town.[111] In Valencia, then, it was in the first quarter of the fourteenth century that private assarting initiatives, exercised

---

[108] Archives of the Cathedral of Valencia, perg. 2333 (1242).

[109] A good example of the grant of *bovalar* to the *populatores* of Cullera in 1252 in Huici and Cabanes, *Documentos de Jaime I*, vol. 3, p. 70. The text is quite precise: 'Damus et assignamus . . . medium milliarium boalarii . . . extra terram que vobis fuit sogueita pro vestris jovatis; in quo boalario totum bestiarium de Cullera . . . paschat libere et franche . . . et aliud bestiarium aliorum hominum, qui non sint populatores de Cullera . . . non paschat in dito boalario sine voluntate vestra'. For the rest of the land not *sogueiata* (that is, which had not been measured by the royal *partidores* to be granted to the colonists), the king took in effect a right of *herbatge* on the flocks he authorised to use them as natural pasture, which might belong to the local inhabitants or to the *cabañas* of transhumant cattle.

[110] José Hinojosa Montalvo, in *Nuestra historia*, vol. 3, p. 123.

[111] Archivo Municipal de Valencia, Manuals de Consell, 1, fo. 256r.

within the context of grants of new colonising plots by the king or his bailiffs, obliged the municipal authorities to tackle the problem.

Valencian communities during the movement of seigneuralisation from the fourteenth century to the beginning of the modern period

For much of the thirteenth century, as indicated above, the feudalisation of the kingdom remained weak, the Muslim threat obliging the king to retain strict military control over the majority of castles, structured by the system of the *alcaidías*. The same general conditions must have been favourable to maintaining most Christian communities in direct vassalage to the king. After the suppression of the great revolt of 1276–7, the danger was substantially diminished, and there followed a process of seigneurialisation which, as we have seen, had important consequences for the evolution of the Muslim communities.

Though not feeling the effects as rapidly or as strongly, the Christian communities were equally affected. It is difficult to make comparisons between periods for which the volume of surviving documents, not to speak of their nature, are dissimilar; it seems, however, that the proliferation of acts of homage at all social levels expresses, by the first half of the fourteenth century and in comparison with the earlier period of the establishment and consolidation of the kingdom, a strengthening of feudal forms linked with the extension and consolidation of seigneurial structures and constraints. Whilst the more important localities generally remained attached directly to the crown, a certain number of small rural communities passed into seigneurial control. The economic condition of the vassals was probably not, in the short run, significantly altered. It was now seigneurial, not royal, bailiffs who collected rents, and later often the regalian impositions progressively alienated by the king, such as the *tercio diezmo* and the *monetatge*.[112] At the beginning of the modern period, as has been

---

[112] On the *Monedage* or *Morabatí*, see the discussion and bibliography in Burns, *Medieval Colonialism*, pp. 150–3, and Pedro Lopez Elum, 'El impuesto del Morabatí', *Anales de la Universidad de Valencia*, 139 (1972), 6–19. The *tercio diezmo* (*terç de delme*) corresponded to a third of the ecclesiastical tithe which, in the Reconquest states, had been granted to the kings by the Papacy. The principal fourteenth-century alienations of these rights are deposited in register 614 of the *Real Patrimonio*, in the Archives of the Kingdom of Valencia.

well shown by Eugenio Ciscar Pallarés, the seigneurial rents and taxes in the Valencian region still do not seem, especially as regards the Chistians, to have constituted an intolerable economic burden on the vassals.[113] There was, however, perhaps especially in the ecclesiastical lordships – and it is for them that we have most information – a determined effort on the part of the lords to raise progressively the level of their revenues by losing no opportunity to increase existing charges or impose new ones.[114]

Of the various forms taken by the strengthening of seigneurial power over the communities, the alienation by the crown of its judicial prerogatives – essentially the *merimperi* – seems to have been amongst the hardest for the vassals to bear. The proliferation of lesser seigneurial justice noted in the case of the Muslims also affected the Christians, as the Alfonsine jurisdiction of 1328–9 benefited not only the lords of three *casas de moros*, but also those with seven *casas de cristianos*.[115] The documents reveal sporadic resistance by the communities to the process of seigneurialisation and feudalisation. At Corbera, for example, which had hitherto depended directly on the king, the *justicia*, the jury and the *pro-homs* of the community refused to render to Dalmau de Castelnou, the noble Catalan to whom the castle had been granted, the oath and homage he demanded.[116] The example of the neighbouring locality of Sueca, studied by Antoni Furió, clearly reveals one community's refusal to enter into a sort of chain of circumstances involving an increase in seigneurial justice, structures of landownership and the feudal system. This example is perhaps all the more significant in that it concerns not a royal locality but an old lordship which had belonged to the Hospitallers since the conquest, where the hardening of the seigneurial regime in the first half of the fourteenth century can clearly be observed. The occasion for the conflict was provided by the transfer of the property of the Hospitallers to the new Valencian military order of

---

[113] Ciscar Pallarés, *Tierra y señorío*, pp. 90, 94 etc.

[114] Good examples of the increase in seigneurial pressure in the fourteenth century for Sueca and Almusafes, which belonged, respectively, to the order of Montesa and the monastery of Valldigna, in Furio, *Camperols del Pais Valencia* and García 'La incorporació d'Almusafes'. For the beginning of the modern period, a fine study in Ciscar Pallarés, *Tierra y señorío*, pp. 88–113, but dealing principally with the Muslim lordships.

[115] See Romeu Alfaro, 'Los fueros de Valencia y los fueros de aragon'.

[116] ACA, Reg. Canc. 85, fo. 128r (analysed in Gallofre Guinovart, *Documentos del reinado de Alfonso III*, p. 425, no. 2063).

Montesa, created by the pope in 1317 following the suppression of the Templars at the request of the king of Aragon.[117] The *justicia* and the jury of Sueca turned a deaf ear to the demands of the commander of Montesa to do homage to the order, on the grounds that the *merimperi* of Sueca had, at the time of the Templars, belonged to the king. After some months, the representatives of the inhabitants, threatened with the confiscation of their property by virtue of the feudal *commissio*, had to end their opposition and the ceremonial oath-swearing by all those holding land in Sueca, could take place, though with the *merimperi* being retained by the king. A few years later, however, we see the order attempting to usurp the exercise of criminal jurisdiction, and, in 1343, the *merimperi* of Sueca was finally sold to Montesa by the king.[118]

The resistance of the communities to the increase in seigneurial power continued throughout the fourteenth century. Again at Sueca, we see the inhabitants refuse to send men to participate in an expedition against the kingdom of Granada in 1344, claiming an agreement of 1280 between the Hospital and the inhabitants, according to which the latter did not owe the service of host except in case of war against the Muslims in the kingdom of Valencia.[119] Growing seigneurial pressure no doubt explains the popular and anti-seigneurial aspects which characterised the movement of revolt called 'of the Union', which affected the kingdom of Valencia in 1348, and which has been the subject of recent studies which call into question the traditional interpretations of this phase of disturbance affecting the region in the mid fourteenth century.[120] A little later still, it seems that various Christian communities rose once more against seigneurial power, profiting in particular from the wars against Castile which were also, as indi-

---

[117] The order of Montesa acquired the lands of both the Templars and the Hospitallers in the kingdom of Valencia. It was, from the fourteenth century on, one of the principal seigneurial powers in the region.

[118] Furio, *Camperols del Pais Valencia*, pp. 96–103, 164–77.

[119] *Ibid.*, p. 171.

[120] Matue Rodrigo Lizondo ('La Unión valenciana y sus protagonistas', *Ligarzas* (Valencia, 1975), vol. 7, pp. 133–66) shows that the war of the Union was a true civil war, in which can be seen a massive adherence of the Valencian nobility to the monarchy, while the revolutionary forces, though they included some knights, were essentially part citizen and part popular in character. Furio's work on Sueca clearly reveals the rural anti-seigneurial character the revolt assumed (pp. 171–2).

cated above, the occasion for numerous revolts by Muslim communities.[121]

The confrontations between seigneurial power and rural communities in the kingdom of Valencia experienced another heightened phase at the beginning of the modern period, with the movement of the *Germanías* of 1519–22, contemporary with that of the *Comunidades* of Castile, well studied by Ricardo García Carcel.[122] It was above all on the occasion of these disturbances and their repression that the question of the mode of election of the representatives of the communities was clearly formulated, by both the rebels and the aristocracy.[123] After the defeat of the *Germanías*, a few isolated movements apart, there were no further armed disturbances of the same type; the resistance of the communities took other forms, not, of course, hitherto unknown, such as the threat to abandon their lands, thus depriving the lord of all revenue. It was by this means that, in the second half of the fourteenth century, the Christians of Amulsafes compelled the monastery of Valldigna to renounce its intention of raising from one sixth to a quarter the proportion of the grain harvest due by the inhabitants according to the terms of the *carta puebla* granted in 1281.[124] This desperate solution seems only to have been employed following the failure of an action against the lord taken before the Procurator General of the kingdom regarding various abuses alleged against Valldigna by the syndics of the community.[125] It was, in effect, by means of legal actions of this type that the protests of the communities of Valencia against the constant pressure of seigneurial power were primarily expressed at the end of the Middle Ages and the beginning of the modern period.[126]

The resistance of the Muslims, then of the Moriscos – who were in no position to abandon their lands[127] – also took the form, at this

[121] Furio, *Camperols dels Pais Valencia*, p. 172.

[122] R. García Carcel, *Las Germanias de Valencia* (Barcelona, 1976).

[123] The *agermanados* demanded the suppression of the system of the *insaculación*, employed for the choice of the municipal authorities, considering it too favourable to them; the seigneurial powers imposed a modification of the system in operation, in a sense more favourable to lordship, at Sueca in 1523 (Furio, *Camperols del Pais Valencia*, p. 176).

[124] Ciscar Pallarés, *Tierra y señorío*, p. 128

[125] Garcia, 'La incorporació d'Almusafes', pp. 268–75.

[126] Furio, *Camperols dels Pais Valencia*, p. 177; Ciscar Pallarés, *Tierra y señorío*, pp. 126–33.

[127] By the thirteenth and fourteenth centuries, the freedom of movement of those

period, of numerous legal actions in which the *aljamas* opposed their lords. There was never, however, any coming together of the opposition of Muslims and Christians against seigneurial power, but rather, on the contrary, permanent hostility, open or latent, between the two groups. The violently anti-Muslim character of the uprisings of the Christian communities, particularly those of the *Germanías* which were accompanied by numerous attacks on the *morerías*, is well-known; it led to the forced baptism of the Muslims, a key event in the evolution of the kingdom of Valencia because it was from that moment that the insoluble Morisco problem dated. This radical and religious opposition, which both heightened and complicated the conflict between the seigneurial class and the peasant communities, no doubt facilitated the steady increase in the power of the lords, even though, as we have seen, the weapons of the communities were, to begin with, far from negligible.

It might perhaps be useful to complete this paper by emphasising some of the common elements which can clearly be detected in the two histories – *a priori* very disparate – of the rural communities of Catalonia and Valencia: common elements which may indicate a model of evolution (perhaps verifiable elsewhere?).

What is most immediately striking is the cohesion of the communities before the establishment of the seigneurial regime. This cohesion is apparent in the case of the Valencian *aljamas* before the conquest, and also appears in the case of the very oldest Catalan communities (in the ninth, tenth and even early eleventh, centuries); it can even be seen in the first Christian settlements in Valencia (immediately after the conquest). In all these cases, the communities were responsible only to the public authority; they controlled a large (sometimes predominant) part of the means of production and defence; they often owned the places of worship; and, lastly, they were largely self-administering under the authority of the 'notables', the 'good men' and the 'elders'.

Muslims not subject to a status which, in itself, implied non-freedom (slaves and Aragonese *exaricos*) was in practice progressively reduced, in spite of texts (in particular charters of capitulation) which affirmed it in principle (see Boswell, *Royal Treasure*, pp. 293–321). At the beginning of the sixteenth century, one of the characteristics of the status of the mudejars, then of the Moriscos after the conversion, was 'servitude of the soil' (Ciscar Pallarés, *Tierra y señorío*, p. 84).

These powers were invariably diminished with the establishment of a lordship. Some communities simply disappeared (as did many of those in the Huerta of Valencia). Others survived with reduced rights. If they survived, it was often – as with the Catalan *sagreres* – as organisms of resistance (sometimes active, mostly passive) to aristocratic domination.

The constraints to which the communities were henceforward subject were not only seigneurial in nature, but also truly feudal. In Valencia, we should note the exact parallel between the expansion of the system of fiefs (according to the custom of Barcelona) and the entry of communities into dependence by means of collective homages (with, in consequence, the threat of confiscation of the property of the community's members). The repercussions of the phenomenon of feudalisation were even more marked in Catalonia; there, the fief was very much the preferred method for redistributing between the members of the dominant ('seigneurial') class the major part of the powers, rights and revenues previously possessed by the members of the village communities.

9. From one servitude to another: the peasantry of the Frankish kingdom at the time of Hugh Capet and Robert the Pious (987–1031)*

Discussing the peasantry at the time of Hugh Capet and Robert the Pious, though they constituted at least nine-tenths of the population of the kingdom, is a hard task. Nor is it made easier by the fact that it fits ill into the context of a celebration of the millenary of the Capetians, for the obvious reason that the vast majority of the peasantry was probably totally ignorant of the events to be discussed. Certainly, everyone knew there was a king, but what picture could they have of him and how many of them even knew his name? We will never know. The task is made all the more difficult, finally, by the relative paucity of evidence.

The narrative sources devote little attention to the lot of the peasantry, for whom the chroniclers (and, more generally, the educated) almost invariably professed hostility and contempt. The peasant was the *animal brutum* of Bernard of Angers,[1] the *rusticus piger, deformis et undique turpis* of Adalbero of Laon,[2] a creature whose behaviour demonstrated *agrestis ferocitus* to William of Jumièges.[3] The chroniclers hardly mention peasants other than in exceptional circumstances, such as, for example, the catastrophic famines of 1005 and 1031–2, or the uprising in rural Normandy in 996–7.

The archival documents are not, as is too often claimed, rare, but they are very unevenly distributed – several hundred, even several thousand, tenth-century charters have been preserved for regions such as the Mâconnais or Catalonia; for large areas, in contrast, the silence is total or very nearly.[4]

---

* To appear in the proceedings of the *Colloque Hugues Capet, Paris, June 1987*.

[1] *Liber miraculorum sanctae Fidis*, I, 7, ed. A. Bouillet (Paris, 1897), p. 33. This section was written by Bernard of Angers between 1013 and 1020.

[2] 'the lazy, misshapen and, in every respect, vile peasant', *Carmen ad Robertum regem*, verse 37, ed. C. Carozzi (Paris, 1979), p. 4.

[3] *Gesta Normannorum ducum*, ed. Migne, *PL*, 149, cols. 823–4.

[4] For Quercy, for example, only one tenth-century charter survives (will of Ranulf of Fons, BN, Doat archive, 126, fols. 32–42).

A last, and particularly striking, characteristic of these sources is that they give us not one but many pictures of the peasantry, highly dissimilar and even antithetical, presenting it sometimes as an anaemic mass, weak in mind and body, sometimes, on the contrary, as a dynamic, even conquering, class. I will respect these contrasts since they represent, I believe, an accurate reflection of reality. The year 1000 was a moment in history when the peasant condition hovered between many possibilities, when the fate of the peasantry hung in the balance, when an ancient social order was dying while the new was still undefined. It was an 'intermediate' period, and a period of change (in some places relatively slow, elsewhere rapid and violent). It was an age not devoid of hope; as is shown by the immense processions of relics which traversed the kingdom, testifying to a passionate longing for peace – peace for souls in search of salvation, for bodies wracked by infirmity, for a society rent by violence. But we should remember that such hopes were rooted in anguish and misery.

A wretched and unfree peasantry

Jan Dhondt's formulation is well known: 'Carolingian man was a famished creature who lived surrounded by woods.'[5] I will leave aside, for the moment, the second proposition, regarding the omnipresence of the forest; though no doubt true of Charlemagne's time – of which the author was speaking – it is much less applicable to the time of Hugh Capet.

Hunger, however, remained: an obsessive hunger which, in some years (1005–6, 1031–2 and 1032–3), reached peaks of horror. I need only cite three texts:

1005–6: There raged at that time a very serious (*praevalida*) famine . . . such that no region was spared lack of food; amongst the people, many died, worn out by privation. And even, in many places, a terrible hunger (*fames horrenda*) drove them to consume as food not only the flesh of vile animals and reptiles, but also that of men, women and children.[6]

[5] *Le Haut Moyen Age (VIIIe–XIe siècles)*, French edition revised by M. Rouche (Paris, 1968), p. 104.
[6] Raoul Glaber, *Historia*, ed. M. Prou (1886), II, 9, p. 44. There are many texts referring to famines in the collection of F. Curschmann, *Hungersnöte im Mittelalter* (Leipzig, 1900), an essential work of reference for this subject (see, in this particular case, pp. 108–9). With respect to the famine of 1005, it should be noted that Raoul Glaber does not give it a precise date: the expression *quinquennio*

1031–2: There was, this year, such a famine in Gaul that in certain places it was with difficulty that some abstained from the flesh of others.[7]

1032–3: The horrors which marked this dismal year are described at length in a famous passage in Raoul Glaber, with impressive precision as to the effects of hunger:

Only pale and emaciated faces were to be seen; many had a skin distended by swelling; the human voice became shrill, resembling the cries of dying birds. The corpses of the dead, which their great number meant had to be abandoned anywhere, without burial, served as fodder for wolves, who for long after continued to seek their prey among men.

This whole text merits study and commentary.[8] Let us note only that it also cites numerous cases of cannibalism.

Such texts (to which others could be added)[9] call for some remarks of a methodological nature. They should not, of course be taken entirely literally. It is doubtful, in particular, if cannibalism became general in the France of Hugh Capet and Robert the Pious, as suggested by Raoul Glaber. But neither should we simply reject this evidence by dismissing it as no more than unfounded rumour uncritically repeated by the chroniclers. A careful reading reveals no special taste on their part for the mor-

which he employs expresses a duration rather than a date and implies that he thought it lasted for five years. Nevertheless, if we take account of the dozens of references to it in other chronicles and annals, it is reasonable to conclude that, after several years of poor harvests, it began soon after the catastrophic harvest of 1005 and ended with the harvest of 1006.

[7] *Eodem anno tanta fames fuit in Gallia ut etiam in quibusdam locis vix alter ab alterius carnibus abstineret.* This sentence is given with a rather vague reference in Curschmann (p. 112). In actual fact, it appears in the margin of a calendar of the cathedral of Auxerre (Paris, BN MS. Latin 5253, fol. 65r); I would like to thank D. Iogna-Prat and G. Lobrichon for this reference.

[8] IV, 4, ed. Prou, pp. 99–102 (Curschmann, pp. 112–13). Translation from G. Duby, *L'An Mil* (Paris, 1967), pp. 112–16.

[9] For example, a sermon by Adémar of Chabannes referring to acts of cannibalism in Saintonge at an unspecified date (after 994 but before 1028; perhaps the famine of 1005?) (L. Delisle, 'Notice sur les manuscrits originaux d'Adémar de Chabannes', *Notices et extraits des manuscrits de la Bibliothèque Nationale*, 35 (1896), 293). Similarly, two stories in the *Liber miraculorum sancte Fidis* (I, 14, 15) reveal that processions were organised in Rouergue to bring about the end of 'a famine of unspeakable cruelty' (before 1013, therefore very probably in 1005–6). The horrors of the years 1031–3 (cannibalism, psychological distress, appalling mortality) are referred to by Andrew of Fleury, who confirms for the Orléanais Raoul Glaber's observations for Burgundy (*Les miracles de saint Benoît, ecrits par Adrevald, Aimon, André, moines de Fleury*, ed. E. de Certain (Paris, 1858). Briefly discussed in E. Pognon, *La vie quotidienne en l'An Mille* (Paris, 1981), pp. 28–31.

bid, rather great repugnance in reporting facts which were terrible to them, and which they recorded only because of their notoriety. Some, like the scribe of Auxerre already cited, even opted for ironical understatement. These texts should be compared, finally, with earlier annalistic references which clearly indicate, for example, for the years 793, 850, 868 and 896, a desperate resort to cannibalistic practices.[10]

How, in these circumstances, are we to estimate the degree of gravity and determine the frequency of famines? It can only be done by distinguishing, as, in general, did the chroniclers, between two types of penury: temporary shortages (called simply *inopiae* or *fames* without qualification) and the 'great famines' (*fames maximae, praevalidae, horridae, crudelissimae* etc.). The former, which occurred in late spring and early summer, might be frequent, but were rarely deadly: relatively brief, they also happened at a time of year when nature was productive, and when gathering in the *saltus* might compensate for lack of bread. The latter were famines which began the very day after the harvest, when only seed-corn (or even less) had been harvested and it was essential to keep everything for the next sowing;[11] long lasting, they were all the less tolerable because they raged throughout the winter, and thus generated high mortality. With this distinction established, we are in a better position to judge both the frequency and the causes of the famines.

If we take as reference point the forty-six years of Charlemagne's reign (768–814) and compare them with the forty-six years subsequent to the accession of Hugh Capet (987–1033), we see that the grip of famine was tending, despite serious setbacks, to slacken: eight years of *fames praevalida* in the earlier period,[12] three in the later.[13] In other words, if the horror of

---

[10] Curschmann, pp. 90–104. Also, a brief passage in Adémar of Chabannes recording a *fames vehementissima* occurring between 909 and 916 (probably in 910): 'Amongst the people there occurred a famine so violent that, something previously unknown, people pursued each other and many, by putting others to the sword, fed on human flesh like wolves' (Adémar of Chabannes, *Chroniques*, ed. J. Chavanon (Paris, 1897), p. 144). On this subject, see P. Bonnassie, 'Consommation d'aliments immondes et cannibalisme de survie dans l'Occident du Haut Moyen Age', *Annales,* 5 (Sept–Oct. 1989), pp. 1035–56.

[11] This is clearly indicated by Raoul Glaber for the year 1032. Cf., for the Carolingian period, the famine of 792–3 which began *statim tempore messis*.

[12] In 779, 789, 792, 793, 794, 805, 806 and 807.

[13] In 1005, 1031 and 1032. The number might even be reduced to two, as references to 1031 and 1032 could apply to the same year; but with little justification since

hunger (*horror famis, terror famis*) did not diminish in intensity, its manifestations grew fewer. It is clear that the chroniclers were aware of this; the annalist of Saint-Gall, for example, described the famine of 1005 as *fames qua per secula non saevior ulla*.[14] Indeed, at that date, no comparable mortality had been known for two generations (since 941–2).[15]

The two famines of the reign of Robert the Pious were, in fact, the last to demonstrate that truly appalling character which had marked the 'great famines' of the early Middle Ages; they were the last at any rate, to give rise to aberrations of behaviour such as recourse to cannibalism.[16] Unlike earlier famines, they seem due less to a general inadequacy of agricultural production (which had, it seems greatly improved) than to intermittent failures.[17] Agriculture was now capable, in normal times, of supporting a relatively large – or at least steadily growing – rural population, but it continued to suffer – and here nothing had changed since Charlemagne's time – from extremely irregular yields. These, which in good years and on the more fertile soils might reach 3:1,

Glaber declares *a contrario* that this famine, certainly very long, lasted for three years. It seems reasonable to assume that it began soon after the harvest of 1031 and did not end until the harvest of 1033.

[14] *MGH, SS* I, 81 (Curschmann, p. 109).

[15] The second half of the tenth century seems to have seen a clear remission in the history of mortality due to hunger. This is suggested by a calculation of the number of *fames praevalidae* in the period 750–1050, based on Curschmann: second half of eighth century: six (763, 779, 780, 792, 793, 794); first half of ninth century: eight (805, 806, 807, 820, 821, 822, 843, 850); second half of ninth century: four (868, 873, 874, 896); first half of tenth century: three (910, 941, 942); second half of tenth century: none; first half of eleventh century: four (1005, 1031, 1032, 1044). The definition used for years of 'great famine' is conformity to at least three of the five following criteria: references in several chronicles, descriptions of famines as *praevalidae, maximae* etc., indications of serious mortality, evidence of the consumption of *immundicia* or human flesh, evidence of legislative or conciliar measures to alleviate the effects of famine.

[16] After 1032, a single, quite isolated, reference, in 1146: it applies, what is more, to the county of Hainault, not part of the kingdom (*MGH, SS* VI, 453, 15; Curschmann, p. 142).

[17] Georges Duby makes a clear distinction between the famines described by Raoul Glaber and those of the later period: 'The tragic picture drawn of the 1033 famine in Raoul Glaber's account shows that these disasters were taking place in an economic climate that was already singularly volatile . . . This was a changing world, and the calamities afflicting it were in reality the price of demographic expansion which was possibly too rapid and at all events unregulated, but which may be regarded as one of the first fruits of economic growth.' (*Guerriers et paysans* (Paris, 1973), translated by Howard B. Clarke as *The Early Growth of the European Economy* (London, 1974), p. 159).

even more (perhaps much more: who knows?),[18] were also liable to fall below 2:1 and even 1:1, thus triggering off cataclysmic famines. The cause of these periodic collapses of cereal production are well known; they were the result of men's impotence in the face of climatic hazards, an impotence itself rooted in the persistent weakness of agricultural techniques (even though the latter – a point to which I shall return – were tending to improve).

But there was another reason for these periodic failures of agricultural production. This lay in the archaic modes of exploiting the soil, or at least, in some of them, those which continued to be based on forced labour.

The persistence into Merovingian and Carolingian times of a type of servitude derived from ancient slavery no longer, I believe, needs to be proved.[19] It is still clearly attested around the year 1000. The antithesis *ingenuus/servus* occurs constantly in charters, whether royal diplomas or private acts, and marks a cleavage still strongly felt between two categories of human being.[20] Rural slaves continued to be the object of transactions between their masters: between 990 and 1007, for example, the noble Garnier gave sixty *mancipia* to Saint-Bénigne of Dijon;[21] round about 1000, two landowners from the Auvergne sold two slaves, Gaubert and Rigaud, who, they said 'came to us from our parents; we got

---

[18] I do not wish to get involved here in the controversy over 'average yields' in the Carolingian period; the debate has only limited significance since, as Pierre Vilar has observed, 'men do not live on averages'. In any case, the sources do not really lend themselves to such calculations. The only reliable figures are provided by Italian polyptiques (recently republished: *Inventari altomedievali di terre, coloni e redditi*, A. Castagnetti and others, Rome, 1979) and in particular that of San Tommaso of Reggio Emilia. For one unspecified year in the tenth century, this document makes it possible to calculate yields on the various demesnes possessed by the monastery varying between 1.7:1 and 3.3:1 (or, possibly, 3.8:1). See, most recently, M. Montanari, 'Techniche e rapporti di produzione: le rese ceralicole dal IX al XV secolo' in *Le campagne italiane prima e dopo il Mille: una società in trasformazione* (Bologna, 1985).

[19] See chapter 1 above, 'Survival and extinction of the slave system in the early medieval West'. As early as 1958, Georges Duby wrote 'like Roman Gaul, like primitive Germany, France in the year 1000 was a slave society' (G. Duby and R. Mandrou, *Histoire de la civilisation française*, vol. 1 (Paris, 1958), p. 15).

[20] 'This was the fundamental division, compared with which all other distinctions were only relative, the only one which had a juridical basis' (G. Duby, *La société aux XIe et XIIe siècles dans la région mâconnaise* (Paris, 1953), p. 118).

[21] J. Chevrier and M. Chaume, 'Cartulaire de Saint-Bénigne de Dijon' in *Analecta Burgundica*, vol. 2 (Dijon, 1943), p. 8, no. 198 (act cited by R. Doehaerd, *Le Haut Moyen Age occidental* (Paris, 1971), p. 187).

thirty *sous* for them'.[22] Such examples could be multiplied, just as it would be easy to enumerate references to *mancipia*, *servi* and *ancillae* occurring in descriptions of the movable and landed property composing the great country estates; if we confine ourselves to deeds executed by Hugh Capet or Robert the Pious, such references are found in diplomas of 988, 989, 990, 993, 999, 1002, 1003, 1004, 1005, 1007, 1014, 1022, 1026, 1027, 1028 and 1031.[23]

Indeed, the idea that servitude was and should be the lot of the peasant remained very strong amongst the ruling class, including in the royal entourage. It was nowhere better expressed than in the famous *Poème au roi Robert* of Adalbero of Laon. He employs only the word *servus* to indicate peasants (verses 285, 289, 290, 292) and he includes in the *servilis conditio* (verse 255), the *servorum divisio* (verse 285) all those who 'tilled the soil, followed the ox's tail . . . riddled the wheat, and cooked by greasy cauldrons' (verses 245, 249), in brief, those who 'were soiled by the filthy world' *(mundana sorde)* (verse 244).[24]

But the picture of an entire peasantry perpetually groaning in servitude *(servorum lacrimae gemitus non terminus ullus)*,[25] if it conformed to the world-view of the well-born, of whom Adalbero was here the interpreter, no longer really corresponded to the realities of the period in which it was formulated. Though rural slavery in the ancient tradition still survived at the end of the tenth and beginning of the eleventh centuries, it increasingly appeared vestigial.

This can be seen by an examination of the vocabulary in charters. The three Latin terms – *mancipium*, *servus* and *ancilla* – which had always been employed to indicate a slave (male or female) certainly continued to occur from time to time in the writing of the scribes, but with unequal frequency. The neuter

---

[22] C. Lauranson-Rosaz, *L'Auvergne et ses marges (Velay, Gévaudan) du VIIIe au XIe siècle: la fin du monde antique?* (Le-Puy-en-Velay, 1987), p. 390, no. 291. We should note, however, that these two slaves were promised enfranchisement.

[23] *Recueil des Histoires des Gaules et de la France*, 10, *Regis Hugonis Capeti diplomata*, nos. 3, 5, 7, 9, 11; *Roberti regis diplomata*, nos. 4, 8, 10, 11, 12, 13, 18, 22, 23, 28, 33, 34, 39, 41, 47, 53.

[24] Ed. C. Carozzi, pp. 18–19 (the poet is, in fact, describing in this passage the order of the *oratores* and it is so as to emphasise the sanctity and purity of this order that he refers, as a foil, to the condition of the peasantry; the clergy were those 'who did not till the soil, follow the ox's tail etc.).

[25] *Ibid.*, p. 22, v. 294.

word *mancipium* – the one whose use most clearly indicates a slave-owning mentality – steadily lost ground, and this over several decades. Throughout the ninth and into the first third of the tenth centuries, its use was regular in 40 to 50 per cent of royal diplomas; the frequency of occurrence falls to around 20 per cent under the last Carolingians (Louis IV, Lothar, Louis V) and to 17 per cent under Hugh Capet and Robert the Pious; it was only 1.5 per cent under Henry I and Philip I.[26]

The use of the words *servus* and *ancilla*, on the other hand, varied according to region. Throughout the south, they disappeared – as, indeed, did *mancipium* – very early. They last appeared in 988 in Septimania,[27] 1035 in Catalonia,[28] and 1031/1055 in the Auvergne.[29] In all these regions, the old slavery had disappeared without trace. Further north, these words continued in use,[30] and this persistence proves that some *familiae* of ancient origin had been able to survive even beyond the year 1000, sometimes to the end of the eleventh, even into the twelfth, centuries.[31] But they were, nevertheless, increasingly rare, evidence of them sparser, and the word *servus* tended, even in the very conservative vocabulary of the charters from the north of the kingdom, to indicate a new reality, bearing no relation to ancient or even Carolingian slavery.

Everywhere, then, there was manifested (with great vigour in the Midi, but also elsewhere) what an edict of Otto III promulgated at Pavia in 998 called the *appetitum libertatis* of the last descendants of the last slaves.[32]

---

[26] Chapter 1 above, especially Table 2, p. 57.

[27] E. Magnou-Nortier, *La société laïque et l'Eglise dans la province ecclésiastique de Narbonne (zone cispyrénéene) de la fin du VIIIe à la fin du XIe siècle* (Toulouse, 1974), p. 223.

[28] Bonnassie, *La Catalogne*, vol. 1, pp. 300–1.

[29] Lauranson-Rosaz, *L'Auvergne*, pp. 393–4.   [30] See above, note 23.

[31] The *terminus ad quem* varies according to place. The last use of the word *servus* in the Mâconnais was in 1105 (Duby, *La société mâconnaise*, p. 249). In the Parisian basin, on the other hand, the use of *servus* (and *ancilla*), without being exactly common, was by no means unknown at the end of the eleventh and in the early twelfth centuries; one or both words appear in 23 of the 171 acts drawn up by Philip I (*Receuil des actes de Philippe Ier, roi de France (1059–1108)*, ed. M. Prou (Paris, 1908)). Further north, in the region of Namur, these words survived even later (L. Genicot, *L'économie rurale namuroise au Bas Moyen Age*, vol. 3, *Les hommes. Le commun* (Louvain–Brussels, 1982), pp. 207–38 and tables 15–16).

[32] Capitular, *De servis libertatem anhelantibus* (*MGH, Constitutiones*, vol. 1, ed. L. Weiland (Hanover, 1893), no. 21, pp. 47–8).

Another image of the peasantry thus emerges (or, rather, should be added to the first): an image of liberty and its active pursuit.

A free and dynamic peasantry

It is a far from easy task to seek first to define peasant liberty and then attempt to estimate the proportion of the rural population who, round about 1000, enjoyed this condition. There are four major criteria, however, which may help us to formulate an answer: economic, judicial, military and cultural.

The economic situation of peasants derived, to a large extent, from their position in relation to the land they cultivated. At the risk of hugely oversimplifying, we can distinguish two conditions: that of the allod-holder and that of the tenant.[33]

The general tendency of research over the last twenty years has been to emphasise the importance of the peasant allod, and this in the most diverse regions. This small peasant property was clearly predominant in the colonising regions, where it might represent as much as 80 per cent of the plots (though not, it is true, of the cultivated area) in some Catalan territories.[34] But it was also found in the interior of the kingdom: in Berry, where Guy Devailly confessed himself 'struck by the abundance of allods';[35] in the region of Charente, where André Debord noted 'an almost unbelievable proliferation of tiny allods;'[36] and in the Auvergne, where Christian Lauranson-Rosaz, not content with discovering unmistakable evidence of allods, could follow, year by year, the acquisitions of plots made between 1022 and 1033 by a couple of peasant allod-holders, Emmenon and Gaudence.[37] The allod even appears where least expected: thus in Picardy, land *par excellence* of the 'demesne system', Robert Fossier could conclude, on the basis of a detailed enumeration of donations of plots, *villulae*,

[33] This is a classic, but unreal, distinction. Many allod-holders supplemented their holdings by renting land from neighbouring large estates. Many tenants were also sole proprietors of a plot of land. It may well be that the majority of (free) peasants were simultaneously allod-holders and tenants.

[34] Bonnassie, *La Catalogne*, vol. 1, pp. 224ff.

[35] G. Devailly, *Le Berry du Xe siècle au milieu du XIIIe* (Paris–The Hague, 1973), pp. 217: 'One particular characteristic immediately stands out when we read cartularies containing acts from this period: the abundance of allods . . .'

[36] G. Debord, *La société laïque dans les pays de Charente, Xe–XIIe siècles* (Paris, 1984), p. 295.

[37] Lauranson-Rosaz, *L'Auvergne*, pp. 397–9.

portionculae, that there was a 'preponderance of the small property' in the ninth and tenth centuries.[38]

The allod was omnipresent, but also fragile. Nothing, in fact, was more unstable than this form of land-holding, which both progressed and regressed during the course of the tenth century. The peasant allod continued to proliferate as a result of assarting;[39] but it shrank no less steadily through absorption into the great estates. Every subsistence crisis (and we have seen how deadly these could be) had the effect of compelling peasants to sell all or part of their plot,[40] or mortgage it to secure a loan which would never be repaid,[41] or even give it (to some potentate or some church) in return for temporary help or the promise of protection. The result was always the same: the transformation of allods into tenures.

This trend towards the erosion of the small allodial property, though it sapped the economic independence of the free peasantry, did not, in the short run, affect its condition. The lot of the tenant did not, around 1000, appear fundamentally different from that of the allod-holder, at least in those cases (which seem in a majority) where the tenure took the form of a lease or share-cropping.[42] The point at issue here is not to establish the geographical distribution of these two types of exploitation, nor even to estimate the weight of the ground rent they bore.[43] What is

---

[38] R. Fossier, *La terre et les hommes en Picardie jusqu'à la fin du XIIIe siècle* (Paris-Louvain, 1968), pp. 210–11.

[39] See below, p. 303.

[40] Hence the striking proportion of acts of sale of allods in the original documentation of the tenth century (between 60 per cent and 80 per cent, according to decade, in the parchments of Catalonia). Not all these acts were drawn up in favour of the large landowners, it is true, but this was often the case (Bonnassie, *La Catalogne*, vol. 1, pp. 236–42, and vol. 2, diagrams, pp. 885–94).

[41] There are many examples in the Catalan documents (*ibid.*, pp. 404–6). On peasant indebtedness, its causes and consequences, see also the suggestive remarks of J.-P. Poly and E. Bournazel, *La mutation féodale (Xe–XIIe siècles)* (Paris, 1980), pp. 366–7.

[42] For land held at rent, see, for example, Devailly, *Le Berry*, p. 219: 'After the allod, the form of landholding which most often appears in the charters of the Berry region in the tenth and eleventh centuries is land held for rent'; see also A. Chédeville, *Chartres et ses campagnes, XIe–XIIIe siècles* (Paris, 1973), pp. 257–8; similarly, on the edge of the kingdom, J.-P. Poly, *La Provence et la société féodale (879–1166)* (Paris, 1976), pp. 105–7. For share-cropping, very common in the south, see, among others, Poly, *ibid.*, pp. 107–8; Bonnassie, *La Catalogne*, vol. 1, pp. 248–54.

[43] The level of rent is difficult to establish in cases where it was fixed; it was very variable, and might be stipulated in head of cattle (in Provence, the customary

crucial is to note that these forms of land-holding left great liberty to the cultivator vis-à-vis the proprietor. Once the rent or share of the crop had been paid, the former owed the latter nothing, except possibly a few days' work or minor services. And this autonomy was all the stronger by reason of the growing fragmentation of land holding. The tenant no longer, in many cases, cultivated one holding held of one single master, but a collection of plots belonging to different proprietors.[44] We are thus a long way, in 1000, from the manse burdened by labour services described by the polyptiques, which, even at the time of Charlemagne and Louis the Pious (and except in the Parisian region), must have been the exception rather than the rule.

In the judicial domain, too, it would be a mistake to generalise on the basis of the Parisian example. It appears that in the region of the Seine, as a consequence of specific circumstances linked to the genesis of the demesne system, harsh constraints were imposed very early on the free peasantry.[45] Very early means by the

rent seems to have been a sheep at Whitsuntide and a pig on All Saints Day), in poultry and eggs, in amounts of grain or wine, sometimes already in cash. For share-cropping rents, the calculations are easier, even though the levels were also very variable. Lowest was the *tasca* (one eleventh), very common in the Mediterranean zone; but the rate of one-tenth (the tithe on land) was also common ('it seems to belong to a group of rural traditions common to both East and West', R. Doehaerd, *Le Haut Moyen Age occidental, Economies et sociétés* (Paris, 1971), p. 197). Towards 1000, rates seem to have become much heavier; a quarter for the grain harvest, a third or even a half for the wine harvest. Such levies, common in Latium from the mid tenth century (P. Toubert, *Les structures du Latium médiéval* (Rome, 1973), vol. 1, pp. 540–5), became increasingly common in Provence (Poly, *La Provence*, p. 107) and Catalonia (Bonnassie, *La Catalogne*, vol. 1, p. 254) at the end of the tenth and in the early eleventh centuries. In the twelfth century, in Rouergue and the Toulousain, the render of a quarter of the crop had become so common that it came to indicate the land granted as a tenure: *terra cartiva, camp quartiu, fevum quartanerium* (P. Ourliac and A.-M. Magnou, *Le Cartulaire de la Selve: la terre, les hommes et le pouvoir en Rouergue au XIIe siècle* (Paris, 1985), pp. 57, 70, note 141). The levels of the *agriers* and *terrages* (also very widely found share-cropping rents) are obscure and also very variable according to region and period (generally between one-tenth and one-quarter). We can only note the extreme age of these forms of rent: the *agrier* appears as a customary rent in Merovingian Touraine (G. Gasnault, *Documents comptables de Saint-Martin de Tours à l'époque mérovingienne* (Paris, 1975), *passim*). For an overall view, see *Les revenues de la terre, complant, champart, métayage, en Europe occidentale (IXe–XVIIIe siècles)*, Flaran 7, 1985 (Auch, 1987).

44   For example, Magnou-Nortier, *La société laïque et l'Eglise*, pp. 147–52.

45   A. Verhulst, 'La genèse du régime domanial classique en France au Haut Moyen Age', *Settimane* (1965), pp. 135ff. See also the comments of Poly and Bournazel, *La mutation féodale*, pp. 356–8.

Merovingian period; the Frankish kings and their auxiliaries, who had established their residence in this region, managed to subject the free-born colonists to forced labour, tending (without ever quite succeeding) to assimilate their condition to that of the *servi casati*. In the same way, the royal *ban* – prefiguring, at some distance, the seigneurial *ban* – was able to impose on these same free tenants a system of sanctions which were very heavy and, in any case, derived from common law. There was, as a result, a generalisation of corporal punishments, excessive use of which Charles the Bald tried tentatively to limit, when, in 864, he prohibited beating slaves *and colonists* with a big stick, advocating only the use of rods.[46]

Elsewhere, it appears that the free peasant was still not generally subject to the power of correction of any lord at the end of the tenth century or the beginning of the eleventh. He continued to depend upon public justice, even if this was fragmented, frequently corrupt, and dying. Public courts and the public *mallus* still met in the Mâconnais, the Auvergne and, of course, in Septimania and Catalonia.[47] Peasants, singly or in groups, made their voices heard in vicarial courts, even occasionally appeared before comital or episcopal courts.[48] Like the other suitors, they normally – at least in the southern regions – enjoyed guarantees recognised by the law, the Theodosian code or Visigothic law.[49] They might, further, feel encouraged by the presence in these courts of *boni homines*, *boni viri* or *scabini*, rural notables recognised for their

---

[46] Edict of Pîtres, c. 15, *MGH, Capitularia regum Francorum*, ed. Boretius-Krause, 2, p. 311.

[47] Duby, *La société mâconnaise*, pp. 103–5; Lauranson-Rosaz, *L'Auvergne*, pp. 345–51; Magnou-Nortier, *La société laïque et l'Eglise*, pp. 263ff.; Bonnassie, *La Catalogne*, vol. 1, pp. 183–203.

[48] This was common in Catalonia, *ibid.*, pp. 197–8. For an example of legal proceedings instituted and won by peasants against the count of Barcelona himself, in his own court: ACA, perg. Ramon Borell, no. 104 (text published in *Les marches méridionales du royaume aux alentours de l'An Mil: inventaire typologique des sources documentaires*, under the direction of M. Zimmermann (Nancy, 1987), pp. 91–4).

[49] The Theodosian Code was still explicitly cited in the Auvergne in 1021 (Lauranson-Rosaz, *L'Auvergne*, p. 212, with references also to Roman and Salic Law). In Septimania, Visigothic law was more commonly applied, but reference was also made to Roman and Salic Law (Magnou-Nortier, *La société laïque et l'Eglise, passim*). In Catalonia, only Visigothic Law was used, and was constantly quoted (M. Zimmermann, 'L'usage du droit wisigothique en Catalogne du IXe au XIIe siècle', *Mélanges de la Casa de Velazquez*, 9 (1973), 233–81; Bonnassie, *La Catalogne*, vol. 1, pp. 136–44.

competence, active or passive witnesses of the judicial procedure.[50] The free peasant thus continued to be judged, if not by his or her peers, at least in their presence.[51]

If his person and his rights continued, to a certain extent, to be respected, it was because he was still – at least in some places – armed. Very little is known about peasant arms. A major investigation of this subject is needed, on the basis of texts (which exist),[52] iconographical representations,[53] and archaeological finds.[54] We may guess that the results would be extremely diverse. Sometimes, the peasant had absolutely nothing with which to defend himself; he was truly the *inermis* of the Councils of Peace. Sometimes, he possessed military equipment which was, if not complete, at least relatively effective: a sword or a javelin, sometimes a helmet. Between these two conditions (perhaps most often?), we might suppose him to possess the traditional popular weapons, '*guisarmes*':[55] iron-shod pole, sling, club (*tinel*), not forgetting bow and arrows. It is clear that this weaponry, inherited from a distant past, in which iron (too dear) played only a very small part, appeared increasingly derisory compared with that possessed by the professional warriors, the *milites*. This did not prevent the service of peasant host from continuing, in some regions, to be performed in person. In the 'public expeditions'

---

[50] *Scabini* in the Mâconnais, for example, '"good men" who were also small men' (Duby, *La société mâconnaise*, p. 104); *boni homines, boni viri* in Catalonia, Languedoc, and many other places.

[51] Cf. the type of judicial organisation found at the same period in Anglo-Saxon countries, which was the basis of the frankpledge system.

[52] I am thinking of the earliest wills of Catalan peasants, some of which include donations of weapons. These documents have now been published: A. Udina Abello, *La successió testada a la Catalunya alto medieval* (Barcelona, 1984); see, in particular, nos. 112, 121, 122, acts dating from 1018 and 1022.

[53] Biblical miniatures in particular; the Bible known as that of Maréchal de Noailles (actually of Sant Pere of Roda) is very rich from this point of view; it can be dated to the mid eleventh century (BN Paris, MS. latin 6) and has many pictures of scenes of combat.

[54] Such as those made on the submerged sites of Charavines. It is, unfortunately, difficult to define the social status of the men whose arms have been recovered (Renée and Michel Colardelle, 'L'habitat médiéval immergé de Colletière, à Charavines (Isère): premier bilan des fouilles', *Archéologie médiévale*, 10 (1980), 167–203).

[55] The word *guisarmes* has to be understood in its etymological sense: what is used 'in the guise of' arms (the meaning found, for example, in the description given by Wace of the arms of the Norman peasants who revolted in 996–7: *Roman de Rou*, verse 885). The word later indicated a particular type of weapon (an asymetrical iron pike).

which the count of Barcelona led onto Muslim soil, at least till about 1020, *minimi* figured alongside the *maximi*;[56] when, also towards 1020, the sire of Anduze stormed the castle of Loupian, in Languedoc, his troops included as many *pedites* as *equites*.[57]

Peasant freedom, finally, might depend on the exercise of solidarity (particularly in the context of the parish), itself cemented by a common culture. We will never know very much about the peasant culture of the year 1000; it certainly, for all that, existed and expressed the claim to an identity. Two very similar stories, contained in the Books of Miracles of Ste Foy[58] and St Vivian,[59] illustrate this well. In both cases, entry to a pilgrim sanctuary was refused to a crowd of country pilgrims who, when night fell, stationed themselves outside. But a miracle happened: the doors of the church, though locked, opened of their own accord; by the wish of the saint, the peasants entered the sacred edifice. Why had their access been prohibited? Because, we are told, the rustics, when they were allowed to enter, disturbed the solemnity of the sacred vigils by singing *cantilenas rusticas* and *incompositas cantationes*, which were seen by the monks as 'savage vociferations' (*ferales rusticorum vociferationes*) producing an inappropriate tumult (*tumultum ineptum*). No clearer opposition between two cultures, one learned, the other popular, nor more total incomprehension between those belonging to the one and the other, could be envisaged. The fact remains that these

---

[56] Udina Abelló, *La successió testada*, no. 95, p. 258.

[57] *Liber miraculorum sancte Fidis*, III, 21, p. 163. The large number of combatants (1000 *equites* and 1000 *pedites*) is certainly much exaggerated, at least for the former. For other late examples of levies of foot-soldiers (*publicae collectae*) and the performance of the service of host by peasants, see Poly and Bournazel, *La mutation féodale*, pp. 74–80. Such practices must, of course, be compared with the institution of the *fyrd*, still very much alive in Anglo-Saxon England at this period.

[58] *Liber miraculorum sancte Fidis*, II, 12, pp. 120–2. This story, collected on the third pilgrimage of Bernard of Angers to Conques, in 1020, refers to events which took place much earlier, 'at the time of the monk Gimon', that is, about 970–80.

[59] *Sancti Viviani episcopi translatio in coenobium Figiacense et ejusdem ibidem miracula* in *Analecta Bollandiana*, 8 (1889), 257–7. The miracles of St Vivian relate to events which took place in Quercy and the Auvergne in the late tenth and early eleventh centuries. In the instance referred to here, it was the inhabitants of the parish of Saint-Santin (Saint-Santin-Cantalès or Saint-Santin de Maurs) who, having come to Figeac on pilgrimage under the leadership of their priests, found themselves refused entry to the church of the monastery where the relic of St Vivian was housed.

'uncomposed songs' of the peasants of the Rouergue and of Quercy are evidence of a living folklore, which is for us, unfortunately, irrevocably lost.

But peasant culture consisted of more than just songs. It also comprised knowledge born of experience and labour. The crucial question here is to discern what, in the technical innovations of the early Middle Ages (and, in particular, of the tenth century), derived from the reflection and directives of the great landowners – lay and ecclesiastical – and what should be credited to peasant empiricism. Such a study – analogous to those conducted, for example, into Andalusian agriculture[60] – would certainly show that most technical improvements had their origin in a patient accumulation of observations and adaptations made on a daily basis by the practitioners themselves, that is, the peasants (and more particularly, it is safe to assume, the free peasants working on their own account): increasingly refined knowledge of soils, adaptation of systems of ploughing to different environments (including the most stubborn and the most fragile) experimentation with new methods of harnessing, also with a reasoned alternation of types of grain, development of small-scale hydraulic schemes (drainage and irrigation canals), improvement of slopes through the construction of terraces etc. It is not only major advances, such as, for example, the adoption of the heavy plough (*charrue*) which can be attributed to such peasant pragmatism; the complicated science of oblique ploughing could only have developed on the basis of a patient experimentation with different angles of attacking the soil, before eventually resulting in the addition of a mouldboard to the plough.[61]

Whatever their rhythm and their nature, these improvements to equipment and cultural practices determined, at least in part, the first manifestations of agrarian growth, which occurred, it is clear,

---

[60] L. Bolens, *Agronomes andalous du Moyen Age* (Geneva–Paris, 1981). See, in particular, p. 220; 'If we try to summarise the progress realised in medieval agriculture . . . we must emphasise primarily the slowness of the rhythm of progress or, more exactly, the unspectacular character of a progress affecting minute elements, whose accumulation constitutes its significance.'

[61] For such questions, publication of the thesis of Georges Comet, *Le paysan et son outil: essai d'histoire technique des céréales (France, VIIIe–XVe siècles)*, submitted to the University of Provence in 1987, is eagerly awaited. Excellent though it is, the work of Perrine Mane, *Calendriers et techniques agricoles (France–Italie, XIIe–XIIIe siècles)* (Paris, 1983) is no help for the period under consideration here.

before the year 1000, often even before 950.[62] What motivated these first assarts? Was it the search for higher profits on the part of the aristocracy? Or, more simply, the struggle for survival of the mass of the humble? Without it being possible to say definitively, it is nevertheless logical to think that fear of hunger, the *terror famis*, impelled peasants to produce both more (by the conquest of uncultivated soils) and better (by improving their tools and practices). Amongst the first assarters, we may surely include many of the escaped slaves, the *servi in fuga lapsi*, refugees from the large estates who hid in the depths of the forests, where they opened up new clearings;[63] also many 'outsiders' (*albani*), who, come from no one knew where, were confined to the lands on the edges of the forest.[64] But, more simply, in most cases, assarts must surely be credited to the small allod-holders or tenants who, year after year, enlarged their fields by uprooting the surrounding scrub or created new fields by burning a few trees.[65] These early assarts are, in most regions, difficult to trace. How could it be otherwise? Spontaneous, not organised, often clandestine, they were not destined to leave traces in the archives; infinitely less, at any rate, than the planned enterprises of the lay or ecclesiastical lords of the subsequent period.

[62] Research into the origins and early development of the expansion of agriculture, carried out in a random manner, has never really been synthesised, but see *La croissance agricole du Haut Moyen Age: causes, modalités, chronologie, géographie*, Flaran 10, 1988 (forthcoming). For example, it is remarkable that the period of most intense assarting in Catalonia was between around 870 and 950/960 (see, in particular, the works of R. d'Abadal, *Catalunya carolíngia*, vols. 2 and 3, also the collection of his articles, *Dels Visigots als Catalans*, 2 vols. (Barcelona, 1969–72)). More generally, see Duby, *The Early Growth of the European Economy*, Part 1: Foundations (seventh and eighth centuries).

[63] For the flight of slaves: *Cartulaire de l'abbaye de Beaulieu en Limousin*, ed. M. Deloche (Paris, 1859), nos. 55, 186. For the famous example of the meeting between Gerald of Aurillac and the colonisers who had fled his demesnes to create their own holdings elsewhere: *Vita S. Geraldi*, PL 133, col. 656. On this subject, Poly and Bournazel, *La mutation féodale*, pp. 201–2.

[64] *Albani* are mentioned in a diploma of Lothar from 979 relating to the estates of Epône and Méziers (Ile de France) (*Recueil des actes de Lothaire et de Louis V, rois de France*, ed. L. Halphen and F. Lot (Paris, 1948), p. 133).

[65] Thus, in 1013, the metaphor of the oak burned by the slash-and-burner came naturally to the mind of Bernard of Angers when he mentioned the body of a man struck by lightning: 'Ita miser . . . arsit igni divio, ambustumque cadaver in carbonem unum reliquit, assimilis ipse ingentis roboris trunco, quem improbus agricola bene exercitatam novalem diu occupasse dolet. Ille summis viribus enisus, certat eum volvere, forasque extrudere. Sed ingenti mole victus, plurimo igni undique succenso, postremo mediis nigrantem deserit arvis' (*Liber miraculorum sanctae Fidis*, I, 12, pp. 44–5).

Nevertheless, by around 1000, the results were apparent; they were manifested, in particular, in the phenomenon described above – the increasing rarity of major famines. In this regard, comparison of texts from the ninth and the early eleventh centuries is illuminating. In the former, the scourge is referred to only very briefly by the annalists (and not at all by the chroniclers): famine, in their eyes, merited at most a mention; it did not constitute, properly speaking, a memorable fact; it was part of the natural order of things. After the year 1000, in contrast, the 'great famines' gave rise to detailed and, above all, terrified, descriptions; they appeared as extraordinary events signifying a disturbance to the order of values, a return to primal chaos.[66] This is a clear indication that, after the first third of the eleventh century, after the great 'tribulation' of 1031–2, the French countryside was heading towards a relative equilibrium with respect to the supply of food. Better times were on the way.

Protected or oppressed, rebellious or subject?

Towards the year 1000, then, the issues were clear. On the one hand, the burden of servitude, legacy of Antiquity and the Carolingian age, was tending to lighten, even disappear; in large parts of the kingdom (in effect, the entire south), there no longer existed, with rare exceptions, any other judicial status for the peasantry than freedom. On the other, the considerable efforts made by the peasantry, for decades, even centuries, to escape from poverty and misery, had begun to bear fruit; dramatic setbacks notwithstanding, production was set to increase by a large amount over a long period. A double opportunity was thus offered to the peasantry: relative emancipation and an amelioration of their material and moral conditions of existence. That this prospect was perceived by large sectors of the rural population is hardly in doubt, as the ferment then gaining ground in many parts of the countryside goes to show.[67] But even a very partial realisation of such hopes supposed two preconditions: that the peasantry obtained guarantees against the arbitrariness of the

---

[66] *Estimabatur enim ordo temporum et elementorum . . . in chaos decidisse perpetuum* (Glaber, *Historia*, IV, 4, 12, p. 102).
[67] See below, pp. 309–11.

powerful, and that the fruits of its labour were not confiscated by increased levies. Neither of these conditions was fulfilled.

Guarantees and protections: from whom could these be expected? Not, apparently, from kings; no gesture in favour of the peasantry was made by Hugh Capet or Robert the Pious. Nor from the territorial princes; here, too, there was silence, if not contemptuous hostility, as in Normandy, at least if we believe Wace.[68] Alone, in the south, the count of Barcelona continued to grant franchises to rural communities,[69] here perpetuating an old Carolingian practice,[70] and took pains to protect them from abuses of power by the nobility; but this attitude resulted from particular circumstances (a frontier county which needed all its men to combat the Islamic threat) and was not long maintained after 1050.[71]

Was the indifference (or impotence) of the superior authorities compensated – as has often been said – by the solicitude of more local leaders, that is, the castellans set fair to become the sole masters of the *ban*? We encounter here the ancient and edifying image of the protective castle, shelter and safeguard of a frightened population: an image no doubt correct for the fortresses of the early Middle Ages (some of them at least), vast enclosures built in the tradition of the pre-Roman *oppida*, which could retain – at least in the Merovingian period – their role as collective refugees;[72] and an image which would once more achieve some truth in the twelfth century, when aristocratic violence had abated and when castles tended to become focuses of settlement, attract-

---

[68] *Roman de Rou*, verses 916, 919–21.

[69] Font Rius, *CPC* vol. 1, nos. 9 (986), 15 (1025). The latter charter, granted by Berenguer Ramon I, was the more important since it confirmed the status of franchise which was enjoyed by all the inhabitants of the county of Barcelona and its marches (by specifying that, in matters of justice, they were answerable only to the public courts regularly instituted by the count). See also *ibid.*, nos. 7, 10.

[70] There is in practice no break between the privileges granted to the *Hispani* by Charlemagne and his successors (*ibid.*, nos. 1, 2) and the comital charters of franchise granted from the end of the ninth to the beginning of the eleventh centuries.

[71] The last active intervention by the count designed to compel respect for the village franchises on the part of the aristocracy can be dated to 1052, at least outside the comital domain properly speaking (Bonnassie, *La Catalogne*, vol. 2, pp. 677–80, and, more recently, chapter 5 above, 'The formation of Catalan feudalism and its early expansion').

[72] G. Fournier, *Le peuplement rural en Basse-Auvergne durant le Haut Moyen Age* (Paris, 1962), pp. 330ff.; *idem*, *Le château dans la France médiévale* (Paris, 1978), pp. 32–4, 46–8.

ing the rural population into sub-castral *bourgs*.[73] But it was certainly false for the period under discussion here.[74] The castles which proliferated at the end of the tenth and the beginning of the eleventh centuries, with the assent or against the will of the public authority, appear essentially to be the bases for and the stakes in the private wars in which family fought family and which had as a consequence the desolation of the countryside. Directly or indirectly, these castles constituted, for the peasantry, centres of violence. The establishment of a 'castral system' even constituted the chief instrument in the subjection of the free peasantry to the power of the lords.[75] This took, in the short run, two principal, and frequently described, forms: on the one hand, the subjection of former free men to seigneurial authority in matters of justice, on the other, the imposition of new obligations, often very heavy, and in any case lacking juridical basis; these were at first simply called *usaticos* or *consuetudines*, but, systematised and priced, they would become the *banalités*. This process – which resulted, amongst other things, in the almost total disappearance of the peasant allod[76] – is well known and need not be described here. It is enough to say that it began in the reigns of Hugh Capet and Robert the Pious: the first references to *malae consuetudines* were

[73] The problem of the birth and development of castral or sub-castral villages has been much studied in recent years by both archaeologists and historians. There are good surveys in *Châteaux et peuplements en Europe occidentale du Xe au XVIIIe siècle*, Flaran 1, 1979 (Auch, 1980). It should be noted that if it is argued that the castle protected the village in the twelfth and thirteenth centuries, the inverse proposition – that the village with its own enclosure constituted the outer defence of the castle – can equally well, in many cases, be formulated (see, on this subject, the remarks of B. Cursente, *Les castelnaux de la Gascogne médiévale* (Bordeaux, 1980), especially pp. 98–9).

[74] At least in France, Italy, with its more precocious *incastellamento*, has a slightly different chronology (Toubert, *Les structures du Latium, passim*).

[75] Since Duby's *La société mâconnaise*, this thesis has been repeatedly illustrated and confirmed by numerous regional studies. There are brief but lively syntheses in G. Duby, *Les Trois Ordres ou l'Imaginaire du féodalisme* (Paris, 1978), translated by A. Goldhammer as *The Three Orders: Feudal Society Imagined* (Chicago, 1980), especially section entitled 'The Feudal Revolution', and in Poly and Bournazel, *La mutation féodale*, pp. 59–103: 'De la paix publique au système castral'.

[76] Even in the Midi, contrary to the received idea. See, for Catalonia, chapter 7 above; for Languedoc, M. Bourin-Derruau, *Villages médiévaux en Bas-Languedoc: genèse d'une sociabilité (Xe–XIVe siècle)* 2 vols. (Paris, 1987), vol. 1: *Du château au village (Xe–XIIe siècle)*; also M. Roche, *La société languedocienne d'après les testaments (813–1270)*, thèse 3rd cycle, University of Toulouse–Le Mirail, 1986, vol. 1, pp. 57ff.

in c. 994, in the Auvergne,[77] 1000 in Anjou,[78] 1016 in Burgundy,[79] c. 1020 in Champagne,[80] 1029 in Poitou etc.[81] By 1005–6, a diploma of Robert the Pious addressed to the abbey of Fécamp referred to the *uses indebitus quem coustumam vulgo nuncupant*.[82]

In these circumstances, the only tangible protection to be hoped for was from the Church, which put the defence of the *inermes* and the fight against the 'bad customs' on the agendas of its Councils of Peace. It is clear, in fact, that a certain number of prelates – and not the least among them – took to heart the difficult struggle against the growing exactions of the new masters of the *ban*; Gombaud of Bordeaux, Guy of Le Puy, Berenguer of Elne, Oliba of Vic, Jordan of Limoges, Aimon of Bourges, not forgetting Abbot Odilon of Cluny. But, whatever their prestige, they did not represent – by a long chalk – the whole of the clergy and, even in their most modest attempts to limit the prevailing brutality, they came up against the stubborn resistance, even open opposition, of a good number of their brethren, as – it goes without saying – of the military aristocracy.[83] This explains the numerous hazards

---

[77] Lauranson-Rosaz, *L'Auvergne*, pp. 407, 456.

[78] O. Guillot, *Le comte d'Anjou et son entourage au XIe siècle* (Paris, 1972), p. 371.

[79] E. Magnou-Nortier, 'Les mauvaises coutumes en Auvergne, Bourgogne méridionale, Languedoc et Provence au XIe siècle: un moyen d'analyse sociale' in *Structures féodales et féodalisme dans l'Occident méditerranéen (Xe–XIIIe siècle)* (Rome, 1980), p. 146.

[80] M. Bur, *La formation du comté de Champagne (vers 950–vers 1050)* (Nancy, 1977), p. 365.

[81] R. Sanfaçon, *Défrichements, peuplement et institutions seigenuriales en Haut-Poitou du Xe au XIIIe siècle* (Quebec, 1967), p. 17.

[82] *Recueil des Historiens des Gaules et de la France*, vol. 10; *Roberti regis diplomata*, no. 15, p. 587.

[83] One of the most characteristic examples of such opposition concerns the assembly of Saint-Germain-Laprade in Velay (one of the first, possibly the first, assemblies of Peace), dated to between 975 and 993, probably between 975 and 980, by Christian Lauranson-Rosaz (*L'Auvergne*, pp. 414–15). The story (summarised), as told by Marc Bloch in *Feudal Society* (pp. 414–15) goes as follows: 'Guy, bishop of Le Puy, assembled his diocesans, both knights and villeins [*milites ac rustici*], in a meadow and "besought them to pledge themselves by oath to keep the peace, not to oppress the churches or the poor in their goods, to give back what they had carried off . . . They [the *milites*] refused". Upon this, the prelate summoned troops whom he had secretly concentrated under cover of darkness. "In the morning he set out to force the recalcitrants to take the oath of peace and give hostages; which, with the help of God, was done."' The text is in *Chronicon monasterii Sanct Petri Aniciensis*, ed. O. Chevallier, in *Cartulaire de l'abbaye de Saint-Chaffre du Monastier* (Paris, 1884), p. 152. Bloch, though correctly perceiving the significance of the story, unfortunately, like everyone before or since until 1976, confused this assembly of Laprade with the synod

which impeded the Movement of Peace in the beginning,[84] as also the very limited, even derisory, character of the protection it afforded to the peasantry.[85] In point of fact, in the climate of violence which characterised many places at the end of the tenth and the beginning of the eleventh centuries, it appears barely credible that the promoters of the Peace could have achieved any results, however slight. Their relative success can only be explained by the exceptional popular support which they enjoyed and which was demonstrated by the, often very large, crowds of peasants at the meetings of the Peace; these often met – the fact is significant – in open country, in the 'meadows',[86] and were thus not without analogies with the *conventus* and *conciones*, the

called of Le Puy (in fact of Saint-Paulien) some years later (c. 994). The correct sequence of events was established by Canon A. Fayard, then Christian Lauranson, *L'Auvergne*, pp. 412–20

[84] The bishops gathered at Charroux in 989 referred to the 'great delay with which this synod happened', a delay due to 'certain events which in these times of corrupt morals multiplied in our regions' (Mansi, *Concilia*, 19, cols. 89–90). The meeting of the synod of Saint-Paulien (Le Puy), around 994, also seems to have encountered serious difficulties; the charter referring to this assembly (*Carta Widonis, Aniciensis episcopi*) does not constitute – as tends to be assumed these days – the 'acts' of the council; it consists of a letter of convocation, drawn up by Bishop Guy, approved by the archbishops of Bourges and Vienne, and addressed to an unspecified number of bishops. In this charter has been inserted either an agenda (the programme of action proposed by Guy to his correspondents) or – but if so at a later date – the summary of the decisions taken by those bishops who had responded favourably to the convocation: eight altogether, of which only two came from the province of Bourges and two from Vienne. The aristocracy, in fact, is conspicuous by its absence; of the *principes* and *nobiles* convoked, not one, significantly, is named in the charter. The *carta Widonis* has recently been the subject of two new publications: E. Magnou-Nortier, 'La place du concile du Puy (c. 994) dans l'évolution de l'idée de paix' in *Mélanges offerts au professeur Jean Dauvillier* (Toulouse, 1979), p. 489, and C. Lauranson-Rosaz, *L'Auvergne*, p. 421. The critical study of this difficult text is, however, still far from complete.

[85] At Charroux, the clergy were protected from aggression, but not the peasantry: as far as they were concerned, only thefts of cattle were forbidden, and this only on condition that the theft 'was not the victim's own fault'! At Saint-Paulien (Le Puy), the capture and ransom of villeins of either sex was prohibited, except on the holding of the captor, and except on land which was the subject of litigation (which amounted to saying that taking peasants hostage was accepted in the context of private wars between lords).

[86] For example: 'the meadows of Saint-Germain' in Velay (Saint-Germain-Laprade); 'the meadow of Saint-Félix' in Rouergue (near Rodez: 1004/5); 'the meadow of Toulouges' in Rosselló (diocese of Elne, 1027). Other rural 'synods': Coler (Colin, near Laroquebrou, Auvergne, before 994) and Lalbenque (Quercy, 1000/1010), cited as sites of assemblies of the Peace in the Book of Miracles of St Vivian (see note 59), not to mention Saint-Paulien, Charroux, Anse etc. Adalbero twice (verses 159, 414) refers to these assemblies as *rura*,

'parliaments' held at this period in the 'woods' and 'plains' by the Norman peasants sworn to defend their liberties.[87] The assemblies of Peace might well, in large measure, represent the emergence at the institutional level of a vast resistance movement by the (still) free peasantry against the attempts being made to subject them.

A resistance movement, thus subversive; the age of Hugh Capet and Robert the Pious seems to be marked – more than any other for some time – by a powerful wave of peasant rebelliousness, whose manifestations were as varied as they were numerous.[88]

A first indication of the state of mind of the rural masses is provided by Adalbero of Laon, who refers us to those 'rustic songs' denounced as unsuitable by Bernard of Angers. Adalbero has the merit of acquainting us with at least one such song (and the choice is significant); describing the grotesque world, the world upside down, which, according to him, was being constructed by Odilon of Cluny and other trouble-makers in the Movement for Peace, he declared:

> The bishops, naked, have only for ever to follow the plough,
> Singing, goad in hand, the song of our first parents.[89]

This song, which, for Adalbero, served to characterise peasant mentality, was none other than that song which, faithfully transmitted from generation to generation, would again be heard during the insurrectional movements of the fourteenth century, in France and in England:

> When Adam delved and Eve span
> Who was then the gentleman?[90]

condemning the bishops who either organised or participated in them:

> Pontifices unquam celebrent non rura deinceps
> Si sue iura tenent

castigating in particular the role played by his enemy, 'king' Odilon of Cluny.

[87] William of Jumièges used the terms *conventus* (and *conventicula*), *conciones* and *coetus* to describe these gatherings (*Gesta Normannorum*, cols. 823–4); the word 'parliament' appears in Wace (*Roman de Rou*, verse 824: 'Unt tenu plusurs parlemenz', also verse 931).

[88] Robert Fossier has drawn attention to some of these ('Les mouvements populaires en Occident au XIe siècle' in *C.r. de l'Academie des Inscriptions et Belles-Lettres* (1971), pp. 257–69; also his 'Remarques sur l'étude des commotions sociales du XIe siècle' in *Cahiers de civilisation médiévale*, 16 (1973), 45–51.

[89] Nudi pontifices sine fine sequantur aratrum,
Carmina cum stimulo primi cantando parentis. (*Carmen*, verses 41–2)

[90] M. Mollat and Ph. Wolff, *Ongles bleus, Jacques et Ciompi* (Paris, 1970), pp.

It was a song which denied all hierarchy (who was then not only the 'gentleman' but the baron, the bishop or the king?), was radically egalitarian, but also affirmed the dignity of labour – for all.

These same demands for equality, liberty and human dignity were expressed by the Norman peasants in 996–7. Certainly, the speech (or rather, the cry of anger) put into the mouths of the rebels by Wace, comparing themselves to their lords:

> We are men like them
> We have the same limbs
> And just as big hearts . . .[91]

is hardly to be trusted, as too 'worked over' and reported too tardily. But William of Jumièges, though violently hostile to the rebellion, emphasised the desire of the conspirators to be free (*iuxta suos libitus vivere decernebant*), noted the massive and unanimous nature of their movement (*rustici unanimes*) and described the type of representative organisation they had evolved: local assemblies (*plurima agentes conventicula*) met in the fields and each elected two delegates (*ab unoque coetu duo eliguntur legati*) charged with presenting the decisions (*decreta*) of their various meetings to a general sovereign assembly held in the middle of Normandy (*ad mediterraneum roborando conventum*).[92]

Another province, another type of rebellion: in Champagne, it was heresy which erupted towards the end of the year 1000. Leutard, a villager of Vertus, *homo plebeius*, not content with burning the crucifixes in the churches, incited his compatriots to stop paying tithe ('a superfluous and groundless tax'), thus criticising, at least implicitly, the wealth of the clergy.[93] His preaching was heard, since it convinced 'a not inconsiderable part of the

---

192–4. This 'song of our first parents' forms the theme of the sermon preached on 13 June 1381 by John Ball to the rebellious peasants camped at Blackheath outside London.

[91] *Roman de Rou*, verses 867–9.

[92] *Gesta Normannorum*, cols. 823–4.

[93] Glaber, *Historia*, II, 11: *decimas dare dicebat esse omnimodis superfluum et inane*. Georges Duby (*L'An Mil*, p. 122) refuses to see Leutard as a peasant: 'though he came from the people, he was educated and thus belonged to the ecclesiastical order'. This argument is not wholly convincing, since Leutard's education hardly came from books (according to Glaber, he quoted the Scriptures without ever having learned them). It matters little, in practice; what is important is to note the success his teaching enjoyed amongst the peasantry.

people'.[94] Similar ideas (refusal to pay alms to a too opulent church) circulated in Rouergue (and neighbouring regions) in the years 1010–20.[95]

Finally, the movement of the Peace of God itself was radicalised under peasant pressure. In Berry, a 'multitude of men of the people' (*multitudo populi, multitudo inermis vulgi, plebeia multitudo*) set out under the leadership of Archbishop Aimon and, though virtually unarmed, began to assault castles, those haunts of violence. Not, in fact, without some initial success: aghast at their numbers, many castle garrisons fled and the tower of Bennecy was taken and burnt. But in attacking the powerful lord of Déols, the Peace militia overreached itself, and, on 18 January 1038, it was cut to pieces at the battle of Châteauneuf-sur-Cher.[96]

These peasant movements all ended in disaster. In Normandy, the conspirators could not withstand the army of knights (*militum multitudine*) sent against them by Duke Richard and commanded by Raoul, count of Evreux. The latter seized all the delegates (*cunctos legatos*) of the clandestine assemblies and many other peasants and had their hands and feet cut off to make an example of them.[97] In Champagne, Leutard, captured by Bishop Jéboin,

---

[94] Glaber, *Historia: Cujus etiam fama . . . in brevi ad se traxit partem non modicam vulgi.*

[95] This was the purport, in particular, of the preaching of the cleric Odalric (*sceleratissime* according to Bernard of Angers) which was not totally unsuccessful in attracting an audience since it provoked a fall in the volume of offerings to Ste-Foy (*ut offerentium prorsus inhibuisset frequentiam*), *Liber miraculorum sancte Fidis*, I, 13, pp. 48–9.

[96] According to Andrew of Fleury, 'Cinquième livre des Miracles de Saint Benoît, ed. de Certain, S. H. F. (Paris, 1858), pp. 192–7. Relying on another source (the Chronicle of Déols), G. Devailly gives a different interpretation of this episode; he sees it as part of the conflict between the viscount of Bourges and the seigneur of Déols for possession of the fortress of Châteauneuf. From this perspective, the peasant militia of Archbishop Aimon appears only as an additional supplementary force alongside the troops engaged by the viscount of Bourges against Eudes of Déols (Devailly, *Le Berry*, pp. 146–8). There are difficulties, however, in thus reducing these events to no more than a 'feudal quarrel'. The objectives of the Peace militia and those of some baron of Berry (in this case the viscount of Bourges) may well have coincided, but there is no justification for saying that the 'peasant army' had been brought together by any such person. It can even confidently be asserted that in attacking (with, what is more, a suicidal courage) Eudes of Déols, it had not mistaken its enemy (see below, pp. 312 and notes 102–3). Most recently, on this affair, see M. Aubrun, *La paroisse en France des origines au XVe siècle* (Paris, 1986), pp. 104, 218–19, with partial translation of the text of Andrew of Fleury.

[97] *Cunctos confestim legatos cum nonnullis aliis cepit, truncatisque manibus ac*

committed suicide by throwing himself into a well.[98] In Berry, the battle of Châteauneuf-sur-Cher ended in carnage; hundreds of peasants, driven back to the river, were trampled underfoot or drowned; the rest were put to the sword by the *milites* of Eudes of Déols.[99] In fact, as early as the year 1000, the balance of power between an aristocracy exclusively devoted to war, and accordingly trained and equipped, and a peasantry increasingly unarmed, was too unequal for these attempts at resistance to have had any chance of success.[100]

The free peasants were thus subjected, some, indeed, were already enserfed. By 1020–30, in effect, in certain regions, we can discern a trend which transformed power over men, assumed by the masters of the *ban*, into possession of men. Certainly, this was still small-scale, and confined to the regions where force had first been employed, where the 'bad customs' denounced by the assemblies of Peace had first been imposed. It was the case in Poitou, where the expression *homines proprii*, characteristic of the new servitude, appeared by 1032;[101] also in Berry, at least in those parts adjoining Aquitaine, where five charters of the seigneurs of Déols (them again!) from before 1040 comprise donations of free men:[102] in 1027, for example (the earliest document of this type?), Eudes of Déols gave the monks of Issoudun 'all his free men' (*omnes homines suos ingenuos*) and his 'culverts' (*collibertos*: descendants of enfranchised slaves) and all his men (*homines suos*)

---

pedibus inutiles suis remisit (William of Jumièges, *Gesta Normannorum*, loc. cit). Wace adds all sorts of other atrocities.

[98] Glaber, *Historia*, loc. cit.

[99] *Miracles de saint Benoît*, pp. 196–7. Exactly the same outcome is recorded in the Chronicle of Déols (Devailly, *Le Berry*, p. 147, note 6).

[100] This inequality was accentuated by the recruitment from within the rural population of the armed auxiliaries of the *seigneurs banaux*. The *milites* who composed the castle garrisons were, at least for the most part, in origin none other than young peasants, doubtless singled out by the castellan for their strength and agility, that is for their aptitude for fighting on horseback. These mounted combatants probably also included men capable of providing their own arms and mount, that is from the richest strata of the allod-holding peasantry. The peasant world could only be weakened by the desertion of its richest and most dynamic elements, who, as a consequence of their new position, turned against it through their active participation in its subjection. On this subject, see the excellent synthesis in Poly and Bournazel, *La mutation féodale*, pp. 101–3, 129–36.

[101] 'Chartes et documents pour servir à l'histoire de l'abbay de Saint-Maixent', ed. A. Richard, *Arch. Hist. du Poitou*, 16–18, no. 91 (1886), 111.

[102] Devailly, *Le Berry*, p. 213.

for them to possess (*possideant*) 'in all quietude and freedom'.[103] Thus there began, by the reign of Robert the Pious, a movement which would become widespread from the mid eleventh century: former free men were given or sold by 1050 in the Auvergne,[104] by 1051 in Septimania,[105] and by 1054 in Catalonia.[106]

From one servitude to another: thus can the history of the peasantry in the reigns of Hugh Capet and Robert the Pious be schematically summarised. Too schematically, perhaps; the old slavery was already in its death throes in 987, whilst enserfments of free men were still rare before 1031. And, even after that date, not all of the peasant class was affected.[107] Nevertheless, the years before and, above all, immediately after, 1000, appear as a turning-point in the history of the rural societies of the Frankish kingdom. Eventful years, rarely happy, often tragic; the latter sometimes the product of the perverseness of a nature still not fully subdued (meteorological disturbances generating famines), sometimes of the appetite for power and riches of the new masters of the *ban*. They were all, in any case, painfully experienced by a peasantry less resigned and bewailing than has often been claimed, composed of men and women who worked hard and not without a spirit of initiative, and who sought, sometimes with suicidal courage, to organise together to combat the injustices which oppressed them and the miseries which perpetually threatened. It was a time of change, even of upheaval: one world died, another was born amidst violence.

The laws withered and any peace vanished.
The ways of men changed as did the order [of society].[108]

---

[103] *Cartulaire des seigneurs de Châteauroux (967–1789)*, E. Hubert (Châteauroux, 1931), V, 7 (act quoted by Devailly, *Le Berry*, p. 213, note 3).

[104] Lauranson-Rosaz, *L'Auvergne*, p. 407, note 366.

[105] Magnou-Nortier, *La société laïque et l'Eglise*, p. 226, note 97.

[106] Bonnassie, *La Catalogne*, vol. 2, pp. 812–13.

[107] Although, on this point, since Marc Bloch (and his critic, Leo Verriest), the question remains open; see chapter 10 below.

[108] Tabescunt leges et iam pax defluit omnis
Mutantur mores hominum mutatur et ordo. (Adalbero, *Carmen*, verse 302–3) The last verse can bear this interpretation. Claude Carozzi does not translate *ordo*: 'Ways have changed as has *Ordo*' (p. 23). Robert Boutruche proposed: 'The ways of men change, as does the division of society' (*Seigneurie et féodalité*, vol. 1 (Paris, 1959), p. 371).

10. Marc Bloch, historian of servitude: reflections on the concept of 'servile class'*

The problem of servitude haunted Marc Bloch. His first piece of research, published in 1911, was about the serfs of the chapter of Notre-Dame of Paris at the time of Blanche of Castile.[1] One of his last articles, published posthumously, was about slavery in the early Middle Ages.[2] In between came his thesis, *Rois et serfs*,[3] nine articles (amongst the most important he wrote)[4] and several crucial chapters in his major works, *Les caractères originaux*[5] and *La*

---

* First published in *Marc Bloch aujord'hui: histoire comparée et sciences sociales*, Actes du colloque Marc Bloch, Paris, 1986 (Paris, E H E S S, 1990), pp. 363–87.

[1] 'Blanche de Castile et les serfs du chapitre de Paris', *Mémoires de la Société de l'histoire de Paris et de l'Ile-de-France*, 38 (1911), 242–72; reprinted in M. Bloch, *Mélanges historiques* (Paris, 1963), vol. 1, pp. 462–90; translated by William R. Beer in *Slavery and Serfdom in the Middle Ages* (London, 1975), pp. 66, 163–77.

[2] 'Comment et pourquoi finit l'esclavage antique', *Annales* (1947), pp. 30–43, 161–70; reprinted in *Mélanges historiques,* vol. 1, pp. 261–85; translation in *Slavery and Serfdom*, pp. 1–31.

[3] *Rois et serfs: un chapitre d'histoire capétienne* (Paris, 1920). The plan for Marc Bloch's initial thesis (modified and limited due to the 1914–18 War) was entitled *Les populations rurales de l'Ile-de-France à l'époque du servage*.

[4] *'Serf de la glèbe: histoire d'une expression toute faite' (1921); 'Un aspect de la société médiévale: rois et serfs' (1921); *'Les transformations du servage; à propos de deux documents du XIIIe siècle relatifs à la région parisienne' (1925): 'Collibertus ou Culibertus' (1926); 'Servus glebae' (1926); *'Les colliberti: étude sur la formation de la classe servile' (1928); 'Un problème d'histoire comparée: la ministérialité en France et en Allemagne' (1928); *'Liberté et servitude personnelles au Moyen Age, particulièrement en France' (1933); 'De la cour royale à la cour de Rome: le procès des serfs de Rosny-sous-Bois' (1938); 'The Rise of Dependent Cultivation and Seignorial Institutions' (1941). All these articles are reprinted in *Mélanges historiques*; the four asterisked are also translated in *Slavery and Serfdom* (to which later page numbers refer); the last article is chapter 6 of *The Cambridge Economic History of Europe*, vol. 1, ed. M. M. Postan (2nd edn Cambridge, 1966).

[5] *Les caractères originaux de l'histoire rurale française*, 2 vols. (2nd edn 1952–6); volume 1 has been translated into English by Janet Sondheimer as *French Rural History* (London, 1966) (to which later page numbers refer); see, in particular, pp. 64–101 ('The *seigneurie* down to the crisis of the fourteenth and fifteenth centuries') and pp. 102–12 ('Legal changes affecting the *seigneurie*; the fate of serfdom'), also, in vol. 2 of *Les caractères originaux*, pp. 80–5 ('Le declin de l'esclavage') and pp. 143–7 ('Servage et sociétés rurales').

Société féodale:[6] in all, he devoted many hundreds of pages to this absorbing question: the enserfment of man by man.

Bloch's principal ideas

'Slavery and serfdom: a historical contrast':[7] if there was one idea which Marc Bloch held dear, which he never ceased to assert with growing conviction, and demonstrate with increasing rigour, it was that of the radical transformation experienced by the Middle Ages with regard to servitude. He placed this transformation firmly in the tenth and eleventh centuries, a period of 'great social disorder and renewal'.[8]

Ancient slavery survived into Carolingian times. In this respect, the 'great invasions' changed nothing; there was even an increase in the numbers reduced to slavery in the fifth century. The slave living in the Frankish kingdom was still relegated to the ranks of objects, at best an animal; devoid, at all events, of his individuality, lacking all status, thus any guarantees, he was 'a foreigner'.[9] The decline of the slave system came about for a number of reasons, amongst which one of the most important was the practice of settling slaves on holdings. It usually took the form of enfranchisement *cum obsequio*, motivated by economic factors. In the ninth century, as the polyptiques reveal, manumissions had already had an effect; slaves constituted only a minority amongst the tenants of the great estates.[10]

Several centuries later, around 1200, servitude existed but was

[6] *La société féodale*, 2 vols. (1938–40); translated by L. A. Manyon as *Feudal Society* (London, 1961) (to which later page references refer); see, in particular, chapter 19 ('Servitude and Freedom').

[7] This was the sub-title given to the first section of 'Personal liberty and servitude' (*Slavery and Serfdom*, pp. 33–91).

[8] *Ibid.*, p. 75. In many of his works, Bloch did not really date the period of the transformation, placing it without further specifying between the end of the eleventh century and the beginning of the thirteenth, but when he refined his analysis (as in the instance quoted here), he placed it unhesitatingly in the tenth–eleventh centuries.

[9] *Ibid.*, p. 35. It is remarkable to note to what extent this definition of the slave by Bloch prefigures that given by contemporary ethnologists, who emphasise the phenomenon of the 'desocialisation' of the slave (see C. Meillassoux, *L'esclavage dans l'Afrique noire précoloniale* (Paris, 1975), p. 21).

[10] For a more detailed analysis of Bloch's views on the decline of ancient slavery, see chapter 1 above, 'Survival and extinction of the slave system in the early medieval west', especially pp. 2–16.

no longer the same. An old name - *servus*, serf - concealed a new reality: serfdom was not (contrary to the writings of, for example, Fustel de Coulanges) the continuation of slavery. In the first place, it affected a much larger number of people: 'the majority of manorial subjects'.[11] Further, it was different in origin; if some ('a small number') descendants of the slaves of the early Middle Ages were found amongst the serfs, the majority of them ('the greatest number' by far) had as their ancestors *coloni, lites*, [freedmen, small allod-holders], in a word, men considered [in the Carolingian period] as legally free'.[12] The process of enserfment took place within the framework of the *seigneurie*: it resulted from 'pressure exerted through promise or threat' on the mass of the humble and led to the creation of a single category of humble personal dependants.[13] This is how the servile class was formed. And it was a class: 'Serfdom in fact presented this double character truly essential to its nature of being at one and the same time a bond between men and a class institution.'[14] Finally, this 'new kind of servitude' was defined by 'almost entirely new criteria',[15] the most important of which were the payment of chevage, prohibition of *formariage* and *mainmorte*.

Bloch's supposed errors

Marc Bloch's ideas about the survival of ancient slavery into the Carolingian period and its subsequent decline have been little contested. True, they upset some common assumptions and caused some perplexity amongst specialists (it was so convenient for ancient slavery to disappear along with Antiquity), but the latter have, in general, been content to leave the question open or veil it in an obscurity which is itself significant. But no one has openly denied the validity of Bloch's hypotheses and the most recent research seems to have given them striking confirmation.[16]

---

[11] *Feudal Society*, p. 262. The idea appears in many other of his written works.
[12] 'Personal liberty and servitude', p. 69.   [13] *Ibid.*, p. 78.
[14] *Ibid.*, p. 65. The concept of 'servile class' is a constant presence in Bloch's work. It assumed such importance in his eyes that it appeared explicitly in the title of several of his works: 'The *Colliberti*. A study on the formation of the servile class', 'Personal liberty and servitude in the Middle Ages . . . contribution to a class study'; and vol. 2 of *Feudal Society* is entitled 'Social classes . . .'
[15] *French Rural History*, p. 90; *Feudal Society*, p. 263.
[16] See chapter 1 above. What follows relates only to the serfdom of the eleventh to thirteenth centuries.

The same is not true of his ideas about serfdom. These were criticised, with unusual vehemence, by the legal historian, Leo Verriest, in his *Institutions médiévales* which appeared shortly after Marc Bloch's death.[17] Forty years on, we may consider that this savage attack (there is no other word for it) deserves to be quietly forgotten. But this is hard to do because Verriest's criticisms, by their very virulence, their peremptory character and their scholarly apparatus, had a profound effect; even today, many medievalists regard the conclusions of Marc Bloch as having been 'undermined' to the point of being 'no longer credible'.[18]

For Verriest, Marc Bloch was wrong on every aspect of the history of serfdom and his mistakes only grew worse as his work progressed.[19] In the first place, Bloch was mistaken in his definition of serfdom. Chevage, the prohibition of *formariage* and *mainmorte* could not be regarded as the specific obligations of serfdom. They very often also bore on villeins who might be considered, absolutely unequivocally, as free men.[20] When, in the thirteenth century, charters of customs, or rather '*chartes-lois*', abolished these charges, they were addressed not to serfs but to 'the population of the free villeins of the *seigneuries*'; Marc Bloch had crudely confused these texts with acts of manumission.[21] When groups of peasants remained subject to these obligations (and particularly to *mainmorte*) down to modern times, we should not see them as serfs. Voltaire himself got it wrong when he wrote his *Mémoire pour l'abolition de la servitude en France*: he was only fighting, in practice, for 'pretend serfs' and infected later historians with the same error, Marc Bloch amongst them.[22]

Secondly, Bloch was equally mistaken as to the number of serfs. The name 'serf' should be reserved for those men whom medieval charters continued to call by the name of *servi* or (but they were

---

[17] *Institutions médiévales. Introduction au 'Corpus des records de coutumes et des lois de chefs-lieux de l'ancien comté de Hainaut* (Mons, 1946). The criticism of Bloch's views appears in pp. 171–248.

[18] 'Undermined' for Robert Boutruche (*Seigneurie et féodalité*, vol. 2 (Paris, 1970), p. 75), 'no longer credible' to Robert Fossier (*Enfance de l'Europe*, vol. 1 (Paris, 1982), p. 577).

[19] Though relatively indulgent towards the ideas expressed by Bloch in *Rois et serfs*, Verriest tore his later positions to shreds ('his doctrine') as it appeared in *Les caractères originaux* and, above all, in 'Personal liberty and servitude'.

[20] *Institutions médiévales*, pp. 232–4.

[21] *Ibid.*, pp. 219ff. Verriest objected to the expression *charte de franchise*, expressed some reservations about *charte de coutumes*, and accepted only *charte-loi* (p. 219, note 1).   [22] *Ibid.*, p. 173, note 2.

the same) for those called *homines de corpore* (words unequivocally implying personal dependence).[23] Defined in this way, serfs
constituted only a tiny minority of the rural population. In which
case, to talk of 'servile masses' or of a 'servile class' was a
nonsense.

Thirdly, Marc Bloch was wrong about the origins of serfdom.
Having hugely enlarged the concept of serfdom, he had to seek
various provenances for it, incorporating into the serfs numerous
descendants of ancient freedmen and ancient free men (both allod-
holders and tenants), creating a 'macédoine' as inadmissible as the
'magma' to which it gave rise.[24] In fact, the few *servi* of the
thirteenth century descended quite simply from the equally rare
servi of Carolingian times. 'The serfs of the late Middle Ages were
purely and simply the fruit, perpetuated without any discontinuity,
of the female servile bellies of the Frankish period.'[25] The continuity was complete and we can manage without the 'great revolution in the index of social values' attributed by Bloch to the tenth
and eleventh centuries[26] in favour of a history that stands still!

Reading Marc Bloch today

When, forty years on, we read both Verriest and Bloch, we cannot
but be struck by the differences of viewpoint, evidence, method
and, in a word, sense of history, separating the two men; on the
part of the former, a punctilious erudition, but limited to fixed
categories of document (polyptiques, cartularies and royal
charters) and put to the service of concerns of a strictly juridical
kind; on the part of the latter, an equally impeccable erudition,
but applied to an immense field (from Antiquity to the French
Revolution), making use of the most diverse materials, extending
far beyond the frontiers of the history of law in an attempt to
examine mentalities and understand the realities of behaviour, and
depending, lastly, on new studies, in particular linguistic.[27] Over-

---

[23] *Ibid.*, pp. 176–7, pp. 200ff. We may remark, in passing, that the identification of
the *homines de corpore* with the *servi* is accepted by Verriest without its being
specifically demonstrated by any text. If the logic of this author was pushed to its
limits, the former could be excluded from the category of the serfs – a paradox, if
ever there was one!

[24] *Ibid.*, p. 179 ('alleged servile macédoine'); pp. 200–1 ('jumbled servile
magma').   [25] *Ibid.*, p. 236.   [26] *Feudal Society*, p. 261.

[27] One cannot but be struck today by the attention Bloch paid to the evolution of
language, seeking to discover through the history of words the history of the

all, if Verriest was occasionally right in his criticisms of Bloch,[28] if he sometimes 'ploughed the cartularies better', it is nevertheless Bloch's intuitions which tend, sometimes in striking fashion, to be receiving confirmation today.

ON THE 'HISTORICAL CONTRAST'

Let us look first at the central problem, the problem which Bloch highlighted in all his works on servitude: continuity or rupture? Marc Bloch suspected, but was unable to describe, the 'great upheaval' of the tenth and eleventh centuries, as a result, he said, of the documentary 'twilight', the 'large obscure gap', which, according to him, as to all his contemporaries, characterised this period.[29] He deplored, in particular, the scarcity of information about the regions of the Midi for which, he said, 'the whole question is still to be studied'.[30] Over the last twenty years, a mass of converging research, bringing to light a considerable quantity of unpublished or little known documents, has illumined these 'obscure' centuries, especially as regards the southern regions: Latium,[31] Provence,[32] the Biterrois,[33] Catalonia,[34] Auvergne,[35]

social realities they reflected. On serfdom, in particular, his argument was as much of a linguistic as a juridical order. See, especially, 'Personal liberty and servitude', pp. 71–5.

[28] As, apparently, at least, on the endlessly discussed problem of the 'specific obligations'. He proved, very clearly (*Institutions médiévales*, pp. 204–19), that men called 'villeins' or '*manants*' were subject to *mainmorte*, payment of chevage and prohibition of *formariage* (or to all three simultaneously). But it is no less clear that texts exist (and Bloch published some quite conclusive ones) which show that prohibition of *formariage* and *mainmorte* were sometimes considered as sufficient to establish the condition of *homines de corpore* (see, for example, the deposition of Gilles Cornut, Archbishop of Sens, 27 November 1252, concerning the men of Orly: *Mélanges historiques*, vol. 1, p. 479). In practice, Verriest only evaded the problem; was the status of the *homines de corpore* not *also* that of many 'villeins' and *manants*? Where, then, should we set the limits of serfdom? There lies the problem.

[29] 'Personal liberty and servitude', p. 34.

[30] *Ibid.*, p. 213, note 107.

[31] P. Toubert, *Les structures du Latium médiéval*, 2 vols. (Rome, 1973).

[32] J.-P. Poly, *La Provence et la société féodale* . . . (Paris, 1976).

[33] M. Bourin, *Villages médiévaux en Bas-Languedoc: genèse d'une sociabilité (X–XIVe s)* 2 vols. (Paris, 1987).

[34] Bonnassie, *La Catalogne*.

[35] G. Fournier, *Le peuplement rural en Basse-Auvergne durant le haut Moyen Age* (Paris, 1962); complemented by C. Lauranson-Rosaz, *L'Auvergne et ses marges (Velay, Gévaudan) du VIIIe au XIe siècle: la fin du monde antique?* (Le Puy-en-Velay, 1987).

and the Charentais.[36] What they all show is the late survival in the areas studied of structures of the ancient type,[37] and their brutal collapse, often in the space of a generation (at the end of the tenth or at various times during the eleventh centuries), concurrently with the establishment, in the wake of the violence, of a system of a radically new type. This was the age of what we are now learning to call the 'feudal revolution'[38] or the 'feudal transformation'.[39]

Amongst the institutions which foundered in this upheaval, slavery was one of the foremost. Long undermined by its failure to adapt to new economic conditions, weakened by those enfranchisements *cum obsequio* whose importance Marc Bloch had correctly perceived (and whose underlying purpose, we now know, was to assure the mobility of labour required for growth),[40] servitude of the ancient type disappeared, lock, stock and barrel. The last references to *servi* date from the end of the tenth or, at the latest, the first third of the eleventh centuries.[41] Throughout the whole of the southern sector of Christendom, the rupture suspected by Bloch has been demonstrated: the great gap separating the slave from the feudal age. In northern Europe, the transformation was less clear-cut and residual groups of *servi* were able to survive beyond the year 1000 (they still constituted about 9 per cent of the rural population of the England of Domesday Book),[42] even into the twelfth and thirteenth centuries.[43] It was only the existence of

---

[36] A. Debord, *La société laïque dans les pays de la Charente, Xe–XIIe siècles* (Paris, 1984).

[37] Hence the title given by Christian Lauranson to his recent thesis on the Auvergne from the eighth to the eleventh centuries – see note 35 above.

[38] G. Duby, *Les Trois Ordres ou l'imaginaire du féodalisme* (Paris, 1978), translated by Arthur Goldhammer as *The Three Orders: Feudal Society Imagined* (Chicago, 1980), part 3, chapter 3: 'The feudal revolution', pp. 147–66.

[39] J.-P. Poly and E. Bournazel, *La mutation féodale* (Paris, 1980).

[40] This idea is developed for Italy by Toubert in *Les structures du Latium*, pp. 471ff., and also 'L'Italie rurale aux VIIIe–IXe siècles: essai de typologie domaniale', *Settimane*, 20 (1973), p. 105ff. More generally, chapter 1, above pp. 41–6.

[41] *Ibid.*, pp. 55–6.

[42] Figure taken from F. W. Maitland, *Domesday Book and Beyond* (republished Cambridge, 1960). The figure of 9 per cent is perhaps too low, as some *servi casati* may have been listed as *bordarii* by the Domesday commissioners: see R. H. Hilton, *The Decline of Serfdom in Medieval England* (2nd edn, London, 1983), pp. 14–19.

[43] L. Genicot, *L'économie rurale namuroise au Bas Moyen Age*, vol. 3: *Les hommes, Le commun* (Louvain–Brussels, 1982), especially pp. 207–38 and tables 15 and 16.

this residual slavery which enabled Verriest to contest Bloch's arguments on discontinuity.

ON THE ORIGIN OF THE NEW SERVITUDE

On this question too, Bloch was quite clear. The serfdom of the eleventh to thirteenth centuries emerged in the context of the *seigneurie*: 'Without any special agreements, the majority of manorial subjects . . . slid gradually, through the agency of prescription, of violence, and of the changes that had come about in legal opinion, into this [servile] condition.'[44] This was, for its time, a truly remarkable claim given the obscurity surrounding the concept of lordship, and more particularly given that no other form of lordship than 'land lordship', distant heir to the Carolingian *villa*, was known. In these circumstances, to detect the appearance of fundamentally new social relations in a context so antiquated testifies to a rare intuition. All became clear with the emergence of the concept of the *seigneurie banale*, proposed by Georges Duby[45] in 1953 and increasingly clearly defined since; *banal*, or 'jurisdictional', or better, perhaps, 'castral' lordship now appears as the keystone of the establishment of a feudal society. It was the castellan's *ban* – the power to constrain, extra-economic in character, and exercised within the framework of the districts subject to the castle by the new masters of military force and their auxiliaries – which submitted the peasants to the 'arbitrary will' (the expression is Bloch's)[46] of the lords. Peasants who had recently been free (allod-holders, tenants or descendants of freedmen) were now subject to the arbitrary power of a lord.[47]

---

[44] *Feudal Society*, p. 262.

[45] *La société aux XIe et XIIe siècles dans la région mâconnaise* (Paris, 1953), pp. 205–29 ('Le pouvoir sur les paysans: l'installation de la seigneurie banale').

[46] 'Personal liberty and servitude', p. 47. See also p. 59, where, on the basis of a discussion of the works of Jacques Flach, Bloch makes violence 'a significant characteristic of eleventh-century judicial life' and explains the genesis of 'servile status' by the helpless subjection to 'brutality and arbitrariness'.

[47] See, most recently, Duby, *The Three Orders*, pp. 159–60: 'Previously, the obligation to toil in order to feed a master had been relegated outside the sphere of the "people": it fell upon slaves. After the year 1000, with the increased weight of the power of the ban, this burden came to be borne by all "rustics". Toil was the common fate of all men who were neither warriors nor priests. Some peasants might well claim to be free; they were nevertheless like the others subjected to the new seigniory.'

The mechanisms and the various modalities of peasant degradation in the eleventh century have been too often described in recent works for it to be necessary to spend much time on them here. The *rusticus*, now subordinated to a leader who enjoyed over him a power of command (*bannus*, *mandamentum*) and punishment (*districtus*), lost even the appearance of liberty; he became the man of his lord, sometimes his 'homme propre', bound to him by a 'servile' homage.[48] The exactions of the *ban*, originally multiform (new customs, new usages, bad usages of every type), gradually turned into more or less 'specific' obligations: tallage at will,[49] but also limitations on the right to marry,[50] and certain archaic forms of *mainmorte*.[51] Soon, at least in some places, *rustici*, ancient free men, might be given, exchanged or sold with their *consuetudines* or their *usaticos*, that is, with the *banal* rights applying to them: by 1050 in the Auvergne,[52] and by 1060/80 in Catalonia.[53] A last threshold would be crossed when the land

[48] In Poitou, the earliest reference to *homines proprii* was in 1032 (*Chartes de Saint-Maixent*, no. 91, p. 111: reference kindly supplied by G. Pon). In Catalonia, a homage was imposed on certain peasants by 1045/6: Alamany de Cervelló and his wife Sicards described as *omines de nostro ominatico* the peasants subjected to the *ban* of their castle (Bonnassie, *La Catalogne*, vol. 2, pp. 582, 815, also p. 224 above). In this region, from the beginning of the twelfth century, the expression *homines proprii et solidi* (own and liege men) was applied to all the men subject to a servitude of a personal kind.

[49] Marc Bloch (approved in this at least by Verriest) excepted arbitrary tallage from the 'specific obligations' of serfdom. Yet, in actual fact, there are regions (in fact, the whole of southern France, from the Rhône to the Atlantic) where its payment was enough to indicate a serf (the *questal*). References are very frequent for Languedoc, Béarn, the Bordelais etc.

[50] Examples for the Auvergne: 'servicio de viris vel feminis maritandis' (1094, *Recueil des chartes de Cluny*, 3681), 'nupcias et . . . que offerunt mulieres surgentes a partu' (1131/7, *Cart. de Sauxillanges*, no. 918) (quoted by Lauranson, *L'Auvergne*). For Catalonia: 'presentalias de ipsos aut ipsas qui duxerint maritos vel uxores' (1067), *presentalias* (1127), 'presentalges' (1130) (references in Bonnassie, *La Catalogne*, vol. 2, pp. 592, 827, also p. 235 above). Thus the origin of the right, arrogated to himself by the lord, was the introduction of the future spouses (hence the choice of spouse) and the tax linked to this right.

[51] Obligatory bequests (*lexivos* or *lexivas*) levied on peasant inheritances regularly figured among the revenues of the Catalan *seigneuries banales* (from the 1050s (Bonnassie, *La Catalogne*, vol. 2, pp. 592, 826, also pp. 234–5 above. They are at the origin of the Catalan *exorquia* and also, probably, the Languedocian *escaducha*.

[52] (*c*. 1050): 'dono . . . consuetudines et vicarias ibidem pertinentes . . . et quinquaginta rusticos cum consuetudinibus quas debent . . . et quinquaginta porcos, totidem multones' (*Chartes de Cluny*, no. 3315, quoted in Lauranson, *L'Auvergne*).

[53] 1063: 'donamus vobis II homines, Arnal Pere et Arnal Iover, ab lur servidi'; many other examples from the second half of the eleventh century. Such dona-

(allod or tenure) of the enserfed man fell, in its turn, under the discretionary power of the master, and was affected by a servile taint:[54] to personal servitude was added bondage to the soil.[55]

Such a schema can, of course, accommodate many variants. It is even the case that the process of enserfment was not always and not everywhere pressed to its ultimate conclusion. Even in the worst period of *banal* constraints, even when subject to, for example, *mainmorte* and arbitrary tallage, men so subject to seigneurial pressure were able, in some regions, to retain some semblance of liberty; at least no one went so far as to give or sell them like the *servi* of ancient origin. Does this mean we should not therefore use the expression 'new servitude' to define their condition.[56] The

tions and sales of peasants might apply to individuals or to whole communities: *homines qui ad ipsum castrum pertinent, homines infra prefatos terminos habitantes* (Bonnassie, *La Catalogne*, vol. 2, pp. 812–13, also pp. 221–2 above).

[54] A typical example of servitude creeping from the man to the land (to land, what is more, still called allodial): (1087) *domanus vobis tres pagenses cum illorum decimis et serviciis et cum illorum alodiis et domibus* (*ibid.*, p. 814, also p. 222 above).

[55] This extension – from man to land – of the servile system was clearly observed and described by contemporaries: as when, towards 1130, Peter the Venerable remarked that powerful lay lords claimed 'the property at the same time as the persons, the persons at the same time as the property' (quoted by Duby, *La société mâconnaise*, p. 592). In the Mâconnais, this tendency for the peasant's master to assume control of the land is visible by the beginning of the eleventh century ('At the beginning of the eleventh century, the allod of the serf, that of the commended free men, was controlled and exploited by the lord of the person; similarly – and here copying the evolution of the feudo-vassalic relationship – the services of the 'man' were gradually transferred to his agricultural holding, which, whether allodial or rented, bore the charges imposed on it by his dependence') and the phenomenon reached its ultimate conclusion in the 'seizure of manses' of the beginning of the thirteenth century (pp. 592–7). The evolution was very similar in Catalonia, except that the establishment of 'serfdom of the soil' (which was also effected through 'seizures of manses') was even earlier (first half of twelfth century) (Bonnassie, *La Catalogne*, vol. 2, pp. 820–4, also pp. 228–32 above).

[56] For the region of Namur, Genicot rejected the 'theory of the new serfdom' (*L'économie rurale namuroise*, vol. 3, pp. 214–15). This is to be explained by the fact that here (as in Verriest's neighbouring Hainault) there was a late survival of residual groups of *servi* and *ancillae* descending (very probably) from the *familiae* of the early Middle Ages: it is to them alone that he believed the concept of serfdom should apply. The real problem is to know whether or not the (very numerous) *homines* who suffered all the *banal* charges and were called *hommes de taille, de poesté, de basse loi, levant et couchants* also suffered some form of servitude. Should we then distinguish 'serfdom' (in the narrow sense) from 'servitude' (in a wide sense)? This risks embroiling us in endless controversy, of the kind which has split (and often still continues to split) medievalists over the use of the terms *féodalité* and *féodalisme*; the sterility of such battles of words hardly needs emphasising.

charters which, even in the region of Namur, describe as *rustice servitutes* the obligations weighing on them hardly seem to challenge the phenomenon of enserfment.[57]

ON THE CONCEPT OF 'SERVILE CLASS'

As for the number of men thus enserfed, Marc Bloch has, since Verriest, been much criticised for having exaggerated. In which case, his concept of the 'servile masses' and, above all, of the 'servile class' becomes unfounded. We need, therefore, to consider this question with the utmost care.

The problem of determining the proportion of serfs or of men regarded as such within the peasant population is extremely difficult. Who was a serf? If we renounce the 'classic' criteria for the definition of serfdom (chevage etc.), we have to rely – as, in fact, Verriest proposed – on what we can learn from the medieval vocabulary. Only those described by their contemporaries as serfs should be regarded as such. This is an excellent principle, but how is it to be applied? Which words indicate serfdom? The answer to the question posed will depend on how wide is the choice of these words. But the choice is not easy, as the meaning of words varied as a function of many factors: the nature of the texts in which they were employed (charters, juridical writings or literary works), or the period or the geographical area where they occurred, and, last but by no means least, the language in which they were expressed (whether, that is, in the Latin of the clerks, or the Romance languages at their different stages of evolution). That the history of serfdom relates in such a crucial way to that of language – as Marc Bloch so clearly perceived – shows in itself that it was not a marginal institution but truly integral to medieval societies.

Three groups of words can perhaps be regarded as characterising the servitude of the eleventh to thirteenth centuries in its different degrees and modalities:

1. *servus* and its derivatives in the Romance languages (serf, *sers*, *siervo* etc.).
2. '*Homo*, with or without a qualifier: *de capite*, *de corpore*, *de casalagio*, *de redimentia* etc.

---

[57] *Rustice servitutes quae ultra censum debitum terrarum a rusticis exiguntur* (Genicot, *L'économie rurale namuroise*, vol. 3, p. 1: the expression is taken from a charter of 1243).

3. Terms with an apparently more general meaning ('*manant*' and 'villein'), but which might, at least in the case of the former (*homines commanentes*) be attached to the preceding group.

The semantic evolution of the word *servus*/serf deserves particular attention because it was his observation of this word that led Marc Bloch to formulate the concept of 'servile class'. The word *servus*, he commented, escaped the obsolescence which afflicted the other ancient words indicating dependence (*mancipium* and *colonus*, for example) and this because it assumed 'class value'. 'The tendency', he went on, 'to assimilate all seigneurial dependants to the *servi* quickly went beyond the level of language.'[58]

If we confine ourselves solely to the vocabulary of the charters (to be precise, the Latin charters from between the Loire and the Rhine), Marc Bloch was wrong. It is, indeed, on the basis of the analysis of this type of document that Verriest based his case: undoubtedly, the creatures called *servi* in cartularies compiled in the twelfth and thirteenth centuries, far from constituting the mass of the peasant population, were only a minority.[59] But, as soon as we enlarge our field of observation, even if we still confine ourselves to occurrences of the scholarly form of the word (*servus* in Latin), the perspectives change. This applies in the case of texts of an ideological character, and, first and foremost, in the celebrated passage in the *Carmen* of Adalbero of Laon defining the tripartite social order: 'The society of the faithful forms only one body, but the State comprises three orders': *oratores*, *bellatores* and *servi*. Not *laboratores*, but *servi*; Adalbero does not employ the word inadvertently; he uses it four times in ten verses, and it alone, to qualify the third order: the *servorum divisio*.[60] The word clearly here has, if not a class value, as Bloch claimed, at least the connotation of an order, something which is perhaps even wider.

---

[58] 'Personal liberty and servitude', p. 73.

[59] Which is confirmed, more recently, by Genicot, *L'économie rurale namuroise*, vol. 3, pp. 20–738.

[60] Nobilis et servus simili non ege tenentur

. . .

Altera servorum divisio conditium:

Hoc genus afflictum nil possidet absque dolore:

Tesaurus, vestes, cunctis sunt pascua servi,

Nam valet ingenuus sine servis vivere nullus.

Much later, at the beginning of the thirteenth century, the same very wide meaning was attributed to the word *servus* by those jurists who had rediscovered Roman law, at least by some of them, and amongst the most eminent. The English example is significant in this regard; in England – and this has been particularly clearly shown by the work of Paul Hyams[61] – the word *servus*, in its ancient sense, was quite deliberately applied by the legists of the years 1220–50 to the whole of the abundant group of 'villeins'.[62] It was even by reference to the status of the slave, as defined in the Institutes, that the status of villeinage was defined.[63] To read the finest spokesmen for the prevalent ideology, from Adalbero to Bracton, it is quite clear that, if all peasants were not born *servi*, all had a vocation to be so, and ought, so far as was possible, and for the common good, to be treated as such.

If we leave the Latin of the clerks for the language in common use, we cannot but be struck by the vitality of the derivatives of *servus*. In the literature of the *langue d'oïl*, 'serf' was in frequent use, as a noun or as an adjective (*la gent serve*),[64] in a literal or in a figurative sense,[65] and there is no doubt that its meaning was much wider than that attributed to *servus* by the charters. The concept of 'serf' might even extend – as Marc Bloch emphasised[66] – to all who

---

[61] P. R. Hyams, *Kings, Lords and Peasants in Medieval England: the Common Law of Villeinage in the Twelfth and Thirteenth Centuries* (Oxford, 1980).

[62] This was so, in particular, in the *De legibus et consuetudinibus Angliae* which gives the most elaborate formulation of the common law of villeinage. This work has always been attributed to Henry of Bracton; but its most recent editor (S. E. Thorne (Cambridge, Mass., 1968–77)) thinks that it was produced, in its original form, in the years 1220–30 by one or more anonymous authors. For reasons of convenience, it is still generally called 'Bracton's treatise' (Hyams, *Kings, Lords and Peasants*, pp. 82–9).

[63] Bracton started from the premiss formulated in the *Institutes*: *omnes homines aut liberi sunt aut servi*. Having some difficulty, nevertheless, in completely identifying the English villein with the Roman slave (*servus*), Bracton got round the problem by specifying that the villein was free with respect to the whole world except his master, but a slave (*servus*) with respect to his master (who could, therefore, among other things, sell or give him like a beast).

[64] For example, *Roman de la Rose*, verses 7837–8:

Vos volés que j'oneure et serve
Ceste gens qui est fausse et serve

[65] For example, *ibid.*, verses 19436–7:

Briefment tant est chetis et nices
Qu'il est sers a trestous les vices

[66] 'Personal liberty and servitude, p. 72.

engaged in 'servile works'; that is to all who toiled in the fields in the service of someone else.

The word's evolution is even more revealing in the *pays d'oc*. There, the word *servus* had completely disappeared from the charters by the beginning of the eleventh century; to read only them, there were no more serfs. But the derivative *sers* remained alive in the spoken language. Peire Vidal, for example, used it to describe Philip Augustus, the evil king, the 'hypocritical', 'cowardly', 'false', 'limp', 'squatting' king, who was assuredly not part of the *'gentz'*, the nobles, but behaved *'atressi cum sers o borgès'*.[67] In the social stratification here outlined by the troubadour, the word *sers* had certainly assumed 'class value'.

In these conditions, the concept of servitude (or, if preferred, the semantic field of the word 'serf') encompasses very diverse situations and applies to men – *homines*, 'men', in the vocabulary of the charters – whose dependence clearly derived from very different juridical categories. Amongst these figured, to be sure, first and foremost, the *hommes de corps* the 'bondsmen', whose servile condition has never been doubted. But it also extended to 'men' who were attached to the land they, or their ancestors, possessed, such as the *hommes de caselage* of Languedoc, serfs *de bien* whose status puzzled Marc Bloch;[68] but also to 'men' whose dependence was both personal and to the land, such as the *hommes naturels* of Rouergue who were listed in the patrimony of lords and given or exchanged with their holdings,[69] or the Catalan

[67] 'A per pauc', str. 3, verse 23 (*Les poésies de Peire Vidal*, ed. J. Anglade (Paris, 1913), poem 32; most recent ed. A. S. Avalle, *Peire Vidal, Le poésie* (Milan–Naples, 1960). The descriptions applied to Philip Augustus are taken from various poems of Peire Vidal, in particular 'A per pauc' and 'Deu en sia grazitz' (*'rei aunitz'*, *'flac rei apostitz'*, *'flac acrupitz'*, *'flac avars'*, *'cors de ven'* etc.).

[68] 'The status of men de casalage appears shadowy' ('Personal liberty and servitude', p. 55). See also *Rois et serfs*, pp. 100–1, and 'Serf de la Glèbe', in *Slavery and Serfdom*, pp. 179ff. Since Bloch's death, the problem has been illumined by various studies on serfdom in Languedoc, in particular, P. Ourliac, 'L'hommage servile dans la région toulousaine' (*Mélanges Louis Halphen* (Paris, 1951), pp. 551–6), 'Le servage à Toulouse aux XIIe et XIIIe siècles' (*Mélanges Perroy* (Paris, 1973), pp. 249–61) and Bourin, *Villages médiévaux*. Other studies are in preparation.

[69] P. Ourliac and A. M. Magnou, *Le Cartulaire de la Selve. La terre, les hommes et le pouvoir en Rouergue au XIIe siècle* (Toulouse, 1985). Curiously, the authors reject the appellation 'serfs' for the *hommes naturels* because of the nature of their dependence, that is attachment to the land, although they were owned and alienated at will by their masters (pp. 25–6).

remença peasantry very numerous till the fifteenth century, whom
the jurists took care not to call *servi* but who were, for all that,
subject to extremely harsh constraints (the five *mals usos* and the
remença).[70] To all these dependants were added those whose
servitude cannot be explained (but is this not so of the previous
groups?) except by their residence within a seigneurial district, and
their subjection to the *potestas* of a local leader. The *hommes de
poesté* or *de pôté* of the Mâconnais[71] or of Champagne,[72] among
others, provide good examples, but also the many *homines* or
feminas to whom the charters give no qualifying epithet, but who
were given or sold with or without their possessions.[73]

Should we go further and incorporate into the servile group the
villeins and *manants*, whose subjection equally clearly depended
on their residence within a *seigneurie*? Marc Bloch dared not go so
far, remaining faithful on this point to an old tradition of legal
history.[74] There are, indeed, texts (though always in Latin) which
preserve a distinction, even mark an opposition, between *homines
commanentes* and *servi* (but not truly between *villani* and *servi*).[75]

[70] The five *mals usos*, see chapter 7 above, pp. 217–37.
[71] Duby, *La société mâconnaise*, pp. 247–50; where he says that, by the dawn of the
    twelfth century, nothing any longer distinguished the *hommes de pôté*, former
    free men subject to the seigneurial *ban*, from serfs of ancient origin.
[72] 'Coustume est en Champagne que hons de poesté ne peult avoir franchise ne ne
    doit ne ne se puet appeler frans, s'il n'a dou don dou signor lettres ou privilaiges'
    (article of the Ancient Custom of Champagne, quoted and discussed by P. Petot,
    'La preuve du servage en Champagne', *Revue Historique de Droit français et
    étranger* (1934), pp. 464–98). More recently, A.-M. Patault, *Hommes et femmes
    de corp en Champagne méridionale à la fin du Moyen Age* (Nancy, 1978), pp.
    27ff.
[73] Amongst a host of examples: 'Ego Poncius de Verneto et ego domina Jusiana
    . . . vindimus vobis . . . quemdam hominen nostrum nomine Martinum Ysarnum
    de Ortaphano et uxorem eius Mariam et omnem suam prolem . . . et omnia bona
    eorum mobilia et immobilia . . . pro precio octingentorum L solidorum
    Malgorensium' (1236), taken from S. Caucanas, *Introduction à l'histoire du
    Moyen Age en Roussillon, recueil de textes commentés* (Perpignan, 1985), p. 93.
[74] Since *Rois et serfs* (p. 21), Marc Bloch regarded the *vilains, manants, hommes
    levants et couchants* as free men (and this constitutes, perhaps, the flaw in his
    argument). He kept to this afterwards, except as regards the villeins of England.
    He quoted, for example, the canon of Hereford who, at the end of the eleventh
    century, in his *Roman de Philosophie*, contrasted 'villein' and 'free man'. For
    the thirteenth century, he did not hesitate: the English villeins 'were considered
    henceforth deprived of liberty; they were often subjected to the old servile
    burdens' ('Personal liberty and servitude', p. 91).
[75] *Homines commanentes/servi* and *homines commanentes/homines de corpore*
    oppositions are recorded for the Parisian basin and Hainault by Verriest (*Institu-
    tions médiévales*, pp. 222–30) and for the region of Namur by Genicot,

But there is much evidence, conversely, which points to an identification of villeinage and serfdom. This was obvious in thirteenth-century England.[76] In France, though barely evident in the Latin charters, it was almost general in writings in the popular tongue, a better pointer to the concrete realities. The case of the peasants of Orly, carefully studied by Marc Bloch, is extremely significant in this regard.[77] Two types of document describe the conflict which, in 1251, opposed the peasants against their lords, the canons of Paris. On the one hand, there are the records of the legal action which was held, after many twists of fortune, at the behest of Blanche of Castile, and consist of several dozen depositions, transcribed in Latin, and intended (though, in the event, without success) to define the juridical condition of the *homines commorantes apud Orliacum*, no one knowing precisely whether they were *homines de corpore* or not;[78] on the other, there is the account given in the *Grandes Chroniques de France*, not overly concerned with subtleties, as is shown by the statement attributed to the canons in their response to the queen, who had just offered her good offices:

The canons replied that it was not her (the queen's) affair to deal with their serfs (*sers*) and their villeins (*vilains*), whom they could seize, or kill, or upon whom they could make such judgement as they wished.

Serfs or villeins? This war of words must, in practice, have mat-

---

L'économie rurale namuroise, vol. 3, pp. 62–3). These authors do not, however, record any oppositions of the type *villani/servi* or *villani/hommes de corpore*.

[76] Hyams, *Kings, Lords and Peasants*, pp. 1–79 (part 1: 'Chattel ownership and its consequences').

[77] In his first article, 'Blanche de Castile and the serfs of the Chapter of Paris', *Slavery and Serfdom*, pp. 163–77. It might be useful, at this point, to give a brief resumé of events: the men of Orly refused to pay a tallage which the chapter of Paris wished to levy, claiming that they were not liable to tallage at will. The canons imprisoned sixteen of them. The peasants did not give in, obtained the support of neighbouring villages and appealed to Blanche of Castile. The chapter then threw all the men of Orly into prison. The queen intervened by asking the canons to submit their rights to an enquiry. The latter replied by imprisoning women and children. The queen then went in person, with a company of armed men, to the cloister of Notre-Dame, and delivered the prisoners who were in dungeons behind the wine cellars of the cloister. After various negotiations, a court of arbitration was established to hear the depositions regarding the status of the peasants and the rights of the chapter.

[78] The depositions were published by Bloch with the original article, see *Mélanges historiques*, pp. 177–90

tered little to these men, or their families, in the light of the fate which awaited them in the late summer of 1251:

Since a complaint had been made before the queen, the canons imprisoned their wives and children; and they were so overcome by the heat that they had from one another, that several of them died.[79]

Did it matter more to those other peasants mentioned – usually quite incidentally – in literary works, who are indifferently referred to by both, equally pejorative, terms? Was the boorish Liétard from the region of Brie, on whom Renart bestowed both names, plus others, similarly unappealing, a serf or a villein?

Desloiaus vilains, puz et sers . . .
Fil a putain, vilain roigneux . . .
Puanz vilains et ors et lierres . . .
(Disloyal villeins, . . . stinking serf . . .
Son of a whore, mangey villein . . .
Stinking villeins, filthy and thieving.)[80]

The two words, 'villein' and 'serf', seems to be interchangeable in Romance speech. Between *vilenaille* and *servaille*, who can distinguish?

ON THE 'PROFOUND ESSENCE' OF SERVITUDE

An examination of vocabulary thus shows that the concept of servitude passed well beyond the social categories indicated by the terms *servi* and *homines de corpore* alone. How then are we to define the 'new servitude' of the eleventh to thirteenth centuries?

Marc Bloch has been much criticised for his emphasis on the three famous 'specific criteria of serfdom' as determinants. It has justly been said that none of the three (chevage, prohibition of *formariage* and *mainmorte*) was truly characteristic of a particular category of the peasantry (that is, those called 'serfs'), and that, further, many other obligations could contribute to peasant enserf-ment. It has been less noticed that Marc Bloch, by 1933, clearly distinguished between these 'specific obligations', in which he saw

---

[79] *Recueils des historiens des Gaules et de la France*, 24 vols. (Paris, 1738–1904), vol. 21, p. 117.
[80] *Roman de Renart*, Branches X–XI, ed. Mario Roques (1958), verses 10481, 10496, 10510.

only the 'exterior characteristics' of serfdom, and its 'profound essence'.[81] What was this 'profound essence'? Bloch never precisely said, but he suggested some clues to help towards its definition.

Firstly, in his very choice of the 'specific criteria'. We will pass over chevage, about which there is probably too much to be said. But *mainmorte* and prohibition of *formariage* define two of the most restrictive forms of alienation which the enserfed peasant experienced: alienation of his power of production (since he could not possess fully nor will freely the fruits of his labour) and of his power of reproduction (since his right to choose his spouse and retain his children was limited, even denied). Now these two types of alienation are among those most readily accepted today by anthropologists when they define servitude.[82] We may simply note that peasant alienation could experience much more severe forms when it was the actual body of the peasant (or of his wife or children) which might be alienated, by gift or sale etc.: 'the counts, barons and free tenants . . . may legally sell their peasants (*rusticos*) like oxen or cows' declared an English judgement in 1244.[83] Let us note in passing that this reduction of peasants to the level of cattle[84] concerned men who were never, in England, Catalonia or Languedoc, called serfs in charters.

A second pointer is to be found in the last lines of Marc Bloch's study of 'Personal liberty and servitude'. Concluding with the concept of 'servile class', he wrote: 'Human institutions being realities of a psychological order, a class exists only through the idea we have of it.'[85] The formulation is perhaps a little abrupt, but it has the value of indicating that it is in the area of mental images that we must seek one answer to the question posed. How did the masters see the 'men' they possessed? This image emerges clearly from the texts, and it is overwhelming. The servile condition is defined by the crushing 'burden of contempt' (the expression is Bloch's)[86] which the society of the well-born inflicted on those who

---

[81] 'Personal liberty and servitude', p. 58.
[82] For example, Meillassoux, *L'esclavage dans l'Afrique noire*, p. 25.
[83] Quoted by Hyams, *Kings, Lords and Peasants*, p. 3.
[84] 'The villein as chattel' is the title of chapter 2 of Hyams, *Kings, Lords and Peasants*.
[85] 'Personal liberty and servitude', p. 91.
[86] *Ibid.*, p. 65.

enabled it to survive. The evolution of vocabulary once again demonstrates this; think of the synonymy villainy/infamy or of the pejorative derivatives of words like *innobilis* and *rusticus*. In literary works, the words 'serf' and 'villein' are used, after the worst insults have been exhausted, to qualify the most repugnant of people.

Thus Ganelon in the *Song of Roland* (verses 3737–8):

> A une estache l'un atachient cil serf,
> Les mains li lient a curreies de cerf . . .
> (They have bound this serf, fast upon his stake,
> In deer-hide thongs his hands they've helpless made)

Remember the imprecations, four centuries later, of Gloucester in *King Lear* (Act 1, scene 2):

> O villain, villain! . . . Abhorred villain! Unnatural, detested,
> brutish villain! Worse than brutish! . . . Abominable villain!

This infinite contempt had as an implicit consequence the refusal – the psychological impossibility – of according human dignity to the peasant. Texts attributing a bestial aspect to the peasant are legion, beginning with the famous portrait found in the 'Yvain' of Chrétien de Troyes, a portrait made up, indeed, of a veritable montage of characteristics drawn from six different species of animal.[87] More precisely, the assimilation of the serf to the dog ('dog, son of a dog') is a literary commonplace. Thus, in Gace de la Buigne:

> Il rest voir que chien est truant et serf . . .
> Si prend son chien qui est son serf . . .
> (It is true again that a dog is wicked and servile . . .
> And he takes his dog which is his serf . . .)[88]

Starting from such premisses, it goes without saying that the power of correction which the masters exercised over their serfs or villeins had in their eyes no precise limits and needed no justification. Arbitrariness was the corollary of servitude. In Catalonia, the *ius maletractandi* – the right to maltreat without cause – was legalised in 1202 by the Corts of Cervera, but it is clear that this

---

[87] The pack-horse, elephant, cat, owl, wolf and boar (*Yvain*, verses 286–91).
[88] *Le roman des déduis*, ed. E. Blomqvist (Stockholm–Paris, 1951), verses 6196–7, 7927–8.

was only a tardy ratification of a practice regarded as natural.[89] It is no less clear that similar habits existed elsewhere. Marc Bloch, always conscious of the long 'complaint [of the serfs], which the dryness of the texts cannot stifle',[90] quoted some examples of brutality: the female serf Niva whose throat was cut by her lord,[91] and the two men of the chapter of Saint-Père of Chartres mutilated by the lords of Gallardon.[92] We will, in fact, never know how many serfs were mutilated,[93] tortured,[94] burned,[95] or simply (if one can put it that way) hanged: such atrocities cannot, as a general rule, be known except when they concerned individuals who did not belong to the perpetrator of the violence. Only then was there complaint, hence traces in the archives. In almost every other case, silence reigned. It is, nevertheless, not unreasonable to assume that the gibbets adjacent to fortresses were there for more than purely decorative purposes.

But more perhaps than these spectacular punishments, we should bear in mind the harassment which was the habitual lot of the enserfed peasant; that is, the threat of (and sometimes recourse to) the stick or the whip.[96] We here touch on what is

[89] On this subject, see P. Freedman, 'The Catalan *ius maletractandi*', in *Recueil de mémoires et travaux, La Société d'Histoire du Droit et des Institutions des anciens pays de droit écrit*, 13 (Montpellier, 1985), 39–53.

[90] 'Personal liberty and servitude', p. 65.

[91] *Ibid.*, p. 59 (She was 'égorgée par Vial, son seigneur').

[92] *Ibid.*, p. 60 and note 123.

[93] For example: the castellan Guillem Bernard of Odena cut off the foot of a peasant of Sant Cugat (*Cartulario Sant Cugat*, ed. J. Rius Serra (1946), 2, no. 627, dated 1062); the castellan Siger of Conques cut limbs off men belonging to the abbey: *monachos execrabilibu odiis insectari non cessabat, hominesque ejus membris diminuebat* (*Liber miraculorum sanctae Fidis*, ed. A. Bouillett (Paris, 1897), III, 17).

[94] A literary example: 'Tu es mon serf, tu ne me dois riens refuser ne contredire chose que je te commande et se tu ne fais ce que je te commanderé, je te tourmenteré du corps moult aprement' *Le Roman d'Apollonius de Tyr*, ed. M. Zink (Paris, 1982), p. 121.

[95] Evidence in *Roman de Renart*: Renart threatens to denounce the peasant Liétard to the count for a hunting offence (Liétard has some venison in his chest). The punishment would be the rope or the stake; and even if the peasant had enough to pay a fabulous fine, he would not escape (verses 11206–16, 11327–33).

[96] For example, again from *Roman de Renart*:

Tu antanz or mout a flater,
mes de duel te femai grater
tes tempes et tes poinz destordre
. . .
Certes je te ferai fraper
En une manière ou en deux. (verses 10489–96).

perhaps an essential point as regards the border between liberty and servitude. This frontier has been much discussed and debated by historians but with a view to defining it on the basis of the most abstruse judicial criteria. At the time, it was perhaps rather simpler and it might be argued that only if you could not suffer corporal punishment at the hands of someone else (except as a result of a serious offence and by virtue of a judicial sentence pronounced according to a regular procedure), could you feel free. Conversely, to be beaten (or susceptible of being beaten), at the discretion of the agents of a master, constituted recognition of lack of liberty. As late as the fourteenth century, Froissart recorded this equivalence between a consciousness of servitude and submission to beating when he made the rebellious Jacques say: 'We are called serfs and beaten if we are slow in service to [the nobles].'[97] The image of the thrashed villein, indeed, permeates the whole of medieval literature, and should not be treated simply as a cliché lacking historical significance. Marc Bloch himself invited us to heed it in a famous page of *Feudal Society*, when he called for a history of the body.[98] Such a history should deal not only with the athletic body of the knight, but with the ravaged body of the peasant.

Alienation, humiliation and subjection to arbitrary power (and in particular, to corporal punishment) seem to constitute the sombre triptych which best depicts servitude, especially that known by the Europe of the feudal period. Far from the legalism of the charters and their often misleading vocab··lary, this triple image enables us, it seems, to come closer to the material and moral condition of the man who was enserfed. Is this to say that it applied to the totality – or to the near-totality – of the peasantry, identifying it, by the same token, with Marc Bloch's 'servile class'? To answer this, we need to look once again at chronology.

ENSERFMENT AND FRANCHISES

In their broad outlines, the movements of enserfment and enfranchisement are today fairly well known. The point of departure is firmly situated at the end of the tenth and in the eleventh cen-

---

[97] *Chronicles* (Penguin Classics edition, 1968), Book 2, no. 2, p. 212.
[98] *Feudal Society*, p. 72.

turies. Marc Bloch got it right when he characterised this period in words such as 'roughness', 'brutality', 'arbitrariness' and, above all, 'violence'.[99] The terrible body-blow which the peasantry then suffered (particularly the old free peasantry) is easily explained. When the last vestiges of the slave (or post-slave) system perished, who could the seigneurial class make support the effort of production – an effort which continued to increase as a result of the first manifestations of growth – if not the mass of *laboratores*? To transform these – all of them – into *servi*, was what Adalbero had already done on parchment. In the real world, the establishment of castral (or *banal*), lordship was the instrument of this gigantic enterprise of subversion. Grasping the free peasantry as if in a vice, the *banal* constraints 'rent the old social tissue', despite its long history, and 'destroyed the peasant neighbourhoods'.[100] Although a tiny minority of the inhabitants of the countryside (the richest, or simply the strongest and most agile in combat) moved into the noble camp, to provide its armed auxiliaries (the first *milites castri*), the mass of peasants was subject to such pressures that it lost the most elementary guarantees of its independence.

In these circumstances, it is not unreasonable to talk of a generalised trend towards the enserfment of the peasantry.[101] Nor was this confined to the countries of the Midi, where the phenomenon appears in a particularly harsh light; it occurred also in post-Conquest England,[102] and even in the north of the Frankish kingdom.[103] When all this violence had achieved its end (generally

---

[99] 'Personal liberty and servitude', p. 59. Bloch was influenced here by Jacques Flach who had already put violence 'in the ranks of the significant characteristics of the juridical life of the eleventh century' (*Origines de l'ancienne France*, 1, book 2, chapter 23: 'La surprise et la violence').

[100] Poly and Bournazel, *La mutation féodale*, pp. 101–3, 218–19.

[101] Duby, *The Three Orders*, p. 159 (and see note 47 above). This idea is expressed in a similar fashion in many other places (for example, *Guerriers et Paysans* (Paris, 1973), translated by Howard B. Clarke as *The Early Growth of the European Economy* (London, 1974), p. 168.

[102] Between 1066 and 1086, according to Domesday Book, the number of fully free tenants (freeholders or sokemen) diminished significantly in favour of villeins (in Norfolk and Suffolk, the number in 1086 was only a seventh of what it had been in 1066; in Cambridgeshire, the number fell from about 900 to 200).

[103] Even in the region of Namur, the imposition of *banal* charges, the *consuetudines indecentes*, could only be achieved by the use of force, in a generalised climate of 'brutalities, exactions and depredations' of every sort; in the second half of the eleventh century, 'violence ran riot' (Genicot, *L'économie rurale namuroise*, pp. 1–19).

around the year 1100: last third of the eleventh century or the beginning of the twelfth, according to place), the distress of the humble and their subordination were such, almost throughout western Europe, that the term 'servile class' used to denote the vast mass of the rural population does not appear particularly outrageous.

But things changed; during the course of the twelfth century, in the euphoria of a growth now well under way, the conjuncture of circumstances improved; while the peasantry benefitted from the side-effects of expansion (even if the chief benefits continued to go to the aristocracy) and thus became more assertive,[104] the masters of the *ban* (and their agents) began to relax their grip slightly. Many factors induced them to do this: a better understanding of their interests, in the first place (a regular and moderate levy on peasant revenues brought in more than rapine, pure and simple), also the need to moderate their demands if they wished to find colonisers for the areas of assarting, and lastly, perhaps, a modification of the way they viewed their 'rustics'.[105]

It was a period of stabilisation of social relations, of normalisation, of a search for compromise, even, if you like, of 'seigneurial benevolence'.[106] It was also a period – and the two are linked – of the regrouping of villages (spontaneous, stimulated or coerced): Languedocian or Provençal *castra*, castral or rural *bourgs* in northern or western France etc.[107] There developed, in consequence,

---

[104] Duby, *The Three Orders*, pp. 175–7.

[105] Contempt for the peasant certainly remained the dominant sentiment in the seigneurial world. The twelfth and thirteenth centuries, however, saw some changes, illustrated by two similar incidents described by Marc Bloch. In the reign of Philip Augustus, the *homines de potestate* of Vernou sought out the king to complain about the bad conduct of their lord, the chapter of Paris; they attracted only the king's wrath and insults: *maledictum sit capitulum si non jactet vos in unam latrinam*! Half a century later, the attitude of Blanche de Castile, who actively intervened on behalf of the men of Orly, was quite different. Even within the chapter of Paris, there was no unanimity; though some canons (in a majority, initially) were in favour of implacable repression, others, who saw themselves as 'good men' (*boni homines*) demonstrated humanitarian sentiments and argued for negotiation: as the months passed, they won the day. ('Blanche de Castile', pp. 173–4; see also, *Mélanges historiques*, p. 483).

[106] 'La bienveillance des seigneurs' is the title of a chapter in M. Bourin and R. Durand, *Vivre au village: les solidarités paysannes du XIe au XIIIe siècle* (Paris, 1984). The authors, it should be said, put the word *bienveillance* in inverted commas.

[107] The case of Latium is exceptional, as a result of the precocity there of the phenomenon of *incastallamento*; the regrouping of villages often preceded (and

the grants of 'liberties', sometimes tacitly, simply by prescription (the lord not insisting on demanding taxes unanimously judged intolerable by his peasants), sometimes by the grant of those charters of liberties to which Marc Bloch devoted a large part of his research,[108] and in which he correctly saw acts of emancipation and not simply codifications of custom.[109]

Fissures opened up in seigneurial arbitrary power. A significant group – growing with the passage of time – amongst the peasantry escaped from the quasi-prison[110] in which the demands of the lords of men and land had tended to confine them, and obtained exemptions from the servitude of the *ban*, often even a statute of autonomy.[111] This privileged (in the literal meaning of the word) sector of the rural population, constantly enlarged, and soon, in many places, in a majority, was now distinguished from those who had retained their ignominious status. This differentiation appeared clearly in the vocabulary of the Romance languages where, in the twelfth and thirteenth centuries, the free/serf antithesis was very marked.[112] It seems that the distribution of the two groups can be

---

determined) the formation of castral lordship (Toubert, *Les structures du Latium*, vol. 1, p. 549, and especially vol. 2, pp. 1274ff.

[108] Beginning with his thesis, *Rois et serfs*.

[109] This was what, perhaps, lay at the heart of the debate between Leo Verriest and Marc Bloch, Verriest seeing the charters (*chartes-lois*) as always granted to 'free men', being unwilling to accept that drawing up a custumal, by the limitations it imposed on arbitrariness, was in itself an act of, at least partial, liberation.

[110] This expression might appear excessive. It follows, however, from the concept of confinement in fixed areas. The prohibition of *formariage*, amongst others, was symbolic of the desire to confine which is implied by the definition of the seigneurial *districtus*.

[111] Catalan charters of franchise, excellently edited by Font Rius (*CPC*, vol. 1, 19; vol. 2, 19), show clearly the two different routes by which emancipation was achieved: the first was the recognition of the village collectively as a juridical personality, the second was liberation from the *mals usos*. These two types of privilege were quite distinct; some villages managed to have themselves recognised as having a true collective identity whilst their inhabitants remained unquestionably subject to the most specific marks of serfdom; conversely, many communities obtained exemption from the *exorquias*, *intestias*, *cugucias* and other bad customs without, for all that, receiving even the most embryonic autonomy of administration. On this subject, see chapter 8 above, 'Rural communities in Catalonia and Valencia (from the ninth to the mid-fourteenth centuries), especially pp. 258–60.

[112] It was the major distinction. Examples are very numerous in the texts. I refer once again to the troubadour Peire Vidal: 'S'anc fos francs, as es sers ses doptanza' (If he was free, he is now a serf without a doubt) (*Les poésies de Peire Vidal*, ed. Anglade, 'Lanza marqués').

related – with reservations – to the movement towards the concentrations of habitat taking place at this period. With, of course, many exceptions, the inhabitants of the new villages seem, in general to have achieved the name and dignity of free men; the regrouping produced strong solidarities which weakened seigneurial constraints. Conversely, the inhabitants of remote places, of hamlets and isolated farms (vestiges of the previous habitat still thinly scattered over the territory of the castellanies) often retained their servile condition.[113]

But we should not be too schematic; the movement from servitude towards liberty was neither linear nor uniform. Two main correctives have to be applied to this over-simplified picture. The first concerns the backwards steps, of which there were major instances. Thomas Bisson and Paul Freedman have recently demonstrated this for Catalonia in the second half of the twelfth and the thirteenth centuries; whilst the franchises which certain groups of peasants (principally on the comital estates) had been able to acquire or preserve were ignored or even destroyed, the jurists elaborated a status of servitude, based on the *ius maletractandi* and attachment to the soil which was applied to increasing numbers of the peasantry, and which was to last until the end of the fifteenth century.[114] England provides a similar example; whilst here, as elsewhere, seigneurial constraints (in this case 'manorial') were loosened during the course of the twelfth century, there was a vigorous and successful counter-attack by the lords of manors from the years 1180–90; a reaction which was assisted by the attitude of the Angevin monarchy, which abandoned all jurisdictional rights over their villeins to lords, and by the care which the lawyers of the royal court brought to the codification of the customs of villeinage.[115] In both cases, the new servitude remained or once again became, in the thirteenth century, a massive reality.[116]

---

[113] See, for Languedoc, the argument of Monique Bourin-Derruau, *Villages médiévaux*.

[114] T. N. Bisson, 'The crisis of the Catalonian franchises (1150–1200)', *Formacio i expansio del feudalisme català*, pp. 153–72; P. H. Freedman, 'Peasant servitude in the thirteenth century', *ibid.*, pp. 437–45.

[115] Hyams, *Kings, Lords and Peasants*. See also Hilton, *Decline of Serfdom*, especially pp. 17–19.

[116] The servile status elaborated by the jurists of the courts weighed most heavily on the English peasantry at the end of the thirteenth and beginning of the fourteenth centuries (Hilton, *Decline of Serfdom*, pp. 25–6), and this despite

The second, and perhaps more important, corrective, relates to the origins of the movement of enfranchisements. It would be wrong to think that it succeeded, in perfect chronological order, the movement of enserfment. In reality, it first drew breath in the struggle of the peasantry to resist the imposition of the *banal* charges. As early as the eleventh century, the new servitude had been contested at the very moment it was being imposed. This was sometimes with a degree of success which, though it may appear to us derisory, was nevertheless important to the men concerned. One of the oldest charters of liberties to survive, granted in 1058 by the abbot of Nonantola (near Modena) to the local inhabitants, is evidence of this; it guaranteed them – its only clause – that they would not be beaten by the agents of the monastery except after a judgement pronounced according to custom.[117] For these poor people, this was to achieve a safeguard for their bodies.

If we choose to go further back in time, we find the revolt of the Norman peasants in 996, magnificently – but, alas, tardily – related by the *trouvère*, Wace.[118] We may guess this conspiracy to be the first – and bloody – riposte to the very earliest attempts to establish the '*banal* order'. What did these 'rebels' voice? Simple demands for human dignity and equality, aspirations based on the assumption – obvious but already denied – that there existed no difference between the body of the nobleman and that of the villein:

> Nus sumes humes cum ils sunt
> Tels menbres avum cum ils unt
> Et autresi granz cors avum
> Et autretant suffrir poum
> (We are men like them
> We have the same limbs
> And just as big hearts
> And we can suffer just as much.)[119]

evidence of very strong aspirations to freedom, which were given concrete form by the creation of free tenures, in derogation of common law, in numerous parts of the country and in particular on assart land (*ibid.*, pp. 19–27). This double phenomenon is equally characteristic of Catalonia (chapter 8 above, especially pp. 254–60).

[117] Document quoted by G. Tabacco, 'La storia politica e sociale. Dal tramonto dell'Impero alle prime formazioni di Stati regionali', in *Storia d'Italia* (Turin, 1974), p. 162.

[118] *Roman de Rou*, verses 815–958. Other accounts in William of Jumièges, Guillaume de Poitiers, Benoît de Sainte-Maure etc.

[119] *Roman de Rou*, verses 867–70.

'And we can suffer just as much': the equality of the body before suffering – we come back to Marc Bloch – was the proof that there were no sub-humans and that the enserfment of man by man was unacceptable. It was this very refusal by peasants to abdicate the human condition – a stubborn refusal, sometimes openly expressed, more often obliquely, but constantly reasserted – which explains why the medieval peasantry was not, at least not for ever and in its totality, relegated to the ranks of the 'servile class'.

Index of persons and places

Glossarial index

acapte 221; see also 220, 227, 252
aemprius 245, 280–1; see also 250
alcadi 264; see also 269
alcaide 264; see also 267–8, 275, 282
alberga 226; see also 158, 219, 220, 232
aljama 263; see also 260, 265–8, 269–72, 286
alquerías 262; see also 263, 265, 267–9, 271, 275, 278
amalgram 264; see also 267
aprisio 45, 248; see also 42, 116, 152
arsina 234–5; see also 219

'bad usages, bad customs' 218–21; see also 58, 122, 165, 178, 188, 232, 236–7, 252, 254, 259–60, 272, 306–7, 322

carta puebla 272–3; see also 276, 277–8, 280–1, 285
castlà 178; see also 109, 161, 168, 179, 184, 188–90, 206–7, 210–13, 217–18, 222, 234
castlania 166, 178; see also 109, 130, 158, 164, 168, 179
cavallaria, caballaria 109, 164; see also 158
cavallarii 161–2
civida 226; see also 190, 220
colliberti, culverts 4, 312; see also 13
comtor 201–5; see also 162, 196–7, 206, 210, 212, 216
cugucia 234–5; see also 164, 190, 219–20, 337 n.111

dret de cuixa 160

estacaments 218; see also 190
exorchia 218, 234; see also 235–6, 260, 322 n.51, 337 n.111

ferma de spoli 234–5; see also 160
fiefs de reprise 110; see also 128–9
fogassa 226
forcia 218; see also 158, 220, 256
formariage 330–1; see also 316–17, 319 n.28, 337

guaita 218; see also 190, 226

homines de corpore, hommes de corps 58, 224, 318, 324, 327–9, 330
homines proprii, hommes propres 58, 159, 222–4, 231–2, 312, 322
homines solidi, 224, 231, 322 n.48, and see 'solid' homage, below

intestia 234–5; see also 260, 337 n.111
iova 227; see also 190. 220, 272 n.82
ius maletractandi 256, 332; see also 338

lexivos 218; see also 234, 322 n.51

manimorte 330–1; see also 236, 316–17, 319 n.28, 322–3
mals usos 234–5; see also 160, 164–5, 217–21, 232–7, 254 n.41, 256, 328, 337 n.111
merimperi 268; see also 269, 283–4
moverías 267; see also 286

'new usages, new customs' see 'bad usages' above

preguera 218; see also 220 n.74
presentalia, presentalges 160, 218; see also 322 n.50
pressura 45; see also 116

questia 218; see also 110, 158, 220 n.74, 221 n.75, 226–7, 256, 258–9

receptio 226

349

Past and Present Publications

General Editor: PAUL SLACK. *Exeter College, Oxford*

351

The English Rising of 1381, edited by R. H. Hilton and T. H. Aston*

Praise and Paradox: Merchants and Craftsmen in Elizabethan Popular Literature, Laura Caroline Stevenson

The Brenner Debate: Agrarian Class Structure and Economic Development in Pre-Industrial Europe, edited by T. H. Aston and C. H. E. Philpin*

Eternal Victory: Triumphal Rulership in Late Antiquity, Byzantium, and the Early Medieval West, Michael McCormick†*

East-Central Europe in Transition: From the Fourteenth to the Seventeenth Century, edited by Antoni Mączak, Henryk Samsonowicz and Peter Burke†

Small Books and Pleasant Histories: Popular Fiction and its Readership in Seventeenth-Century England, Margaret Spufford**

Society, Politics and Culture: Studies in Early Modern England, Mervyn James*

Horses, Oxen and Technological Innovation: The Use of Draught Animals in English Farming 1066–1500, John Langdon

Nationalism and Popular Protest in Ireland, edited by C. H. E. Philpin

Rituals of Royalty: Power and Ceremonial in Traditional Societies, edited by David Cannadine and Simon Price

The Margins of Society in Late Medieval Paris, Bronisław Geremek†

Landlords, Peasants and Politics in Medieval England, edited by T. H. Aston

Geography, Technology, and War: Studies in the Maritime History of the Mediterranean, 649–1571, John H. Pryor

Church Courts, Sex and Marriage in England, 1570–1640, Martin Ingram*

Searches for an Imaginary Kingdom: The Legend of the Kingdom of Prester John, L. N. Gumilev

Crowds and History: Mass Phenomena in English Towns, 1780–1835, Mark Harrison

Concepts of Cleanliness: Changing Attitudes in France since the Middle Ages, Georges Vigarello†

The First Modern Society: Essays in English History in Honour of Lawrence Stone, edited by A. L. Beier, David Cannadine and James M. Rosenheim

The Europe of the Devout: The Catholic Reformation and the Formation of a New Society, Louis Châtellier†

English Rural Society, 1500–1800: Essays in Honour of Joan Thirsk, edited by John Chartres and David Hey

From Slavery to Feudalism in South-Western Europe, Pierre Bonnassie†

*   Published also as a paperback

** Published only as a paperback

†   Co-published with the Maison des Sciences de l'Homme, Paris